Münster:
The Way it Was

—Heinz Hessling (The original is hanging in the Münster Museum)

Ian Hawkins

Münster:
The Way it Was

Edited by RICHARD H. PERRY

Robinson Typographics
ANAHEIM, CALIFORNIA

Library of Congress Catalog Card Number: 85-051125

I.S.B.N. Number: Regular Edition: 0-918837-00-6
Deluxe Edition: 0-918837-01-4

Printed in the United States of America

Robinson Typographics
1614 South Clementine Street
Anaheim, California 92802

For Ahmed Kambal of Jeddah, Saudi Arabia, and for the late Mr. Walpole Lewin, C.B.E., M.S., F.R.C.S., Neurosurgeon and senior Vice-President of the Royal College of Surgeons, formerly of Addenbrookes Hospital, Cambridge.

Suaviter in modo, fortiter in re.

Author's Note

Among the very many kind responses which I have gratefully received from those who were directly involved in the events described in this book was an hour-long tape recording from Major General John B. Kidd, U.S.A.F. (Ret'd.), the former Operations Officer of the 100th Bombardment Group at Thorpe Abbotts, Norfolk.

Part of Major General Kidd's tape recording states:

> There is great meat here for telling the story of air warfare . . . philosophising about warfare . . . about the courage, and the lack of courage, of men . . . about the humorous and tragic incidents . . . certainly the tragic isn't hard to find. But there is also a need for a balanced treatment in this kind of story.
>
> I have read other books along the lines of this one, and I must say that authors have had torches to bear and points of view to be supported and I think a lot gets lost in trying to foist one's views, distaste, etc., concerning warfare off on the public through this kind of vehicle.
>
> If, and I'm sermonising here I appreciate, if the story can be told just as it was, for good, for bad, and without embellishment, it seems to me that a greater service is done.
>
> How does one go back in time nearly forty years and recall one's frame of mind, the precise details, the feeling that prevailed in the latter half of 1943?
>
> Many, many of the things I'm going to talk about are extremely vivid to this day, in my mind . . . but it's asking a bit much to sit down, with the pressures of current everyday matters etc., etc., and put oneself back instantly almost forty years and rattle off the way it was.
>
> Well, here is an attempt . . .

Introduction

Most accounts of historic battles of past wars have been the result of research and interpretation of scanty records of events long forgotten. The authenticity of such accounts can be evaluated and debated only by those who also have studied the records and accounts. World War II has passed into history, but not so far that there aren't many who can still recall vividly the details of their participation.

Mr. Hawkins has taken advantage of this fact in writing a history of a major battle that took place during this great war, and in my opinion probably the most vicious single air battle of that war, or of all time. In addition to the most detailed record research, he has based his effort upon the personal accounts of the participants. The story is particularly significant in that it relates to events as they actually occurred and to the people who were involved, the bomber crew members, the ground crews, the fighter pilots on both sides as well as those of the civilian population who were involved in the attack. This is a story as told by the Lieutenants, Sergeants, Privates and the man in the street; those doing the shooting and getting shot at. This is a story of the men who prepared the aircraft, dropped the bombs and of those upon whom they fell, and of the courageous people who risked their lives aiding those who evaded capture as opposed to a review of the records and recollections of senior officers as contained in their memoirs. This is a story of incredible courage and ability displayed by young unprofessional men from all walks of life with limited training, while performing in a hostile environment, over a hostile nation, and the fantastic reliability and capability of their equipment. This is a story of the test of a theory espoused by men like Billy Mitchell, Trenchard, Portal, Arnold, Spaatz and many others, opposed by foes greater than the Third Reich. A theory that a nation could be brought to its knees by air power, a theory that a determined air attack cannot be stopped, and that no war can be won without control of the skies. The validity of this theory in the eyes of many hinged upon the outcome of this battle.

Any event appears different depending upon the location of the observer. In terms of an aircraft mission over enemy territory, the degree of roughness of the mission would depend therefore on one's location. The loss of one aircraft and it's crew would be as rough as it possibly could be to the members of that crew. To the Squadron Commander this loss would represent a significant portion of his strength (12% in the case of these missions) and a personal loss as well due to the intimacy within the Unit. To the Group Commander it is a regrettable loss and to the Air Force Commander it might be thought of as an easy mission when considered in terms of the total force involved.

There undoubtedly will be those who will disagree with my views, earlier expressed, that the mission described by the author was one of the toughest, if not the toughest flown from England by the Eighth Air Force during World War II. It certainly was from the viewpoint of the thirty crews that went down; it probably ranked high in the eyes of the Squadrons and Groups involved, and it probably was the worst single loss suffered by the 13th Combat Wing, though not by the Eighth Air Force. This mission plus those immediately preceeding and the one following represented it's most difficult period of operations. It was of sufficient impact to cause grave concern regarding the future of daylight bombing in Europe as night flying practice was begun with the possible view to joining with the Royal Air Force in it's night operations.

My view regarding the mission that the author describes so vividly is based upon several factors. First, it took place relatively early in the daylight bombing effort. German fighter pilot experience was high, and the bomber force small and largely unescorted. Since there was no blind bombing capability, all missions were conducted in clear weather, which greatly aided the Luftwaffe's rapid take off, landing and refueling capability. Such was the situation at Münster. The raid penetrated a heavily defended area and withdrew, following the same general route permitting fighters to remain in contact with the bombers while staying in the immediate vicinity of their home bases. This mission was the third in a series of four conducted in a period of seven days. Crew members were weary and aircraft numbers were reduced. We were pushing ourselves to the maximum as were the Germans. It was a concentrated demonstration of force, will and determination during an unusual period of good weather prior to the onset of winter. It was a sort of do or die effort on our part, and Germany it seems, was determined to do everything in its formidable power to stop it.

The fighters literally appeared as swarms. The attacks were pressed home viciously, to the extent that the bomber defenses were saturated. In other words, often the fighters did not leave the range of the bomber guns to repeat attacks. I heard one bombardier say that he shot down an FW-190 that was flying in the same direction as his bomber and at a range of less than one hundred yards.

More aircraft were lost on the following raid to Schweinfurt, but the flight was of greater duration and it appeared to me to be more of a running battle. There is no intent here to belittle its intensity, but the concentration of fighter forces in the target area at Münster permitted pilots to pursue attacks in force during a very vulnerable span of the mission and for a longer period.

The situation changed after October 1943, slowly at first and more rapidly as 1944 progressed. Inclement weather slowed operations; the size of the bomber force increased significantly; and the long range P51 escort fighter entered operations in large numbers. The German fighters were up in great numbers also, but the aggression and the determination seemed to have lessened. I recall returning from Munich in mid-1944, the weather was clear and not a German fighter in sight, a confident American voice came over the radio and said, "Goering, where is the Luftwaffe?". Needless to say, this sort of invitation would not have entered anyone's mind a short time earlier. Bomber crews began to worry more about anti-aircraft fire than fighters, and the number of missions to complete a tour increased to thirty and then to thirty five.

It is ironic and most appropriate that Mr. Hawkins chose this particular battle for his work as it represented a high point in the evolution of air power; a power over-shadowing that of armies and navies; air power spawned and produced by the two nations whose leaders established its principles and had the belief, courage and determination to pursue to victory their objectives against the criticisms of not so peaceful adversaries at home and a determined enemy abroad. The launch of such power from England could not have been more appropriate, nor could it have been possible from any other location at that point in time.

In an informal conversation with General Adolf Galland, the Commander in Chief of the Luftwaffe fighter forces, shortly after the end of World War II, I asked him why he had not concentrated and directed his fighter effort such that he could have destroyed all or a majority of the bombers on one or more occasions when he had the capability to do so, and did he realize the impact of such an action. In his reply he indicated that his fighters were divided between a ground support role and an air-to-air role such that the necessary concentration could not be accomplished. He was somewhat vague, in my opinion, upon the impact of the results of such a course of action.

In answer to a related question as to why the Me 262 jet fighter was not used to a greater extent in the air-to-air role he indicated that Hitler had directed its use in support of ground troops. I concluded from General Galland's remarks that either the Luftwaffe was insufficiently schooled in air power theory to make a convincing argument on it's behalf or there were more convincing arguments on behalf of the army that caused the nation's air power to be so misused. Had things been otherwise I doubt that the outcome of the war would have been altered in the long run. It was certainly in the best interest of the Allied effort at that time that such was not the case.

—Major General Thomas S. Jeffrey, Jr., United States Air Force, (Retired)
Former Deputy Group Commander 390th Bombardment Group (H)
(March 1943 - May 1944)
Group Commander 100th Bombardment Group (H)
(May 1944 - March 1945)

Foreword

Following the dedication of the 100th Bombardment Group's Memorial Air Museum at their long-abandoned airfield at Thorpe Abbotts, Norfolk, on 25 May 1981, the Group's former Ground Executive Officer, Major Horace Varian U.S.A.F. (Ret'd), read out the following letter:

Dear Ladies and Gentlemen,

On the occasion of the dedication of the Air Museum and Memorial to the fallen airmen, both Allied and German, of the Second World War, here at the former Control Tower of the airbase in England, I send you my warmest and sincerest greetings.

All Nations are scarred from the terrible aftermath of the Second World War. We cannot overcome the past by forgetting the discord and sorrow which war has brought, but by willingness to reconciliate we can ensure peace for the present.

So it pleases me, on this day of dedication, to represent the bond of friendship between our peoples.

May the merciful God hold His hand over us so that we are guided in His way and seek for peace which He has prepared for us.

With my sincerest blessings,

Yours,

Dr. Reinhard Lettmen, Bishop of Munster.

In preparation by the same author:

The 95th Bomb Group Anthology

Judder In Jeddah, Before And After

An Illustrated History of the 13th Combat Bomb Wing

Table of Contents

We should listen to the old people, for they have been where we have not. They have seen what we shall never see. They have heard the sound of silence. And when they go, things will never be quite the same. They are a dying breed. It is sad but it is so.

—*Michael Watkins,* This Other Breed, East Anglians.

There are men here tonight with mental and physical scars obtained during those dark days who could tell any 'Peacenick,' far better than I could, that there is no glory in war.

—*Roger Freeman, St. Louis, Missouri, U.S.A., 8 October 1977.*
(From his address at the U.S. 8th Air Force Historical Society's 3rd Annual Reunion.)

Only the Control Tower is in anything like its original condition, although if you ascend the iron staircase be careful. You might end up writing a book about it.

—*Len Deighton,* Bomber.

Prologue

DURING that fine and endlessly sunny September of 1979, while farmers throughout England strenuously strove to harvest the broad acres of ripened corn, three American tourists, each edging past middle age, re-visited three ancient English villages, set deep since time immemorial, among the gently undulating farmlands of the East Anglian countryside.

They came, on seperate occasions and completely unknown to each other, back to their former bomber airfields at Thorpe Abbotts, Framlingham and Great Ashfield which now bore very little resemblance to what they once were, thriving, noisy and bustling front-line bases spearheading the theory of daylight strategic aerial bombardment.

They walked again along cracked and crumbling perimeter tracks, wide runways flanked by flat fields which stretched away to wooded horizons and whose only inhabitants were now wheeling gulls, startled lapwings, scuttling partridges and the occasional scampering rabbit. For these were now lonely places. Gone forever were the huge formations of the Allied air fleets, vast aerial armadas which presented a sight and sound never to be forgotten by a whole generation of East Anglians. Very few of the large circular concrete hardstands remained where once stood the four-engined B17 Flying Fortress bombers, one of the most famous and effective aircraft of the Second World War. They had gone to war over Occupied Europe bearing expertly painted 'nose-art' of scantily clad, glamorous young females and adorned with not-so-glamorous names such as *Piccadilly Lily, The Vibrant Virgin, Our Gal Sal, Miss Behavin', Pistol Packin' Mama, and Calamity Jane*. Now only the distant hum of combine harvesters and the harsh snarl of far-off tractors broke the silence.

The visitors paused occasionally to peer into gloomy, derelict and ruined wartime buildings, feeling strangely apprehensive. But there was nobody there of course. The last American airman had driven out through the main gates of these airfields during the summer of 1945 leaving behind the ghosts and the memories of all that had gone before.

Winton MacCarter at Thorpe Abbotts and Stanley Smith at Framlingham discovered the former Control Towers, the nerve centres of any operational airfield, being renovated to become Memorial Museums as permanent reminders of those long gone days. Also still standing at Framlingham is the massive, Cathedral-like aircraft maintenance hangar which, in September 1944, had echoed to the cheers of 3,000 young American airmen as they showed their appreciation to the legendary Glenn Miller and his Army Air Force Band as he led them through such timeless arrangements as "Moonlight Serenade", "American Patrol", "In The Mood" and the rest.

At Great Ashfield John Pettenger presented a sizeable cheque to the Clergy of All Saints Church, on behalf of the 385th Bombardment Association in the United States who make annual donations to the 12th century Church, which maintains the Group's memorial to those who didn't return.

The three quietly spoken, warm and modest United States 8th Air Force veterans had first arrived at their respective bases in England during the early Summer of 1943, fresh from training schools in America. Within a few short and traumatic weeks of their arrival each had become fully conversant and hardened with the stark reality, the sights and the sounds, of war in the perilous skies high over Occupied Europe.

There were several other things they shared in common quite apart from being former crewmembers of the rugged B17 Flying Fortress and being drawn back, as if by some unseen magnet, to their long abandoned airfields in Suffolk and Norfolk. One factor above all others, bound all three together with an invisible bond.

Each, in their different way, had survived what a much respected and authoritative aviation historian has described as, "Probably the most concentrated air battle fought by a B17 Combat Bomb Wing during the Second World War."*

*Roger Freeman

Chapter 1

TO nine-year-old Sammy Hurry it was like a dream come true. He had overheard his father, who worked for the Air Ministry maintenance unit at nearby Pulham St. Mary, mention to his mother that two old cottages at Grove Wood were being pulled down as part of the site clearance for a new airfield. The cottages were bounded by the South Norfolk villages of Thorpe Abbotts, Billingford and Dickleburgh, Sammy's village.

The arrival of several official-looking men in Air Ministry cars some time previously had sparked off rumour and counter-rumour among the villagers. The strangers brusquely set up their tripod-mounted surveying instruments, took innumerable dimensions with long, linen tapemeasures, while accompanying workmen dug numerous trial holes to ascertain the nature of the soil strata at varying depths, and hammered countless wooden marker stakes into the ground. Within a short time, the surveyors had completed a thorough inspection of the site, and had reported to the Air Ministry in London, who quickly arranged purchase of the land at the pre-war price of £35 an acre.

Construction of the huge airfield began in the late Summer of 1942. A small army of workmen with strange sounding accents descended on the area, travelling daily in buses from hastily arranged lodgings in the nearby country towns of Scole, Diss, Harleston and Eye. Twenty or thirty caravans arrived with temporary accommodations for use as site huts. One storey wooden buildings provided office space for the site manager, engineers, trades foreman and the Air Ministry clerk-of-works and his staff.

Six massive caterpillar tractors hauling box-scrapers snarled their way up and down the future runways and around the perimeter track, gouging out by sheer force the topsoil which they stockpiled, ready to be dispersed to make up the levels in the low parts of the site, or to be hauled away and used in the construction of the bomb storage area, the shooting-in butts, and on the many blast proof air raid shelters.

A fleet of trucks, raising clouds of dust as they sped through the narrow, winding country lanes, hauled countless tons of sand and stone to supply the voracious appetite of the concrete batching plants. Large gangs of fit, tough specialists working a ten-hour day, seven-day week, dynamited trees, uprooted hedges and filled in existing ditches to clear the site of all obstacles. They dug trenches to receive some 23 miles of water main, rainwater and sewerage pipes which were laid to specified gradients. They poured half a million square yards of concrete to provide the hardstands, perimeter track and three runways thick enough to withstand the sudden jarring impact of the wheels of a thirty-ton bomber landing at a speed of 95 miles an hour.

Eleven miles of single-track concrete roads were constructed. In addition, almost four and a half million bricks were devoured in the construction of a whole alphabet of buildings: Air raid shelters, briefing hut for combat crews, control tower, dining rooms, engineering workshops, fuel compounds, guard house, hospital, interrogation block, jail, kitchens, link trainer, transport office, night flying store, operations building, photographic section, quarters for the airmen, radio and radar sections, squadron offices, teleprinter section, uniform store,vehicle maintenance compound, water pumping station, X-ray unit, Y.M.C.A. hut, and a zebra-striped airfield control post.

All these buildings, and many more, were in instant communication with each other by an overhead cobweb of telephone and power lines.

Black corrugated-iron Nissen huts suddenly appeared as if by magic, like schools of stranded whales, among the trees. Two enormous aircraft hangars, each half the size of a football field, rose rapidly — structural steel skeletons at first, then weatherproof caverns as each section of corrugated cladding was methodically bolted into position. The hangars easily overlooked the trees in nearby Billingford Wood.

A wartime airfield cost about a million pounds to build.

At suitable locations throughout Eastern England the huge programme of building urgently needed airfields for an expanding Royal Air Force Bomber Command, Royal Australian Air Force, Royal Canadian Air Force, and the United States Eighth Army Air Force, the largest of the American Overseas Air Commands, rapidly gained momentum.

Some idea of the gigantic scale of wartime airfield construction in Britain can be gauged from the huge quantities of asphalt laid by Wimpey's, one of the country's leading civil engineering contractors. This firm laid and rolled no less than 16 ½-million square yards of 'blacktop' on the runways and perimeter tracks of their alloted airfields.

Of 50 new airfields occupied by the USAAF in Eastern England, 36 were built by the Air Ministry, 14 by the US Army Engineers, and numerous existing RAF airfields were also occupied by the American Air Force.

Former British Air Ministry resident engineer, W.R. "Bill" Race, was in charge of construction of the four-squadron heavy bomber station at Metfield, Suffolk, until shortly before handover to the Americans in August 1943. Overall construction of the airfield took about nine months. An American Fighter Group with Thunderbolts moved in first, and the bombers came later.

Said Mr. Race:

The runway excavation was done by caterpillar scraper units of seven-cubic-yards capacity. The concrete laying machines ran on rails and these were fed by dumpers from the batching plant. The 'as raised' ballast or gravel was imported to the site by about 30 Air Ministry lorries with local firms supplying the gravel from their pits on a sub-contract basis.

The practise of lorries being checked in at the gate two or three times, then making their circuits without unloading applied to us as it did to many other airfields under construction at the time. I only hope that it became too well known to last in practise for any length of time.

There were about 800 Irish labourers encamped on the site, some of whom came to me and complained of the 'hardness' of the Site Agent, Mr. Curzon, but there was never any real trouble. The labourer's rate of pay was one shilling and threepence an hour, equal to seven new pence today. I didn't envy Mr. Curzon his job at all!

My job was to keep an overall eye on affairs, mainly to keep the thing going at full capacity. How lucky I was to have such an excellent staff in all sections, other than one of the Foremen of Trades. There were rumours of his having sold two or three lorries at the end of the contract!!

Recalled former Suffolk schoolboy John Watson:

At the time, I heard of a fairly typical haulage contractor who, after one of his lorries had made about ten or twelve circuits of an airfield without unloading, although collecting a ticket at the gate each time for the same load, reprimanded his driver by saying, "You had better tip that load off next time round . . . I can see grass starting to grow on it!

Farmer Percy Kindred of Parham, near Framlingham, remembers the Air Ministry requisitioning some of his father's land for an airfield in 1942 at an annual rent of 15 shillings an acre. He explained:

In those days, of course, we didn't have any choice and cooperated to the full. We were only too pleased to do what we could to aid the war effort. Although things were very much in the balance at that time, some of the really big landowners complained that the presence of an airfield on their land would disturb the pheasants and partridges.

I had four horses and carts which I hired out to the building contractors during the cold, wet winter of 1942/43. This was the only way they could move their heavy loads of building materials because of the muddy conditions. I also had a tractor which had spade grips on its iron drive wheels. This tractor proved its worth when, time after time, it easily pulled bogged-down lorries out of the mud.

I still marvel that the building of Framlingham airfield was ever completed.

The local Home Guard units had many tales to tell of those action-packed war years. David Warne, a veteran of 'J' company, 4th Suffolk Home Guards, remembers events during the construction of Horham airfield in 1942:

The first occurrence happened during the laying of the concrete runways. It was in the early hours of the morning and the job was progressing very well. Fortunately, the construction gangs didn't work after dark with floodlights like they do today, and they always parked their machinery and trucks around the perimeter of the 'drome until the next day's work began at dawn.

About one or two o'clock one morning, a German bomber dropped what must have been one of those landmines right on the point where the main East-West runway intersects with one of the two shorter ones. It made a crater some 60 feet across and 30 feet deep, and the force of the blast actually sucked the subsoil out from beneath adjacent undamaged concrete bays causing them to crack, which of course meant that these too, had to be broken up and re-laid. It meant a lot of extra work, but the huge crater was filled with concrete before construction could recommence two or three days later.

At about that time, another large bomb landed quite close to the cottage of a friend of mine, Roger Coleman, who lived almost on the airfield. Luckily the bomb — I believe it was a 1,000-pounder — didn't explode, and the bomb disposal people took it away. It took them almost a week to dig it out and make it safe. Brave chaps, those.

Another incident happened one night when a German airman, who had apparently bailed out of his damaged plane, tried to give himself up to a Home Guard Private. The poor Home Guardsman, who was on his way home from guard duty — or the pub — and in full uniform, promptly leapt from his bicycle and fled into the night! Two Irishmen who were walking back to the airfield, then met up with the German and took him to Hoxne police station. He gave the Irishmen his compass which was on a strap like a wrist-watch, but had been worn around the thigh, just above the knee. It was luminous. It subsequently changed hands several times on Horham airfield, and that's how I came to see it.

For Sammy Hurry and his 11-year-old friend Billy Taylor, who lived almost beside the new Thorpe Abbotts airfield, the hectic building activity was of constant fascination.

Never before had they seen such awesome power as generated by the huge earthmoving equipment, the concrete laying machine, or the spectacular chain of explosions each time trees were blasted out of the ground in rapid succession.

The bulk of the construction work was completed by April 1943, an incredible feat of civil engineering considering the extremely adverse weather conditions prevailing that winter.

April coincided with the arrival of American administrative personnel of the 100th Bombardment Group (Heavy), and soon the construction equipment, trucks and workmen moved on to build yet another airfield in West Norfolk. Only a few small gangs of bricklayers, carpenters, plumbers, painters and labourers remained to complete their outstanding work, while technicians installed standby generators, telephone exchange, boilers, water pumps and radio equipment.

The 100th Bomb Group had been officially activated at Walla Walla Air Base in Washington State on 14 November 1942, and Col. Darr H. Alkire was appointed its first Commanding Officer. The Colonel had been a Flying Fortress man ever since the airplane had been adopted by USAAF in the late 'thirties.

He was a forceful individual who quickly won the respect of the men in his new command. The day following his arrival at the Walla Walla Base, he assembled the entire command in the base theatre and let them know what they could expect in a colourful and strongly-worded walk by way of self- introduction. He began:

> The ground crews are the backbone of this outfit. Without them the flying Prima Donna's aren't worth a damn . . .

He went on to explain why.

To the combat aircrews, Colonel Alkire spoke with chilling simplicity about the stark reality of the task that confronted them:

> Don't get the idea that your job is going to be glorious or glamourous. You've got dirty work to do, and you might as well face the facts. You are going to be baby-killers and women-killers, because the enemy started this bombing of cities and we're going to finish it. We're going to beat them at their own game, and we can't let pity for non-combatants hold us back in this business of destroying the enemy's war potential.*

One of the original 100th B.G. ground crewmen was Sgt. Robert Spangler from Pennsylvania, who had enlisted in the Army Air Corps in February 1940.

He said:

> I'll always remember the time when I had just graduated from Technical Training School. I took my tool kit out to begin maintenance work on an airplane and reported to a Technical Sergeant. His first words to me were: 'Go back and get a bucket of soapy water and some clean rags. You won't be needing that tool kit for a while.' It seemed that one needed to be at least a Corporal before you were allowed to change a spark plug or a cotter pin on an airplane. The training was very, very thorough, and by the end of it we knew every single part on a B17, its function and how to replace it.
>
> In January 1942, I was a Private, 2nd Class, Air Mechanic. By November 1942, I was a Master Sergeant, Line Chief, and was assigned to the 551st. Squadron, which was commanded by Captain (later Major) John B. Kidd, of the 100th. Bomb Group at Walla Walla, Washington.
>
> During the next two weeks, about 90 mechanics arrived fresh from Aircraft and Engine Schools. They had received about a month of basic training and five months of A & E schooling. They came from every walk of life, bank clerks, ranch hands, salesmen, cowboys, farmers, students, etc. That's how the engineering outfit of the 551st got started under the

---

***Contrail 6: The History of the 100th Bomb Group*

command of Lt. William Carleton. The Group's three other Squadrons took shape in the same way.

Our B17's arrived straight from the Boeing factory, Seattle, and our Group went on to various bases in the United States for further specialized training prior to moving overseas in early summer of 1943.

Ellis B. Scripture, a 21 year old administrator in the Y.M.C.A., recalls the rigorous training of the flight crews for the 95th Bombardment Group (Heavy):

Each of us volunteers for flying duties were a real bunch of greenhorns when we began our pre-flight training in February, 1942, at Santa Ana, California. When we arrived, there were less than 1,000 people on the base. Within three months there were 50,000 there and you can imagine the frantic activity that took place in order to build this installation, and many similar installations around the country, as the United States mobilized for war following the Japanese attack on Pearl Harbour the previous December.

We were given rough training and we were treated like the scum of the earth when we were Cadets. This, of course was absolutely necessary to instil into our minds the fact that military discipline is most important for the task that lay ahead. We were drilled continuously and we lived in very rustic barracks. This moulded us into a cohesive group of young men, all dreaming dreams of flying for the United States Army Air Corps.

During our training we were separated into three groups; pilots, bombardiers, and navigators. Of course, every young man joined the Air Corps with the idea that one day he was going to be a pilot and I was no exception. But it was necessary for the Air Corps to develop a full crew and they used their best judgement in dividing us into three different categories.

We survived our Cadet training and in early July 1942 some of us were transferred to Mather Field, near Sacramento, California, to begin our specialized navigational training. It was rigid, it was tough, it was difficult and it was an entirely new discipline for each of us. We had a great many things to learn very quickly. We got very little flight time and by the time we graduated I recall each of us had spent a maximum of 35 hours in the air. We were commissioned 2nd Lieutenants and were given our assignments.

The ideal situation on receiving our commission was to be assigned to Air Transport Command. This Command was responsible for moving airplanes all over the world and all of us who had worked hard at Navigational Training School had hoped that we would have an opportunity to see the world. However no one from our class joined A.T.C. All of us were assigned to Combat Units which were being put together in great numbers at this time.

A group of us were assigned to the 95th Bombardment Group at Geiger Field, Washington, in October 1942. I became a member of a brand new

Group that was just being formed under the command of Colonel Alfred Kessler. A vastly experienced but small group of men assisted him in putting together, in a few short weeks, a fully fledged combat Group from comparatively young and raw material by demonstrating excellent and superior leadership themselves. Colonel Kessler, a West Point Graduate, Class of 1922, was assisted in his immediate task by men such as Jack Gibson who had flown some 10,000 hours as an American Airlines pilot after having been an Army Air Corps pilot back in the early days, Dave McKnight who had joined the 95th after having had very thorough flying experience with the Royal Canadian Air Force, the Hamilton brothers who were also vastly experienced pilots as was Dexter Snedley, another pilot from the R.C.A.F.

These sort of people knew airplanes and they knew how to fly airplanes, in particular they knew how to fly the B17. But the great majority of the young pilots who made up the original 95th Group were men who had been rushed through flight training, just as we had been rushed through our navigational and bombardier training.

My original pilot, Charlie Reuben, had a total of something less than 150 hours flying time including primary, basic, advanced and four engine bomber training when he arrived at Geiger Field. Our co-pilot, Willie Wilson, had even less and so it went through all of our original flight crews.

We were young, we were eager and we wanted to do the job but we didn't really know what it was all about or what to expect. Under the experienced and dedicated leadership by the men in charge we were able to form a reasonably good combat team in a very short while.

This was how the 95th Bomb Group began and many other Groups took shape in exactly the same way. Among the several close friends I had made at Mather Field was my room-mate Harry Crosby, later to become Group Navigator of the 100th Bomb Group. We subsequently "sweated" each other through many tough missions when we were flying with the 13th Combat Bomb Wing in the European Theatre of Operations.

Chapter 2

IN mid-June 1943 the B17 Flying Fortresses of the 100th Bomb Group appeared over Thorpe Abbotts. One by one each of the 42 aircraft pealed off gracefully from the circling formation and landed on the main runway. They then taxied to their respective dispersal points under directions radioed from the control tower.

All except one:

Said pilot Lt. John Brady:

My crew was issued a brand new B17F at Kearney, Nebraska. From there we flew in stages to Selfridge Field, Michigan, to Presque Isle, Maine, to Goose Bay, Labrador, to Reykjavik, Iceland, and on to Prestwick, Scotland. We then took off again for Podington, England, where we remained for several days before proceeding to Thorpe Abbotts, Norfolk.

On arrival over our permanent base we found that we couldn't get our landing gear down. We were then directed to the repair depot at Warton where we proceeded to make a wheels-up landing, thus ending the career of that particular plane. We had previously made another wheels-up landing in the United States, but that was in the Rocky Mountains. Fortunately, the snow had been so deep and soft that not even the ball turret was damaged. That airplane lived to fly again as it was subsequently dis-assembled and trucked out of the mountains. Both crash-landings were made without injury to the crew.

I found the B17 a very forgiving airplane to fly. It would almost fly itself, and was so stable that it would absorb quite unbelievable damage in battle during subsequent combat missions over Europe and still function.

Farmer Percy Kindred remembers:

The first Fortress Group to arrive at Framlingham temporarily, was the 95th. They flew two or three missions in early June. Then on Sunday 13 June, about 18 of their B17's took off on another mission to Germany. Only six came home. Of those that had survived, one crash-landed and the rest were literally shot to pieces.

That was one of my first sights — virtually outside my front door — of what those men were going through. I was stunned. What I saw that evening I won't forget . . . ever . . . . .

Then came the 390th, and so it went on.

Most of the American airmen I met were nice fellows and extremely generous. In fact, they were the most generous people I have ever met. If we were ever short of anything and they had it you could be sure that they would share it with you. They behaved like gentlemen, and if ever they set a foot wrong I would only have to whisper, and they never did it again. They were young men in a strange land, fighting for this country, and it goes without saying that I held them in the highest regard.

Sgt. James Johnson of the 95th Bomb Group's Intelligence Section recalls:

We had been transferred from Alconbury to Framlingham on 12 May 1943. That same evening, 'Lord Haw Haw', broadcasting from Berlin, announced on our radio, "Welcome to your new airfield at Framlingham men of the 95th Bomb Group . . ."

We were constantly warned that "Careless Talk Cost Lives" by posters and signs virtually everywhere we went, and security was generally speaking, rigidly observed.

However, we had been at Horham for quite some time when two of our S-2 (Intelligence Section) people went to London on a 48-hour pass to get some much needed rest and relaxation. On the train from Diss to London, one of them got talking with an RAF officer the way airmen do. During their conversation, our man casually mentioned some aspects of our method of decoding the Field Orders when they came in via teletype machine from Divisional Headquarters prior to a mission.

On arrival at Liverpool Street Station, the RAF officer immediately summoned two military policemen and ordered them to arrest our man. He was subsequently court-martialed and served a lengthy sentence at Leavenworth Prison, Kansas.

» » » « « «

The construction of bomber and fighter airfields for the 8th Air Force, mainly in East Anglia, was not without incident. At Framlingham, a dozen or so miles from the east coast, and while the air field was nearing final completion, a crippled four-engine B17 Flying Fortress returning from a raid on Germany, approached the completed main runway. Its two inboard engines, propellers "feathered" (blades turned edge-on to the airstream), trailed long plumes of smoke as two red flares, signalling that the aircraft carried wounded crewmen, arched up into the late afternoon sky from the stricken plane.

Percy Kindred, working in an adjoining field, watched horrified, as a building contractor's lorry drove slowly towards the runway's threshold, its driver oblivious to the approaching B17. For what seemed an eternity, the staggering aircraft continued on its collision course with the truck. At the last possible moment, the pilot pulled the giant plane up and veered off, its two remaining engines roaring in tortured protest as the pilot slammed the throttles forward. There was no alternative but to go around again and attempt another approach.

The Fortress* had gained precious little altitude when it suddenly nosed up, stalled, rolled completely on its back and plunged to the ground in a shattering explosion, its roaring engines its own executioner. A funeral pyre of oily black smoke and red flames leapt skywards from the blazing wreckage of the B17, instantly incinerating its ten-man crew.

Percy Kindred swallowed hard as he heard the wailing sirens of the ambulances racing to the scene but he knew it was hopeless. The human body does not survive the crushing impact of being hurled to the ground at a speed nearing 200 miles an hour.

"You're too late," he whispered, "too damned late . . ."

The truck continued slowly on its way around the perimeter track to its destination of the far side of the airfield, its driver still seemingly oblivious to the stark tragedy he had unwittingly caused.

» » » « « «

Britain had already endured almost four long years of war. East Anglians had heard their wireless sets tell them heart-rending accounts of the bombings of London, Coventry, Bristol, Manchester and many other British cities and towns, including Norwich and Ipswich, the County capitals of Norfolk and Suffolk respectively. They had endured strict food and clothing rationing, the blackout, and all the other accom-

---

*This Fortress, piloted by Lieutenant Melton Wallace, was B17F 42-3212 from the 379th bombardment Group, Kimbolton, Huntingdonshire. It was returning from a raid on Kassel, Germany. The date of this tragedy was 30th July 1943. The charred bodies of all ten crewmen were recovered from the smouldering wreckage and were later buried at the American Military Cemetery at Madingley, Cambridgeshire.

panying discomforts, privations and hardships of wartime Britain.

Probably the worst of the many bombing raids on the nation's capital occurred on the night of Sunday, 10 May 1941, when 1,200 German bombers attacked the heart of London. The glow from the ensuing raging fires could be seen quite clearly in the night sky above the burning capital from Ipswich, 70 miles away. The civilian casualties amounted to about 1,800 seriously injured and 1,436 killed — excluding those of the injured who died later.

Among the many historical landmarks and famous monuments badly damaged by the high explosive and incendiary bombs which showered down in thousands, were the Houses of Parliament, Westminster Abbey, British Museum, Mansion House, the churches of St. Clements Danes, All Hallows and the Temple.

That night, Nazi radio in Berlin broadcast to the world that the City of London had ceased to exist.

Sgt. Ted Lucey, a radio technician based at Horham with the 95th Bomb Group, relates his impressions following a visit to a blitzed London in October 1943:

> I took the underground train to Marble Arch. As always, it was sad to see hundreds of civilians camping in subway stations for the night. First arrivals got cots which were hinged to the station walls; others whatever platform space they could find. Some people had gone through this ordeal since the beginning of the blitz in 1940. Little children slept somehow oblivious to the noise and bustle going on around them. Train services ceased at 2300 hours so there was relative quiet for these poor people until the early morning.
>
> I went for a long walk in the St. Paul's Cathedral area. Neither the cathedral nor the buildings facing it had been badly damaged. On the other three sides, however, virtually nothing was left standing. Just a huge desert of broken bricks, caved-in walls, steel girders twisted by the heat and very little wood; that had been consumed in the fire-storms. Here and there odd things came into view. High up on a jagged wall a toilet bowl was held in place by its pipework . . . no floor . . . no ceiling. What a horrible experience for these unfortunate Londoners. And we were here to do the same thing to the Germans.

Sergeant Bob Banta, a B17 Radio Operator with the 390th Bomb Group at Framlingham, expresses his thoughts on bombing Germany:

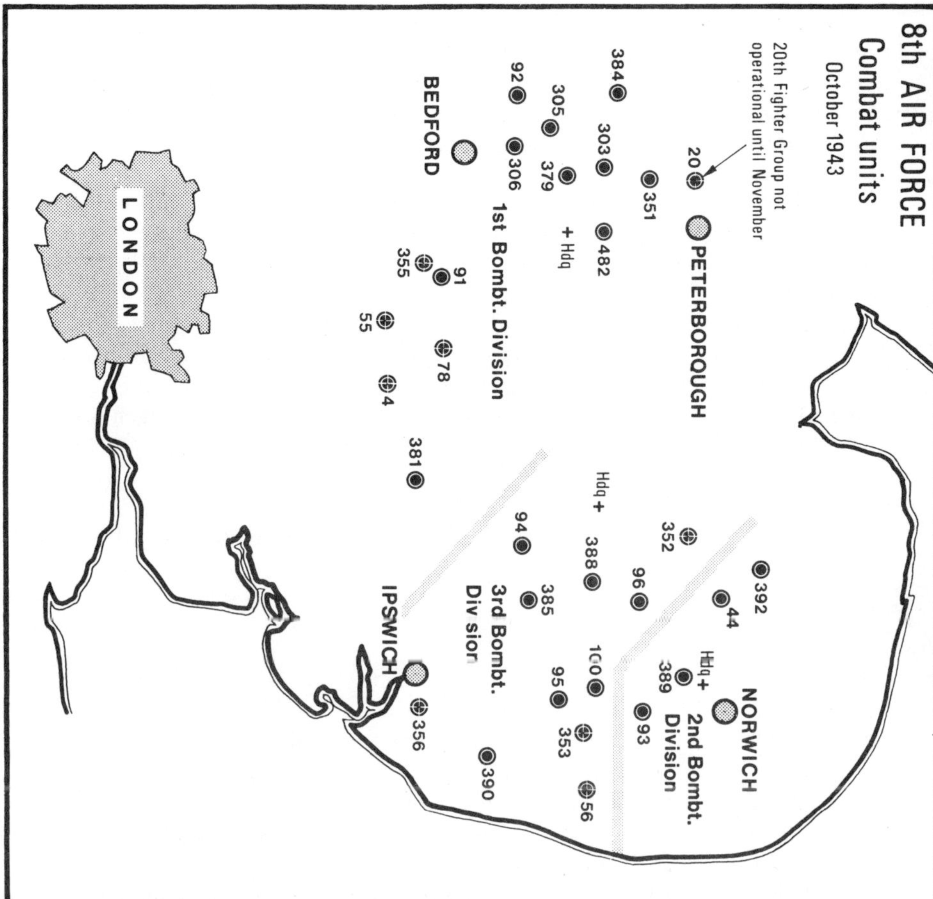

4 FG	Debden	P-47
20 FG	Kings Cliffe	P-38
44 BG	Shipdham	B-24
55 FG	Nuthampstead	P-38
56 FG	Halesworth	P-47
78 FG	Duxford	,,
91 BG	Bassingbourn	B-17
92 BG	Podington	,,
93 BG	Hardwick	B-24
94 BG	Bury St. Edmunds	B-17
95 BG	Horham	,,
96 BG	Snetterton Heath	,,
100 BG	Thorpe Abbotts	,,
303 BG	Molesworth	,,
305 BG	Chelveston	,,
306 BG	Thurleigh	,,
351 BG	Polebrook	,,
352 FG	Bodney	P-47
353 FG	Metfield	,,
355 FG	Steeple Morden	,,
356 FG	Martlesham	,,
379 BG	Kimbolton	B-17
381 BG	Ridgewell	,,
384 BG	Grafton Underwood	,,
385 BG	Great Ashfield	,,
388 BG	Knettishall	,,
389 BG	Hethel	B-24
390 BG	Framlingham	B-17
392 BG	Wendling	B-24
482 BG	Alconbury	Pff B-17

Location of Eighth Air Force combat units which were operational in October 1943.

My country requested that I help it in a conflict that it deemed necessary. I obeyed that call to arms. But my willingness really came from a selfish desire to be or do something special and the inborn craving for adventure. I was proud of my technical achievement and involvement as a member of a Fortress crew and the adventure inherent in such duty, so much so that all other considerations were ignored.

The airplane, of which I was part, would be carrying bombs which would cause much death and destruction among the German people. I didn't hate the Germans. How then, could I justify my part in helping to kill them?

Germany was a nation that had been taken over by a minority group who simply terrorized or killed their opposition. They thrived on power, greed and the brutally sadistic treatment of others. They had deprived other nations and other races of their freedom, employing methods never before dreamed of. But I still could not bring myself to hate the average German, because I knew that they were pawns just as I was a pawn in something far greater than the individual.

But Germany had to be stopped. Otherwise my country's freedom, as well as my own, would also be threatened eventually.

« « « » » »

The bomber airfields themselves occasionally came under attack, as Lt. Jack Nosser, 390th Bomb Group, recalls:

One night, German bombers dropped a number of anti-personnel bombs on and around our base at Framlingham. Apparently some had landed near the runways and taxi areas. These bombs had thin wire feelers spread out around the bomb and when a feeler was disturbed the small bomb would spring off the ground and explode.

The following day, we had orders to stay out of any rough grassed areas and to keep on the concrete and paved surfaces, until Base Ordnance C.O. Major Harry Price had personally made a thorough search. I always admired that act . . . most Majors would have sent a Private instead!

Lt. Paul Schultz, Lead Navigator, 385th Bomb Group at Great Ashfield, Suffolk, also vividly remembers an attack on his airfield:

Early one morning, I was briefing the navigators for a mission, when an aircraft was heard to 'buzz' the airfield. My assistant, George Dowling remarked, "Achtung, der Luftwaffe!" This brought roars of laughter. But almost immediately there were several very loud explosions. The lights went out, pieces of plaster fell from the ceiling, and we all dived for the shelter of the tables. The lights came back on in a minute or so, and George's first nervous words were, 'Please . . . I was only fooling.'

What had happened was a German 'plane had indeed 'buzzed' the field. The control tower had turned on the runway lights and at the same time the large maintenance hangar opened its doors to roll out a B17. That was all the German pilot needed, he dropped his bombs and left hurriedly for Germany.

« « « » » »

For young Sammy Hurry and his friend Billy Taylor, that summer of 1943 was a time for making friends with the American airmen at Thorpe Abbotts.

Sammy Hurry remembers:

When the Americans arrived at Thorpe Abbotts it changed our lives completely. I had never seen an aeroplane close-up before, and the Flying Fortresses seemed enormous at first, but we soon became accustomed to their great size. And after a little while we were allowed by the friendly ground crews to go inside the B17's and have a look around. What never ceased to amaze me was how these monsters were ever able to get into the air at all.

Billy and I made many friends, notably from the 351st Squadron whose 13 hardstands stretched along the perimeter track for about a mile on either side of the control tower. We spent almost all our time at the airfield, even occasionally playing truant from Dickleburgh School to do so. We would approach the mechanics as they worked on the planes and ask, "Got any gum, chum?" And back would come the reply, "Sure have, buddy. Got any big sisters?"

Because there were no laundry facilities on the base, I soon became a 'laundry boy.' I had a home-made cart, vaguely resembling a Chinese rickshaw, which Billy and I used to haul veritable mountains of laundry home for our mothers to wash and iron for the American airmen. The standard charge for a military issue shirt was sixpence. This extra income was very welcome to our parents as the average weekly wage per household was then very low. We also ran countless errands for the Americans, from collecting and delivering tools to placing flarepaths beside the runways when the weather was bad. We had our meals in the Airmen's Mess (Chow Hall) and were issued overalls. Quite often we were allowed to ride in jeeps and trucks to and from various parts of the base which was, in effect, a small American town.

What impressed me most about the Americans was their sincere and warm friendship and their generosity to us youngsters in particular.

The fire station, which was next to the control tower, was open for mugs of steaming coffee practically all the time. I'd never tasted real coffee before! We also had access to the control tower and to the 'Greenhouse' on top of the roof which contained a pair of binoculars mounted on a stand which swivelled enabling us to see the planes on the far side of the airfield much more clearly. From here we could count the aircraft going out on a mission in the mornings, and in the late afternoon we would count them as they returned, and more often than not they'd suffered losses. We saw some terrible sights, particularly when a crippled Fortress came in for a crash-landing firing red flares as it approached the airfield. The ambulances and crash tenders, sirens blaring, appeared as if by magic beside the bomber as it finally slithered to a stop. Split seconds could often mean the hairline difference between life and death for the bomber crews, some of whom didn't seem to be much older than Billy Taylor.

All this ceaseless, noisy and hectic activity, accompanied occasionally by destruction, injuries and death, which many local people witnessed, was a very strange and vivid contrast to the peace and quiet of an afternoon's fishing for perch at the nearby River Dove.

« « « » » »

During routine maintenance, the ground crew chiefs ground-tested their particular aircraft. It was during one of these pre-flight tests that a very bizarre accident occurred.

A workman, while driving his truck along the perimeter track, failed to notice a Fortress emerge from its hardstand, its crew chief more intent on studying the engine gauges than the path in front. The equally inattentive workman subsequently collided with one of the aircraft's four whirling propellers, cutting the steering wheel off in the startled driver's hand, after first demolishing the front wheels and the truck's engine in a spectacular shower of sparks and clouds of escaping steam, as the crew chief frantically stood on the planes brakes. Miraculously unharmed, the driver emerged slowly from his shattered cab, now at ground level, still clutching half a steering wheel.

When he at last regained his composure after several minutes, the driver strode purposefully to the Adjutant's office and indignantly demanded a new truck. Major Uttley, the Adjutant, patiently listened to both sides of the story, and then offered the workman a deal. He would supply the new truck if he in return, replaced the B17's $10,000 propeller and $15,000 engine. The case was closed.

This incident quickly paled into insignificance, however, compared with the almost daily dramas, tragedies and disasters during the next few months which were to earn the Group the forebodingly grim epithet "The Bloody Hundredth."

John Pettenger, Pilot on 10 October 1943, 385th Bomb Group, 551st Squadron, on perimeter track at Great Ashford, Suffolk, 27 September 1979. Ian McLachlan

Winton MacCarter, Pilot on 10 October 1943, 100th Bomb Group, 349th Squadron, at the Control Tower at Thorpe Abbotts Airfield, 8 September 1979. 100th B.G.U.K.

Stanley Smith, a Waist Gunner on 10 October 1943, 390th Bomb Group, 570th Squadron, at the 390th Group's Control Tower at Framlingham, Suffolk, 16 September 1979. Stewart Evans

Official U.S.A.F. Photo

Miss Fortune ***approaches Framlingham Airfield.***

British Crown Copyright Reserved
R.A.F. Museum

Horham Airfield, Suffolk, under construction on 27 August 1942. Control tower is near the top to left of center and two hangers can be seen at the top right.

Framlingham Airfield (Parham) under construction 16 October 1942. The main runway is from left to right. The perimeter track is 3 1/2 miles in length. The total amount of concrete used in building one bomber field would build a highway 18 ft. wide by 65 miles long.

British Crown Copyright Reserved
R.A.F. Museum

Winter mists at Thorpe Abbotts Airfield.

Sammy Hurry visits the ground crew of Hardstand #13, 100th Bomb Group, 351st Squadron, at Thorpe Abbotts, December 1943. Sammy Hurry

A 390th plane, Sequatchiee *is ready for take-off.* Sequatchiee *was M.I.A. on 22 June 1944 over Paris.*

Schoolboys Leslie Jefferson, Billy Taylor and Sammy Hurry pose near the Fire Station and ambulance sheds in the Control Tower area of Thorpe Abbotts Airfield in September 1943. Sammy Hurry

William Vandivert

Coventry, in England's industrial midlands, was the target for 500 German bombers on the night of November 14, 1940. The city center was almost completely destroyed in a raid which was the worst suffered by an English city during the war.

In the city of London, St. Paul's Cathedral is outlined against the smoke and flames during a night attack by the Luftwaffe on 29 December 1940.

United Press International

388th Bomb Group practice bombing mission over Tollesburg Rande, north of London. Airfield is Bradwell Bay. Nearest aircraft (230215) is the second Slightly Dangerous *which led the 388th Group on the Münster raid.*

100th Bomb Group, 351st Squadron: Left to right, Captain Barker, Squadron Operations Officer; Captain William Carleton, Engineering Officer; Master Sergeant Robert Spangler, Line Chief.

Major John B. Kidd, Operations Officer, 100th Bomb Group.

Everett E. Blakely, Pilot of Just-A-Snappin, *100th Bomb Group, which crash landed after returning from the Bremen raid of 8 October 1943.*

The original crew of Miss fortune, *shot down over Bremen, 8 October 1943 while flying* Blood, Guts and Rust II.

Just-A-Snappin', *a 100th Bomb Group plane, crash landed at Ludham Airfield upon returning from the Bremen raid, 8 October 1943. Maj. Gen. Kidd states: "Someone counted over 800 holes from the radio room back."* Maj. Gen. J.B. Kidd

Another view of Just-A-Snappin' *after landing at Ludham Airfield.*

Official U.S.A.F. Photo

Bombs drop on Bremen, 8 October 1943, from the 385th Bomb Group formation.

Flak near the 390th formation over Bremen, 8 October 1943.

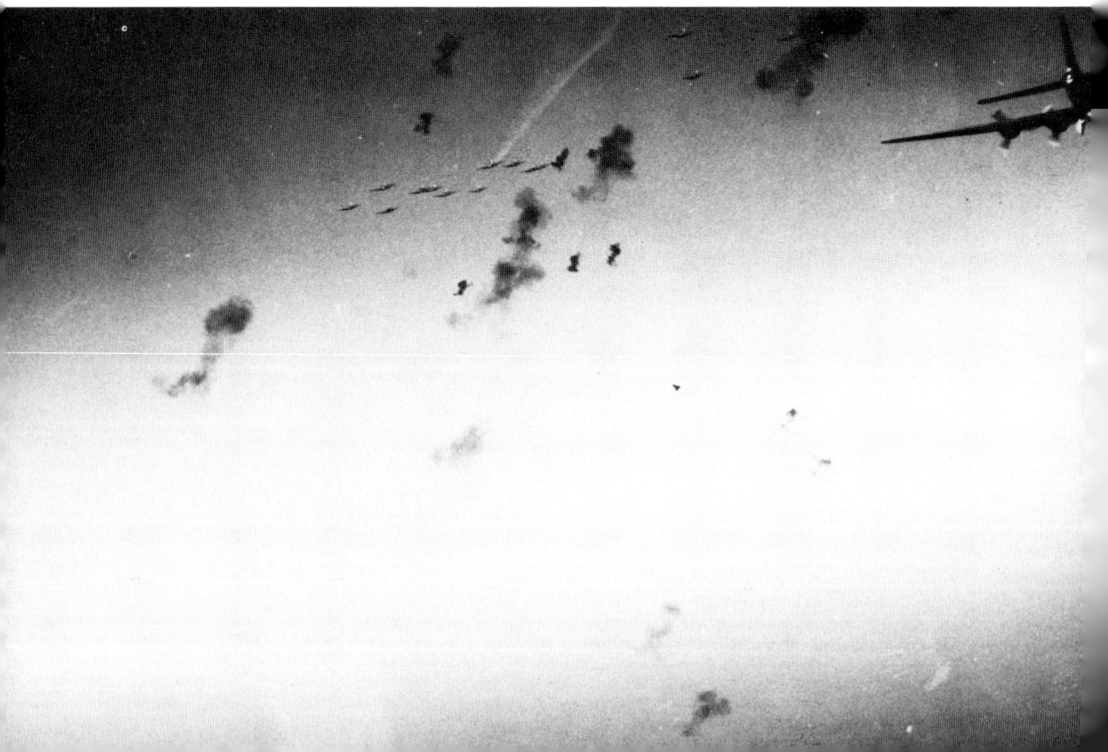

***Stupefier** of the 379th Bomb Group crashed on takeoff for Marienburg with a full load of fuel and bombs, 9 October 1943.*

Official U.S.A.F. Photo

390th formation after the bomb run over Marienburg, 9 October 1943. Official U.S.A.F. Photo

Sergeant Henry Bush, Crew Chief, running up the engine of the P47 Thunderbolt Little Demon *on hardstand in 1943. 353rd Fighter Group, Metfield, Suffolk. Note the B17's flying overhead.* Walter Beckham

P47's taxiing for take-off. The 353rd Fighter Group, Metfield, Suffolk, October 1943. Walter Beckham

Colonel Hubert "Hub" Zemke, Commanding Officer of the 56th Fighter Group.

P47 Thunderbolt (The Jug, as it was known). 61st Squadron, 56th Fighter Group, Halesworth, Suffolk.

A 56th Fighter Group P47 Thunderbolt with 75 gallon belly tank

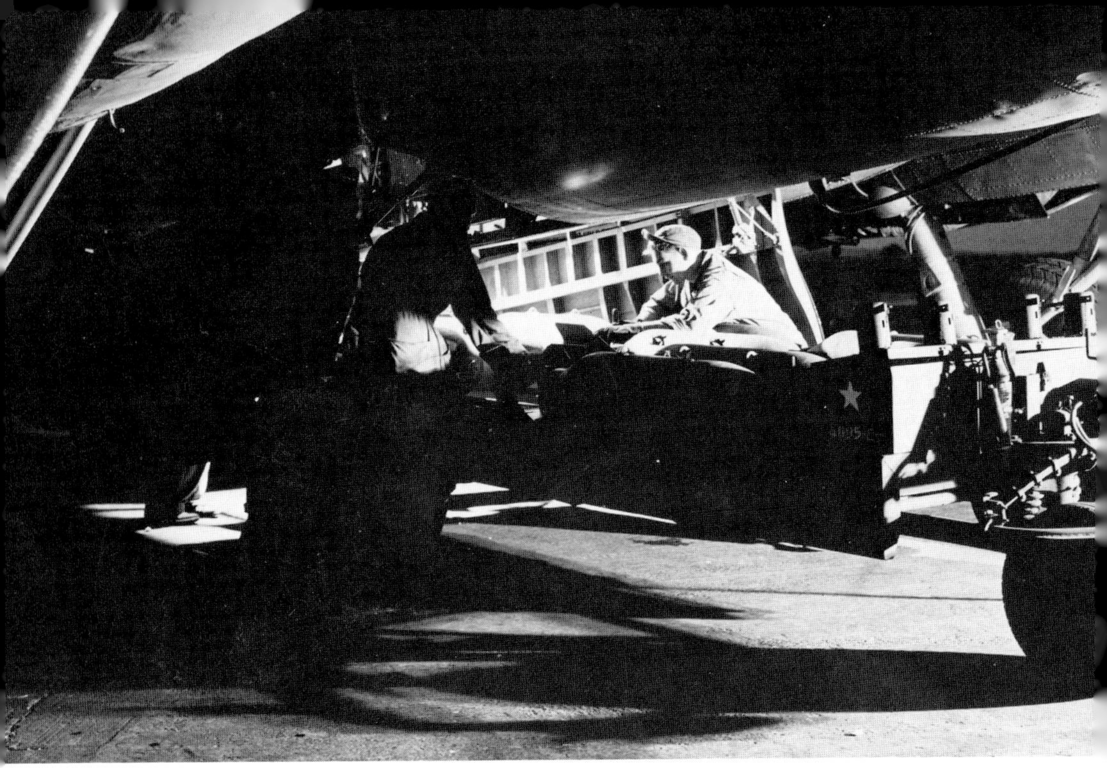

Preparing bombs at dusk for tomorrow's mission. 388th Bomb Group, Knettishall, Suffolk.

Loading bombs at dusk. 388th Bomb Group, Knettishall, Suffolk.

The ground crew working on B17* Miss Carry *of the 570th Squadron, 390th Bomb Group.

Miss Carry *on hardstand at 390th Bomb Group, Framlingham, with ground crew at work.* Official U.S.A.F. Photo

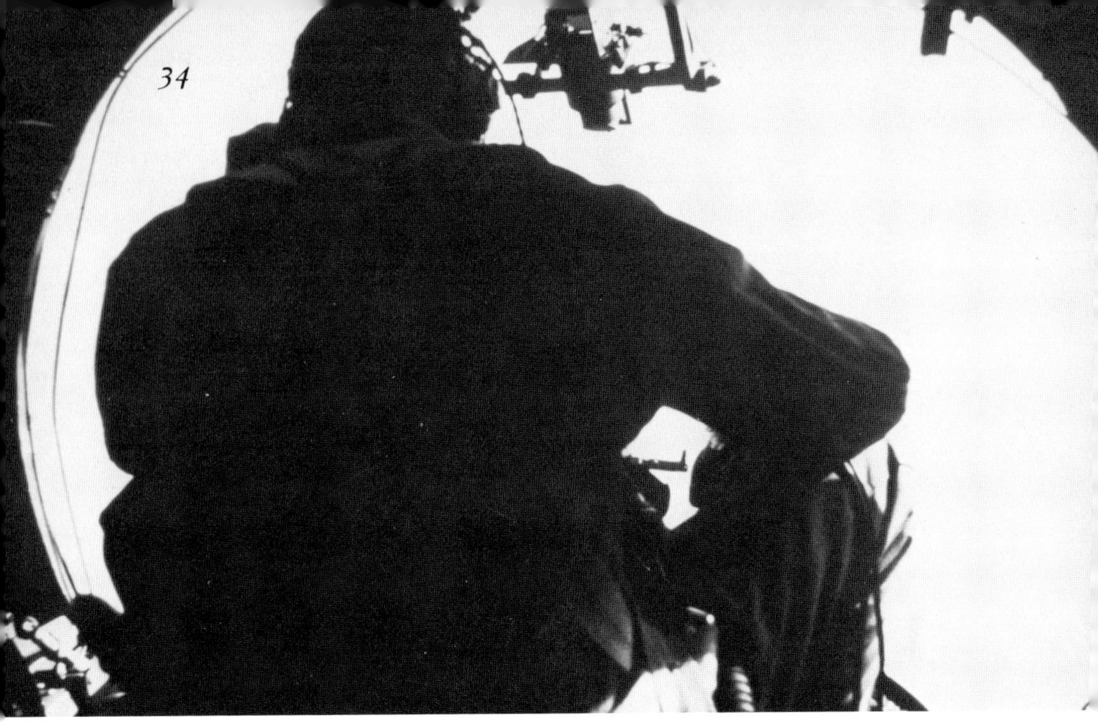

Lt. William Nicholls, Bombardier of Laiden Maiden *of the 385th Bomb Group releases his bombs over Marienburg, 9 October 1943. A falling bomb from another B17 can be seen in the lower right of the photo.*

100th Bomb Group ground crewmen anxiously await their bombers return.

Chapter 3

FRIDAY afternoon, 8 October 1943. For Major John B. Kidd, the 24-year-old Operations Officer of the 100th Bomb Group, it had been an eventful summer and early autumn. He'd flown several missions, some of them rough, and others which he had regarded as "Milk Runs."

He flew, alternating with the Group's Commanding Officer, Colonel Neil B. Harding, and the four Squadron C.O's, on the occasions when the 100th was selected to lead the 13th Combat Bomb Wing, which was comprised of the 95th Bomb Group, Horham; the 100th and the 390th Bomb Group at Framlingham. Both these other Groups were based in neighbouring Suffolk and were within a few minutes flying time of Thorpe Abbotts.

Major Kidd had led the Group on the long shuttle mission to North Aftica on 17 August, bombing en-route an important aircraft factory complex at Regensburg in Southern Germany — a highly accurate attack which, although Allied intelligence were unaware at the time, had destroyed almost all of the fuselage jigs of a top secret jet fighter, the Messerschmitt 262.

It was the Regensburg raid, however, which signalled the start of the 100th Bomb Group's misfortunes. They had lost 9 of the 21 Fortresses dispatched from Thorpe Abbotts. This crippling blow contributed to the highest loss suffered to date by the Eighth Air Force in their daylight strategic bombing campaign against Germany, 60 B17's.

Another vital strike against the German war machine was achieved on the night of August 17/18, 1943. Pathfinders of Bomber Command illuminated the top-secret V2 rocket research establishment at Peenemünde, on Germany's Baltic coast, with flares which enabled the main force of Lancasters, Stirlings and Halifaxs to carry out a highly successful raid which disrupted the development programme for several months. The cost was high. Forty-four Royal Air Force bombers failed to return.

As new airfields became available for new B17, B24 Liberator, and twin-engined B26 Marauder Groups during that Summer of 1943, and they in turn had suffered bitter losses and experiences, it wasn't until the Regensburg raid and shortly thereafter that the 100th Bomb Group established an unenviable 'jinx' which, as no news travels like bad news, quickly became a legend throughout the entire Eighth Air Force.

The briefed target for 8 October, was Bremen in North Western Germany, a well-defended ship-building and industrial town, and nearby Vegesack with its U-Boat building yards beside the River Weser, less than 30 miles from the North Sea.

At precisely 1329 hours, Major Kidd in the co-pilot's seat of Captain Everett Blakely's B17 *Just-a-Snappin'*, crossed the East Anglian coast after gaining altitude and assembling, leading the 13th Combat Wing of 63 Fortresses out over the North Sea. The Wing formed part of the largest task force assembled to date — 399 Fortresses and Liberators, to be escorted part of the way by 274 fighters, the rugged single-engined P47 Thunderbolt, affectionately known by the bomber crews as their "Little Friends."

As the 100th Bomb Group passed over the Initial Point at the start of their bomb run on Bremen, the Fortresses lowered their bomb bay doors. Recalled Major Kidd:

As we approached the target area, everything on this particular mission was going comparatively well. But as we got closer, the hitherto clear sky was literally getting blacker over the target. We could actually feel the whole airplane being thrown bodily upwards as shells burst directly below us, and we heard the accompanying rattle of steel splinters striking the fuselage, sounding just like rice being thrown over an automobile at a wedding. I couldn't help thinking how remote what was going on at that moment was from a wedding . . .

The flak seemed to be coming up in co-ordinated bunches. I learned later that this technique was called a "Box Barrage." It comprised up to 16 radar-controlled guns firing in unison. When the shells exploded all together in a tight pattern of black, smokey puffs, it was rather an exciting spectacle to behold.

During the bomb run, which could last up to five minutes, the pilot turned the control of the aircraft over to the bombardier who then steered the plane via the Automatic Flight Control Equipment for the slight directional changes necessary to hit the target accurately.

For the pilots, of course, this was the most trying time of the mission, when the airplane and the formation were under the control of the Lead Bombardier. There was nothing for the pilots to do except watch and wait. With the flak exploding all around, I could feel the concussion rocking the ship. I think that it was the hardest thing to do during my time on this earth. Shortly after bombs away we were hit, the aircraft lurched and things began to happen.

Among the other 100th Bomb Group B17's which had been caught in that same barrage was a Fortress named *Our Baby* piloted by Major Gale Cleven, one of the four Squadron Commanders at Thorpe Abbotts. His burning B17 crashed near Osnabruck after his crew had successfully bailed out. Another 100th Bomb Group bomber, *Salvo Sal,* went down on the way home near the Zuider Zee area of Western Holland. Three crew members evaded capture and set off down the escape lines to try to reach Spain. Captain William MacDonald, Pilot, and Lieutenant Frank McGlinchey, Bombardier, were unluckily captured at a border post in the Pyrenees Mountains, virtually within sight of freedom. The plane's Navigator, Lieutenant Carl Spicer, was more fortunate.

Major Kidd and Captain Blakely returned in *Just-a-Snappin'* after bombing the target and a running battle with German fighters, with the two engines on the right wing shot out and useless and five of the crew injured — Waist Gunner Sgt. Lester Saunders fatally. By the skillful navigation of Lt. Harry Crosby, later to become Group Navigator, landfall was made at the coast of North Norfolk at an altitude of 1,200 feet despite the loss of the compass.

As their severely damaged Fortress crashlanded at an unmanned, dummy airfield at Ludham, Norfolk, the completely unmaneuverable aircraft, without brakes, veered off the runway and collided, at speed, with a large oak tree, fortunately without further injury to the crew.

Revealed Major Kidd:

Someone counted over 800 separate holes in that aircraft, and had we been forced to ditch in the North Sea, we would have had only our individual Mae West lifejackets to support us, as the liferafts stowed in the upper fuselage, were literally shredded. Survival in those very cold waters for any length of time, especially during the winter months, was virtually nil.

The Bremen and Vegesack raids had cost the Eighth Air Force 27 B17's and three B24's. From the Liberator's 10-man crews only a total of eight survived to become prisoners of war. This was indeed an ordeal by fire. Most savagely hit were the 100th Bomb Group with seven B17's lost, not including Captain Blakely's wrecked *Just-a-Snappin'*. The 381st Bomb Group based at Ridgewell, Essex, also lost seven Fortresses. Following the evidence recorded by their bomb-strike photographs the 381st Bomb Group was awarded a Distinguished Unit Citation.

Leading the 381st Bomb Group to Bremen was Major Bill Ingenhutt, the Commander of the 535th Squadron at Ridgewell, Essex. Although his Fortress was on fire following flak and fighter hits on his aircraft in the target area, Major Ingenhutt continued leading the remainder of the 381st formation until reaching the Rally Point when the growing intensity of the flames forced all of the crew to bail out.

Flying as Tail-gunner/Observer in the 381st Lead aircraft was Lieutenant Robert Weniger who, while flying co-pilot in another B17, had miraculously survived a mid-air collision with a FW 190 over Amiens-Glisy, France, on July 14th, 1943. The barely flyable Fortress was successfully crash-landed at Manston, Kent.

Among the several battle-damaged B17's to return to Ridgewell was a plane named *Tinker Toy*. A fusillade of cannon shells from a fighter attacking head-on tore off most of the plexiglass nose canopy. Two shells penetrated the cockpit windscreen frame, decapitated the pilot, and made a bloodbath of the cockpit. Co-Pilot Lt. Thomas Sellars, although badly injured, was assisted by Top Turret Gunner and Flight Engineer Sgt. Miller, to make a successful landing at their home base.

That night, 8th October 1943, RAF Bomber Command again hit Bremen, adding to the fires and starting fresh ones blazing in an area attack on Hanover.

The next day, in the early hours of Saturday morning, 378

American bombers were readied and with brimming fuel tanks, set off on the deepest penetration raid yet flown by the Eighth Air Force. The distant targets, beyond Berlin, were in Eastern Germany and the Baltic ports of Gdynia and Danzig.

From a height of 12,000 feet, half their normal bombing altitude, extremely accurate strikes were observed by the crews on the aircraft factories at Anklam and Marienburg.

Lt. Theodore Bozarth, 95th Bomb Group Fortress *Heavenly Daze* Navigator, while flying over Marienburg was able to see an aircraft factory through his binoculars as it was hit by bombs.

He remembers:

> The whole building complex seemed to leap about 50 feet into the air and then begin to disintegrate. Conspicuous smoke and fire afterwards, and very little loss of life on the ground or in the air . . . very satisfying type of warfare . . . and very rare . . .

Another Navigator, Lt. Gordon Wharton of the B17F *Eightball,* 390th Bomb Group, recalls:

> We were at 12,000 feet, a very low altitude as no anti-aircraft was expected at Marienburg. As we approached the target the Lead Group released its bombs. They had been assigned a certain portion of the installations as their target, and they hit it. The bombs hit close together, not simultaneously, but split-seconds apart. Some sent up black smoke, others pale brown. It was like a silent movie. There was little noise at our altitude, except for the roar of our engines, but I could hear a slight crump-crump-crump as our bombs exploded far below.

As we passed over Denmark on our way home our crews reported seeing crowds of people shouting and waving at us. We were flying quite low,and those friendly Danes had probably never seen us that close before.

It was a long, long flight of 11 hours, and the deepest penetration into enemy airspace up to that time. We were exhausted when we returned.

« « « » » »

It was the practice, whenever possible, for a newly-trained replacement crew to fly their first combat mission accompanied by an experienced veteran pilot. Such a crew was that of Lt. William B. Rose of the 92nd Bomb Group, Podington, Bedfordshire, whose assigned target was Gdynia. Despite effective use of smokescreens by the ground defenses they successfully bombed the target, leaving several ships burning in the harbour and dry-dock installations heavily damaged. The 40th Combat Bomb Wing, which included the 92nd Bomb Group, turned for home. Their return route took them across the Danish peninsula where a furious battle developed with German fighters.

To Lt. Rose, sitting in the co-pilot's seat beside a battle-hardened pilot, it was the first time, but by no means the last, that he saw enemy fighters in air-to-air combat with the heavily-armed Fortresses. He recalls:

On the belts of ammunition which fed each B17's 12 heavy machine guns, every fifth bullet was a tracer, and it was an incredible sight to see a veritable hail of tracers racing out to meet the attacking German fighters. It seemed impossible that the fighters could penetrate that shield of defensive fire from the formation, send a Fortress spinning earthwards and get away, seemingly unscathed.

We were flying left wingman and I noticed the pilot's eyes never left the B17 flying the lead of our element of three airplanes thereby maintaining a good close formation, so vital to our survival, despite the tremendous noise of battle going on at very close range.

This was the first time that my crew and I were made very much aware that there was somebody up here who was trying to kill us. It was the point at which we realised that we were in combat for our lives and it brought about a complete change in our outlook and attitude to everything, because up until then it had been countless hours of training and practice.

Sgt. Leo Hotis, B17F *Queen Jeanie* 384th Bomb Group Ball Turret Gunner, remembers:

At the briefing which was at 0500 , we were told that we "might have a little fun today." Not only were we attacking the Arado airplane factory at Anklam, but that we could get even with the Jerries because Anklam was also a training base for "green" fighter pilots. The crews roared with laughter.

We hit the target hard. Only a few enemy aircraft were seen near Anklam, but they made no effort to attack us. Our navigator relayed to us that Berlin wasn't too far away. On our return trip over Denmark, we received stiff opposition from what seemed like dozens of enemy fighters. The Jerries knocked Lt. Calhoun's *Philly-Brooklyn* out of our formation setting it on fire, and I watched four crewmen bail out. Ball Turret Gunner Lopez remained in his gun position and hit several attackers. In 1976, I learned that four others made it and became Prisoners of War, including Sgt. Lopez. Lt. Ingles in *Dallas Rebel* went down in the North Sea. I didn't see any parachutes.

However, our Group faired reasonably well as there were 16 B17's lost from the other Groups over Denmark and the North Sea from the Anklam task force.

Straggling and battle-damaged, the Fortresses and Liberators returned to their East Anglian bases, their landing lights slicing long narrow fingers of brilliant beams of light through the gathering gloom, probing for the wide runways. With fuel tanks almost empty, the crippled craft sought the sanctuary of any airfield. They had lost 25 planes during the 1,500-mile flight, the vast majority to enemy fighters while the bombers were beyond the range of their protective "Little Friends." Commented Lt. Jack Nosser, Bombardier of *Cash and Carrie:*

One of the greatest "highs" emotionally that I have ever had in my life and I'm sure almost every crewman experienced the same ecstatic feeling, was returning safely to base after a mission.

The debriefing rooms at Framlingham were bedlam with everyone wanting to talk at the same time — "run off at the mouth" is perhaps a better way of putting it. The adrenalin was still racing, and a single shot of whisky, furnished by the Intelligence Officer, was sufficient to get merrily drunk on. Everyone was a friend or a buddy. I think some crewmen got to the state where they couldn't live without that strongly-addictive feeling.

Pilot of the 390th Bomb Group Fortress *Miss Carry,* Lt. Paul Vance, added:

I considered the Marienburg raid, and it perhaps can be verified, as the perfect example of American strategic bombardment throughout the entire war in Europe. It was pulled at the lowest altitude that we had ever bombed — 12,000 feet.

I recall the briefing, very early that morning, when it was stated that there was a P.O.W. Camp located on the edge of the Marienburg target. We were told to avoid hitting it if possible. When the results of the raid were evaluated, I learned that not a single prisoner had been killed.

We returned from Marienburg, encountering a few fighters over the Danish peninsula, and for some reason or other my own plane was reported as going down in the North Sea. I was happy to correct this error back at Framlingham.

Brigadier General Curtis LeMay, 3rd Air Division Commander, confirmed the accuracy of the bombing. He said:

I remember that mission because of the exceptionally good bombing as was borne out, not only by the strike photographs, but I remember talking afterwards to an inmate of the Prisoner of War camp right beside the aircraft factory, who reported all bombs falling within the factory grounds and no casualties in the P.O.W. camp.*

During these past two days, the four Groups of B26 Marauders (twin-engine medium bombers) had attacked Luftwaffe fighter bases in France and Belgium. On 9 October, the B26's had flown their last operation as part of the 8th Air Force. On 16 October 1943, they were transferred to the 9th Air Force. Although initially enduring heavy losses since its arrival in England in late 1942, the Marauder ultimately proved to be one of the most successful and effective bombers of the war.

Whilst defending their strategic targets, the Luftwaffe had sustained total losses over the two days of 39 fighters and many more damaged. The Fortress and Liberator gunners, aided by their fighter escorts, had also taken their toll during the vicious air battles in the thin air of the freezing sub-stratosphere. Three P47 Thunderbolts were shot down, all in Holland. Two pilots became POW's and the third, Lt. Patterson of the 4th Fighter Group, Debden, Essex, evaded capture and escaped via Belgium, France and Spain.

« « « » » »

During these large-scale air battles, often fought over an area encompassing hundreds of square miles of airspace, from great altitude down to tree-top level, an increasingly heavy toll was taken of some of the most experienced and accomplished Luftwaffe fighter pilots. The American and other Allied pilots found themselves up against veterans who had seen action during the invasion of Poland, the "Blitzkrieg" of Holland, France and Belgium in 1940, the Battle of Britain, North Africa, Italy and the Russian Front.

One of the German "Aces" to be killed in action during the afternoon of Friday, October 8th, 1943, while endeavoring to defend Bremen was Oberstleutnant (Lieutenant Colonel) Hans Philipp, the Commander of Jagdgeschwader I.

Born in Meissen, Saxony, he was nicknamed "Fips" during his outstanding career with the Luftwaffe. His first air victory came in September 1939 over Poland while flying with I Staffel/Jagdgeschwader 76. "Fips" Philipp was promoted to Staffelkapitan of 4/JG/54 in August 1940 and was awarded

*From a personal letter, General LeMay to the author.

the Knight's Cross on 22nd October 1940 following his 20th air victory. In June 1941, following Hitler's surprise attack and devastating invasion of Russia, Hans Philipp became Commander of I JG/54 in February 1942. On 3rd March 1942 he became the fourth Luftwaffe fighter pilot to achieve 100 air victories while fighting in Russia.

In April 1943 the now vastly experienced pilot was transferred to the West and took command of JG/I. When "Fips" Philipp was shot down by P47 Thunderbolts (possibly from the 56th Fighter Group) he had flown over 450 combat missions and had accumulated no less than 206 confirmed air victories, 29 in the West including one B17, the remainder on the Eastern Front. He was one of the Luftwaffe's most decorated fighter pilots.

« « « » » »

Among the injured crewmen recovering in English hospitals from wounds sustained during previous raids was Lt. James Brown, Navigator of the 100th Bomb Group's plane *Torchy*. He relates:

In mid-October 1943, I was still a patient in the 12th Evacuation Hospital near Thetford, following being wounded on 15 September. On 9 October, my Squadron Flight Surgeon, Dr. McCarthy, had been to visit me and brought me up to date on the 100th's losses, including the seven crews lost the day before.

Group losses were never publicly aired or officially recognised on the base. Living in dispersed squadron areas, it was only by chance talk at the Officer's Club, flight-line gossip and so on, that one learned exactly which crews, and how many, had been lost on a given mission. But the Headquarter's staff were kept fully informed on such matters. Many people seem to have the idea that a list of the crews missing in action was posted on some bulletin board, but this was definitely not the case.

In any event, the visit by Doctor McCarthy (He blew his brains out a year or two after the war. He just couldn't shake clear the war memories from his mind.) brought me up-to-date on my Group's losses and the realisation finally dawned on me that most of my pals, buddies and acquaintances who had formed the original 100th were now Prisoners of War or dead. This awareness caused me, for the first time, to question whether it was possible for me to survive to complete my tour of 25 missions, if somehow I were allowed to rejoin my crew.

« « « » » »

In marked contrast to the hazards and continuous strain of

flying bombing raids, joviality on the ground by combat crews proved a welcome, light-hearted break.

One such example was recalled by Captain Rodney Snow, Pilot of the 95th Bomb Group plane *Herky Jerky II:*

Late one afternoon in the Fall, the Armament Officer casually mentioned to my friend Bill Lindley and I, that he'd seen quite a few ring-neck pheasants near our base at Horham. We promptly borrowed his jeep, let the windshield down, took a couple of shotguns and a handful of shells, and drove into the surrounding countryside to try and locate the beautiful gamebirds. As the jeep is a four-wheel drive vehicle we were able to go anywhere along the hedgerows bordering the fields and the edges of dense woodland.

We flushed out the pheasants which were quite easy to hit since both of us were experienced birdshots and quailshots from the South. We bagged about six in as many minutes. We then returned to base, and by bribing the cook with one of the birds, we were able to plan and prepare for a real feast which would be a pleasant change from the monotonous diet of pork chops and Spam that was wearing thin on our appetites.

It just so happened that one of our senior officers had a brother-in-law who was Colonel of a tank Brigade in the U.S. Army, and who was coming to visit us. We took things in hand and prepared a real feast — roast pheasant, potatoes, an abundance of vegetables and thick gravy. For dessert we had fresh fruit and ice cream made from powdered milk. Long Havana cigars were furnished by Dave McKnight's wife, Grace, who had sent them from the United States. Rare Scotch whisky in wire-encased bottles and with many years vintage behind them, were also put on the table. Any other additional delicacies which we could muster were displayed before our distinguished guest amid profuse apologies for this rather 'ordinary' meal.

The visiting Colonel, who had been on basic 'C' rations and other not-so-palatable items for months, could hardly believe his eyes. He took quite a 'ribbing' as we told him, with tongue in cheek, how bad the food now was in the Air Force, and that these days for some reason, our rations had practically gone to Hell . . ."

After we'd had pheasant two or three times following this treat, the Group's Commanding Officer received a complaint from the Mayor or some local dignitary from Horham, informing him that some of his officers had been seen taking "the King's game" and that this was very much frowned upon. Therefore, he would like our Commander to thwart immediately any further pursuits of shooting "our birds" from wildly-careering jeeps.

Apart from amusing incidents like the above, tension persisted for the flyers. Major Horace Varian, Ground Executive Officer of the 100th Bomb Group, Thorpe Abbotts, was determined to personally experience the tensions leading up to and during a mission.

From the 100th's earliest days, I was aware of a tension between flyers and ground people. It was a little like the ambivalence of personal relationships, a kind of love-hate mixture. It wasn't hard to understand; I did my work in relative safety on the ground, while they fought in the air with the odds, especially in the early days of combat, stacked heavily against them.

I suppose it was a mixture of wanting to see what a combat crew really experienced, and a need to test myself, that made me seek permission to fly a combat mission. I asked my good friend Harry Crosby, the Group Navigator, to arrange one for me, confident that he would wait for a 'milk run' to the French coast. But on the evening he called me into Group Operations, he told me that he'd put me on the crew list for a deep penetration mission to Fulda in Central Germany, which was a 10-hour flight. I noticed a faint smile around his lips, and in his eyes, as he watched my reaction.

It came as a distinct surprise to me that in the few hours I tried to sleep before briefing and take-off, I experienced intense fear and I wondered if combat crews went through this every time they were scheduled to fly. With their greater knowledge of the risks involved, they were probably more frightened than myself.

Once aboard the B17 and in the air, some of the anxiety faded. The mystique of that remarkable aircraft had rubbed off on the ground people as well as the flyers, and I felt almost safe as I sat on a step about eight-inches-high in the nose compartment with the navigator and bombardier. But I was acutely conscious of all the unfamiliar equipment I was wearing and using; winter underwear, a full uniform (so that I wouldn't be taken as a spy if forced to bale out over enemy territory), a heated flying suit and, in case that didn't work, a furlined leather jacket, trousers, boots and flying helmet. Over all that was a steel flak vest and helmet, parachute, and an inflatable 'Mae West' lifejacket.

I wondered whether I could unplug the oxygen mask, the earphones and throat microphone and then the heated clothing quickly enough if we had to bail out. I also realised that the parachute harness strap running between my legs was quite slack, and try as I might, I couldn't tighten it. Each time I thought about what would happen if and when the 'chute snapped open, I broke out in a cold sweat!!

The mission itself turned out to be a relatively routine one, a little flak, but the German fighters kept their distance to my intense relief. As we left the target area, I could hear on the interphone and feel the gradual lessening of tension by members of the crew. The pilot even checked to see whether I had survived. It was good to feel and hear the landing wheels scuff against solid ground as we landed back at Thorpe Abbotts.

I don't think my flying mission brought any spectacular change in my relationship with the airmen, but I hope I understood a little better the tensions which they experienced every day. I think I learned that their courage was not a lack of fear, but rather the ability to live with that fear and do their jobs in spite of it. I was glad I had tagged along on that mission.

A Headquarters Staff Officer of the 95th Bomb Group, Horham, was not so fortunate on his one and only combat mission while flying in Captain Robert Bender's appropriately named Fortress *Spook V*.

Major David McKnight, a 95th Bomb Group Squadron Commander, and later the Group's Air Executive, explained the circumstances:

Captain Bender was a character. His nicknames were "Chief" and "Yip Yip", but I remember him better as "Yip Yip" because it was so aptly descriptive.

"Yip Yip" went through five airplanes in his total tour of 13 missions. His B17's were named *Spook I* through to *Spook V*. The reasons for all these mishaps in such a short space of time varied from highly-spectacular crash-landings, being shot-up beyond repair (except for spare parts) and finally, a ditching. It was after the ditching that we formally declared him to be an "Ace" . . . of the Luftwaffe, that is . . . and relieved him of his flying duties, as by then it was felt that "Yip Yip" had had quite enough emotional experiences for one war as a combat pilot.

Actually "Yip Yip" was a well-liked personality and had many friends. But when he described some of the more eventful combat missions on which he'd participated, in his high-pitched voice, it used to unnerve the replacement crews before they'd even had one mission under the belts. He attributed his personality to being subjected to anti-aircraft fire which he called "The Flaks." For example, during debriefing he would announce that "The Flaks" were really after him that day.

The only experience I had in actually flying with him confirmed to me the things I'd heard. I was the mission Commander, and I was in the right-hand seat of Captain Bender's airplane. The target was a rubber manufacturing plant at Huls, located close to the highly-effective defences of the Ruhr valley. Bender's "flaks" were particularly heavy throughout the Ruhr, and we had more than a few occasions when we could actually see the orange flashes in the middle of the black smoke. Each time one of those shells exploded the airplane rocked noticeably, "Yip Yip" would reach for a feathering button, and I would reach for "Yip Yip." He would point out that the oil pressure gauge or some other instrument was vibrating, but so was everything else on the airplane. As a matter of fact, the only damage we'd sustained was the hydraulic fluid drained from our braking system but the brakes held until we'd completed most of our taxi back to the hardstand after landing. We completed the mission courtesy of our ground crew chief and a tractor.

On his thirteenth mission Captain Bender's airplane was apparently shot up sufficiently to prevent his making the English coast on return. He must have done an excellent piece of flying because he ditched his airplane without loss or injury to his crew. Everybody took to the rubber liferafts, including an officer from our Headquarters, who had also gone along on the mission. As it happened, he clambered aboard the same raft as Captain Bender. Shortly after they got squared away, "Yip Yip" starts screaming that he could hear hissing . . .

It was found that the Headquarter's type had a knife strapped to his thigh and somehow the knife had come out of its sheath and punctured the raft. Fortunately, they had the necessary repair equipment on board and were able to plug the leak in time, while "Yip Yip" continued screaming non-stop at his "super-cargo." They were out there all night before being picked up by the wonderful British Air Sea Rescue launches. They told me that Captain Bender talked all night. He'd had many more experiences during his 13 missions than I had in my total of 41.

Chapter 4

IT is a harsh fact of life that different people react to different situations in different ways, especially those involving extreme stress and danger. Not surprisingly, a few flyers had their own mental breaking point when they were exposed at very close range to the savagely-fought air battles which all too often surpassed fiction with horror-filled reality and regularity.

Following the Bremen raid, a young replacement B17 commander, flying his first mission as co-pilot, had returned to Horham at the controls of a heavily damaged and barely flyable Fortress. The bomber's experienced pilot, a veteran of 23 previous raids with the 95th Bomb Group, had finally cracked at a critical stage of the mission. As he was led slowly and gently to the waiting ambulance, a pitiful stumbling wreck, his glazed eyes bore mute testimony to the silent, deeply-moved and sympathetic onlookers, that he had taken more than enough and that he had nothing more to give.

Major General David Grant, Air Surgeon in charge of the health of the United States Army Air Forces, explained in very explicit terms the daunting problems faced by the bomber crews:

> One look into the pilot's cabin of a B17 will convince you that it's flight is actually an engineering operation demanding manual and mental skills which put the driving of an automobile into the kiddy-car class.
>
> The compartment is lined — front, sides, ceiling and part of the floor — with controls, switches, levers, dials and gauges. I once counted around one hundred and thirty. The co-ordinated operations of all these gadgets would be difficult in the swivel-chair comfort of your office. But reduce your office to a five-foot cube size, engulf it in the constant roar of four 1,000-horsepower engines, and increase your height to around four and five miles. Then get into a flying suit, gloves, and flying boots — all heated by electricity — put on a helmet with earphones, cover your eyes with goggles and the rest of your face with an oxygen mask containing a microphone, strap on your parachute, and it might be well to add on about sixteen pounds of body armour.

That will give you an idea of the normal conditions under which these men work out the higher mathematical relationships of engine revolutions, manifold and fuel pressure, aerodynamics, barometric pressure, altitude, wind drift, airspeed, ground speed, position and direction.

You may have to face an occasional pain from ears, bends or intestinal gas expansion, a touch of dizziness, numbness from cold, or the subtle comatosity of anoxia. There will be interruptions to man machine guns against enemy attacks. Due allowance must also be made for a stream of machine gun bullets and cannon shells, or the burst of flak and air-to-air rockets in your immediate vicinity.

As a final touch to this bizarre picture of intense concentration, add the fear of death.

But sympathetic as the American authorities were to the victims of nervous breakdowns their British counterparts had no such consideration, as Sergeant Roy Smith, an Air Gunner with Bomber Command's 102 Squadron (Lancaster's) pointed out:

The Royal Air Force, I'm afraid, took a very hard line if any aircrew went sick because of nerves. They were graded "L.M.F." (i.e., lack of moral fibre), stripped of their rank and given a ground job. Hence they were branded as cowards for the remainder of their service lives.

I'm sure many crews have gone missing through a crew member being mentally ill. Even when crews knew a member of their crew was cracking they didn't report the fact.

In my first crew we had this happen to a man who went completely. One night, just after take-off, we had to circle for four hours to use up enough fuel to be light enough to land, while maintaining radio silence. It took four crew members to restrain him. He was taken to the hospital, and the last we heard he'd been reduced to the rank of Air-Craftsman II and was working on 'general duties.' For weeks prior to this he'd been standing on his bed at night and jumping off screaming 'Bail Out.' We all knew that it was only a matter of time before he cracked up.

Exceptionally heavy losses were sustained by my first Squadron. During my first tour of operations 117 crews came to the Squadron and only five completed their tour of trips. Of these survivors none were the same as when they'd started, all had suffered losses of various crew members.

Corporal Joe Scarlett, a Technical Instructor with Bomber Command's 103 Squadron, Royal Air Force, Elsham Wolds in Lincolnshire, remembers those wartime bombing raids:

Late one beautiful summer's evening the silence of the surrounding countryside was shattered as about forty Lancasters started up their engines, one by one. They seemed to come alive as they began taxiing, slowly and ponderously, around the perimeter tracks in two long processions prior to setting on another deep penetration raid into Germany. The black, menacing and snarling shapes of all those bombers presented an especially awesome sight, outlined as they were in the gathering dusk.

Aldis lamps flickered briefly from the control tower as each Lancaster reached the end of the runway. Then, one after the other, they surged forward, gathering speed and roared off into the twilight. Each aircraft carried six tons of high explosive and incendiary bombs.

The silence returned and the long hours of waiting began, lasting until the following dawn. And so it went on.

Nobody counted the modest homes in the back streets of towns and cities that were blasted to pieces in the same instant as the factories. By the same token, nobody had the time to take much notice, except the bereaved relatives, of missing bomber crews or the numerous rear gunners as their shredded bodies were lowered from shattered turrets and taken to the mortuary on return to base. The rifle calibre .303 machine guns of the British bombers were pitifully inadequate against the 20-millimetre cannons of the German fighters. Darkness, cloud and altitude were the night bomber's friends against their deadly, radar-equipped adversaries. Remembers Sergeant Ted Lucey of the 95th Bomb Group:

Almost every night we heard the drone of British bombers passing high overhead on their way to Germany. Early one morning, a severely shot-up Lancaster bomber made an emergency landing on our airfield at Horham.

When the ground crews lifted the tail gunner's body from the mangled turret they found he'd been shot eleven times, once squarely between the eyes. The Germans may have been taking a beating but they still fought back.

The survival percentage of Bomber Command crews who successfully bailed out of their damaged aircraft compared very unfavourably with their American counterparts.

The first indications which a Royal Air Force night bomber crew usually had that anything was amiss was an explosion, or series of explosions, as a German night fighter crewed by an expert pilot and radar operator, suddenly poured non-tracer high-explosive cannon shells into their bomber's vulnerable fuel tanks — the attack coming from the undefended and least expected direction — below. Many months were to pass before the Royal Air Force learned the secret of this new and deadly innovation — the fixed upward-firing "Schrage musik" (oblique or jazz music) guns.

It's inventor Feldwebel Paul Mahle, an armourer with a Luftwaffe night-fighter unit, received a written testimonial and 500 marks (about $150) from the German Air Ministry. "Schrage musik" cost the British Air Ministry untold millions of pounds and countless bomber crews.

As the stricken aircraft either exploded, or at best plunged earthwards ablaze and out of control, the occupants, if uninjured, had precious few seconds in which to grope their way past or over unseen obstacles in cumbersome flying clothing and reach frantically for escape hatch handles. Providing of course, the whirling gyrations of the bomber did not pin the airmen against the spinning interior of the aircraft by the overwhelming centrifugal forces. In moments of extreme horrifying danger mere seconds appear to the victim to stretch into endless hours.

In direct contrast, the American daylight bomber crews had the priceless advantage of being able to see clearly all obstacles barring their way to the escape hatches.

« « « » » »

The Flying Fortress was basically an all-electric aeroplane, and had more than six miles of electrical wiring. The radio equipment was powerful enough to transmit back to England from Eastern Europe, and its generators would provide enough power for all the lights in a medium-sized hotel. Into the construction of each went enough aluminium to make 50,000 percolators, enough steel for 160 washing machines, and sufficient rubber on its leading edge de-icing equipment and massive wheels to retread 800 car tyres.

The average age of the men who commanded and flew the B17 was 21 years.

The peacetime occupations of the Fortress crews were as varied as their ages. Lt. Robert Haughy, 23, a former San Francisco salesman, had successfully trained as a pilot and was assigned to the 379th Bomb Group, Kimbolton. His crew included a 32-year-old ball-turret gunner who had been a truck driver in Pennsylvania, and a 20-year-old bombardier, formerly a mechanic, whose home state was West Virginia. Other crew members were former: student, carpenter, mechanic, grocer, salesman, truck driver, and design engineer, now co-pilot.

Said Lt. Richard Perry, a 390th Bomb Group Co-Pilot:

The interior of the B17 was rather drab and nothing like modern airliners. It was just sheet metal, aluminum sparring, many control cables and various coloured electrical wires running along the top and sides of the fuselage. There were aluminium oxygen tanks in assorted sizes fitted to the bulkheads, many 50 calibre machine guns, and long, looping belts of ammunition. Despite this somewhat cluttered interior, when I sat in my armour-plated seat in the cockpit with my gloved hands on the wheel and throttles, and my feet on the rudder pedals, I felt that there was no better warplane. I had complete confidence that it would carry me to our assigned targets and back.

« « « » » »

The fighter which was most employed to provide protective escort to the American heavy and medium bombers during daylight raids on Occupied Europe in 1943 was the P47 Thunderbolt. The fighter's development is described by Colonel Hubert "Hub" Zemke, Commanding Officer of the 56th Fighter Group, *Zemke's Wolfpack:*

In the Spring of 1942 word began to leak out about a 'Super Fighter' being developed by the Republic Aircraft Company which had a 2,000 horsepower radial engine, could fly at 400 m.p.h. on the straight and level, and reach a higher altitude than any other American escort fighter.

When I first saw and flew the P47 Thunderbolt in mid-1942 I was very disappointed. It looked twice as large as any conventional fighter of other nations. It was a monster, weighing around seven tons, and it took off and climbed like a water-logged goose on a fledgeling training flight. It accelerated like a logging truck dragging timber through a swamp.

Certainly this wasn't an Interceptor Fighter as the Spitfire had been during the Battle of Britain. We were told that it was a Strategic Escort Fighter but performance feed-back and study of relevant charts gave the P47 only a 175 mile radius of action when considering all the factors.

On top speed at altitude the Thunderbolt managed 400 m.p.h. if first entered into a dive then levelled off. Once top speed had been attained the aircraft held it. Dive with throttle open could be very dangerous if held for any length of time because, in those days, very little was known about compressibility and the speed of sound. At the conclusion of one of these test flights in November 1942 Lt. Dyar and Lt. Comstock decided that they should indulge in a little 'rat-racing' while descending to the air base. What then transpired turned out to be a new world record for aircraft in a terminal dive. They landed safely, both scared out of their wits, with two very warped P47's which never flew again. Gad . . . We instantly knew that the monster was a demon on a down-hill slide . . .

Learning these things, and a few more, those of us who knew we'd have to use this 'Flying Jug' in combat quickly concluded that we'd have to develop tactics employing the advantages of the P47, not the disadvantages. Taking a well trained pilot from Flight Training School with 350 or more airborne hours, and stressing the superior qualities of the P47 very favourable combat results were eventually forthcoming.

The superior characteristics of the Thunderbolt when compared with the Me 109 and FW 190 can be generalised as; (a) Superior top speed above 22,000 feet. (b) Superior acceleration and diving speed at any altitude. (c) Superior rate of roll and turning radius above 22,000 feet. (d) Good rate of roll with relatively light stick and rudder control at any altitude, provided the air-speed was kept up. (e) Since such an out-standing diving speed could be attained it was assumed that an outstanding zoom back to altitude would automatically follow. With application of engine power to recover in the zoom climb this outstanding asset proved itself. Zoom recovery was excellent. (f) Fire-power with eight 50 calibre heavy machine guns was devastating if a favourable position on an enemy aircraft could be attained. At a range of 250-300 yards, with minimum deflection, most enemy aircraft were mortally wounded by a relatively short burst from the eight guns. Perhaps 'despatched' is the word.

With the technical modifications of a 'paddle-blade' propeller, fuel injection, auxiliary fuel tanks, and bomb racks the capabilities of the P47 in combat were very considerably enhanced.

The Thunderbolt's ability to absorb punishment was legendary, claimed Sgt. Leo Lester of the 56th Fighter Group, Halesworth, Suffolk.

I've seen P47's come home with whole cylinder heads shot away from their engines. The airframe was exceptionally sturdy as was proved the day a P47 landed with a large indentation in the leading edge of its left wing and trailing several telephone wires. It transpired that the plane had collided with a telegraph pole at high speed while strafing a train.

Major Walter Beckham, one of the 8th Air Force's outstanding fighter pilots, gives his views on the Thunderbolt:

The P47 was delightful to fly, it handled impeccably and I loved it. Comparison with the German FW 190 and Me 109 is difficult. I always had full power on in combat situations and I felt that the P47 could out-turn either of the German planes at any altitude. But who knows? I never knew if the opposing pilot was a veteran or inexperienced, good or bad, or whether he had full power on or not.

Two factors, I feel, operated greatly in our favour. First, the eight fifty-calibre machine guns which we had, each one fired at a rate of about 800 rounds a minute. The opposition's two cannons were probably more effective against their prime targets, our Fortress, Liberator, and Marauder bombers. Secondly, and most of all, our P47's had a superior diving speed over any of the German planes. This great asset, in addition to the fact that we usually joined in fights from an altitude of 30,000 feet plus, was of immense value both in the offensive and defensive roles. This in spite of the dangerous characteristic of the Thunderbolt, compressibility in a high-speed dive, which made it impossible to pull the plane up in time.

My first-cousin, Lowery Brabham, explained to us at Milleville, New Jersey, in early 1943, 'Just wait,' he said, 'and don't tuck in too much elevator trim, otherwise you will bend the airplane, and yourselves, when you get down to lower altitudes.

I must have lived a good life, as I never experienced the nightmare of compressibility.

Chapter 5

ON the night of 9 October 1943, the teletype machine in the Operations Building at Horham Airfield, Headquarters of the 13th Combat Bomb Wing, clattered out the first indications of yet another operational mission, the third in three days.

As there were only 13 hours of daylight in this the second week of October, it left precious little time for the specialist ground crews to work on aircraft maintenance before dusk quickly turned to darkness, necessitating the use of lights in a calculated risk against possible night attacks by German bombers.

Captain John Miller, the Assistant Operations Officer of the 95th Bomb Group, read the short cryptic message. From that moment the base was on "Alert."

It had originated at "Pinetree", the code name for the 8th Air Force Headquarters at High Wycombe, Buckinghamshire, about 30 miles northwest of London and near the Headquarters of RAF Bomber Command, which at that moment was itself a hive of activity finalising details for tonight's raid on Berlin.

Further details of the American's daylight mission for tomorrow were transmitted throughout the night and early morning to the three Air Divisional Headquarters located at Brampton Grange, Huntingdonshire (1st Air Division); Ketteringham Hall, Norfolk (2nd Air Division) and Elveden Hall, Suffolk (3rd Air Division Headquarters). Thence in a matter of minutes to the different airfields concerned.

For the third night running the ground crews at the numerous 8th Air Force bases all over East Anglia worked long and hard until dawn and well into the following morning. A multitude of tasks had to be performed to ready the bombers and fighters for the pending mission. There were empty oxygen cylinders to be replenished, so vital for the combat crews at the altitudes the bombers flew in the rarified atmosphere five miles above the earth. Thousands of gallons of petrol were pumped into near-empty wing tanks from mobile bowsers, their crews ever mindful that the slightest spark would mean certain oblivion. Armourers installed snakelike belts of heavy point-five machine gun ammunition to replace the thousands of expended cartridge cases littering the floors of the Fortresses and Liberators. In the armouries, the guns themselves were being stripped, cleaned, oiled and re-assembled.

Problems regarding the point-five calibre machine gun, which weighed 64 pounds and was the defensive weapon installed in all heavy and medium American bombers, are outlined by Captain Roy Crist, a 2nd Air Division Gunnery Officer:

> A common cause of failure of our guns was ice forming and freezing the oil on the open bolt at altitude. Some Groups solved this problem by charging the guns before take-off, or soon after, despite the inherent danger of accidental firing. Another problem was the feeding mechanisms which led to guns jamming at critical times during combat, the very time when they were needed most of all. This too, was eventually solved by relatively simple modifications.
>
> Perhaps boys who had been born and brought up on farms were the best shots, but anyone who had considerable experience in hunting or target shooting with any weapon was able to absorb the specialised gunnery training that much faster. Probably the very best were those individuals who were able to remain relatively calm and workmanlike under the extreme pressures and stress of high altitude combat.

Cigar-shaped bombs, ranging in size from 100-pound incendiaries to 1,000-pound high explosives were hauled from the bomb dumps on tractor-drawn trollies, and in turn positioned and winched up slowly and carefully into the gaping bomb bays. Each large bomb, as it was inched into position and the shackles took its weight, caused a distinct swelling to the side walls of the two main landing gear tyres. Sweating crew chiefs supervised these three main tasks to their own aircraft.

The size of bombs to be dropped on a particular target varied from Group to Group.

In the hangars, damaged aircraft took priority. The specialist ground crewmen, working against the clock, performed minor miracles in the repair and renewal of complete engines, and such diverse necessities as the replacement of damaged turbo-superchargers — whose whirring, fanlike blades forced compressed air at high altitude into the straining engines to provide sea-level air pressure — the delicate and sensitive instrument repairs and adjustments, and sheet metal experts skilfully riveted replacement sheets of aluminium onto the damaged exterior surfaces of the bombers.

Some engineering problems were described by Engineering Officer Captain William Carleton of the 100th Bomb Group:

In many cases the battle damage was severe, but the B17 lent itself for a fairly rapid replacement of wings, tail or fuselage. It was a most durable aircraft, and could sustain tremendous damage and still fly. On two separate occasions we had a plane return without a horizontal stablizer (rear tail section) on one side. This had been broken off right at the fuselage due to being struck by German fighters going through the formation.

We were losing several airplanes because the bomb bay doors would not open in the normal manner, making it necessary for the pilot to "salvo" his bombs. In that instance, the doors dropped and it was then necessary to re-engage the doors with a hand crank. This took many minutes, since the gear ratio was such that dozens of turns were necessary. With the doors open, the speed of the aircraft was reduced five to 10 miles per hour, and this might force the plane out of the defensive formation of the Group. And if you dropped out of formation you were a 'sitting duck' should enemy fighters be around.

The problem was that the doors always worked perfectly when on the ground. In fact, they functioned perfectly during test flights. Eventually, it was discovered that the culprit was the 'relief tube' which was in the bomb bay. Our flights were normally quite long, with take-off at six in the morning and possibly a return 10 hours later. Even a short mission would last four or five hours. The combat crews wore sheepskin clothing, and while using the relief tube they balanced on an eight-inch-wide beam between the bombs. Since they were in flight, they could be bouncing around quite a bit, and as a result the limit switches might get a bath that had not been planned. With temperatures of 30 to 60 degrees below zero, these switches immediately froze and the doors would not then operate. Perhaps many lives were lost because of lack of foresight on such a simple thing.

The ground crews had a very close personal relationship with their flight crew. The loss of their bomber was always a personal tragedy, but the hope always existed that they had bailed out in time and were Prisoners of War.

We had a further engineering problem concerning aircraft tyres. It was a 56-inch rim, and the plane rode on two main wheels and a smaller tail wheel. Fully loaded the B17 weighed about 58,000 pounds, and it had been designed in the 'thirties for around 36,000 pounds, but subsequent models beefed it up to carry a heavier bomb load — up to 20,000 pounds — with larger engines, but the same tyres.

To add to the problem, British airfields were not as well-graded as those in the United States.

British runways were more apt to follow the contours of the earth. Also, wartime workmanship added another rough, and sometimes bumpy surface. The local aggregate contained a lot of flint which could lead to blow-outs. Take-off speed was about 110 to 115 miles an hour, but the greatest danger occurred around 60 to 70 miles an hour when the plane had less lift but a lot of bounce to the ounce. The side-walls of the tyres would often deflect with a consequent constant danger of punctures which could cause an aircraft to 'ground loop' with a possible loss of both lives and plane.

The solution was two-fold. In typical Army Air Force style, we received a shipment of tyres that should have gone to Alaska. However, these tyres had a steel mesh in them to give added traction on icy runways. What it did for us was to prevent the penetration of flint stones into the tyres. There was also less deflection leading to fewer blow-outs.

All our B17's were equipped with inflatable de-icer boots on the leading edges of the wings and tail. This equipment cost thousands of dollars, but added hundreds of pounds in weight and decreased flight speed. They were removed and stored away.

A further problem that might be termed very lowly was the condition of the airfield itself. Due to the loamy soil and heavy moisture content, the grassy portion of the airfield would not support our planes.

On take-off, pilots would be nervous, and when taxiing many of them were careless. Consequently, quite a few taxied off the concrete perimeter track, and as soon as one of both wheels went over the soft ground, they sank in as deep as two or three feet. Digging them out was a Herculean task, since the bombs had to be unloaded, but we couldn't always get the bomb doors open. Likewise, the 2,800 gallons of gasoline had to be pumped out of the wing tanks to lighten the craft. Even then, when we tried to jack up the plane, we found that all we did was to jack the jacks themselves into the mire. Sometimes the planes were stuck so far in that we could not position the jacks under the wings to start with.

Also, if the pilot had not run the plane completely off the taxi-way, he could hold up the entire operation by blocking off part of the field.

This problem was resolved in part by large air bags which were developed for this purpose by the Royal Air Force. We borrowed some of these bags, slid them under the wings, and pumped them up with an air compressor. The distribution of the load was such that the plane could then be raised.

Sergeant Robert Spangler, the 351st Squadron's Line Chief at Thorpe Abbotts, remembers the maintenance procedures:

The bombers returned from the raids either during the late afternoons or early evenings. As soon as the aircrafts taxied to their respective hardstands, Captain Bill Carleton, the Engineering Officer, and myself would begin our rounds of all returning planes.

By this time, our Crew Chiefs would have their pilot's report on their bombers' condition. After reviewing each plane with its Crew Chief, we were then able to determine, depending on its condition, how many from our Squadron would be ready to take part in another mission on the following day.

Minor repairs and replacements like instruments, spark plugs, oxygen system leaks, brake or tyre changes, exhaust stack repairs, etc., would all be completed that same evening.

The number of aircraft available would then be sent to Group Headquarters and passed on to 13th Wing Headquarters. Every effort was made to get all the bombers in flying status in time for the next day's mission.

The supply of spare parts was quite a problem. Anything at all which we could lay our hands on and acquire illegally was most jealously guarded. The problem was in concealing these excess parts from the Wing Headquarters' Inspectors, who regularly checked that we held no extra equipment. At a conservative estimate we had three times our quota of spare parts.

I went over to the aircraft 'graveyard' at nearby Pulham and found four B17 tail wheels, complete with tyres and axles. Otto Dietrich, our expert welder, had found an old farm trailer with iron wheels which, of course, sank deep into the mud. Otto welded the high-tensile steel of the B17 tail wheels onto the iron of the trailer. We then mostly used the trailer to haul spare parts back and forth from the flight line.

When inspection time came around everything we weren't supposed to have was loaded onto the trailer and covered with tarpaulin. We put a man on the tractor during inspection. He would then drive around the perimeter track on the other side of the base. The problem was solved.

Sgt. Spangler related one of several very amusing incidents that happened early one morning prior to a practise misson. He said:

Sgt. Parmentier, Crew Chief on number three hardstand, was testing the engines of his airplane when he noticed an officer go into the latrine at the back of the hardstand among the trees. The sides and roof of the latrine were built from wooden packing cases nailed to four posts which had been driven loosely into the ground.

As Sgt. Parmentier ran-up each engine in turn, the slipstream caused the flimsy latrine to slowly raise up from the ground, and when he throttled back it settled slowly down again. One red-faced officer emerged from the latrine angrily demanding to know, 'Just what the hell is going on around here?' Tears of laughter were streaming down my face as I walked quickly away.

« « « » » »

That Saturday night, 9 October 1943, with each hardstand ablaze with powerful floodlights running off portable generators, the ground crews worked feverishly through the small hours in a race against time. Mercifully, there was no wind or rain. The unpredictable English weather was not always this kind. More often than not, they had to labour under hastily improvised canopies slung over 'H' frames around each engine in turn, for protection against the chilling east wind and driving rain or sleet.

Sparking plugs had to be meticulously checked, carburettors, magnetos, fuel and oil lines, filters, pumps, and a bewildering multitude of no less vitally important items of precision engineering were scrutinised for potential signs of wear and tear, and replaced where necessary.

Every two or three hours, the mechanics would snatch a quick break for a mug of steaming coffee and sandwiches in the wooden shack made out of used packing cases and bomb boxes, in the shelter of nearby trees beside the hardstand. Going all the way to the mess hall for a snack, often a mile or so from the flight line, took up valuable time. More than one of these shelters had disappeared in a spectacular blaze, more often than not as a result of a carelessly thrown cigarette end or while heating food on the crude stoves.

The ingredients of tired men working all night until dawn surrounded by equipment of such a highly-volatile nature, was bound sooner or later, to result in tragedy. Barely four months previously, a 95th Bomb Group B17 at their host Alconbury base, was being loaded with 500 pound bombs when in an instant 18 men were no more and many others were seriously injured. In the massive explosion, four adjacent B17's were completely wrecked and 11 more were badly damaged. Said Lt. Waldo Cleveland:

> The cause of the accident was never determined. However, bombs were not afterwards fused until they had been loaded and secured. Prior to this tragic accident, fuses were screwed in while the bombs were on the ground beneath the bomb bays.

An example of the hidden dangers involving human fallibility in the routine servicing of the Fortresses, is outlined by Radio Technician Sgt. Ted Lucey of the 95th Bomb Group:

Sgt. Rossignal and I teamed up to pre-flight a B17. While I was checking the flight engineer's interphone, Rossi was examining the fuses on the bulkhead in front of the bomb bay. This should never be done while the power is switched on. He unintentionally caused a short circuit resulting in a vivid flash of flame.

I stood staring and waiting, not so much scared as angered, because the accident had been so unnecessary. Fright came later on thinking things over. There were twelve 500-pound demolition bombs on board. And all around us were full oxygen tanks. Even the slightest leak from one of these — not at all unusual — would have most certainly triggered off a massive explosion.

At Thorpe Abbotts, under a nearly full moon, the 100th Bomb Group ground crews were only too well aware that the coming mission might well be cancelled at a moment's notice if the weather experts forecast a sudden deterioration. They would then be faced with the tedious and dangerous task of unloading the bombs, but the good weather showed no sign of moving away.

« « « » » »

In the Operations Building at nearby Horham Lt. David Henderson of the 95th's Photographic Section selected the relevant Target Folder marked MÜNSTER from the filing cabinet.

He sat down and quickly thumbed through the pages which described the target, its location, industries, defences, and its importance to the Third Reich. Also in the file, were the most up-to-date aerial photographs of Münster. In the top right-hand margin of each photograph was a secret code number. The photographs had been taken by the RAF's reconnaissance units with specially trained crews equipped with fast and high-flying Mosquitos.

After referring to the cypher book to de-code the number specified in the Field Order, Lt. Henderson then chose the relevant photograph and placed it carefully under a rectangular plastic transparency which was divided by both vertical and horizontal grid lines. It was exactly the same size as the seven by five-inch photograph. Also on the Field Order, were two numbers which were to be used in conjunction with the grid. Where the vertical and horizontal numbers on the grid intersected over the photograph was the planned Mean Point of Impact (MPI). This was to be the aiming point for the Lead Bombardier. The other bombardiers would then release their bombs immediately the Lead Fortress unloaded over the target during the bomb run. This meant that a pattern of bombs fell rather than each individual plane aim for the same point. Each Bomb Group was assigned a different MPI within the target area and when a group of 18 Flying Fortresses, in good formation, released their combined bomb loads, totalling 54 tons of high explosives and incendiaries from an altitude of approximately five miles the results were quite devastating.

Lt. Henderson meticulously lined the edges of the grid up with those on the photograph underneath. He suddenly straightened up when he saw where the grid lines intersected. Doubting what he saw, he studied the photograph for a second time. He repeated the procedure for ascertaining the MPI, but came up with the same result. There had been no mistake.

« « « » » »

In 1943, a combat crewman stood a one in three chance of completing his tour of 25 missions. So after his eighth daylight raid he was living on borrowed time . . . and by the Grace of God. Newly-arrived replacement crews were told, "Some of you may have no religion, well now is the time you would be well advised to get some."

As on other nights preceding a raid, the combat crews slept uneasily that night. Some had difficulty sleeping at all.

Lt. Jack Nosser at Framlingham, Suffolk recalls:

> The sounds in the Nissen huts on mission nights were always different. The ceaseless movement of prowling cats and their occasional squealings as they roamed outside. Muffled coughs and the clearing of dry, tickling throats, gathered together for a spasmodic symphony of fear within. Matches flared brightly and briefly, leaving the pale orange glow of cigarettes floating in the darkness. A loud groan or a plaintive cry deep from a troubled dream would cause a sudden, startled hush from the sleepless, and would suspend the moment, then gradually movement and noise would again prod the night along.

Chapter 6

AT the Casablanca Conference on 4 February 1943, the Allied political leaders issued the following directive to Royal Air Force Bomber Command and the United States Army Air Forces operating from England:

Your primary objective will be the progressive destruction and dislocation of the German military, industrial and economic system, and the undermining of the morale of the German people to a point where their capacity for armed resistance is fatally weakened.

The directive continued with chilling simplicity:

Within that general concept your primary objectives will for the present be in the following priority
(a) German submarine yards.
(b) The German aircraft industry.
(c) Transportation.
(d) Oil plants.
(e) Other targets in the German war industry.

Ever since the outbreak of war, the industrial Ruhr in Northwestern Germany had been considered a prime target. It was a huge, sprawling and vital area, its cities ringed with a powerful and accurate range of anti-aircraft guns defending the blast furnaces of Dusseldorf, Essen, Dortmund, Wuppertal, Cologne and the rest which, night and day, churned out all the paraphernalia of modern warfare beneath tall, smoking chimneys.

Even the steel hulls of the submarines which had almost brought Britain to its knees during the Battle of the Atlantic, were fabricated by Krupp, a name inexorably linked with every European struggle from 1870 onwards. The insidious tentacles of this huge armaments empire reached out to every city, port and town of the Third Reich.

In Poland and eastern Germany, under a thin veil of secrecy, the chimneys above the ovens of the concentration camps were smoking with soot and a fine grey dust of a very different kind, as a whole racial minority were being systematically annihilated.

On the night of 5 March 1943, the Battle of the Ruhr began. In one half an hour Lancasters, Stirlings and Halifaxes of RAF Bomber Command unloaded a thousand tons of high explosive and incendiary bombs on the enormous Krupp armament plant at Essen, the most heavily-defended target in Germany. The following months saw other Ruhr cities bombed incessantly in a series of attacks, including the incomparable accuracy of the "Dam Busters" raid in May, led by Wing Commander Guy Gibson, which disrupted production lines significantly, but only temporarily.

« « « » » »

Barely 35 miles from the Dutch border and a similar distance to the North of Dortmund, is the historic City of Münster with its army garrison swelling its wartime population to 155,000 inhabitants. Founded about the year 804, Münster received its City Charter in 1137, and in 1815 became capital of the Province of Westphalia. In the middle ages a brisk trade had flourished at this natural crossroads where German iron met Flemish cloth, Brussels lace and English wool. Throughout its long history, however, the Horsemen of the Apocalypse had ridden roughshod over this city, so rich in architectural gems. In the 16th Century it came under the domination of the Anabaptists who composed the fanatical wing of the Reformation, and the bloody dictatorship of "King" Johann van Leyden. During the Seven Years War, in the mid-18th Century, the city was under siege and captured by the allied English and Prussian troops, and in Napoleonic times it was occupied by the French army.

Near the centre of Münster, the world-famous City Hall, with its beautiful Gothic gable-end towering over surrounding ancient houses along the cobbled Prinzipalmarkt, housed the Hall of Peace — the old council chamber — which in 1648 had witnessed the Peace Treaty, when the whole of Europe was at war, granting the Netherlands national independence. Oak panelling covered the 12th Century stone walls, sumptuously adorned with friezes and figures. Münster woodcarvers had created this outstanding artistry of the late Gothic and early Renaissance styles in the 16th Century. The signing of the Treaty had been witnessed by contemporary oil portraits of the signatories gazing down solemnly from the walls.

In the very centre of the city stood the thousand-year-old Cathedral, with its medieval stone sculptures of the Apostles and Saints looking out with unseeing eyes over the flat farming plains of Westphalia and scattered villages with their moated manor houses.

The winding River Aa threaded its narrow way through the city centre. The Aa Lake lay surrounded by idyllic meadows, and the nearby man-made Dortmund-Ems canal, opened to barge traffic in 1899, connected the smoky industrial Ruhr valley with the River Ems which flowed into the North Sea after passing the main port of Westphalia, Emden, a hundred miles North of Münster.

Supplementing the Dortmund-Ems canal, were the bustling, sprawling railway marshalling yards. Münster's railroad workers, track maintenance gangs, signalmen, porters and administrators saw endless wagons loaded with imported Swedish iron ore pass southwards on the last leg of the journey to the ever busy smelting furnaces of the Ruhr. From the opposite direction behind puffing, whistling steam engines, came long flat-cars bearing the finished product — brand new 50-ton tanks, trucks, diesel engines, guns and ammunition, bound for the German forces.

Before the war, Münster had been a fine example of the beautiful old cities of Western Germany. There were churches, museums, convents, a University in the city centre, and many fine old gabled buildings. Its predominately Catholic population, however, were no friends of the now all-powerful Nazi regime. During the 1932 election campaign in Germany Münster's citizens had pelted Hitler with rotten eggs and over-ripe fruit. The Fuhrer never forgot that and he vowed never again to set foot in the city. To him, it was the "Black City" because of the priests black cassocks and robes, and the influence of the widely respected Clemens-August von Galen, Bishop of Münster, who made several anti-Nazi speeches which were widely reported to an unheeding world. Despite these blatant gestures of hostility towards the 'New Order,' when it came to the vote in early 1933, 40% of Münster's citizens sided with the Nationalsozialisten. Little did they realise what the uncertain future held for Germany under Nazi rule.

With one third of Germany's dispirited work force unemployed and experiencing bitter hardships and deprivations in 1933 there was little to suggest that within six short years Hitler's Germany was to achieve full employment and possess one of the most powerful, formidably equipped and superbly trained Armed Forces in the world at that time. An Army, Navy and Air Force had been built up with the utmost stealth and secrecy despite the almost total restrictions imposed on the German nation at the end of the First World War.

Among the terms of the Treaty of Versailles in 1919, signed by the American President Woodrow Wilson, French Prime Minister Clemenceau and British Prime Minister Lloyd George, the victorious Allies demanded that Germany make huge and totally unrealistic reparations payments, surrender or destroy their entire Air Force, their fleet, their artillery and their tanks. The Allies also prohibited the Germans from ever again building up an armed force larger than the absolute minimum necessary for the maintenance of Germany's internal law and order.

"Germany," the Allies asserted vengefully, "would be squeezed until the pips squeaked."

When Marshall Ferdinand Foch, Commander in Chief of the Allied Forces, who had seen a hundred blood-soaked battlefields between those ghastly war years of 1914 and 1918, heard the details of the Treaty, he observed with stunning accuracy, "This is not Peace. It is merely an Armistice for the next twenty years."

When Adolf Hitler came to power in January 1933 the leaders of the British Government thought that he, as the leader and head of a modern and civilised nation of eighty million people would not be all that different from all the others with whom they dealt.

Sir Horace Rumbold, the vastly experienced and astute

August von Galen, Bishop of Münster, Died in 1946.

Painting a curb at the Ludgeristreet in Münster, December 1939.

W. Beer

Unteroffizier Voigt, FW 190 Pilot, 4 Staffel, JG/126, was shot down and killed in action a few weeks after the Munster raid.

Squadron Leader Ronald Hawkins, R.A.F., Commanding Officer, Squadron No. 3 (Typhoons), Killed in Action 5 October 1943 near Ghent, Belgium.

R.A.F. Number 3 Squadron Typhoon, Manston, Kent, October, 1943.

Seymour "Buck" Feldman, an American volunteer who flew Typhoons in the R.A.F. No. 3 Squadron, Manston, Kent. Taken 5 October 1943.

Gerd Wiegand of JG/26, an FW 190 pilot who shot down a 95th Bomb Group B17 on 10 October 1943 while flying this FW 190.

Seymour "Buck" Feldman receives the Distinguished Flying Cross from King George IV, July 1944.

FW 190 pilots awaiting orders to "scramble" make conversation around their planes.

Flight line on an FW 190 field.

390th Bombardment Group, Framlingham, Suffolk. During the very early morning hours the combat crews of the 390th Bomb Group receive their briefing prior to a daylight mission. Date of this photograph is unknown, but is probably late 1943 or early 1944.
Official U.S.A.F. Photo

Captain Ellis B. Scripture, Group Navigator of the 95th Bomb Group, briefs navigators and bombardiers for an earlier mission in July, 1943. **Official U.S.A.F. Photo.**

Captain Ellis B. Scripture, Group Navigator of the 95th Bomb Group and Lead Navigator on the Münster mission.

Lt. Jack Nosser, Bombardier of the 390th Bomb Group's Cash and Carrie.

On the left is Major John Egan, a Squadron Commander of the 100th Bomb Group who flew the Münster raid as Group Leader. At right is his good friend, Major Gale "Bucky" Cleven who was shot down on 8 October 1943 on the Bremen raid.

Crews of the 92nd Bomb Group, Podington, being briefed for a mission sometime in 1943. John Copper

The 390th Bomb Group crew, headed by Pilot Robert Schneider, assigned to fly the 100th Bomb Group plane Little Mike *on 10 October 1943.*

The crew of the 385th Bomb Group B17 headed by Pilot William Whitlow.

Captain Richard H. Perry of the 570th Squadron, 390th Bomb Group and Co-Pilot of the Fortress Eightball *on the Münster raid.*

A B17 takes off from the main runway of the Framlingham Airfield from which the 390th Bomb Group flew.

Taxiing along the perimeter track at Framlingham Airfield before a mission. The nearest plane is Skippy *which was damaged in both the Bremen and Marienburg raids. It returned early from the Münster raid with mechanical problems.*

The 390th Bomb Group B17 Eightball *in formation over Suffolk.* Eightball *returned from Münster 10 October 1943 badly damaged.*

381st Bomb Group B17F The Hellion, *based at Ridgewell, Essex, over the patchwork quilt of the English countryside. Note the edge of the airfield at the left of the picture and the edge of the town of Great Dunmow at the right.* Official U.S.A.F. Photo

The 390th Bomb Group formation over the North Sea in September 1943. The lead plane is Pistol Packin' Mama. Paul Vance

From the cockpit of Lt. MacCarter's **Oh Nausea** *of the 100th Bomb Group in September 1943.*

Flak can be seen in this photograph taken on the same mission.

Another photograph of the 100th Bomb Group formation taken from Lt. MacCarter's Oh Nausea.

Contrails from the 100th Bomb Group formation.

Colonel John K. Gerhart, Commanding Officer of the 95th Bombardment Group. Col. Gerhart led the 95th and the Eighth Air Force to Munster on 10 October 1943.

Colonel Gerhart greets two of his ground crewmen.

Captain Keith Harris, Pilot of Spot Remover. Stewart P. Evans Collection

The crew of Spot Remover *of the 390th Bomb Group was assigned to fly B17G* Stork Club *in the 100th Bomb Group formation on 10 October 1943. Sergeant Stanley Smith, Waist Gunner, is kneeling in the front row, third from the right.*

Major William Lindley, Lead Pilot of the 95th Group on 10 October 1943 (then a Captain).

The crew of The Zoot Suiters, *the Lead Plane on the Münster mission. Captain Lindley is at the left in the back row. Lt. O.G. Tigerman, the Co-Pilot flew the Münster mission in the Tail Gunner position as Col. Gerhart was in the right hand seat as Task Force Commander.*

Luftwaffe Flak (l. to r.) Hessling, Föcuing, Schembeuer, Feidler, and Stemmer relax on a bridge over the Dortmund-Ems Canal in October 1943.

British Ambassador in Berlin at that time, disagreed. Reporting to London on Hitler's successful election campaign, recently over, he said, "The speeches of Nazi leaders would be regarded in most civilized countries as deliberate incitements to violence."

In a dispatch to the Foreign Office in London, dated July 30th, 1933, after surveying Hitler's first six months in power, Sir Horace wrote,"I have the impression that the persons directing the policy of the Hitler Government are not normal. Many of us have the feeling that we are living in a country where fantastic hooligans have got the upper hand."

Sir Horace Rumbold's early warnings of impending disaster had also gone unheeded.

The Nazi regime, by 1939, was now in a position to turn the thoroughly unjust and humiliating Versailles Treaty of 1919 on its head. They set about their expansionist policy with a vengeance and a ferocity that is unsurpassed in history.

History itself has proved, down through the ages, that all that is necessary for evil to prevail and triumph is for good men to do nothing.

By 1943 the citizens of Münster had to cooperate with their Nazi rulers or face the consequences. The daunting prospect of vicious and bloody reprisals, deportation to a labour camp or worse, hung like a dark shadow over every anti-Nazi home in Germany. The ominous flag of the swastika drooped over the doorway of the Gestapo offices in Gutenbergstrasse as a grim reminder.

Despite this, Bishop von Galen publicly denounced, and openly accused the Nazi officials and doctors as "inhumanly criminal," the euthenasia programme then being carried out at Hadamar, a small town to the southeast of Cologne, among Germany's psychiatrically ill.

"Who doesn't work, shall not eat or be fed by the community," said the Nazi creed, resulting in the mass murder of helpless unproductive "Volksgenossen".

The Nazi's reply to the Bishop's plea was a swift condemnation of "this morass of traitorism," but they were afraid to arrest this revered man and secretly transported their defenceless victims to Eastern Poland for extermination there.

Because of its strategic position, Münster was also a garrison city of the German army, second in size only to Potsdam near Berlin. The garrison surrounded the city with installations and barracks for infantry, artillery, an ordnance depot in the city centre, cavalry, Corps Headquarters, construction service, transportation depot and workshops, District military hospital and Recruiting District Headquarters. Münster was also the centre of communications and administration for both army and air force for Gau-Westfalen-Nord (District of Westphalia).

Münster's garrison also included a Corps of the German Sixth Army, the bulk of which had perished in the Arctic conditions at Stalingrad, on the Russian Front, during the previous winter. This titanic battle was perhaps the turning point of World War II that signalled the beginning of the end for Hitler's Third Reich.

Two airfields were situated close to Münster, Loddenheide and Münster-Handorf, from which in the Summer of 1940, lumbering Junkers 52 transport aircraft had flown countless missions carrying tons of supplies and highly-trained paratroops during the "Blitzkreig" of France, Belgium and Holland. Münster-Handorf was now a fighter base equipped with both day and night fighters, Focke Wulf 190's and Messerschmitt Bf109's. Heavy anti-aircraft guns defended both airfields and other areas of the city, including the numerous garrison installations.

Münster's industries ranged from wheelwright and wagon builders which catered for the needs of the surrounding farming community, to a factory complex sited conveniently beside the main North-South railway line, manufacturing light and heavy wing components for the Messerschmitt Aircraft Company. But many of the city's working population were employed at the busy and efficient railway junction, the remainder at the hospitals, schools, or in the various administrative offices one would expect to find in a provincial capital.

This then, was Münster, a seemingly well-defended city of questionable allegiance to the Nazi cause.

Submarine yards, aircraft industry, transportation, said the directive . . .

Chapter 7

TWENTY-ONE year old Felwebel Gerd Wiegand, a Pilot with the FW 190 equipped 4 Jagdgeschwader/ 26 (JG26) based at Lille-Nord airfield in northwestern France, recalls the days leading up to 10 October 1943:

My previous aerial engagement had been on 5 October while flying a borrowed aircraft.

Unteroffizier (Corporal) Voigt was a newly-arrived "Baker's Boy" (as they were called by the senior pilots in our Group) and he was entrusted to me for his first flight from Lille-Nord. We took off after breakfast. There was quite low cloud and undercast. I planned to show him our most important and prominent orientation points of our tactical area, the railway line which runs between Lille and Brussels, the Wester-Schelde and Kanal Knie (Channel Knee) from Ostend to Boulogne on the Northern coast of France.

As we approached Kortryk we received a radio message, " . . . Two Indians in MF8 heading southeast . . ." We immediately gave chase and steered a course of 270 degrees. I ordered weapons loading by hand signals so as not to break radio silence. Almost immediately we saw them, two Royal Air Force Typhoons straight in front of us flying low, just below the undercast. They were now heading north.

The leading machine immediately pulled up into the clouds, the other was about to start a low-level attack on a barge moored on a narrow canal. I only had to bank slightly to the right to position myself directly behind and above him. We fired simultaneously — he at the barge, and me at him. He fell immediately and crashed near his intended target. It happened near the village of Mennin.

The whole episode, from the radio message to the bitter end, lasted less than 30 seconds. It was my sixth air victory.

The surviving RAF Typhoon pilot remembers:

On the morning of 5 October 1943, we were briefed for another "Rhubarb." We were to fly at tree-top level from our base at Manston, Kent, and hit the Luftwaffe airfield at Courtrai (Werelgem), Belgium. The order also included hitting targets of opportunity, including trains, shipping and canal traffic, motor vehicles and anything else that moved.

I set off from Manston with Flying Officer 'Johnny' Foster. Shortly after crossing the Belgian coast and approaching the Courtrai area, we were jumped by two FW190's. I saw the mottled greens behind us and reported them to Foster. He acknowledged and said, "I'll meet you above the clouds."

I never saw him again.

That same day, we lost our Commanding Officer, Squadron Leader Ron Hawkins and Warrant Officer La Rocque, a Canadian, to heavy flak while dive-bombing the oil refineries at Ghent, Belgium.

Concluded Flight Lt. Seymour "Buck" Feldman, an American volunteer Pilot with the RAF's No. 3 Squadron:

1943 was a rough year on aircrews. Plenty of wonderful fellows got the "chop," especially on the shipping attacks at low-level around the North Sea and the Channel. The flak was really quite accurate.

Feldwebel Wiegand resumes his story:

So Unteroffizier Voigt still received his orientation training and could report back to Hauptmann Ebersberger, our Staffelkapitan (Squadron Commander), that he'd also flown his first operational mission at the same time.

The following three days were unusually quiet until 8 October.

It was late afternoon when I inadvertently created the "Airmans Monument" which comes from taxiing too quickly and carelessly over a recently filled-in bomb crater. This practice was against regulations and strictly forbidden, needless to say, because the tail of the aircraft rapidly rises and a plane standing on its head always leads to the extreme disapproval of the pilot's superior officers.

My beloved "10" . . . what did she look like? What could I do now?

Fortunately, there were 12 mechanics close at hand and they soon brought my bird to a more dignified posture. Apart from several filthy remarks they made the following summary:

- All three propeller blades were slightly bent at the ends.
- The aircraft pilot's nose was distinctly white.
- There was sand in the plane's BMW 801 engine (relatively easy to remove).
- Leading edge of the left wing was dented.
- Hauptman Ebersberger was away on a short holiday and not due back until late the next day.
- Crankshaft and oil sump undamaged. Engine started and functioned perfectly.
- The Chief Mechanic's idea was "The engine has exceeded its hours and urgently needs an overhaul. It could be replaced immediately if the aircraft can be flown to the workshops at Vendeville."
- The choice was three days under close arrest or I could risk the flight to Vendeville.

I chose Vendeville, and with a lot of luck and "Kupferbolzen" (Copper

Bolt) — an expression used to describe the feeling of absolute fear — I coaxed my faithful "10" into the air. In the gathering dusk and flying low, I got my aircraft to the repair depot at Vendeville where I had a new engine fitted in return for my one day's willing help with fitting a new airscrew ... makes sense!

So the Deutsche Luftwaffe, without knowing it, had one criminal procedure less, and on 10 October 1943, a recently flown in "10" with accompanying pilot, was ready for action. Hauptmann Ebersberger never learned of the aforementioned. Two weeks later, he encountered a Spitfire Squadron while flying alone and was shot down and killed.

Chapter 8

TO the 95th Bomb Group, Headquarters of the U.S. 13th Combat Bomb Wing, fell the responsibility of leading the fifteen other selected Bomb Groups from the 1st and 3rd Air Divisions to Münster in two Air Task forces. Three more Groups from the 2nd Air Division, equipped with B24 Liberators, would form a Third Task Force, and fly a diversion route over the North Sea in a north-easterly direction, then change course at a specified time in a feint thrust towards the Bremen, Emden and Hamburg areas of Northern Germany before withdrawing. This, the planners believed, would split the German fighter defences and divert their attention from the main force attacking Münster, which would have six P47 Thunderbolt Fighter Groups escorting them. Three Groups at different rendezvous points on the way to the target, and the other three during the withdrawal. In addition, five squadrons of short-range RAF Spitfires would further cover the Bomber's withdrawal from the Dutch coast across the North Sea. The Thunderbolts, now equipped with 75-gallon pressurised drop tanks, could reach Münster as it was within their 340-mile operating range.

Very early on Sunday morning, 10 October 1943, the tired combat crews were rudely awakened from their sleep by operations personnel who went around each barracks in turn with the depressing news that the mission was "On," and that briefing was at 0715 hours, considerably later than the four to five a.m. briefings of the two previous days.

At that very moment, the engine sounds of the Fortresses, Liberators and Thunderbolts being given their pre-flight warm-ups by Crew Chiefs, could be heard on many East Anglian airfields.

The crews soon trudged through the cold, damp, early

morning mist to the mess halls for a breakfast of cereal, powdered eggs, toast and coffee. After breakfast, many crewmen sought comforting solace in chapels of their various denominations where the Base Chaplains held services to help soothe jangled nerves. The airmen were only too aware that this could be their last day on earth.

Then it was off to the briefing huts.

At Horham, when the curtains in front of the briefing room were pulled aside to reveal a large-scale map of Central Europe, there were audible groans from the flyers. Every head followed the red lines on the map. One line went from England's East Coast across the North Sea and Holland, to a point just inside the German border where it swung northeastwards for a short distance then a straight course westwards, parallel to the outward leg and return to England. But it was a far shorter mission than the previous day's deep penetration raid to Eastern Germany and occupied Poland.

Major Donahue began:

> Your target for today, gentlemen, is Munster. (Pointing it out on the map with a billiard cue.) It is a vital rail junction between Germany's northern coastal ports and the heavy industries and munition plants of the Ruhr valley immediately to the south of your primary target. Through these marshalling yards, each day and each night, roll hundreds of tons of armaments and war materials produced in the Ruhr valley destined for all points North, West and East.
>
> However, unlike all previous military and industrial targets attacked to date by the 8th Air Force, today it will be different . . . very different . . . because today you will hit the centre of that city, the homes of the working population of those marshalling yards. You will disrupt their lives so completely that their morale will be seriously affected and their will to work and to fight will be substantially reduced.
>
> Should the primary target be obscured by cloud or industrial haze, the secondary target is Hamm, located in the Ruhr valley itself, and as a last resort, any industrial town in Germany.

There was a stunned silence among the crews as the enormity of this sudden and complete change in strategy was set before them in such cold and clinical terms. Momentarily, it was quiet enough to notice the sounds of the countryside. A skylark's shrill twitter, a distant rook's harsh caw and a blackbird's vibrant song drifted through an open window. It was hard to believe that here in this quiet sleepy Suffolk village plans were being made, and instructions issued, for a city's destruction in the centre of Europe that very day.

There was a murmur of conversation which was cut short as the crews received further specialised briefing. Assembly points, map co-ordinates, route to and from the target, rendezvous points and times with their fighter escort, numbers of known enemy fighter airfields within a radius of a hundred miles of their route, known anti-aircraft gun emplacements to avoid, the turning point for the bomb-run onto the target known as the Initial Point (I.P.), which in this case was the small town of Haltern to the southwest of Münster, and the Mean Point of Impact (M.P.I.). Bomb release time—or Zero Hour — was 1500 hours. Watches were synchronised.

Lt. Mills, from the Group's Weather Section, pointed out the weather prevailing and forecast favourable conditions with good visibility over the mainland of Europe, but some low stratocumulus over the North Sea and possibly stretching five or ten miles inland on return.

Major Donahue emphasised the need for security, and pointed out the best routes for evasion, known border checkpoints, in case they were shot down over occupied territory. A Communications Officer briefed the crews on the call signs for bomber/fighter inter-communication, radio frequencies. The radio operators were issued their code sheets printed on edible rice paper in case of capture.

After the briefing, the co-pilots collected each of their fellow-member's escape kits. These comprised a silk map, both sides of which were relevant to the occupied areas flown over, a button-sized compass, concentrated high-energy foods in tubes, anti-fatigue tablets, water purifying pills, language phrase cards and money in currencies of the enemy-held countries. The navigators and bombardiers collected their navigational charts and target maps after their own short, specialised briefing.

Captain Ellis Scripture, the 95th Bomb Group Lead Navigator, recalls:

I had been raised in a strict Methodist home. My parents were God-orientated people and were quite active church members. I was shocked to learn that we were to bomb civilians as our primary target for the first time in the war and that our aiming point was to be the front steps of Münster Cathedral. I was very reluctant to fly this mission. In fact it turned me off completely.

I approached Colonel Gerhart and told him that I didn't think I could fly this particular raid and I explained my reasons. His reaction was exactly what one would expect (in retrospect) of a career officer and a very fine Commander.

He said, "Look Captain, this is war . . . spelt W-A-R. We're in an all out fight; the Germans have been killing innocent people all over Europe for years. We're here to beat the hell out of them . . . and we're going to do it.

"We have, to date, been very diligent and concentrated all our efforts on U-Boat yards, aircraft plants, oil installations and other industrial targets connected with the German war machine. We have astutely avoided the possibility of bombing civilians.

"This decision has only been reached after great consideration. It has become very apparent to the Allied leaders that we must now carry the war to the German people to make them realise that there is a war going on and that they are the victims of their own military leadership in Germany. People there are beginning to have real doubts about the Nazi's capability of winning this war. All of us are well aware of the countless atrocities committed by the Nazis in the name of the German people.

"Now, I'm leading this mission and you're my navigator. You're leading this mission also . . . any questions?"

I said, "No Sir," and that ended the incident.

Captain William Lindley, the mission's Lead Pilot, recalls:

About the only thing I can remember about the briefing was this was the first American mission where the target was the city itself, and not an industrial complex. One of the purposes of the strike was to destroy a University located in the centre of the city. Apparently it was being used as a centre for developing hardline Nazis.

Reactions were mixed at the other American airfields. Major John Kidd, 100th Bomb Group Operations Officer, explains the prevalent mood of the time thus:

At Thorpe Abbotts during the late summer and fall of 1943 we had a complete turnover of combat crews in fourteen weeks. This didn't make for prolonged friendships, but what it did do was that very close and intense friendships developed among those crewmen who defied the odds and managed to stay around a little longer.

Combat crews came and went. I vividly recall the occasion when a replacement crew arrived at the base late one night and we had to send them on a mission the very next day. They didn't even have time to unpack their luggage and personal belongings.

They didn't come back.

Major John Egan, a 100th Bomb Group Squadron Commander, had recently returned from a 48-hour pass to London. On learning that his close friend Major Cleven had been lost over Bremen two days previously, he demanded, and received, permission to lead the Group in the attack on Münster. Said Major Egan:

The briefing was the same as usual until the Intelligence Officer, my good friend Miner Shaw, flashed a photograph of the target on the screen with his slide projector. The Aiming Point and the Mean Point of Impact (M.P.I.) were the centre of the city of Münster.

Shaw's voice droned on that we were going to sock a residential district. At this point I found myself on my feet, cheering. Others who had lost close friends in the past few raids joined in the cheering because here was a chance to kill Germans, the spawners of race hatred and minority oppression. It was a dream mission to avenge the death of a buddy.

The mission had not been set up for me to kill the hated Hun, but as a last resort to stop rail transportation in the Ruhr valley. Practically all of the rail workers were billeted in Münster. It was decided that a pursuit and fighter-bomber attack could not effectively stop up the Ruhr valley. A good big bomber raid could really mess up the very efficient rail system by messing up its personnel.

People who never saw bomber pilots taxi out for a mission in the European theatre of operations during the summer and fall of 1943 really missed seeing boys who were, for a short time, big men. Mind you, all of these boy-men weren't fighters, that is professional soldiers or adventurers. They were people who were in the Air Force for various reasons: better food, better pay, better ratings, better glamour, better kind of discipline, better chance to slug Adolph, better chance of being killed . . .

These boy-men commanded no less than nine other individuals and booted 4,000 horses in the tail with their right hand to get their B17's into the air and keep them there in the face of the toughest, roughest opposition mankind has ever faced.

However, among the many 100th Bomb Group crewmen who remained seated throughout the briefing, was Lt. George Ziegler, a 349th Squadron Bombardier. "It proved to me," he said, "that the political leaders of our country were just as bankrupt in ideas as the leaders of other nations. I'm not as bitter as this sounds but I know that power corrupts."

A 390th Bomb Group Pilot, Captain Keith Harris, added, "I was very suspicious and apprehensive about this mission from the start. It was a Sunday afternoon, and our M.P.I. was the steps of the Cathedral."

At the 385th Bomb Group base at Great Ashfield, Pilot Lt. William Whitlow, who had flown the long, tiring mission to Marienburg the previous day, made a prophetic statement, "Give me a short, hot mission to the long dreary one any time."

Because the Eighth Air Force was on its third successive maximum effort daylight raid, some flyers didn't even know or care where they were going. Said Sergeant John Leahy, a 385th Bomb Group Radio Operator:

I was exhausted and completely drained emotionally. I assumed that we were continuing our strategic bombing of military targets. By then, of course, we were living on borrowed time — our crew was on it's 19th mission — and quite frankly I didn't expect to complete my tour.

It seems strange, in retrospect, but no-one paid much attention to the thousands of civilians and slave labourers, both men and women, who undoubtedly died at work or in the air raid shelters of German tank, submarine and aircraft factories during the Allied bombing campaign.

For some there was a momentary surprise at hitting the centre of the city. Explained Lt. Paul Perceful, a 95th Bomb Group Co-Pilot:

In my case it was only a momentary question mark, because by October 1943, our Group's losses were almost 100%. We had also heard stories concerning the Luftwaffe's lack of chivalry, not to mention how the German Army was conducting itself. In the early days we might have had second thoughts, but not at that point.

95th Bomb Group Navigator, Lt. T.H. Bozarth, commented simply, "We were just too tired to care much one way or the other."

Captain Frank Murphy, Navigator of the 100th Bomb Group's B17 *Aw-R-Go,* recalls:

Compared to our 11-hour deep penetration into German airspace to distant Marienburg the previous day which I flew in the 100th's lead B17 with our Commanding Officer, Colonel "Chick" Harding, Münster, which is just beyond the Dutch/German border, didn't appear to be a particularly alarming or hazardous mission at that time.

Despite the fact that we were to have fighter escort virtually all the way to the target that day, I was always very nervous and apprehensive before every combat mission which I flew over Occupied Europe. We all knew that our lives were very much in danger each time we went out, and we were very much aware that each town in Germany was a known flak area.

I had logged considerable combat time with the crew of Captain Charles

Cruikshank, a fine, skilled and thoroughly dependable pilot. This was to be our crew's 21st mission since arriving at Thorpe Abbotts in June. Very few of the original crews remained.

I don't recall any particular feelings one way or the other as to the target being city centre of Münster itself. I had seen no signs from the Germans that there were any sporting rules in the game. To me a target in Nazi Germany was a target. Incidentally, my grandfather was born in Germany.

B17F *Cash and Carrie* Bombardier Lt. Jack Nosser of the 390th Bomb Group, remembers smiling wryly to himself at the briefing.

I'd noticed that the Intelligence Officer had said, "If we can do a good job today . . . " but then had switched to, "Your M.P.I . will be . . ." and "You are going to bomb the workers' homes . . . "

Even saying we would bomb only military targets was not truly realistic. Most of our military targets were factories and plants situated in cities and towns anyway, and with a whole Air Division of perhaps nine or ten Bombardment Groups all attempting to hit a specific point accurately from an altitude of five miles, and with cross winds gusting up to more than 100 miles an hour, errors were bound to occur. And very often they did, despite the computerised bomb sight.

I remembered our first mission in early August to Bonn. The target was an optical instrument factory, but a fair proportion of the bombs carried over and landed in the nearby residential district of the city. Most certainly the population of Bonn got it, just as the population of Münster were about to get it. Saying we were after a military target doesn't change the results or morals of the end product. However, I felt that the Germans got what they deserved, and many of them received a good deal less than they deserved.

Recalled Lt. Robert Sabel, Pilot of the 390th Bomb Group's B17F *Rusty Lode,* "It was Sunday, and many of the crews at Framlingham had deep reservations about bombing anywhere near churches."

Captain Rodney Snow, Pilot of B17F *Herky Jerky II,* 95th Bomb Group:

Reaction at the briefing really didn't register for a while. What got to me was that it was a Sunday mission, and probably the only one I flew on the Sabbath. Being of Scots-Irish descent and a regular Presbyterian, did give me some deep reservations about the need for Sunday bombings.

Quite frankly, my first concern was my position in the formation. Leading the third element of three airplanes in the High Squadron is the worst position in the Group. You are on the whip-end, which means to say that when the Group Lead airplane makes a turn to the left or right you have to anticipate and react very quickly or you find yourself out of the formation and all alone.

There was another flyer who was not at all concerned about the mission's civilian target. He was Lt. Howard Hamilton, Bombardier of the 100th Bomb Group's Lead B17 *Mlle. Zig Zag*.

Being at that time a very young man, I felt I was there to help win the war, if possible. I had been bombed myself when in London on leave, and had personally seen the results of the indiscriminate German bombing there.

The basic problem in trying to bomb a railway system is that if sufficient labour is available, railroad tracks can be repaired in short order. We were told that the idea of bombing these railroad workers' homes was to deprive the Germans of the people to do the repair work.

Lt. Richard Perry, Co-Pilot of the 390th Bomb Group's Fortress *Eightball* recalled:

It didn't seem to be a very difficult mission. It wasn't like going to Schweinfurt or Regensburg. My main concern before setting off on all my missions was for good weather and hoping that no mechanical problems would befall our aircraft.

Lt. Bohn Fawkes, Pilot of a 379th Bomb Group Fortress named *Tondelayo,* remembers:

I was disappointed, although I had strong suspicions that not all our bombs fell directly on our assigned targets. The smug assertion we aimed only at military targets was comforting. However, I don't believe I held the German civilians entirely blameless in the state of affairs which brought me to that unhappy task. My primary responsibility was for our aircraft. At times this was a full-time job.

Sergeant Bob Banta, Radio Operator of the 390th's *Rose Marie,* recalls:

After flying two tiring missions on the two preceding days and being up early on the third consecutive morning, we were understandably very tired. At the briefing there were moans and groans from the flyers when the curtains were pulled aside and the map revealed another tough target in the Ruhr area. The gloomy forecasts quickly abated however when we were told that P47 Thunderbolts would cover us all the way to Münster, at that time the deepest penetration by our escorts. That really caused some appreciative noises!!

After collecting their cumbersome flying gear, parachutes, Mae West life jackets, flak vests and helmets, sheepskin jackets, trousers and boots from the equipment stores, the crews were driven out in jeeps and trucks to their waiting Fortresses. Then began the long "Readiness" wait — a tense and trying period of time.

For Sergeant Warren Thomas, Radio Operator of the 95th Bomb Group B17 *Fritz Blitz,* this was to be his 25th mission and completion of his tour. After it was over he could spend the remainder of his Air Force career on the ground, and after all, there were 314 separate occupations and skills an enlisted man could choose from.

> Upon arrival at the *Fritz Blitz* I stowed my gear, triple-checked my parachute and began the dreaded waiting period until take-off time. This count-down was always the worst part of every raid for me personally. Mission doubts, the ever-lengthening odds on returning, and other black thoughts clouded all other mind matters. The longer the wait, the worse my condition of mind. The summons to board the bomber was always a very welcome call. The actions required to taxi, take off and assemble were the ideal antidote to clear the nagging doubts and fears.

At 1020 hours Captain Howard Keel, at the controls of a 100th Bomb Group B17 named *Little Mike,* took off from Thorpe Abbotts for the short flight to Framlingham where Lieutenant Robert Schneider and his crew of the 390th were assigned to fly the mission in his aircraft as a "spare" B17.

As take-off time approached, Lt. Winfrey "Pappy" Lewis, Co-Pilot of *Royal Flush* at Thorpe Abbotts, wandered away from his fellow crew members to be on his own for a few minutes before boarding the aircraft. Their regular B17, *Rosie's Riveters,* had been flak-damaged over Bremen and was undergoing repairs in one of the hangers. As he looked up at the cloudless morning sky over Norfolk, he whispered, "Lord God of Host, be with us yet. Lest we forget, lest we forget."

At Horham, Colonel Gerhart, the Task Force Commander sitting in the co-pilot's seat of *The Zootsuiters,* read off the pre-flight checklist to his Pilot, Captain William Lindley. "Catfish" Lindley, as he was known to his close friends, was one of the 95th's "characters" and completely fearless. When the Group Navigator had asked him on one occasion if he was interested in any particular period of past history, he replied, in his deep Southern drawl, "No, not really . . . y'see, 'Scrip' . . . ah'm too busy makin' it."

Prior to starting the four great engines in sequence; the two pilots worked smoothly and unhurriedly in completing the twenty-six steps on the B17 starting check list. The low whine of the fuel booster pump which supplied 100 octane petrol was quickly drowned by the higher whine of the electric/inertia starter and as the pitch increased the starter switch to Number One engine was turned in the "engage"position. With raw fuel now injected through the intake pipes of several cylinders on the engine, the quarter-ton propeller initially jerked around in slow motion until the engine coughed, caught, snarled angrily and then roared, transforming each propeller in turn into a blurring 12-foot-diameter silver disc, amidst belching blue exhaust smoke which was instantly whisked behind the giant aircraft by the gale-like slipstream. The crew chief on the hardstand, unplugged the electrical lead of the trolley generator from the trembling fuselage of the bomber. This additional power boost prevented an excessive drain on the B17's batteries.

Captain Lindley minutely adjusted the throttles until the quivering guages indicated 1,000 rpm to gradually warm up the engines, checking that the propeller-feathering mechanisms were functioning correctly. He then advanced the throttle of each engine in sequence to maximum power to test the turbo-superchargers and the magnetos.

Using the two outboard engines to maneuver after the brakes were released, he guided the Fortress from its hardstand onto the perimeter track and taxied at walking pace towards the end of Horham's mile-long main runway. As they passed each hardstand another Fortress would join the ever-lengthening line. The ground crews waved and wished them luck. On the far side of the airfield, the two other Squadrons were creeping around to the end of the take-off runway. The surrounding countryside reverberated to the booming sound of scores of 1,200-horsepower Wright Cyclone engines as the 22 B17's continued their ponderous procession.

« « « » » »

At the 12th Century St. Mary's Church in nearby Horham village, the parishioners congregated for the morning service. They came dutifully from their picturesque thatched pink cottages and more modern brick red-tiled houses. Tough, ruddy-faced farm workers with gnarled hands calloused from a lifetime of long, hard hours at the plough, pitchfork, and a variety of patiently learned skills ranging from shoeing a horse to hurdle-making. They came with their families, clothed in their Sunday best. Smartly pressed suits and colorful coats, despite the meagre clothing coupons allowed each household. The small children were giggling and chattering to themselves above the harsh engine sounds coming from the direction of the airfield. Local tradesmen and landowners, as their forefathers had done for generations before them, took their places in the polished oak pews.

Softly-coloured shafts of sunlight from the stained glass windows beyond the altar added an air of serene beauty to the church's interior as the soft notes of the organ announced the beginning of the service.

About 300 miles due East, and almost within the same degree of latitude, Clemens-August-von Galen, Bishop of Münster, was completing the sacraments of Holy Communion to the last of his congregation in the magnificent Cathedral. Some of the communicants — and the Cathedral — now had less than four hours to live.

Chapter 9

CAPTAIN Lindley turned the growling Fortress into the slight breeze at the end of the wide runway. A green flare curved up into the bright morning sunlight from the distant control tower, and at precisely fourteen minutes past eleven he began the long take-off run, advancing the throttles smoothly and gradually to full power. Colonel Gerhart monitored the main engine instruments, revolutions, oil and fuel pressures, boost and temperature gauges. He tersely called out the rapidly increasing airspeed to the pilot who had his eyes fixed unwaveringly at a point on the horizon beyond the runway's end which raced closer with every passing second. The bellowing engines had reached 2,700 rpm, and gradually and grudgingly the tail wheel rose clear of the solid concrete runway.

". . . . ninety . . . . hundred . . . . hundred and ten . . . .," reported Col. Gerhart.

Captain Lindley eased back the control column slightly and felt the reassuring sensation of smooth flight instead of the comparative bumpiness of the runway's imperfections which the two main wheels had transmitted through the aircraft.

"Gear up."

Col. Gerhart flipped the landing gear switch on the central control pedestal to "Up" and gently dabbed the brakes twice to stop the huge wheels spinning before they entered the two inboard engine nacelles with a satisfying clunk.

Twenty-six tons of highly-volatile Flying Fortress was now committed to flight, its engines roaring at maximum power, the four blurring propellers clawing the air, as it slowly rose from the runway as if on an invisible ramp. Green and brown fields, hedges, cottages with well-maintained and colourful gardens, tall groups of trees and trimly-thatched corn stacks slid easily and rapidly beneath the giant bomber, its shadow leaping and hurdling across the patchwork Suffolk landscape.

After reducing power slightly, Captain Lindley began a slow, left-hand turn with a 150 miles-an-hour indicated air-speed, and continued to climb at 300 feet a minute. At 30 second intervals the Group's remaining aircraft took off. Each Fortress announced its arrival at the runway's end by flashing its Squadron code letter to the control tower. Soon, all 21 planes, plus a spare one, were circling the base, straining for altitude.

After reaching 10,000 feet the crews turned on their life-sustaining oxygen equipment. For every thousand feet they gained, the temperature dropped 2 1/2 degrees centigrade. The ideal outside temperature for structural icing to rapidly form on the leading edges of an aircraft is minus six degrees centigrade. To avoid the temperature conducive to icing, the plane has to either climb or descend.

Each crewman had his own private thoughts as the B17's reached for the skies. The two Pilots busily engaged in flying each bomber were constantly aware that any sudden maneuver could easily result in a mid-air collision, and the Navigators checked each landmark as it passed below their briefed assembly route. For the remainder of each crew there was little to keep their minds occupied until later.

Lt. Jack Nosser describes his thoughts and fears during these moments:

> I watched the earth dropping away, beginning to change from sharply-defined details to a chequered pattern. The last detail was a glimpse of a boy leading a cow towards an open barn door. The sight made me momentarily forget the dull roar of the engines and I suddenly started wondering, "Why am I in this plane and not down there leading that cow? Why must I be in this game of chance played on this field of disaster with the gruesome rules of kill or be killed? Why must I be food to feed this parasite of civilisation that gilds the lucky few with glory and consumes the multitudes with death? What and where will I be this evening when the boy again milks that cow? Will I just be a toast in a bar, a tear in an eye, a sudden thought in a mind?"

The 95th Group's last aircraft finally reached the specified altitude of 24,000 feet about an hour and a half later. At almost five miles above the earth, the planes were able to complete their bombing formation into High, Lead and Low Squadrons. Captain Lindley then set course for the "Buncher" radio homing beacon at Great Yarmouth for Wing Assembly with the 390th and 100th Bomb Groups.

Explained Major J.B. Kidd:

The process for forming the Combat Wing, and then the Wing into a stream of the Air Division, before tacking the Divisions together, was quite a complex and time-consuming procedure. It was all laid out on charts with very precise times, assembly points and adjoining angles. Due to the weather over England, the visibility frequently wasn't too good. Sometimes the atmospheric conditions were such that the heat from our engines

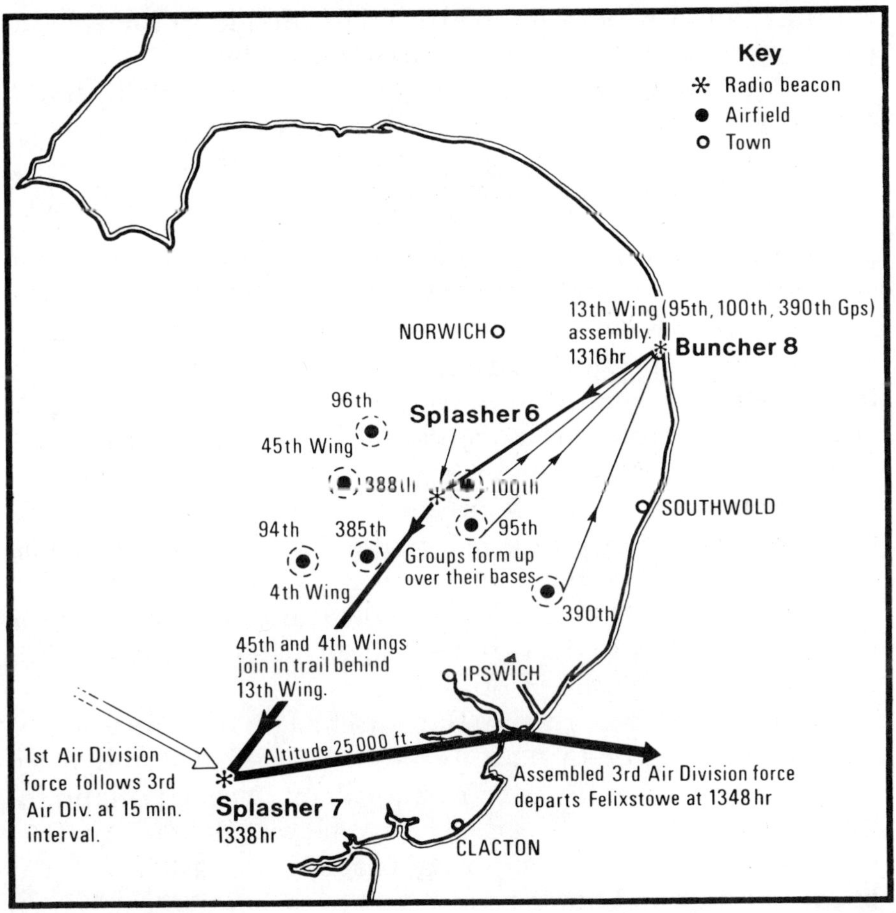

Assembly route of the 13th Combat Bomb Wing for the Münster raid of 10 October 1943.

would form condensation trails (contrails) resulting in complete cloud decks through which we had to fly while circling for altitude. It was possible that entire Groups could be on a collision course, so to minimise that risk, Groups were instructed to join the main stream at a very acute angle so that a very slight turn would bring the Groups together.

Timing was all-important, and a matter of 10 or 20 seconds off from arrival at a precise location meant that you had to catch up on a turn and add a little more throttle. Adding throttle in the lead plane of 21 meant that the other 20 aircraft had to follow suit, and this wasn't very good for maintaining a tight and compact Group formation.

Extremely favourable atmospheric conditions on that Sunday morning over East Anglia, meant that there were no contrails, but further inland ground fog and low clouds hampered take-off at some 1st Air Division airfields.

Lt. Paul Vance at the controls of *Miss Carry,* a 390th Bomb Group Fortress, had an early indication of things to come:

Three members of my crew spotted a lone German Messerschmitt 110 at high altitude which was observing the Groups forming up into a Task Force. Waist Gunner Ross Farris called on the interphone and remarked, "The Jerries will be up waiting for us today." Possibly at the time he did not realise what a prophetic statement this would turn out to be.

Quite apart from the enemy intruder, the German Radar stations along the Dutch coast were keeping a watchful eye on the American formations assembling high over East Anglia. Deep in the reinforced concrete bunkers beneath the huge revolving Freya and Wurzburg scanners, great skeletal bowls seven metres across, the radar screens told their story. At 1323 hours nearly half an hour before the American bombers had crossed the English coast, the Luftwaffe controllers at Stade in Northwestern Germany, telephoned advanced warning of the impending attack to the various fighter airfields and the pilots were immediately placed on readiness.

Green and red recognition flares arched up into the sub-zero temperatures of the thin air as the 13th Combat Bomb Wing completed its assembly over Yarmouth and headed inland for the rendezvous with the other two Wings of the 3rd Division at another radio homing beacon, "Splasher 7" near Braintree, Essex. They passed over "Splasher 6" near Dissen route.

The remaining two 3rd Air Division Combat Wings were

the 4th, comprising the 94th Bomb Group (Rougham) and the 385th Bomb Group (Great Ashfield); and the 45th Combat Bomb Wing (C.B.W.), which encompassed the 96th Bomb Group (Snetterton Heath) and the 388th Bomb Group (Knettishall). All were Suffolk airfields with the the exception of Snetterton which was in South Norfolk.

Lt. William Goldenberg, Lead Navigator with the 388th Bomb Group, later described the assembly procedure:

Our standard Group formation comprised three six-ship Squadrons, High, Lead and Low, with about 500 feet of altitude and distance separating each Squadron. A three-ship element provided replacements for airplanes aborting the mission — "fill in's" as it were. To attain mission altitude and to form up in elements, Squadrons, Groups and then Combat Bomb Wings, we spent time over East Anglia flying between "Splasher" radio homing beacons, using our radio homing compass.

During this phase, our Group Leader and Deputy Lead aborted. The 388th Group Commanding Officer, Colonel Bill David, then called us by radio and, after ascertaining that we had a bomb sight on board, instructed us to take over the Group Lead position. By this time, perhaps not surprisingly, we were scattered like a flock of pigeons and were too far behind the 96th Bomb Group — the other Group in the 45th C.B.W. — to assume the Wing Lead as had been scheduled. Consequently, we were told to pull up and form the Low Group behind the 96th Bomb Group.

The awesome responsibility of shepherding this aerial armada of B17's, each of which was valued at a third of a million dollars, quite apart from the inestimable worth of their highly-trained ten-man crews, fell on the shoulders of Captain Scripture, the Lead Navigator, riding in the Fortress *The Zootsuiters* with the Task Force Commander.

From Braintree, the 3rd Air Division swung eastward and passed over Felixstowe on schedule. The time was twelve minutes to two. The Dutch Coast was now a mere thirty minutes flying time away. Simultaneously, the small diversion force of 2nd Air Division B24 Liberators droned out over the shimmering North Sea from Cromer on the Northeast coast of Norfolk. The overall plan called for the leading B17's of the 1st Air Division to follow the lead Fortress of the 3rd Air Division over Felixstowe at a time interval of 15 minutes. This meant a bomber stream 75 miles long. At this spacing the target would be under continuous bombardment from the 16

Groups in turn for 30 devastating minutes.

It was now all too apparent to the Luftwaffe controllers that this was no practise mission. The very size of the bomber formations now streaming over the North Sea heading on a direct course towards Holland, a mere half-hour flying time, meant that the time had come to order the alerted fighter pilots to board their planes.

By this stage of the war, the German air defence system was well experienced and honed to a very fine degree of efficiency. From five strategically-placed locations in mainland Europe highly-trained Luftwaffe personnel issued a constant stream of very precise and explicit instructions to the fighter interceptors, guiding them with unerring accuracy to both the day and night bombers. These specialists operated from large and complex reinforced concrete bunkers with massive 12 foot thick camouflaged walls and roofs.

The five German Air Divisional Headquarters were at Deelen, near Arnhem in Holland, Stade on the lower Elbe River in Northwestern Germany, Metz in Northeastern France, Doderitz near Berlin, and at Schleissheim near Munich in Southern Germany.

At Stade, as at each of the other four "battle opera houses", a huge vertical frosted glass screen with a gridded map of mainland Europe dominated the nerve centre. On this screen, Luftwaffe women auxiliaries plotted the movements of friendly and enemy aircraft. Each girl was linked by telephone with a radar station on the coast. She in turn projected the information as it was received onto the relevant grid square with narrow-beam hand-held torches. The ground control and liaison officers were thus able to see at a glance the direction of the main thrust. Being in direct contact with the airfields and airborne fighters, they conducted the air battles in the sub-stratosphere — like some gigantic airborne orchestra — although they were perhaps more than 200 miles from the action. The science of highly-sophisticated radar had made giant strides in barely five years.

From the air defence centre bunkers of Stade, codenamed "Socrates", the short cryptic message, "Pilots in cockpits,"

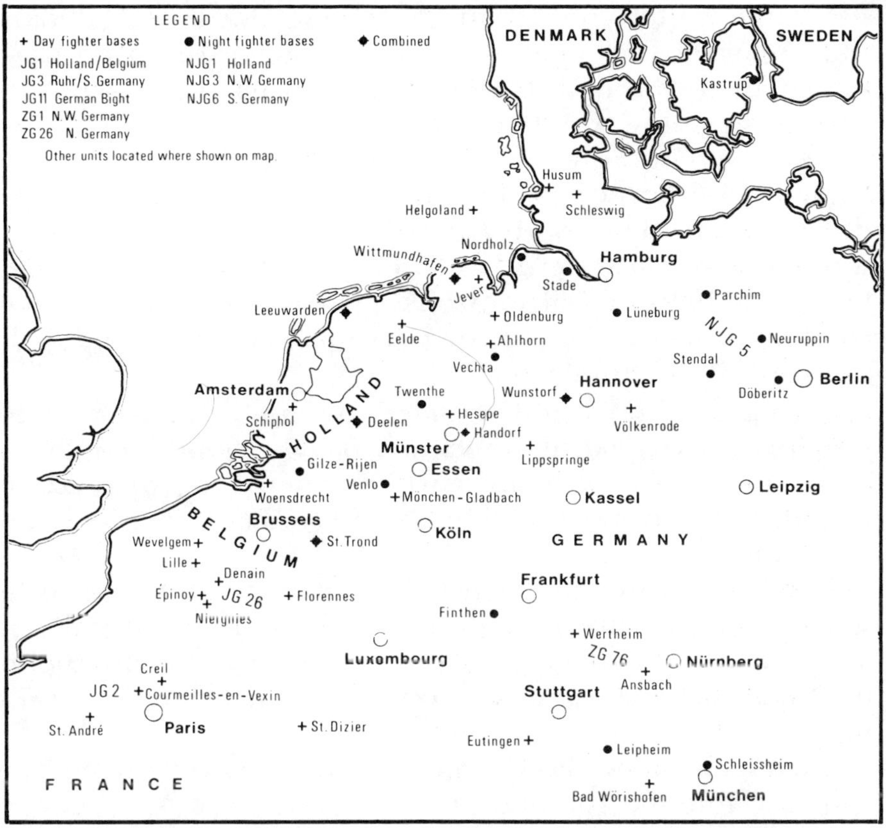

German Air Force Combat Units, October 1943.

was sent out. This order sent to the Luftwaffe's twin-engine fighters of the 2nd Division in the Low Countries and Western Germany, was despatched at precisely 1354 hours, six minutes after the first of the American bombers had crossed the coast of East Anglia.

There was no hurry, no rush. The probing invisible eyes of the long-range radar scanners now reflected growing numbers of clear sharply-defined snow-white blips on the darkened screens as the B17's of the 2nd Air Task Force appeared, following behind those of the 1st. The curvature of the earth could only hide them for so long.

Orders were also transmitted to the ground defences from the Dutch coast to well inside Germany itself. Numerous flak sites came to life as men went about their alloted tasks. Radars warmed at the flick of a switch, shells were fused, covers were pulled off guns and the barrels elevated menacingly skywards. Coastal shipping was alerted.

Two Staffeln (Squadrons) of twin-engined Me 110's from Stade were airborne by 1415 hours. Ten minutes later, another three Staffeln flew south from the Luftwaffe base at Leeuwarden in Northwestern Holland. At 1408 hours, three Staffeln of Me 109's were already on their way to patrol the Dutch coast and shadow the 3rd Air Division's Fortresses and their escorting P47 Thunderbolts.

A complex and highly-efficient air and ground defence system, which stretched from Scandinavia to Southern France, awaited every Allied bomber which entered the air space of Continental Europe. And Sunday, 10 October 1943, proved no exception.

At that moment, the civil defence and rescue teams, garrison soldiers and fire brigades, police force and hospital staffs of Münster were blissfully unaware that during the afternoon their considerable resources would be stretched to the breaking point.

But much blood, both American and German, would be spilled before the afternoon turned to evening.

Said German Fighter Pilot Feldwebel Gerd Wiegand:

We always had adequate warning of the next big bomber raid. Our Headquarters were, at all times, aware of the "Dicke Autos" (Fat Cars: our name for four-engined bombers) as they assembled in the very early hours over East Anglia.

On 10 October, after a very nervous breakfast, we took off from Lille-Nord and landed at Deelen, Holland, to help in the defence of the Reich. We were fighter pilots out of passion, the prospect and situation of man-to-man combat fascinated us at that young age. However, each one of us had our "Kupferbolzen" (Copper Bolt) when attacking the "Dicke Autos", which can be easily explained.

Each B17 had 12 heavy machine guns which could fire accurately and score hits at a range of 600 metres. When we attacked a formation of from three to six Flying Fortresses it meant that we had to fly through the fire from anywhere between 36 and 72 guns to make an effective attack, often closing to within 200 metres of less, in order to get enough strikes sufficient to shoot down a B17 . . . who would relish that?

After the usual queuing at the latrines and singing or humming such calming and reassuring songs as *Sing, Nachtigall, Sing* or *Ich Weisse, es wird ein mal ein Wunder geschehen (I Know That One Day Something Wonderful will Happen),* then what always seemed to be an eternity of waiting, always the worst part of any action, we at last received the order for our Staffeln, part of Jagdgeschwader 26 (we were eight or ten aircraft? I can't remember), to take off at 1420 hours with Jagdgeschwader 1, who were based at Deelen. But what I do remember though, is that I was flying my faithful "10" with a brand new engine.

Mechanical difficulties, oxygen failures and interphone problems took their toll of the U.S. 13th Combat Wing as aircraft were reluctantly forced to abort the mission one by one. Particularly hard-hit was the ill-fated 100th Bomb Group. One Fortress failed to take off because of engine trouble, and six others dropped out of their formation, including one of the two 390th stand-in B17's, over the North Sea and shortly after they had crossed the Dutch coast at 1420 hours.

Lt. James Brown, a Navigator who had arrived at Thorpe Abbotts in June 1943 and had been injured by flak during his 13th mission the following September, summarises the problems, both human and mechanical:

There were, I am certain, cases of aborts not caused by aircraft failure but by personnel failure. They were few but they were there. During my own detailed research of the 367 original 100th Bomb Group air crew personnel, I have found only *one* pilot who could be tarred with the "Lack of Moral Fibre" (LMF) label and he, after five combat missions and one very "close call", simply refused to fly any further combat missions. There are about 20 of the 367 whose "fate" I have not yet discovered. Of these, there may be a few "LMF's" but, more likely, their records, when and and if discovered, will show that they completed their tour, were transferred to other Groups, etc.

I cite the above simply to show that the "White Feather" was present in only a very small degree. This is not to say that on any given mission a pilot, when faced with a mechanical problem, might decide to return to base rather than proceed, whereas another pilot, when faced with the same problem, might choose to proceed to the target rather than return. This could reflect momentary cowardice or panic but it could also be just the difference of attitude of the individual concerned. One man might be slightly more rash or "brave" and another more steady or "careful."

The B17's were very well maintained considering the exposed conditions under which the ground crews had to work. But troubles did occur and it is my considered belief that most aborts (perhaps 90%) can be said to be legitimate, and 10% or less called questionable. As to what occurred on the Münster mission, I would not even venture a guess. But what we do know is that from 3 September 1943 through to 9 October 1943, the 100th Bomb Group lost 17 aircraft. So on 10 October the Group must have been scraping the bottom of the barrel to get 20 ships together for the mission. This could well mean that a few aircraft might have been "borderline" mechanically.

Captain Keith Harris, Pilot of the 390th Bomb Group Fortress assigned to the 100th's formation, states:

Lt. Rosenthal's ship and my ship made up the entire High Squadron. The other twelve planes in the Group formed the Lead and a Low Squadron of six ships each. Due to our regular ship, *Spot Remover,* being damaged over Bremen two days before, we were flying one of the new B17G's which had an extra two guns in a chin turret up front.

The 95th Bomb Group in the lead position, also had its share of ill fortune. Captain Rodney Snow remembers:

The mission looked relatively short in duration, although we knew that we would be in for considerable trouble any time we penetrated Germany. This was my 21st mission, and I was to lead the third element in the High Squadron. Shortly after take-off my two wingmen, Lt. Smith in *Slightly Dangerous* and Lt. Tucker in *Cuddle Cat* developed engine and oxygen trouble respectively and were forced to abort. In addition, Lt. Glenn Infield piloting *Peggy Ann,* which was was one of the spare B17's, had to turn back with his interphone out. That left me flying alone as an element in the High Squadron, so I elected to fly the diamond behind Captain Lindley's Lead Squadron of six aircraft — i.e., I was flying low behind the second element of three ships.

Things proceeded normally when I suddenly noticed that my mixture control was too rich and I had burned up way too much fuel if the mission was anywhere near as long as indicated at take-off. Our gasoline tanks were filled with only about half-an-hour or so more capacity than the mission called for; that is, if the mission was of six-hour duration we would have enough fuel for about seven hours at the most. I cut the mixture back and decided that maybe I could go ahead and complete the mission with the remaining fuel on board. We proceeded across the North Sea, where the gunners tested their machine guns to ensure they were functioning properly, and crossed the coast to Holland.

Being an unusually clear and beautiful Autumn day for flying with not a cloud in the sky, we could see for about 40 to 50 miles from our altitude of 24,000 feet.

Each Fortress carried twelve 50 calibre heavy machine guns capable of firing 14 rounds a second, with a highly destructive range of 600 yards. Even at a distance of four miles, the two-ounce bullet leaving the air-cooled barrel at a speed approaching 2,000 miles-an-hour was enough to kill a man.

The bomb arming procedure is described by Lt. Clifford Milburn, Bombardier in the 100th Bomb Group's airplane *Royal Flush:*

I had pulled the 12 safety pins from the bombs while we were over the North Sea to arm the bombs and pre-flighted the highly accurate Norden bombsight. The sight consisted of two major parts, the optical sight itself, which was about 15 inches in length and eight inches in diameter, and the stabilizer which was permanently attached to the floor in the nose of the airplane and connected to the Automatic Flight Control Equipment (A.F.C.E.). The gyro optical sight was fitted onto the stabilizer. This then controlled the A.F.C.E. through the actions put into it by the Bombardier.

As in all problems, there are certain factors which are variable and unfortunately some highly unpredictable. For example, the trajectory of various bombs were tested and found to do certain things. These were recorded in tables. The important variables were air and ground speed, drift caused by the wind, and altitude.

The sequence of pre-flighting the Norden was thus: I matched the serial numbers of the sight issued with that of the stabilizer, locking it in an upright position, and switched it on to activate the gyro. Then I set the drift, altitude and groundspeed, that had been obtained at the morning briefing. These were refined to the actual conditions over the target, because often the wind changed direction and velocity in the meantime.

As they passed high over Schouwen Island, bursts of inaccurate flak blossomed up to meet them. The red, crimson and orange bursts left black puffs of smoke which looked harmless as they slid below and behind the bomber formations, but the crews knew that with each seemingly innocuous explosion hundreds of potentially lethal steel splinters were streaking out in all directions from its centre, mostly upwards.

Soon they were over the mainland of Occupied Holland, and the flat panoramic view of the land of dikes, windmills and windswept canals appeared. Far below was the Walk River, its barge traffic seeming like matchsticks, one behind the other, on the narrow band of waterway.

Shortly after crossing the Dutch coast, P47 Thunderbolts of the 352nd Fighter Group from their base in Bodney, Norfolk, rendezvoused on schedule with the Fortresses of the 3rd Air Division. They were under strict orders to stay with the bombers unless attacked themselves, and not to go looking for trouble thus leaving the B17's without escort. Bitter experience had shown what could happen when German radar became aware that the fighter escorts had been drawn away from their charges. Accordingly, one Squadron of 12 fighters flew top cover, 3,000 feet above the bombers, while the remaining two Squadrons flew on either side of the long column of B17's grinding their remorseless way towards Münster at a cruising speed of 155 miles an hour. Due to the considerable difference in cruising speed between the fighters and bombers, the P47's were forced to weave from side to side in order to stop them from rapidly overtaking their "Big Friends."

The seven-ton Thunderbolts carried tremendous fire-power in their eight fifty calibre machine guns, while their keen-eyed highly-trained pilots had to be accomplished marksmen, navigators, radio operators and even bombardiers.

Sergeant Bob Banta, Radio Operator of *Rose Marie* a 390th B.G. Fortress, recalls:

> When the friendly fighters rendezvoused as scheduled they began a criss-cross pattern above us. What a reassuring feeling it gave to see these "Little Friends" spreading over us like a large wing of a protective mother hen. Their lingering contrails gave the impression of permanent protection as we headed for Germany.

As the 3rd Air Division continued across Holland, the 355th Fighter Group which was to have taken over escort of the bombers from the 352nd Fighter Group, were still waiting for the dense opaque ground fog, which was restricting visibility to less than 50 yards, to lift from their base at Steeple Morden in Cambridgeshire.

Quite apart from the loss of fourteen B17's from the 13th Wing and a further thirteen aircraft from the other four Groups which made up the 3rd Air Division, including the Lead Fortress from the 388th Bomb Group, which had aborted the mission, the Division's remaining one hundred and twenty bombers would now be without fighter escort both before and after bombing the target.

Recalls Lieutenant Howard Hamilton, Bombardier in the 100th Bomb Group's Lead Fortress:

> The first indications of the trouble we were really in was when the P47's above us started dropping their belly tanks through our formation, at which point we knew that they were very busily occupied with German

fighters and we couldn't expect any help from them.

The formation was still west of Hertogenbosch, Holland, but the German fighters didn't begin their attacks until the Thunderbolts, their fuel gauges indicating less than half full, very reluctantly turned back at Dorsten, Germany at 1448 hours. Intense and accurate flak had been encountered beginning at the German border town of Cleve, and it continued from every town along the route thereafter.

Captain Frank Murphy, Navigator of *Aw-R-Go* 100th Bomb Group, remembers:

I recall looking through the navigator's astrodome to see where our P47's were. Most of them were turning back to England having reached the limit of their range. I also saw a very large number of German single-engine fighter aircraft climbing to engage us.

As we crossed the border into Germany the intercom suddenly came alive as I counted something over 60 German aircraft climbing and racing ahead of our 13th Combat Wing to begin their standard method of attack . . . head-on, straight and level, coming directly into our formations, veering away, or rolling and doing a "Split-S" at the last possible moment to drop away below us. It very quickly became apparent that we were in for a very difficult time.

Thus began the most intense, determined and relentless fighter attacks that any of us had ever witnessed . . .

Chapter 10

AGAINST the heavy defensive fire power of the Flying Fortresses, the Luftwaffe had amassed nearly 350 aircraft ranging from single-engined machine gun and cannon firing Messerschmitt 109's and Focke Wulfe 190's, to twin-engined air-to-air rocket launching Me 110's, 410's and Junkers 88's. A completely new feature was the appearance of rocket-firing Dornier 217 medium bombers. Some of the single-engined fighters were also equipped with rocket launchers fitted beneath their wings.

Recalled 95th Bomb Group Pilot Captain Rodney Snow:

As we approached the smoky industrial Ruhr area, which we could see quite clearly in the distance, the enemy fighters were concentrated in numbers such as we had not seen on any of my crew's 20 previous missions. I'll digress here for a moment to say that the Luftwaffe were never able to turn back an 8th Air Force bomber effort. I think this particular mission was aimed at turning the attack back. The ensuing events are extremely difficult to describe because of the number of enemy fighters we encountered.

They elected first to take on the 100th Group which was flying Low Group in the Wing. On the first pass I remember there were eight to ten Me 109's, 410's, and FW 190's coming in waves directly through our formation in a frontal attack from twelve o'clock level. Following their first pass, which took out three airplanes from the 100th's Lead Squadron, wave after wave kept attacking these Low Squadrons. I thought that the enemy had successfully shot down all of our 100th Group, certainly most of them were smoking or had exploded in mid-air due to direct hits. American and German parachutes from the planes considerably below were soon visible to my gunners in the rear of our ship.

We were sure these German pilots were the cream of the Luftwaffe as it was evident that the " Abbeville Kids" and "Goering's Flying Circus" were leading this enemy attack because of the gaily-painted engine cowlings on their fighters, and also the scarves and headgear of the pilots.

Against a backdrop of clear blue skies and in the sub-zero

temperatures of the sub-stratosphere, tracer bullets began to stream out from the Fortresses, bridging the rapidly narrowing gap between attackers and attacked. Exploding flak shells vividly formed a deadly curtain of hurtling chunks of steel and splinters interspersed with dark splodges of drifting black smoke.

Captain Frank Murphy, Navigator of B17 *Aw-R-Go* in the 100th Bomb Group, vividly describes the action:

The German aircraft came after the 100th in seemingly endless waves. As one element of fighters broke away, another was turning for a head-on attack far ahead of us, and still others were forming up. Fighter after fighter flew directly into our formation passing by so close that we could distinctly see the German pilots in their cockpits. Although we were firing continuously, and could plainly see our own tracers as well as those from other B17 aircraft seeming to be on target, they had no apparent effect. The fighters came on, at tremendous closing speed, with complete disregard for the curtain of defensive fire from our guns, the leading edges of their wings twinkling and glittering as they fired. Exploding cannon shells "walked" through our formation.

What were my thoughts? Fright, terror, frustration, imminent death, hopelessness . . . all of these. More than once I turned away from the attacking fighters fully expecting a certain head-on collision.

As we proceeded towards our I.P. we began to receive heavy anti-aircraft fire. I clearly recall looking out of the left window of the aircraft and seeing a B17 from our Low Squadron, 500 feet below us, sliding slowly away from our formation with its left wing completely enveloped in flames.

Sgt. Jack Rogers, Top Turret Gunner and Flight Engineer in the 100th Bomb Group B17 090 *El P'sstoffo*, commented:

We were being attacked from six o'clock. I fired a long burst at two Me 410's and they seemed to give off a flash then a large puff of smoke, stall and dive away. I thought that I'd shot them both down, but logic told me I hadn't.

Then Robert Sandy, our Ball Turret Gunner, shouted over the interphone to our Pilot, Winton MacCarter, "Raise up, Mac. Raise up!" He had seen the German planes firing what appeared to be long narrow shells at our ship. They were rockets. Lt. MacCarter successfully avoided the first attack.

About thirty seconds later, came the shout again, "Raise up, Mac!! GO UP!!" I immediately felt the ship climb.

Lt. Winton MacCarter, remembering the incident, said later:

The fighters had tremendous firepower, and Seventeens were dropping away all around us in every stage of distress. My crew was reporting many parachutes while I was trying to maneuver my ship out of the path of the rockets which the gunners were reporting from the rear. Although it was not a long engagement, for many of my buddies and for our ship, it still seemed like an eternity. It was hell!!

Waist Gunner, Sgt. Raymond Manley, takes up the story:

I was shooting at a 190 at nine o'clock and pieces started to come off him when a small glare to the right suddenly caught my eye. A rocket had apparently struck our left wing igniting the main gas tank and our number one port outer engine was also on fire. I called the pilot on the intercom to tell him, and he immediately banked the airplane steeply to the right out of the formation and dived. He side-slipped in an effort to extinguish the flames but fire grew in intensity.

Unable to put the fire out, our pilot then levelled the ship up and rang the bail-out bell. I put my chest pack on and went to the rear escape hatch, pulled the emergency handle and kicked the door out and off the fuselage. I took a breath and discovered that my oxygen hose was still hooked up and had snagged on something. I couldn't breathe. I backed away from the door to let the ball-turret, radio and right waist gunner jump. The tail-gunner had already bailed out on hearing the bell from his own small escape hatch underneath the right stabiliser of the tailplane.

After disconnecting my oxygen mask, I also jumped, with my hands on my parachute. There was no senstion of falling, and it seemed as though I was lying on my back. I fell free for quite a while, and I could hear gunfire and explosions, and then complete silence. I then pulled the ripcord, my chute blossomed out above me and I was yanked up short by the harness straps. I thanked God.

The plane's Navigator, Lt. Harold Weachter, continues the narrative:

On hearing the bail-out bell Lt. Ziegler, our Bombardier, and myself went to the escape hatch behind our stations in the nose. I pulled the cable to release the hinge pin and kicked the door away. After the Bombardier was away I slipped through the hatch. I suddenly remembered that the bomb-bay doors were open and I was concerned about hitting them as I bailed out. I pulled the ripcord soon after I cleared the airplane and saw several other chutes but could not ascertain if Lt. MacCarter, who had held the ship steady while the crew jumped, had gotten out.

As I was descending, a German fighter circled me and I recalled talk that some German pilots had machine gunned flyers as they were floating down in their chutes. As I had absolutely no control over the situation, as a final gesture I thumbed my nose at the pilot. He then made a 180 degrees turn around me, peeled off and away.

I could see our airplane, still on fire but flying normally for quite awhile. Then it suddenly nosed down and exploded on impact. That was

The 95th Bomb Group formation under attack on 10 October 1943.

Official U.S.A.F. Photo

Fighters attacking the formation of the 95th Bomb Group on the Münster raid.

Official U.S.A.F. Photo

B17s under attack near Münster, 10 October 1943. Wilfred Beer

Fighters flying through a formation of B17s near Münster. Wilfred Beer

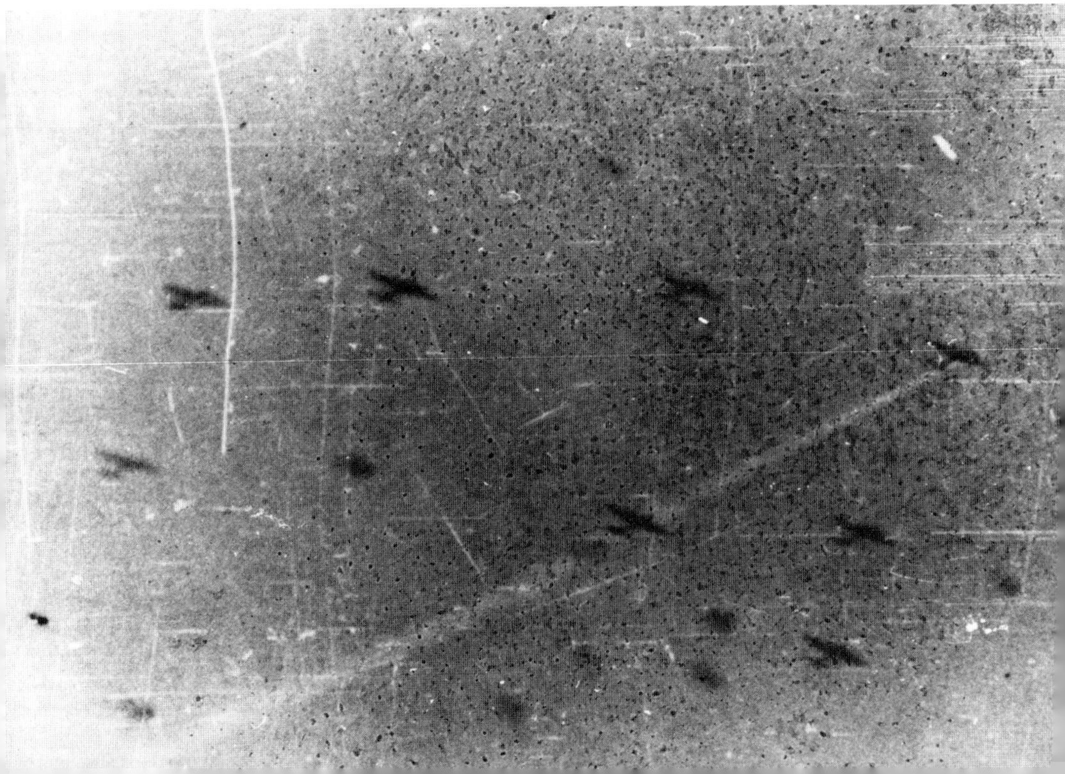

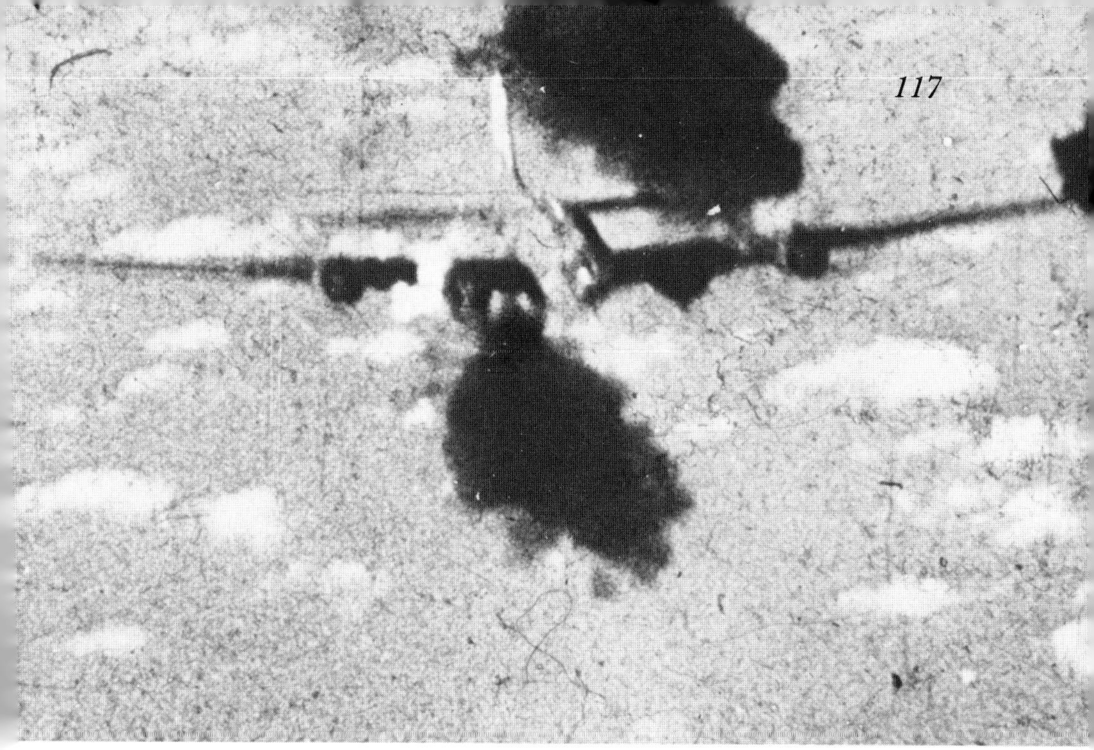

B17, Group and date unknown (probably late 1943), flys through flak and frontal attack (note hits from the fighter's guns between number 3 and 4 engines of the Fortress.)

Joseph Hallerbach, Pilot of an Me 410.

Another view of a B17 formation from a German fighter. Joseph Hallerbach

Fighter attacking the 95th Bomb Group formation over Münster.
Official U.S.A.F. Photo

A gun camera on P47 of Major Eugene P. Roberts, 78th Fighter Group, records this Me 110 taking hits from his guns before going down on 10 October 1943.
Eugene P. Roberts

The crew of the 100th Bomb Group's Mlle Zig Zag *in North Africa after participating in the Regensburg Shuttle Mission of 17 August 1943.*

Lt. Winton MacCarter (second from left in back row) and his crew of the 349th Squadron, 100th Bomb Group. They were flying El P'sstoffo *on the Münster raid, shot down on 10 October 1943 but all bailed out and were made Prisoners of War.*

The crew of Herky Jerky II, *piloted by Rodney Snow, of the 95th Bomb Group.*

Rodney Snow

Captain Rodney Snow, Pilot of Herky Jerky II.

Lt. John Justice, Pilot of Pasadena Nena, *100th Bomb Group, shot down 10 October 1943. Lt. Justice evaded capture.*

Left to right: Captain Frank Murphy, Navigator; Captain Charles Cruikshank, Pilot; of the 100th Bomb Group* Aw-R-Go*, shot down over Münster 10 October 1943; and Captain L. Burr, S-2 Intelligence Section. In front is Lt. Glenn Graham, Co-Pilot.

Frank Murphy

Lt. Lesley Kring, Pilot of* Rhapsody in Flak*, 95th Bomb Group, 10 October 1943. This pilot's B17 took the bomb strike photos of Münster.

Captain Charles Cruikshank, Pilot of* Bastard's Bungalow *and* Aw-R-Go *in the pilot's seat.

A champagne reception for Lt. Paul Pennock on the completion of his first tour of 25 missions. Lt. Pennock was with the 379th Bomb Group.

Otto Schuett and friends in Münster in early November 1943.

"Flak Towers" in Münster in the background as an elderly couple hurry to the bomb shelter.

Lt. Col. David McKnight, Deputy Group Commander, 95th Bomb Group, Horham, Suffolk. (This photograph was presented by Lt. Col. McKnight to Ed Charles, Lead Navigator, 95th Bomb Group.)

B17 Cabin in the Sky, *390th Bomb Group, piloted by Captain Robert Brown.*

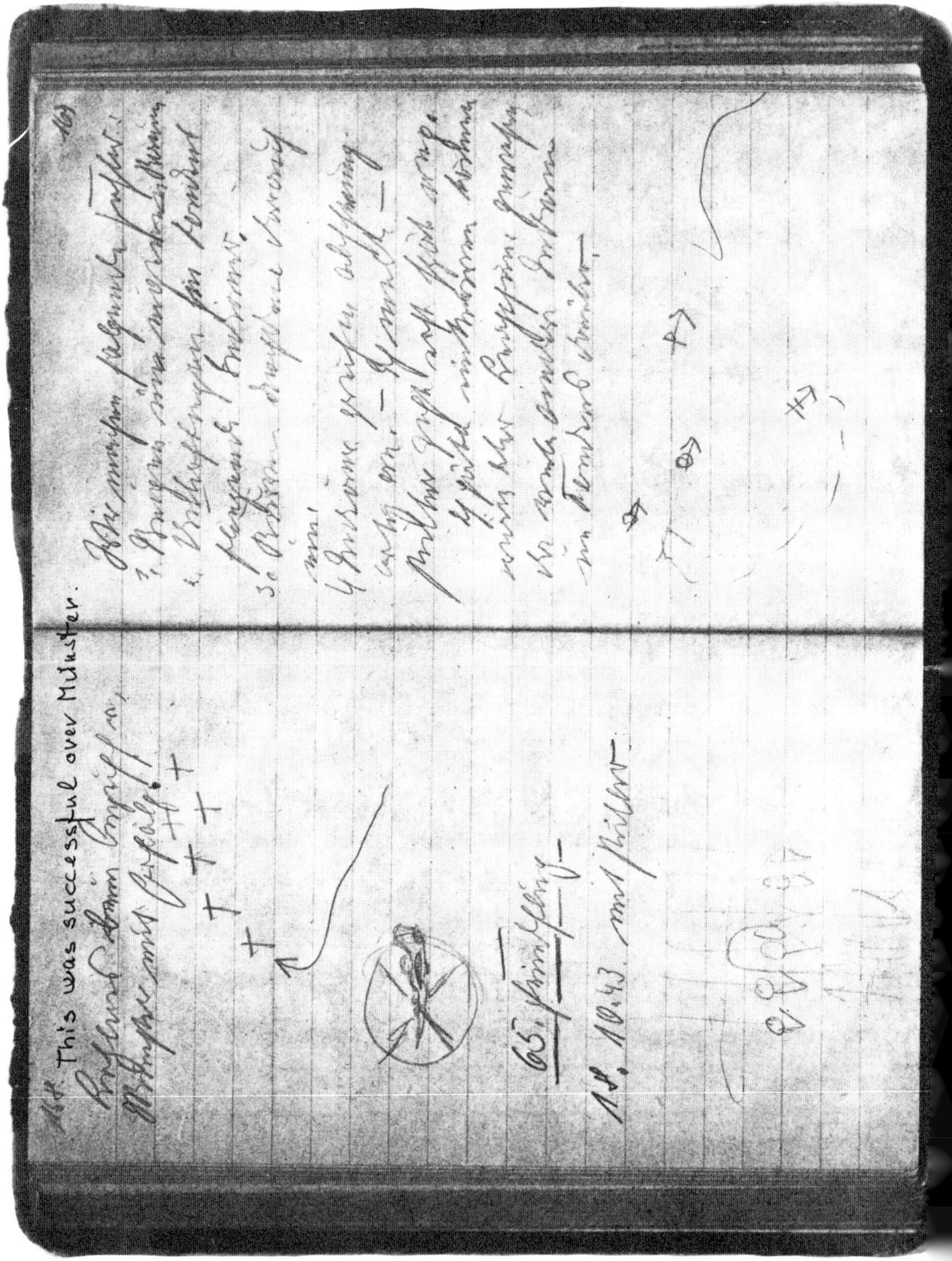

Four pages from Gerd Wiegand's diary of 10 October 1943 describing how he shot down the 95th Bomb Group B17,* Brown's Mule, *Piloted by Lt.

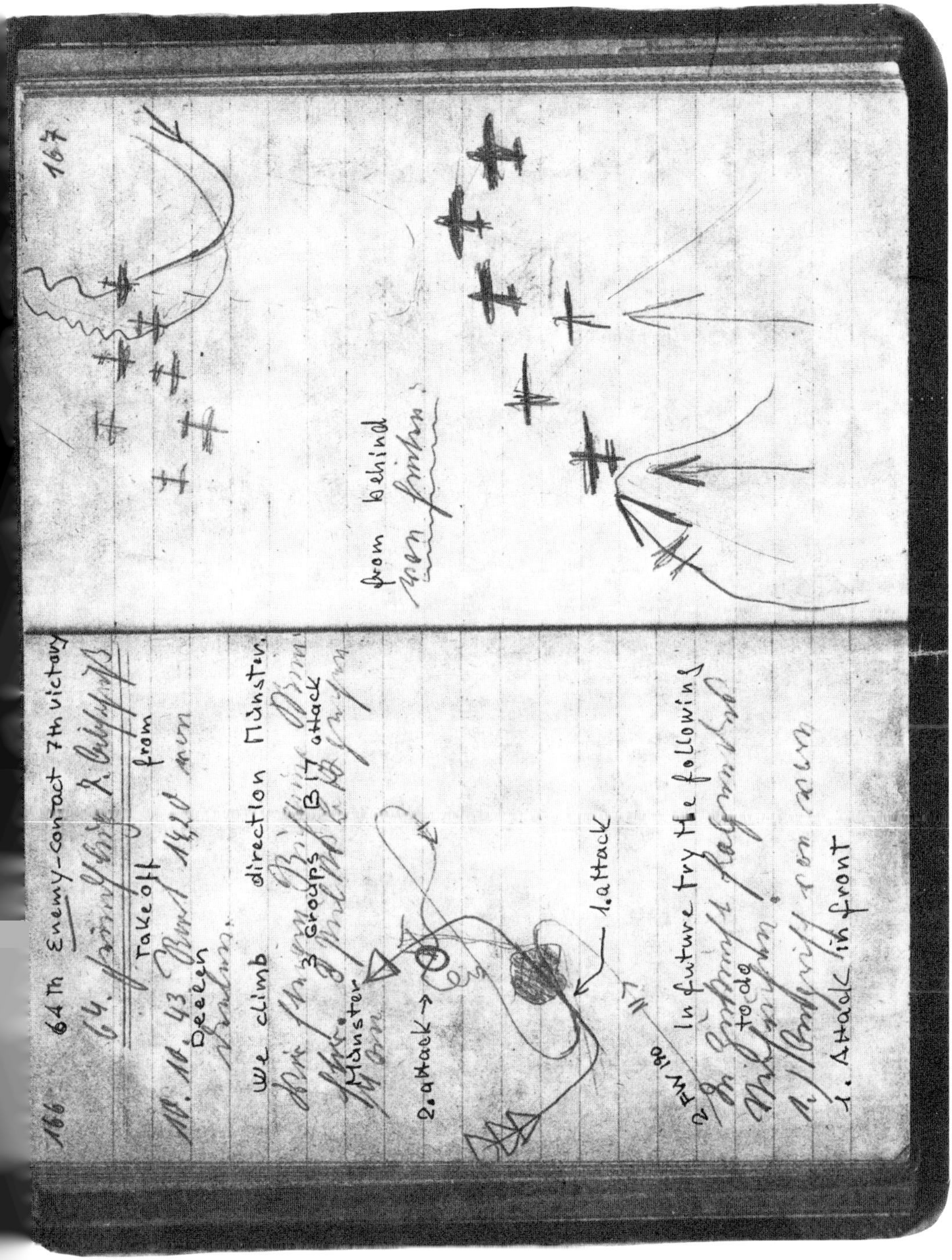

John D. Riggs (a Prisoner of War.)

This is a blow-up of a portion of the lower picture showing two German fighters attacking. From the description in Gerd Weigand's diary it is probable that these fighters are those of Weigand and his wingman Unterfleiger Rossner.

Fighter planes attacking the 95th Bomb Group formation.

Gerd Weigand, Pilot of an FW 190.4 Staffel JG/26, Lille-Nord Airfield.

An Me 109G of the JG/27 in flight.

A flight of Me 110's.

Friedrich Stehle, Me 410 Pilot, ZG 26.

Oberleutient Heinz Knoke, ME 109 Pilot, 5 Staffel JG/11, Marx Airfield, Northwest Germany.

Heinz Knoke

Me 410's in formation.

The crew of the 390th Bomb Group B17 Cash & Carrie, *piloted by Bob McGuire, second from left in front row.*

The crew of Miss Carry *of the 390th Bomb Group piloted by Paul Vance, at right in the second row.*

The crew of **Piston Packin' Mama** *of the 390th Bomb Group. Richard Perry, at far right flew as Co-Pilot on* **Eightball** *on the Münster raid.*

The crew of the **Rusty Lode**, *390th Bomb Group, summer, 1943. Lt. Sabel is in the center of back row.*

the end of *El P'sstoffo* and I feared the worst for Winton MacCarter.

As I came closer to the ground I hovered over a tall, brick chimney of what looked like a brick factory. For what seemed like an hour I could see straight down the inside of the chimney. I thought at the time that it would be utterly ridiculous to land on top of it and then be hung up inside suspended by my parachute. However, I drifted well past it and landed in a farm yard.

The sudden impact broke my left ankle. I tried to get my chute off and head for the nearby woods. The pain was so bad that I had barely got my chute off when a young German boy with a long rifle approached saying, "Pistole? Pistole?" I shook my head and said, "No." Then some men and women, who were obviously farmers, appeared.

Shortly after this, two German soldiers came with our Radio Operator Stanley Sawicki and Flight Engineer Jack Rogers, who had landed in the woods. I couldn't walk, so they loaded me into a crude wooden wheelbarrow with my parachute. They later put me on a bicycle, and as we moved along we met the Tail Gunner, Cosmo Demonico, and Roy Graff, one of our Waist Gunners, who had also been captured soon after they landed.

We were loaded into an open truck and taken to a police station. On the way there, we picked up our Co-Pilot who had apparently landed near a searchlight battery. When we finally arrived at the police station, we were all very relieved to see that Lt. MacCarter had preceeded us and was apparently uninjured. When we were re-loaded into the truck several civilians gathered round and some of them tried to attack us. The guards quickly dispersed them, so saving us from an extremely ugly situation. We were taken to what appeared to be a Servicemen's Club. My ankle was bandaged and taped, then we were put into a brick-built prison with flat board racks to sleep on. The complex was just outside a Luftwaffe fighter base.

After his parachute descent, Waist Gunner Sgt. Ray Manley landed in a field a few yards from a large woods. A woman, about 50 yards distant, walked towards him, so he rolled up his chute and headed towards her thinking that perhaps he had landed in Holland, and there might be a chance of escape. He explained later:

Suddenly, I heard men shouting behind me, and immediately realised my mistake. I turned, and my worst fears were confirmed. Four German soldiers approached me and asked if I was armed. I said, "No," and then one of them replied in perfect English, "For you, the war is over!" Then they walked me to a nearby village where a crowd of people had gathered. We stopped there while the soldiers and civilians talked in German. A little blonde girl, aged about five or six years, stood and looked me over. She smiled at me, the only friendly face there, so I gave her the white silk gloves that I wore under my heated gloves which I was still wearing. I knew that the soldiers would have taken them from me later.

I was re-united with my fellow crew members later that day.

Giving his version of the bail-out, Lt. MacCarter said:

Jack Rogers had salvoed the bombs by the emergency release before bailing out through the bomb-bay. Why we didn't blow up is a wonder. After I had given the bail-out signal I had to order my Co-Pilot, Dan Barna out, as he didn't want to leave the ship just then. Finally, he went out via the bomb-bay. After I'd checked the ship and assured myself that all the others had left, I prepared to go. God must have been with me, because when I grabbed my chest chute off my seat it slipped from my grasp and bounced through the opening between the pilots' seats and came to rest on the edge of the open hatch through which the Navigator and Bombardier had left . . . a horrible moment! Only a right tilt of the airplane prevented it from falling out into space. Needless to say, when I finally got my hands on it, I didn't let go until it was securely fastened to the rings of my harness.

I then bailed out, and my descent was uneventful — apart from being shot at from the ground by 88's. As I look back, I can't understand why I shouted to those gunners, "Stop that shooting at me!" Anyway, it must have relieved me somewhat, because when I landed I was calm, but scared as hell.

About ten Germans — farmers, I believe — were on the ground looking up at me as I hung from my parachute which was caught on a tree branch. Presently, the limb gave way, and I landed in the circle of men. Only the fact that I was unarmed — only one of them had a gun, and the others pitchforks and hoes — prevented anything serious happening. I picked myself up, gathered my chute and took off in the direction they indicated.

My 15th mission was over . . . and so was my freedom . . .

Lt. George Ziegler had a scary descent after he bailed out. His fear was that a German fighter plane which approached him about three times might fire at him, but to his great relief it eventually flew off leaving him unharmed.

But his relief was short-lived. Ziegler landed on his back and was winded by the fall. When he recovered he took off his chute and started running towards a small, forested area. He heard a shot while he was running, and almost immediately felt the air of another bullet as it whizzed past him, and then heard the shot. He halted and looked up a hill to see a group of German soldiers who were obviously doing the shooting. Lt. Ziegler raced for the trees but the next bullet came so close that he stopped and raised his arms.

Lt. Ziegler, hands held high, walked towards the soldiers, and one of them uttered their usual expression in such circumstances: "For you the war is over!" He was then led off to a nearby police station where he rejoined the rest of his crew.

« « « » » »

Shackrat, a 100th Bomb Group Fortress piloted by Lt. Maurice Beatty, leading the second element of three aircraft in the Low Squadron, suddenly exploded over Xanten, West of Haltern, the Initial Point. Only two parachutes, those of Lt. James Dabney, Co-Pilot, and Sgt. Edward Karamol, the Left Waist Gunner, who were literally blown from their positions, emerged from the blazing wreckage before it crashed between Xanten and Vynen. The body of Tail Gunner Sgt. Smith J. Young was recovered the following day from the swift-running waters of the Waal river near Arnhem in Eastern Holland. Waist Gunner Angelo J. Licato's body was also found in Dutch territorial waters on 11 October 1943.

Lt. Thomas B. Casey, a 100th Bomb Group Bombardier, was very fortunate to escape from his B17 after it was hit. Describing the incident, he said:

> We were on our fourth mission and well past the Dutch-German border. Our P47 escort had departed only minutes before when we came under heavy fire from attacking FW 190's, and our crew claimed at least four of them.
>
> Then I saw our element lead B17 explode as a result of a direct hit, apparently by flak, but possibly air-to-air rockets. As it fell, I saw two chutes trailing behind two bodies emerge from the wreckage.
>
> In less time than it takes to tell this, we too were hit by flak. With the controls shot away and our right wing on fire the airplane went into a shallow dive.
>
> Our Pilot, Lt. Robert Kramer, told us over the interphone that he was sorry but we would have to bail out. He then rang the bail-out bell. Lt. Hugh Geiger, our Navigator, followed by me and Lt. Ed Connelly, Co-Pilot, bailed out of the nose hatch.
>
> After my chute had opened, I looked for our airplane but could not see it. I then looked at my watch. It was 1450 hours. We had been due over the target at 1500 hours. Later I was told that a wing blew off our B17 and it went into a flat spin immediately, thereby pinning Lt. Kramer, Sgt. George White, a Waist Gunner, and the Ball Turret Gunner, Sgt. Donald Glaze, inside the airplane killing them when it crashed.
>
> Apparently, Lt. Kramer saw that the two gunners were still in the ship and either held the airplane steady waiting for them to jump, or went back to try and help them, and was caught in the ship when it started to disintegrate.

Lt. Casey's Top Turret Gunner, Sgt. Deane Todd, added:

Lt. Kramer asked the Bombardier to release the bombs after we were badly hit and on fire. Lt. Casey tried to jettison them but the bomb racks wouldn't function, so I released them with the emergency release near the top turret. The Pilot then gave the order to bail out and I left via the bomb-bay.

Radio Operator/Gunner Sgt. James Watkins remembers:

Our Pilot was steadying the ship with one hand and checking his parachute with the other. Lt. Kramer then left his seat and stood just behind the Co-Pilot at the forward escape hatch. He turned and saw that we weren't out yet, and then returned to his seat to steady the ship for us. I bailed out of the waist door behind the left Waist Gunner. But Lt. Kramer, Sgt. White and Sgt. Glaze were trapped in the airplane as it went into a spin within seconds. Then it exploded.

Those first bitter actions signalled the start of the air battle of Münster, fought out five miles above the sun-drenched plains of Westphalia, and which had few equals in its intensity, ferocity, total commitment, courage, endeavour and sacrifice by both sides.

« « « » » »

In the meantime, the 39 B24 Liberators had been spotted by a German patrol ship far out in the North Sea, and their course, altitude and size of formation was radioed immediately to the Luftwaffe controllers. At a point about 120 miles due North of Emden, the Lead Liberator experienced a complete failure of its electrical system and equipment.

Several things happened simultaneously to the B24. It lost all its lights, radio transmitting and receiving capability, bomb release mechanism, warning alarms and signals, electrical instruments, de-icer boot valves and propeller anti-ice pumps, intercooler shutter control, power to its gun turrets, interphone communication between crew members — who no longer had the relative comfort of their flying clothes being electrically heated — also ceased. In that instant too, the power to the propeller feathering pumps and controls stopped, as it did to the automatic flight control equipment, thereby increasing the pilot and co-pilot's workload at a most critical time.

Despite hand signals and firing numerous flares, the Lead

B24 was unable to convey its plight to the Deputy Leader, and the entire formation turned back with the leader thereby abandoning the vital diversion thrust.

As the B24's sudden and unexpected departure became obvious on the German radar screens, the Stade controller wasted no time in vectoring the now airborne fighters from airfields in the Bremen area, Nordholz, Jever and Oldenberg southwards to the Ruhr.

The American's overall plan was beginning to go wrong . . . very wrong.

One of the earliest casualties in the battle was Lt. Paul Vance, piloting a 390th Bomb Group Fortress, *Miss Carry*. He said:

We were not yet at the Initial Point and were under very heavy fire both from fighters and flak. It seemed the enemy fighters were attacking from all directions at the same time. I saw FW 109's coming in at nine o'clock level with their guns spouting and attacking the ship to our left. As I watched their shells pass right through the fuselage of my wingman, I can remember thinking, "They've had it . . ." but incredibly it maintained formation and kept right with us.

Burgess Murdoch, my Co-Pilot, was our fire control officer, aiding our gunners in calling out targets as he spotted them. Interphone chatter was very hectic, animated and hard to stop. As a kill was made it was reported.

Then something struck me in the left leg. Upon being hit, I turned the controls over to Burgess to see what was wrong. My leg wouldn't work. I wasn't in shock, and frankly I wasn't in pain, but I could feel my flying boot filling up with blood. I knew that I'd been badly hit, and if I didn't put a torniquet on my leg I would bleed to death. I took my microphone cord and tied it round my leg above the knee and cinched it up tightly. My leg was still bleeding so I wrapped and tied my scarf round my thigh. It was still bleeding, but not so heavily.

My mind returned to the problems facing us — the Group and Task Force. We were having trouble maintaining a tight defensive formation because of the terribly effective attacks being made on us by the German fighters. The "Yellow Nose Kids," generally thought to be the elite of Goering's pilots, were very much in evidence, and the flak was also very intense at this time. I don't know if I was hit by flak or fighters, but one thing was certainly very apparent. We were in trouble . . . big trouble.

The 100th Bomb Group's Lead Pilot in B17 *Mlle. Zig Zag*, Lt. John Brady, remembers:

We were picked up by the German fighters, and I suspect the size of our Group attracted their attention because things then warmed up considerably. There was a lot of fighter activity as well as increasingly heavy flak as we approached the Ruhr area.

When we were finally hit (we had several flak hits earlier which had not affected the airworthiness of the plane, but had killed Waist Gunner Gene Clanton and wounded Ball Turret Gunner Roland Gangwer), it was on the bottom of the airplane, probably flak, but possibly one of those rockets we had seen. Control cables were severed and an outboard engine was set on fire.

Lt. Winfrey Lewis, Co-Pilot of *Royal Flush* remembers seeing the Lead plane being hit. He commented:

The ship took a direct flak hit in the belly, and numerous shrapnel holes appeared in the roof of the radio room. My thought at that time was that no-one could have been in that compartment and survived. The Lead ship began a slow descent, trailing smoke. I could see Major John Egan, in his unusual light-coloured flying jacket, sitting in the right-hand seat of the Lead plane.

Other pilots also remember the incident. Captain Keith Harris of the B17 *Stork Club* recalls:

When the Lead airplane was hit and began going down, two other B17's followed it. Things then got very confusing in a hurry. The ships which were left milled around trying to form up on a new Leader while under extremely heavy fighter attacks from both sides and the rear.

Lt. John Justice of *Pasadena Nena* recollects:

We were over Germany and had been under attack for some time when the Group Lead B17 was hit and caught fire. The pilot performed the prescribed procedure in putting his nose down and getting away from the formation. His wingman, according to standard procedure, should have then taken over the Lead position, instead both wingmen followed him down. Then German fighters immediately came in at us in overwhelming strength and split the remaining formation all over the sky. We soon found ourselves completely alone.

Captain Charles Cruikshank, Pilot of *Aw-R-Go* added:

I was leading the second element of three airplanes behind the Group Leader's element when he was hit and left the formation. I immediately took over the Lead and continued the route as briefed. Apparently we were the only three ships left. Fighter opposition was extremely heavy at this point and it continued all through our bomb-run to the target.

Recalled Lead Fortress Bombardier, Lt. Howard Hamilton:

After several minutes of attack I was hit in the back by a 20-mm cannon shell. The impact destroyed my flak suit and knocked me flat in the nose compartment. I was also wounded in both hands. At that time, our intercom was shot out and our controls system was damaged beyond use. We began a gradual descent. I knew we had one dead man in the waist compartment, but had no idea who else was wounded or how badly. My wound was quite severe and had punctured my lung. Consequently, my right shoulder hung at a rather odd angle, and the shoulder strap of my parachute harness was hanging down over my right arm.

Our crew Co-Pilot, Lt. John Hoerr, was standing between the Pilot and Co-Pilot's seats, because the Co-Pilot's seat was occupied by John Eagan. I crawled back, looked up at him and he motioned me to bail out. I tried to pull the quick-release mechanism on the nose compartment door, but did not have the strength to do so because of my wounded right arm and shoulder.

I then decided that the only way to get out would be to stand on the door, which opened outwards into the slip-stream, and with my good left hand and arm to open the door, using the regular door handle. The door handle was curved, curving up toward me when the door was in the downward position. I stood on the door, twisted the handle and fell through. Unfortunately, my right shoulder-strap caught on the handle and I found myself hanging outside the airplane with the quarter-ton inboard propeller whizzing round six inches from my head with the 160 mph airstream buffeting and bouncing me around, and several German fighters circling and firing shells into us. It was about this time that I thought I had "Bought The Farm" . . .

Stated Major Egan:

As for our ship, it was obvious that we'd had it. Lt. Brady and I pulled off our oxygen masks to converse. Dave Solomon, our Navigator, came up from the nose looking quite messy to tell us that we had to leave the formation because Lt. Hamilton had numerous holes in him and wanted to go home. I assured him that I'd left the formation. After he left, Lt. Hoerr made certain that Lt. Hamilton in the nose had gotten out, while Engineer Blum checked the after-end of the ship.

Lt. Brady was having difficulty keeping the ship on an even keel while I ran the administrative end of the abandon ship. Then we scrambled to the bomb-bay where we started arguing as to who jumps first. I said, "Go ahead, Brady, since I'm the senior man on board." He said, "No, you go ahead," as it was his crew, and he wanted to be last out. Just then, a row of the nicest spaced holes — about six inches apart and just below our feet — appeared along the entire length of the bomb-bay door. They were 30-calibre punctuation marks. I said, "I'll be seeing you, Brady." I stepped out and pulled the ripcord about the time I passed the ball turret.

The loneliest feeling anyone could ever experience is being suspended in a parachute over enemy territory.

Continued Lt. Hamilton:

Other people were going out the back, through the waist door, the bomb-bay, wherever. John Brady had told John Hoerr to go down into the nose and make certain that I had gotten out alright. He just happened to look down and see me and the door hanging on the outside. The only way he could free me was to operate the quick-release mechanism, but my added weight complicated the situation as Hoerr had to struggle with it for some time. But he finally succeeded. Meanwhile, I think Egan and Brady had bailed out, which left only John Hoerr in the airplane as it got closer and closer to the ground. John did get out eventually, and was awarded the Silver Star for his bravery in freeing me from the door.

Once released I opened my parachute, floated down and landed in a clump of high trees. Due to my injuries I had great trouble in getting out of the trees. I finally got free by swinging back and forth until I was able to clutch a tree trunk and then crawl down.

I knew I was very badly wounded because I was still bleeding heavily and felt very weak. I started walking through the forest and soon came upon two German soldiers who were searching for shot-down airmen. They marched me about a mile to where our Sgt. Roland Gangwer was lying on the ground. He had a very badly wounded leg, and was in fact, ultimately repatriated.

After an hour or two, an ambulance came for the pair of us. Prior to its arrival, a young Dutch girl and her little brother came over to see us and they talked with me. She told me I was on the border between Holland and Germany, and wanted to know if she could do anything for us. I asked her for water which she brought, and after a thankful drink we were placed in the ambulance which contained only a chair and a stretcher. The driver was an old civilian, and was accompanied by his 14 or 15-year-old grandson. The boy had an ancient hunting rifle which he kept pointed right between my eyes during the 30-mile journey to Münster.

Captain Ellis Scripture, Group Navigator, *The Zootsuiters* 95th B.G. pointed out:

While Dewey Johnson, our Bombardier, and I were busy getting to the target and getting in quite a few shots en route, we heard many reports over the intercom regarding 100th Group bombers being hit and going down in every stage of distress. We could also tune in on the command frequency and hear their chatter among themselves and to Colonel Gerhart as the battle continued.

« « « » » »

Four factors, in their own separate ways, contributed to the 3rd Air Division's extreme misfortune.

First, there was the premature withdrawal of the B24 Liberators' diversionary thrust to the north, which would undoubtedly have meant that fewer German aircraft would have been available to the defenders at a critical time.

Secondly, the non-appearance of the 355th Fighter Group, whose 36 eight-gun Thunderbolts were still fogbound and unable to take off from their base in far-off Cambridgeshire.

Then there was the complete absence of clouds over Holland and Western Germany which could have provided sanctuary for the lumbering bomb-laden Fortresses.

Also, the unusually high number of abortive B17's, due directly to the flying of three missions in as many days, leaving insufficient time for adequate maintenance.

In total, the first Air Task Force had 27 abortive Fortresses. This represented a loss of the defensive firepower of more than 300 heavy machine guns.

Such are the fortunes of war.

The Luftwaffe had, up until then, failed to turn back an attack by the Eighth Air Force before bombing the objective during the American strategic daylight bombing campaign against the Third Reich. With overwhelming superiority in numbers over their adversaries, here was that chance.

High over Haltern, the Initial Point, as if throwing down the challenging gauntlet, red and green flares curved lazily up from the Task Force Commander's Fortress *The Zootsuiters,* as Captain Lindley made a gradual left-hand turn onto a new course of 57 degrees magnetic, and led the already badly-mauled and beleagured 13th Combat Bomb Wing to Münster, now a mere 30 miles to the northeast.

The time was 1453 hours

« « « » » »

In October 1943 fifteen year-old Otto Schuett was an apprentice printer, typesetter and book-binder with a Münster publishing company. His German-born parents had met in Münster, became engaged, emigrated to the United States and married in New York in 1926. Otto was born in Brooklyn, New York, in 1928. In 1931 his parents decided to return home to Germany where his father was employed as City Archivist in Lubeck, eventually arriving in Münster in 1939 where he became a Party Member and led the local Cultural Section — full circle.

In addition to his apprenticeship, Otto Schuett had joined

the Hitler Youth Movement and was promoted to Group Leader. He remembers:

We youngsters were taught the virtues of honesty, dependability, dedication to family and friends, cleanliness and so on. As the Allied air raids gradually increased, as the war progressed, our primary task was to assist the authorities during and after bombing raids, fire-fighting, rescuing the injured, and digging out the dead from bomb-shattered houses.

We had lost our first home in Münster, courtesy of Royal Air Force Bomber Command, during a night raid in the late summer of 1941. We lost everything, but at least at that early stage of the war it was still possible to purchase furniture, bedding, clothing and so on. Soon we were almost back to normal in a new apartment.

Besides being the capital City of Westphalia, Münster also has an historic University. It is an administrative centre and the majority of its population were bureaucrats and merchants mostly, dealing with the surrounding farmers. It had no heavy industries to speak of. The predominant religion in Münster is, and always was, Catholic and we were all convinced in the late summer of 1943 that the war would soon turn again and that the final outcome would be favorable to Germany.

By October 1943 Münster had experienced hardly any daylight raids but night raids occasionally occurred, mostly incendiary bombs which resulted in fierce fires restricted to relatively small sections of the City. These were usually contained and swiftly brought under control with comparatively small loss of life.

Many, many times Munster was overflown by Royal Air Force bombers on their way to attack targets in Central Germany and Berlin. The air-raid sirens usually sounded at around 2200 to 2300 hours, the ominous sound of the bomber's engines a short time later. It was with a deep sigh of relief when we heard the droning sound of the bomber stream receeding in the night sky and we realised we were safe . . . at least for the time being.

It was not unusual that the British planes, returning from a raid further inland, would occasionally drop bombs over Münster on their way home to their bases in England. Only when the last flights of aircraft had departed from German territory, and the sirens sounded the "All Clear", could we relax from our vigil and finally go home to bed, usually well after 0300 hours the following morning. I think we were always feeling very tired because "getting up time" for most people was 0600 to 0700 hours or earlier.

Like most things that come your way in life we adjusted to this almost nightly routine. I reached the stage when, by the varying sounds of the bombers engines, I could determine whether or not the planes were still carrying their bomb loads.

It was apparent however that the intensity of the bombing raids was growing more and more, month by month. No longer could we stand out in the streets and watch with fascination while the big bombers made every conceivable twist and turn to evade the probing beams of the searchlights which surrounded Münster in their efforts to escape from the anti-aircraft fire.

The days remained comparatively quiet and calm. This is basically how Münster fared during the first four years of the war. Very soon however, this all came to a sudden screeching halt.

In Münster itself, many of the city's inhabitants, including off-duty soldiers from the garrison, thronged the cobbled streets, the popular meeting place of the market square, or basked in the warm sunshine on the cool grass in the municipal parks. After yet another week of toil at the ever-busy railway junction and sidings, factories and administrative offices of the provincial capital, Sunday afternoon provided a welcome time for relaxation.

Under the watchful eye of their parents, children sailed their toy yachts and boats from the banks of the picturesque Lake Aa on the city's outskirts. Many people wended their way to the railway station, looking forward to an afternoon and evening visit with friends and relatives in the clean and invigorating air of the woods, meadows, farms and villages of the green and lush countryside that surrounds Münster.

Inside the towering Cathedral, Curate Hubert Leiwering busily prepared for Vesper, the evening service. A few young people and their parents assisted him.

Hildegard Kosters, who was 14-years-old at the time of the raid, recalls:

Because of the many previous air-raid alarms, my family was evacuated to Wolbeck, a village 12 kilometers southeast of Münster. Whenever possible, we went to Münster to visit our home in Schillerstrasse which was very close to the railway station.

That Sunday we came home once more by train for a brief visit.

Carl-Friedrich Bell, at that time a 17-year-old student at the Johann Conrad High School in Münster, recollects:

We were sixth-year students, and during the air raids we all had to help in the defense of Münster. Our battery consisted of six 8.8 cm. anti-aircraft guns emplaced in a large reinforced concrete structure with sloping earthen banks situated on the northern outskirts of the city.

Our battery was crewed by 40 regular soldiers, Officers, Sergeants, Corporals and Privates, 60 Air Defense helpers, 16 and 17-year-old boys mostly, and 20 Russian POW's who, in exchange for better food rations, helped handle and carry the heavy shells for the guns.

We students were given such tasks as fuse setters, gun layers and range-finding. This involved using optical instruments which electronically computed the bombers altitude, distance and airspeed. During the previous ten months, I had experienced only night raids by the RAF bombers which flew alone. Then we had to rely solely on our ground radar crews because we could not see our opponents. About this time in the war, the Allied bombers began dropping thousands of small strips of silver foil which greatly affected the radar.

Gerhard Ringbeck, a German soldier on his way from his unit on the Russian Front to attend an Instructor's course in France, had stopped at Münster railway station during the early afternoon in order to change trains. He relates:

We travellers were already being warned by the loudspeakers above the platform that heavy bomber formations were approaching Münster. Then the air raid sirens sounded.

I was very surprised to see how many people were still at the railway station and on the streets, seemingly unconcerned.

After the continual assurances from the Home Air Defence and higher authorities, few thought that the Americans would dare attack on such a clear, cloudless day.

The Air Defence's massive gamble that the bomber's intended target was to be the industrial Ruhr, just a few miles to the south, had been proved disastrously wrong at that instant in time when the droning bomber formation had begun the left-hand turn high over Haltern.

Otto Schuett continues his narrative:

Frequently the weather conditions in Northwestern Germany leave a lot to be desired. But on Sunday, 10th of October the sun rose on a blue and cloudless sky, providing an exceptionally beautiful early autumn day. For Münster and its inhabitants the world was still in reasonable order as people attended the morning Church services, visited relatives and friends and enjoyed walks on the promenades in the warm October sun before having their mid-day dinners on this outstandingly beautiful day. Very seldom (until that day) had the war reached out on a Sunday.

On this day the leaders of my Hitler Youth Movement had been requested to attend a Münster Police Department Horse Show on the southern outskirts of the City. That morning my mother had baked a large plum cake. Before leaving for the Horse Show I had asked if I could have my portion of the cake beforehand, but my very strict father thought that I should wait until my return home later on in the afternoon.

During the morning I had completed one of my chores which was going out into the surrounding fields to gather green feed for our four rabbits which we were raising for the benefit of our dinner table.

After dinner I left our house to meet some of my friends in the Group and after a while we took the streetcar to the edge of town and got off at the final stop. From there it was a fifteen minute walk to the Show Ground, and as we were walking along the wailing sound of the air-raid sirens broke the peace and quiet. Nobody seemed concerned or paid much attention and we continued to our destination. The blue sky remained beautiful, completely quiet and still, with absolutely no sign or sound of any air activity. We remained in a jovial and unconcerned mood. After all, we had been looking forward to the Horse Show for a long time. And what could possibly happen on that lovely Sunday afternoon?

Many times previously the sirens had sounded. When the "All Clear" had followed a little later on we had neither seen nor heard any unfriendly planes. We concluded that nothing at all would happen and that the alarm had sounded because a few enemy aircraft were perhaps on their way into Germany, maybe well to the south or north of us. Nobody, not even remotely, was worried about an attack on Münster . As a matter of fact we could not remember any large scale air raid which had taken place anywhere on a Sunday afternoon in Northwestern Germany.

Another reason why no one seemed concerned was probably the fact that, except for the main railway lines serving the heavy industries of the Ruhr district to the south, Münster actually offered no real military target.

But we soon discovered that we had wrapped ourselves into a sense of totally false security. No sooner had the Horse Show commenced when the approaching roar of aircraft engines began to be heard, growing louder and louder with each passing second.

Chapter 11

THE 95th Bombardment Group's bombing run on Münster was particularly long, confirmed Captain Rodney Snow:

It was the trait of "The Catfish", Captain Bill Lindley, to make a long bomb-run in order to give the bombardiers ample time — too much, I thought — for straight and level flight to ensure that the twelve 500-pound bombs which each Fortress carried would reach their primary objective, the target area.

I clearly remember that on this particular day our bomb-run was nearly six minutes — two minutes longer than we liked to fly straight and level as enemy anti-aircraft fire was quite heavy, as were the fighter attacks, and our evasive action was eliminated during this period. Also, we lowered our bomb-bay doors during the turn over the I.P. thereby creating extra drag which in turn reduced our airspeed.

After they had practically destroyed the 100th Bomb Group in the low position of our Wing, the fighters next concentrated effort was on the 390th Bomb Group, who were flying at about a thousand feet above and behind us. Here again, they took their toll with straight head-on attacks against the three Squadrons of the 390th. The sky seemed full of tracer bullets and burning airplanes, both theirs and ours. It was later estimated that we were being attacked by about 250 fighters all through the bomb-run.

The German viewpoint of this stage of the battle was given by Feldwebel Gerd Wiegand:

We were patrolling south of Münster at a height of 9,000 metres when we saw the "Dicke Autos" (Fat cars). Three "pulks" (boxes) of B17's heading east and coming straight towards us. We didn't know at that stage whether or not they had accompanying "Indians" (fighter escorts). We had hardly sighted them when the three boxes (or Groups) made a distinct turn to their left which indicated an attack on Münster.

In order to attack from the front, we now had to overtake the boxes from the south, which seemed to me to take a long time. I can still picture it, even now, the still intact city which I knew well, with the railway station far below me, and which, in a very few minutes, would be a blazing inferno. I was now very determined, and at last far enough in front to turn with the

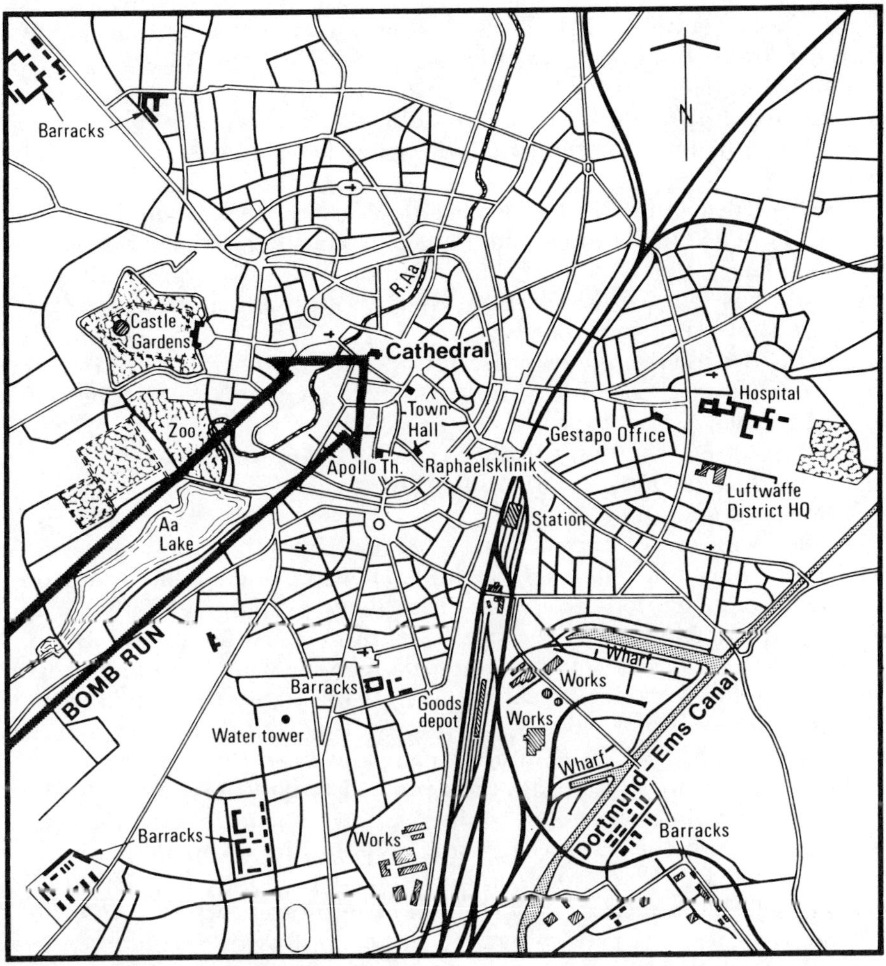

The bombing run of the 3rd and 1st Air Divisions on Münster, 10 October 1943.

others and face the box. With firing buttons pressed we went through the formations, passing so close to two B17's that I almost rammed them. It took seconds, and pulling away while diving I looked around for their fighter escorts. I took a very deep breath.

Lt. Jack Nosser, Bombardier on board Lt. Robert McGuire's 390th Bomb Group B17F *Cash and Carrie,* recalls:

Before we reached the Initial Point I had seen Paul Vance's *Miss Carry* take a direct flak hit just after the heavy fighter attacks had begun. It appeared to me that part of the left side of the cockpit had been blown completely away, and I vividly remember seeing Lt. Vance lying slumped across the lap of his Co-Pilot. It was all over in an instant of time, but his ship continued holding formation.

Our pilots had it drilled into them from the outset, and it was constantly emphasised during each briefing, to hold those airplanes in tight formation, especially on the bomb-run. If things were right, we were practically in each other's laps.

As we turned at the I.P. and headed for Münster, which I could see quite clearly, I opened the bomb doors. I had seen considerable flak during my previous 12 missions, but never this accurate. Suddenly, four shells burst right amongst our Lead Squadron. One hit our number one engine putting it out of action completely.

This is the interphone conversation that I remember:

Lt. Glen Oster, Co-Pilot, almost matter-of-factly, "Number one's hit. Shall I feather?"

Lt. McGuire, "No, don't feather. They'll know we're hurt."

Bombardier to pilot, "Shall I salvo the bombs?"

"No, hold the bombs."

In the cockpit we had an instrument missing from the panel, and I could see Lt. McGuire's face through the hole. He was calm and looked unconcerned. He spoke briefly to the Air Task Force Commander on the command frequency, who was ahead of us with the 95th Bomb Group.

The fighters were making vicious attacks now, coming in four or five abreast and almost ramming us, and I was firing at the one's which I could get the nose-gun on. Suddenly, the pilot yelled, "For God's sake, cut the power on number two, it's running away and I can't hold her!"

Then I heard the screaming, high-pitched wail of the runaway turbo-supercharger which was about to disentegrate. The noise gradually subsided as the power was reduced. With a windmilling propeller, only two good engines, full bomb load, and on fire, we gradually fell behind. I'll never forget Captain Geary, Pilot of our Group Lead ship *Pistol Packin' Mama*. His face was pressed against the plexiglass side window of his cockpit, watching us as we slowly dropped back. The expression on his face, despite his oxygen mask, said it all.

We ended up at the rear of the formation where we received the brunt of the fighter attacks. We were now in a hell of a lot of trouble. There is simply no way that I can begin to describe the God awful noise that was going on. That screaming supercharger, the 20-mm fire from the fighters sounding like gravel thrown on a tin roof coming in waves along the fuselage, the deafening din of all our own point-five's firing, and the constant roar of our two good engines running at advanced power settings. At times, the vision from the nose was obscured by exploding shells. Why *Cash and Carrie* wasn't blown into a thousand pieces, I shall never know.

Lt. Drouhard, our Navigator, moved in back of me and looked over my shoulder with a chart in his hands trying to get a navigational fix on the ground. Then he was hit in the knee by a 20-mm cannon shell and it knocked him across the navigator's table. If the shell hadn't caught him in the knee, then I would have got it right in the middle of my back.

I decided it was in our interest to continue firing rather than assist him. We couldn't hold formation with our reduced power, especially with a full bomb load on board, and we had no chance of getting the bombs to Münster, unless we landed and rented horses and wagons . . .

Suddenly the Co-Pilot screamed over the interphone, "For Christ's sake, get rid of those bombs!"

I salvoed the bombs and got the doors closed again, which was somehow very satisfying because I knew that the open bomb-bay doors caused excessive drag. I discovered later that the bomb explosions had caused some confusion to the Bomb Groups following us.

Those were the last words that came over the interphone to the nose area as communication was shot out soon after. It must have been at about this time that the Pilot gave the order to bail out, and only five men in the rear heard the order. Then the airplane just banked straight over and we fell, I don't know how many thousand feet. I hit blind panic as I struggled against the tremendous centrifugal forces and tried frantically to grab my chest chute and hook it onto my harness.

What had happened in the cockpit was a minor mutiny.

After we had thankfully levelled off at around 10,000 feet I heard another explosion in the aircraft. A 20-mm shell had apparently hit one of the guns in the top turret. The force of the explosion had blown Sgt. Norman Auger from his position. He was normally a Waist Gunner, but was riding Top Turret that day. I then saw an Me 110 at three o'clock turning away after an attack. Presumably this was the aircraft that had knocked Sgt. Auger out of the top turret. I watched the Me 110 hoping that he would go around the nose and I could get a shot at him. Then I heard loud yelling behind me. I turned and saw Sgt. Auger squatting beside the Navigator with blood streaming down his face. The Navigator, obviously in a state of complete shock, was screaming at him, "Get back to your guns or I'll kill you!" He started searching through his gear for his pistol. I looked out of the nose again just in time to see an Me 109 coming in straight ahead and level. I got off about 10 shots at him before the gun jammed. I don't know if I got him or not, but I didn't see him fire before he dived beneath us.

I couldn't see any more enemy aircraft in the area, so I looked round to see what was going on behind me. There was no-one there! I couldn't comprehend what had happened to the pair. I had a moment of panic as I thought I was the only one left in the airplane. I then looked to the hole in the instrument panel and the reassuring sight of Lt. McGuire calmed the panic. I thought we were on our way back to England, with or without the remainder of the 390th formation.

It was about then that all the engines went dead. The only sound was the eerie whistling of the airstream. I looked down and saw the tops of trees silently gliding past just below *Cash and Carrie*. It suddenly dawned on me that we were about to crash and I made a dive for the rear of the nose compartment. I had only just managed to reach the crawl hole behind the armour plating with my outstretched hands when we hit.

I could hear the trees crashing down, shattered fences pinging like taut piano wire as we hurtled through them, and of course the scraping and bouncing over the ground which I thought would never end. Finally there was silence — an astonishing, profound and incredible silence.

Explosion flashed through my mind. I had to get out!

I started for the escape hatch under the nose, but realised that it was jammed against the ground. Next, I remembered my G.I. shoes which were stowed in one of the ammunition boxes. I grabbed the shoes and saw that the plexiglass nose was completely gone. I dived through the opening out onto the ground. While I was struggling to regain my feet, Lt. McGuire raced past me away from the airplane.

The next sequence of events may seem unbelievable and, as I look back, humorous, but they actually happened.

My flying gear comprised helmet, electrically-heated fur-lined flying suit over overalls, shoes, fur-lined flying boots, parachute harness, chest chute and Mae West lifejacket. The Pilot, when he went past me, had on G.I. shoes, shirt, trousers and a leather flying jacket — a weight difference of perhaps 20 pounds. He was ahead of me when I started off after him, still carrying my G.I. shoes. I beat Lt. McGuire to the first fence which stopped him. I cleared the fence like an Olympic hurdler and continued running out into the field. Two men standing on a dirt road at the edge of the field attracted my attention by motioning me in their direction. When I got closer, I could see that one was in uniform and the other in civilian clothes. The civilian levelled a shotgun at me over the fence, and the one in uniform started pulling a bayonet from his belt. I did an immediate about-turn and started back towards the airplane. While I was running I heard a shot.

When I got back to the ship I saw Sgt. Auger, who apparently wasn't seriously hurt, helping the Navigator around a wing. Lt. McGuire and Lt. Oster, who had undoubtedly saved our lives by their remarkable crash-landing, had just arrived and were standing in front of the airplane. I joined them and sat down on the ground to take off my flying boots and light shoes, and put my G.I. shoes on — one of the most difficult operations I have ever performed was lacing and tying those shoes.

Meanwhile, the 13th Combat Bomb Wing, with a grimly determined Colonel Gerhart leading the Task Force, relentlessly headed for Münster, drawing ever closer with each second. Following his Wing were the other Groups of the 3rd Air Division, the 96th and the 388th (45th Combat Bomb Wing) and the 94th and 385th Bomb Groups (4th Combat Bomb Wing), in that order. Behind them came the nine Bomb

Groups of the 1st Air Division, divided into three Bomb Wings. They stretched back 40 miles almost to the Dutch coast. The contrails of the 4th Fighter Group's 48 Thunderbolts from Debden, Essex, streaked out behind them as they crossed the Dutch coast at an altitude of 28,000 feet racing to keep their scheduled rendezvous with the leading 1st Air Division Groups over Haltern at 1509 hours.

The auxilliary belly tanks on the P47's were still being plagued by teething troubles, however, as Pilot Lt. Earle W. Carlow, pointed out:

> I was flying a borrowed "kite" as mine had been shot down with another pilot over Bremen two days earlier. On the Münster "Ramrod" (bomber escort), shortly after crossing the Dutch coast, I had to abort the mission because the pressure line from the belly tank failed to operate and there was no way that I could reach Haltern and return with the gasoline left in my main tank.

Two other 4th Fighter Group P47's had to abort the mission with similar problems. The scattered remnants of the 100th Bomb Group pressed on towards the target.

For Bombardier Lt. Clifford Milburn in *Royal Flush* there was an air of unreality about the events, as he explained later:

> Reflect with me, if you will, my thoughts at that precise moment in time. Here I was, a 23-year-old fellow from Chicago, Illinois, whose only exposure to violence was an occasional school fight. War, and all that it implied, was found in history books or the movies. My personal feelings of the war were more akin to that of a distasteful job.
>
> The orange lights flickering in front of the German fighters could not be real . . . the grey-black puffs of smoke through which we were flying must surely be just that . . . the Fortress below us and on fire must surely have been an accident of some sort . . .
>
> But after one or two loud and heavy thumps on our airplane fuselage all thoughts of war, governments, the rights and wrongs of it all, were instantly erased from my mind, and only one thought predominated . . . survival . . . or more specifically, my survival.

Bomber Pilot Captain Keith Harris, continues:

> At the early morning briefing our Commanding Officer, Colonel Edgar Wittan, said to me, "If things get rough and out of hand, remember we will be 1,000 feet above and behind you; come up and join us."
>
> It seemed to me that things were now well out of hand with B17's going down all around us. Just then, the 390th formation passed slowly overhead

about 3,000 feet above us, and at that point Colonel Wittan's advice seemed very wise. I immediately put on take-off power and climbed as fast as we could. After climbing the first 1,000 feet slowly — too slowly, I thought — I told my Bombardier, Lt. Winspear, to salvo our bombs to give us a better rate of climb. Lt. Rosenthal stayed loose off our right wing and climbed with us.

Fighter attacks became increasingly severe during the bomb run, as Lt. "Pappy" Lewis, Co-Pilot of the 100th Bomb Group's B17 *Royal Flush* well remembers:

I saw one very aggressive Messerschmitt 109 coming in off our right wing. The German pilot expertly positioned himself to fire on us when I shoved hard on the control column, forcing our bomber into a shallow dive — but very steep for such a large aircraft. "Rosie" (Lt. Rosenthal), who was busy flying the airplane, didn't bat an eyelid, nor did he look sideways at me, as though he knew the reason for my otherwise unthinkable action.

The *Miss Carry* Tail Gunner, Sgt. William "Ike" Adamson, remembers flying above the 100th Bomb Group formation and looking down seeing several of their B17's shot down. In a vivid eye-witness account he recalls:

I remember seeing a B17 shot down by an FW 190. Both planes were going through the wildest manouevres that I have ever seen. The fighter was right on the B17's tail, It seemed as if the two airplanes were tied together as they twisted and turned about 3,000 feet right below me. The fighter and the B17's tail gunner were firing at each other at literally point blank range when suddenly both aircraft exploded and disappeared completely in one big ball of black smoke and flames.

Imagine a handful of beans in a glass jar being violently shaken up and down, then try to follow and describe the actions of a single bean. You will then have some idea of the wild melee which took place over Münster. At one stage, for minutes on end, the sky was full of metal from exploding planes, both theirs and ours, smoke, flak, falling spent brass cartridge cases, escape and exit doors and, of course, parachutes. Sgt. Henry Glende, our Top Turret Gunner, said later it was like flying through an aerial junk yard. He was credited with four German fighters including an Me109 which exploded so close to our ship that pieces of it were dug out of our right wing after we had landed back at Framlingham.

I also saw an FW 190 pilot drop back with his engine on fire, turn his aircraft upside down, open the canopy and bail out clear of his aircraft. It was like watching a training film on how to bail out of an FW 190, but when he pulled the ripcord and his parachute started to billow out he somehow slipped clean through his harness. The harness unaccountably broke, or the metal clips weren't fastened correctly. Anyway, he started off on a very fast trip to earth five miles below.

William "Uncle Willie" Kubitzki, our 6 foot 6 inch Radio Operator-Gunner, was tall enough to poke his head and shoulders through his position in the radio hatch and call out targets to the other gunners. Someone said it looked like a turtle's head popping in and out of its shell, and I well remember him hollering through the interphone, "Here come the twin-engines!" My hurried reply was, "If it doesn't have four engines, fire at it!" He was later credited with two fighters.

The German twin-engines would fire rockets into our formation and we would fan out to let the rockets pass. We could see them coming from away back, and I'd instantly relay their trajectory to our pilots up front and they would take evasive action. At that stage I was completely unaware that Lt. Paul Vance, our Pilot, had been seriously injured.

During the bomb run — which seemed to last for hours — I shot down an FW 190 coming in at six o'clock low with his guns twinkling. I could see my tracers bouncing off the armour plate around his engine. The tracer shells had a different trajectory than the explosive and armour-piercing rounds as they changed weight as they burned, but I must have hit him hard because his right wing suddenly snapped off at the root and went fluttering down like a leaf. The fighter's forward momentum took it corkscrewing and cartwheeling underneath our ship and I lost sight of it. This all happened inside seven or eight seconds.

The single-engines would hit us in waves, some with their flaps lowered to prolong their guns bearing time. I have never seen fighters at such close, point-blank range as on that day. The long Regensburg raid to North Africa in August 1943 was rough, the Eighth lost 60 B17's that day, but this was something else. It was more like a vicious bar-room brawl than an air battle, with highly inflammable airplanes being the furniture and long streams of multi-colored tracers and rockets being the projectiles.

I also remember Captain Keith Harris from our Group, but flying with the 100th that day, coming up to join us near Münster. His airplane seemed to be in a level attitude, the nose wasn't pointed up, but it appeared to me that his ship was on a high-speed lift until he found a slot in our formation which he could fly into.

The 390th Bomb Group B17 *Rusty Lode* encountered highly accurate flak about 50 miles west of the target area. The Pilot, Lt. Robert Sabel, remembers:

It knocked out my right inboard engine, but fortunately I was able to feather the propeller while the engine still had sufficient oil pressure to do so, and I shut down power to it.

The Group, because of their superior speed, gradually pulled ahead which made my ship "Tailend Charlie", a sitting duck for enemy fighters. Fortunately we weren't spotted until we had passed the I.P. and were on the bomb run. Several fighters then tried a co-ordinated head-on and tail attack but my gunners kept them away and no further damage was sustained at that time.

One of the Eighth Air Force few NCO bombardiers, Sgt. James Shields, of the 390th Bomb Group recalls:

Our regular ship, *Norma Jane*, was temporarily laid-up for repairs and we were flying one of the new B17G models for this mission. Although the two guns in the chin turret would test fire satisfactorily on the ground, they malfunctioned in the very cold air at high altitude. I learned later that a gasoline truck had backed into the turret shortly before takeoff.

When the enemy fighters really got among our formation during the bomb run, all I could do was call out targets for the gunners and duck down behind the bombsight when the fighters came in from twelve o'clock. Our Tail Gunner, Sgt. McPherson, kept us informed as the ships behind us went down, and it seemed only a matter of time before we would join them.

Then I noticed that our number four engine was on fire. I immediately informed our Pilot, Captain Reilly, who replied that he knew it but was unable to feather the propeller. As I watched, the whole prop assembly slowly tilted back and then came off, crashing into number three propeller and engine which, of course, began to vibrate madly, threatening to wrench itself loose and cause further serious damage to our ship. Fortunately, Captain Reilly managed to feather number three in time. This left us with two engines on the port side, and we slid quickly towards the rear of the formation.

One of the few remaining 100th Bomb Group Fortresses still in the air, *Forever Yours* piloted by Lt. Edward Stork, slowly heeled over on fire and plunged earthwards. Lt. Stork, once a train fireman, had barely 48 hours earlier performed the almost-impossible by bringing home to Thorpe Abbotts a B17 named *Miss Carriage* on only one engine after the other three had been disabled by flak over Bremen — a distance of 400 miles.

Eight parachutes — including Lt. Stork's — emerged and blossomed one after the other from *Forever Yours,* before the wreckage smashed to the ground just beyond the village of Amelsbeuren, six miles south of Münster.

Waist Gunner Sgt. Stanley Smith of the 390th's *Stork Club,* relates:

There were bandit targets all around the clock at this stage as we stood back to back, our feet slipping on the rolling clutter of spent cartridge cases while we tracked our separate targets, or relayed them to each other as they darted over and under our ship. The windstream screamed a banshee wail over the constant roar of the engines as the sub-zero cold tore through the wide-open waist windows, freezing the breath in our oxygen masks and raising ugly red frostbite welts on the tiniest bits of unprotected flesh. Like clumsy deep-sea divers in some intricate underwater ballet, we constantly fouled into each others interphone lines, oxygen hoses and heated suit cords which were our lifelines.

As the 390th formation neared the target, Captain Robert Short's B17F 826 took a hit near it's number three engine. The flames spread rapidly along the right wing threatening to ignite the fuel tanks with each passing second as the bomber spiralled crazily downwards, hopelessly out of control. Nine parachutes emerged from the plane before it exploded. Captain Short, on his 16th mission, was one of the survivors as was photographer Sgt. Joseph Easley, who made up the 11th crew member. Navigator, Lt. Hal Hughes, was severely injured on landing by parachute and died in a German hospital later the same day. Ball Turret Gunner Sgt. Richard Grace, and Radio Operator Sgt. Donald Lowrie, also perished.

For the German pilots too, the battle proved an extraordinary experience.

Said Oberleutnant (1st Lt.) Heinz Knoke, an Me 109 Pilot based at Marx, who two days previously had shot down a B17, his 18th confirmed victory:

> When bombers were expected to attack targets in Central or Southern Germany, we were ordered from Marx in Northwestern Germany to Twente Air Base near Enschede in Eastern Holland. So on this occasion we flew there and awaited further orders.
>
> At 1439 hours we took off, and shortly after sighted a formation of Fortresses in the distance approaching Münster from the south. A Squadron of Me110's was attacking the B17's from the rear with rockets. I knew that the 110's had previously employed this method of attack, but this was the first time I witnessed this extraordinary sight.
>
> Feldwebel's (Sergeants) Barran and Fuehrmann were flying with me. We all watched as the Me 110's launched their rockets in salvoes, and could clearly see the dark smoke trails left by the rockets as they streaked in towards the bombers from behind. The sky seemed full of rockets, and we saw two of the Fortresses going down.

« « « » » »

Although they were surrounded by hordes of German fighters, Major Hansel and Captain Geary in the 390th's Lead Fortress *Pistol Packin' Mama* could now only sit, watch and wait until their bombs were released.

The airplane's Lead Navigator, Lt. Nathaniel "Gus" Mencow, recalls:

Just before we reached Münster I shot down an Me 109, it started smoking and spiralled down to crash west of the city. No one was seen to bail out and I assume the pilot was killed. I remember it clearly. I can recall the sweat pouring down my face and over my oxygen mask. When I glanced at the external thermometer it registered 27 degrees below zero.

Immediately afterwards the Bombardier, Lt. Willms, and I were too busy locating the target to worry about who was shooting at us. It's strange, but to this day I can still hear the roar of the engines and our airplane shuddering with the recoil of all the guns firing as one, sounding like pneumatic road drills hammering in unision. There was also the acrid smell of burnt cordite and scorched oil from the many empty shell cases littering the floor of the nose compartment . . . then we were over the outskirts of Münster.

Hauptmann Walter Hoeckner of 2 Staffel Jagdgeschwader I, resumes the German viewpoint of the action:

At 1431 hours we took off from Woendsdrecht and I led my three Staffeln against the American bombers flying towards the Ruhr. Ground Control led us to three boxes of B17's which we first sighted at 1453 hours. At 1501 hours we attacked the second box from the side, then diving under them I hit the B17 which was last in the formation of the low (third) box.

Diving steeply, and closing to about 80 metres while firing, I saw flames and black smoke pouring from his right wing and right inboard engine. Pieces of fuselage were now breaking off the Fortress. As I dived under him I received hits in my engine, probably from the ball turret, and my cockpit immediately became full of dense smoke and gasoline fumes, forcing me to bail out or fry. As I jumped, my engine seized and stopped.

The B17 exploded in the air and crashed near the village of Hohenhalte, 12 kilometers west of Münster. During my parachute descent, I saw another Fortress on fire and coming down in steep spirals. It exploded in the air after losing its right wing and crashed within a hundred metres of my own landing place in a hedge bordering a meadow. I had to use my knife to cut my harness straps before I could free myself from the hedge.

The two Fortresses and my fighter had all crashed within 800 metres of each other.

It was Hauptmann Hoeckner's 60th air victory, and his kill was a 100th Bomb Group B17F 823, piloted by Lt. Charles Walts, who parachuted to safety, following four of his crew. The second Fortress 734, piloted by Lt. Charles Thompson, which had crashed so close to Hpt. Hoeckner, was also a 100th

Bomb Group B17. Seven of her crew, including Lt. Thompson, bailed out and and became POW's. Lt. Thompson's airplane had been shot down by Unteroffizier Rubbau of 4 Staffel, JG/1.

Hauptmann Hoeckner fired 320 shells from his four 20-mm cannon, and 202 bullets from his pair of 17-mm machine guns during his two attacks. The six guns in his FW 190A were fed four different types of ammunition — tracer (brandgranaten) and non-tracer, high-explosive (minegeschosse), and armour-piercing (panzermunition). With all guns firing accurately, about 70 rounds a second were striking B17F 823. On average, 20 hits from a 20-mm cannon were sufficient to bring down a Fortress.

Captain Ellis Scripture, Lead Navigator of *The Zootsuiters,* resumes the narrative:

We had made all the navigational check points en route and we approached the city from the southwest. Dewey Johnson, our Bombardier, had taken control of the airplane through the A.F.C.E. by this time. Between the Initial Point and the target area, the Wing had encountered intense fighter opposition, and this was the greatest concentration of German fighters we had seen to date. They seemed to lose the classical attack patterns and become a jumbled mass before, over and beyond the target. Tracers filled the air, and it was like shooting at fish in a tank when the slow, heavy twin-engined night fighters became entangled in the bomber formations.

At 1503 hours, three minutes later than scheduled, the bombs curved down and we hit the target hard, in spite of intense fighter opposition. And as we turned away from the target, I shot down a twin-engined German fighter. It was an Me 410, flying every so slowly, as if he was trying to outrun us. At the time, I felt we had to clear him out of the way or run over him!

Quite frankly, I didn't experience a particular thrill over the situation, either at the time or later. As one who had grown up on stories of fair fights in Western novels and stories of First World War "dog fights", I could take no particular pleasure in shooting down a guy who was trying to run away, even though he came in shooting and had probably been firing at other B17's in our formation just previously.

As the bombs dropped from the gaping bomb doors of *The Zootsuiters,* the other 18 Fortresses of the 95th Bomb Group released their loads of twelve 500 pound bombs squarely on the assigned target area from an altitude of 24,500 feet. Forty seconds after release, the first of the bombs, approaching their terminal velocity speed of 750 miles per hour, struck the heart of the city of Münster. The rest followed very quickly.

Then the remaining 16 Fortresses of the 390th Bomb Group unloaded their cargoes of death and destruction into the cauldron of fire and smoke now boiling up from their target.

Following the 390th came the shattered remnants of "The Bloody Hundredth." Only six of their B17's had survived from the 19 Fortresses which had set out from Thorpe Abbotts less than four hours previously, six of these having aborted the mission because of mechanical problems. The mission, however, had been regarded by many veterans of previous raids as comparatively easy.

Lt. Clifford Milburn, Bombardier of *Royal Flush,* 100th B.G.:

Lt. Rosenthal put the airplane on the Automatic Flight Control Equipment (A.F.C.E.) and I took control, sighted through the telescope of the Norden, lined up the target, the bombs trained out and fell in the target area.

The fighters continued their attacks on those of us remaining, flying through their own flak to do so. A sharp left turnafter bombs away, and we were on our way home.

From the Show Ground, approximately three miles to the south of the city centre, Otto Schuett watched the approaching formations of American bombers. He remembers:

It was an amazing sight to behold. The B17's came in at very high altitude (25,000 feet or so) and it took a little time to recognize the bombers configurations as they blended very well into the blue sky. The approaching planes were met with very heavy anti-aricraft fire from the 8.8 cm batteries which were emplaced around Münster. Within a fraction of time sky and earth were transformed into a living hell.

From our position we saw smoke, in dense clouds, erupting which, from a distance, looked more like dust clouds. It took a very short while for me to realise that Münster was under extremely heavy attack, the town centre was being hit severely. At first we could not understand where the dust clouds were coming from. We heard explosions but I didn't hear the whistling sounds that one normally associates with falling bombs. For the first time that day what I heard was a "whooshing" through the air, more like the sound of large calibre artillery shells passing close overhead.

As the bombs dropped closer and closer and as the attack grew in its intensity, we suddenly realised that our lives were at stake. We all started to scatter and race for cover as the bomb explosions and anti-aircraft fire reached a crescendo. I simply sprawled face-down on the ground. Looking upwards I saw, to my horror, bombs and phosphorous canisters coming down and it looked like they were all coming directly towards me. But they exploded thirty to fifty yards away, showers of dirt and bomb fragments went flying through the air above my body while I hugged the ground. I was terrified and as I glanced around me for more secure cover a phosphorous container hit the side of the Geist Kirche, broke apart and the burning phosphorous streamed down the side of the building. The noise of the explosions was deafening. I felt a growing sense of anger and frustration as I lay there in the dirt, expecting death at any minute and being powerless to do anything about it.

Then came a momentary lull for a few brief seconds. I got up and started running, frantically looking for better cover. As I ran I looked up to see if any more planes were approaching . . . there were. Many more . . . but directly overhead was the falling wing of a B17 with its two propellers still turning. The wing came down directly towards me and again I ran for my life. It seemed to be following me. I again hit the ground and thought "It's all over." The wing actually crashed to the ground about thirty yards away, burning fiercely and sending up clouds of black, oily smoke into the sky. *(Author's Note:* This wing probably came from the 390th Bomb Group's B17 826 piloted by Captain Short.)

The anti-aircraft fire remained very fierce. While exploding flak shells give out black powder puffs of smoke I noticed now and then pink puffs. Later on I learned that Russian Prisoners of War, serving as ammunition handlers, had passed exercise ammunition to the gunners, who, in the heat and frenzied activity of battle, did not realise the difference. I never learned if the Russian prisoners had acted purposely or not.

Just previously, over Münster, Feldwebel Gerd Wiegand and his FW 190 had been in a fight for survival of a very different kind. He recalls:

What an incredible sight just above me . . . the sky was full of B17's with their bomb-bay doors open. One Fortress was in flames, another streaming black smoke. Many parachutes were opening below me, flak shells bursting above. Suddenly it was raining bombs all round me.

I immediately banked my "10" over vertically to reduce the chances of being hit by a falling bomb. Luckily, I avoided them, and once clear of the danger I climbed at full throttle back to the safety of altitude for my second attack. While climbing, almost vertically, I was joined by another FW190. It was Unteroffizier Rossner from my Squadron.

Fourteen year old Hildegard Kosters continues her memories of the bombing raid:

Looking out of the windows at home that afternoon, we suddenly saw high above the railway station the dreaded sign of a daylight air attack. Target smoke markers, which we were to get to know as "Leichenfinger" — a corpse's finger — were on their way down and seemed to be coming straight for us.

We ran out into the street and made directly for the nearest air-raid shelter, a huge concrete bunker only 150 metres away, built directly under the station platforms and extending way back beneath the railway lines. In the ensuing panic during the stampede for shelter, many people had their clothes torn to shreds and ruined. New clothing was simply unobtainable in wartime Germany. My family had all the buttons ripped from their clothes in the chaotic melee, but we all reached the comparative safety of the shelter.

The mournful wailing of the air-raid sirens mingled with the deadly whistling of the descending bombs. They exploded massively all around us: the earth shook, vibrated shuddered and heaved from the impact of the concussions. The solid concrete bunker trembled and shook to its very foundations. The railway junction and marshalling yards must have been the target. Suddenly all the lights went out. The people — mostly women and children — huddled together like sheep in a slaughterhouse, praying, crying, and shrieking in terror. Some were mute with fear. It was simply terrifying.

Another eye-witness recalls:

I was five months pregnant at the time, and I left our house in Melchesstrasse with my five-year-old son and a neighbour to catch the 1500 hours train to Handorf. My husband left at the same time to cycle to Hilltrup. He hadn't been drafted into the army because of ill health.

On the way to the station, as we were passing along Englestrasse, the air raid sirens sounded. We ran with our four small children for the train to get out of Münster. We tried to get on the train, but we were pushed away and had to go to the air raid shelter.

We were still on the platform as the first bombs dropped on the opposite platform. Shrapnel was flying all around us. By the time we squeezed into the shelter more heavy bombs were exploding above us. We were only able to shuffle our way along — it was terrifying. Next to us a wounded woman became hysterical. Her back was full of shrapnel. Then the lights went out. The raid seemed to last for a lifetime.

Meanwhile, my husband, on his way to Hilltrup, saw the whole terrible sight as he sought shelter in a roadside ditch.

Gerhard Ringbeck at Münster railway station continues his recollections:

Apparently, a daylight raid on Münster had never happened before, and the local people were not taking the wailing sirens seriously as they nonchalantly strolled about in the warm afternoon sun. Very soon I saw the first units of the bomber formation in the distance coming straight towards Münster. They were being attacked by many of our fighters and as they got closer I could see bursts of anti-aircraft fire from our flak guns south of the city engaging the bombers. Then I saw two or three burning planes diving down out of control

It quickly became apparent, however, that the enemy bombers were not being stopped or diverted by our air defences. Being such a clear day I could see many more bomber units appearing in the distance, all heading directly towards Münster.

It gradually dawned on the people in the streets that they were now in great danger. Then we heard that the air raid bunker beneath the railway station was already full and overcrowded so I ran as fast as I could away from the station and in the direction of the Servatiplatz. Just as I reached the railway administration building the first bombs were already exploding in the direction of the city centre and coming nearer and nearer to the railway station.

I searched desparately for a cellar window at the Reich's railway management building for shelter from the frightening whistling of the bombs, now crashing down with ear-splitting explosions. At last I found a window, kicked it in, and dived through to comparative safety.

What happened next was frightful, it was an inferno, which I'd never before experienced even as a veteran soldier on the Russian Front. I can't recall just how long the rain of bombs lasted. All around me I could hear injured people screaming who were trapped under demolished and burning houses. Almost all of the city centre had been flattened to the ground, and the main railway station had been heavily damaged. Wherever I looked there were injured people including women and children.

Seventeen year old Karl-Freidrich Bell, Air Defense Helper at one of Münster's anti aircraft batteries, recollects:

The 10th October 1943 was the first large-scale daylight raid on Münster. It enabled us to constantly double-check the range and position of the bombers with both optical range-finders and radar.

The raid started at about 1500 hours on a beautiful Sunday afternoon. I will never forget it. The first wave of B17 Fortresses approached from the southwest in a clear blue sky, three boxes of about 20 bombers in each group. They were flying at an altitude of 8,500 metres, only just within the range of our guns which had been manufactured in 1937. Later models of the 8.8 cm. could reach higher altitudes. So the bombers were only within range of our battery for the comparatively short period of time that they were passing over Münster. Soon many more bombers appeared in the distance.

After five salvoes of "Gruppenfeur", all our six guns firing simultaneously, four of the American bombers began burning fiercely, their crews bailing out over or near Münster. At one time the sky seemed to be filled with drifting parachutes. It was an absolutely incredible sight. If there had not been the constant, high-pitched whistling of the falling bombs, the deafening detonations of all our guns firing in unison, the earth-shaking explosions as the bombs struck sending up gigantic smokepalls and dust-clouds from the inner city, you would have thought that the Americans were a force of paratroopers. The noise was indescribable.

« « « » » »

Following the bombing run of the 13th Combat Bomb Wing Sergeant Mackie, Radio Operator in the Task Force Commander's Fortress *The Zootsuiters,* tapped out on his morse key a coded message to 3rd Air Division Headquarters at Elveden Hall relayed to him via interphone by Colonel Gerhart. He sent it slowly, with a distinct spacing between the dots and dashes for each letter, to ensure clarity of the transmission above the static.

"PRIMARY STRIKE SUCCESSFUL STOP DIVISION UNDER SEVERE REPEAT SEVERE ATTACK STOP PRESENT POSITION FIVE TWO ZERO SEVEN NORTH ZERO SEVEN FIVE TWO EAST STOP COURSE TWO SEVEN THREE STOP ALT TWO FOUR STOP IMPERATIVE GET ESCORT REPEAT IMPERATIVE END.

GERHART"

Shortly after the message was received at Elveden Hall it was being relayed to the Thunderbolts of the 56th Fighter Group who were, at that moment, approaching the Holland/German border at an altitude of 30,000 feet. Although the distance between the P47's of "Zemke's Wolfpack" and the B17's of the 3rd Air Division was closing dramatically, they were not yet close enough to establish vocal communication by V.H.F. radio.

« « « » » »

The attack on the primary target developed in three phases. The first and second consisting of general purpose and high explosive bombs, and a third being incendiary bombs. These struck the target in three concentrated and well-defined areas, crossing the city from west to east.

The historical and cultural heritage of Münster, dating back to and beyond medieval times, and preserved over the centuries, disappeared forever in a mere fraction of time. Münster Cathedral, the University, Town Hall and several of the city's churches and places of culture all received varying degrees of damage. Fortunately, the Bishop of Münster was rescued from the Bishop's Palace, located on the Dom Platz, before it was gutted by fire.

In Münster Cathedral, the Sexton's wife and her youngest son, heard the bombs exploding in the near vicinity. As they were coming from the Sacristy in the north tower, carrying the valuable cassocks worn by the celebrants of the Mass, and on their way to the safety of the vaults, a bomb crashed through the roof of the Cathedral and exploded. The 16-year old boy was struck by a bomb splinter and died where he fell. Curate Hubert Leiwering was able to administer the last rites to him before he passed away. The young boy's name was Antonius Gerhard.

An official police report (Stadtische Polizeiverwaltug) graphically describes the conflagrations near the town hall, which was near the main post office and telephone exchange facing the Dom Platz, at the height of the attack:

> All around us the bombs exploded, houses burned fiercely before caving in and collapsing with a sound like thunder. Nearly all the windows and doors of the town hall were shattered and demolished, consequently all corridors, stairways, landings and rooms were filled with dense, blinding, dust-filled smoke and fumes. Each of us had great difficulty in breathing through our dampened handkerchiefs tied to our faces. There was broken and splintered furniture everywhere, and the floors were strewn with broken glass and piles of rubble and debris.

The post office and telephone exchange also received direct hits and were put out of action, disrupting at a stroke Münster's vital telephone communications.

Chapter 12

AMERICAN casualties were particularly heavy during the critical time-span in which they were in the target area, from both flak and incessant fighter attacks.

Sergeant William Ellett, Ball Turret Gunner in the 390th's *Rusty Lode,* recollects:

We had been battling swarms of fighters for what seemed a lifetime, when suddenly below, I saw three 'chutes open. I knew they must have come from our ship, so I climbed out of the ball turret to be certain. Both waist guns were hanging limp from their mounts. I listened for the sound of our other guns, but all I could hear was the grinding of our engines. It felt eerie standing there, rather like being in another world. I went over to the waist guns, breathing from the 'walk-around' oxygen bottle, and then looked back into the tail and found the tail gunner had gone. Then I noticed the torn and bloodstained flak jackets on the floor and realized what had happened.

I almost ran to the radio room but when I opened the door I stopped short. Sgt. McGregor was slumped over his gun — it looked as though a 20mm had burst in his face. I laid him on the floor and then stumbled towards the waist door. All I could think of was getting out. Then I heard the top turret guns firing and knew that the fellows up front were still there and that my place was with the ship. I went back to the waist guns and started firing again.

The bomber's Pilot, Lt. Robert Sabel, remembers:

Immediately after we had bombed the target a very aggressive flight of fighters, FW 190's, pressed home another attack against us destroying our flight control system. However, the auto-pilot was still operational and was successfully engaged after some disturbing gyrations, but our manoeuvrebility remained very limited.

Several large holes appeared in both wings and the fuselage. Another engine, number one, caught fire, but was fortunately extinguished when I feathered the propeller. The fighters continued their attacks, though with less experience, and I guessed that we had been 'handed off' to a different fighter organisation.

At that stage of the battle I was completely unaware that we had lost four

Bombs released by the 95th Bomb Group over open country south of the Aa Lake approximately three miles from the target. The bomb strike photos were taken by a K-10 camera in the B17 **Rhapsody in Flak**, *piloted by Lt. Lesley Kring. The camera takes a photo every 10 seconds.*

Official U.S.A.F. Photo.

Approximately 40 seconds after release the first bombs land on the target at about 750 m.p.h. from almost 5 miles up. The Aa Lake (bottom of picture) and the Dortmund-Ems Canal (upper right) can be clearly seen.

Official U.S.A.F. Photo.

The rest followed quickly at 1503 hours.

Official U.S.A.F. Photo.

Bomb bursts at approximately 1504 hours.

Official U.S.A.F. Photo.

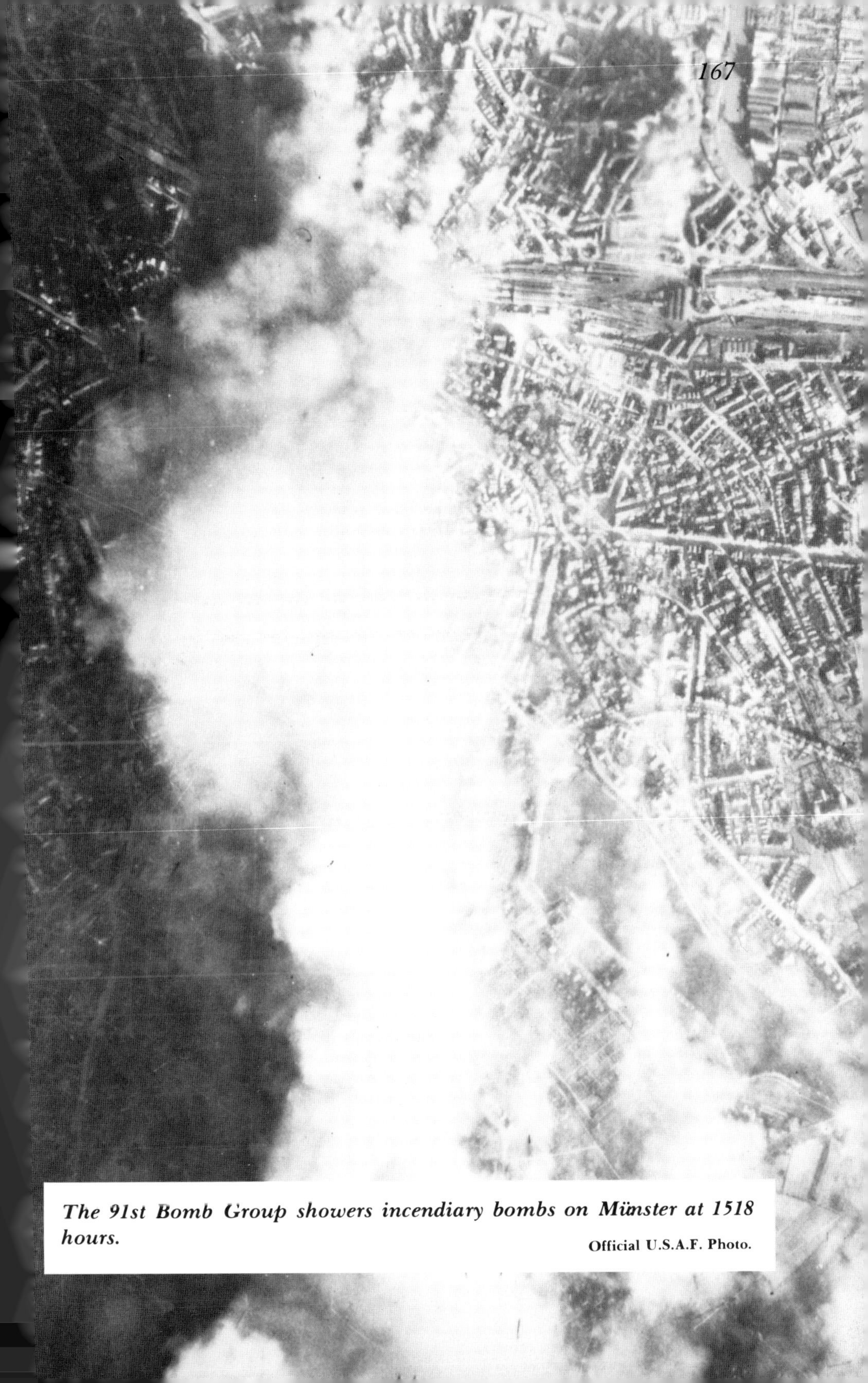

The 91st Bomb Group showers incendiary bombs on Münster at 1518 hours.

Official U.S.A.F. Photo.

Bomb strike photos of Coesfeld.

Official U.S.A.F. Photo.

Manfred Holsbusch.

Manfred Holsbusch.

Manfred Holsbusch.

Manfred Holsbusch.

Manfred Holsbusch.

Manfred Holsbusch.

Interior of the Münster Cathedral after the bombing.

W. Beer.

Münster Cathedral, after 10 October 1943. W. Beer.

As soon as possible the excavator comes to start work on the heavy rubble to rescue inhabitants of the house "Aegidehof" who are buried under the rubble. W. Beer.

From the garden of a bakery, which has not been destroyed, one can see the fire caused by the phosphorous. W. Beer.

A pathway is cleared of rubble at the Clemenskirche.

Manfred Holsbusch.

Statue of a farmer stands erect among the burning ruins.

The Apollo Theater. Manfred Hülsbusch.

Bombed out buildings seen from the Lumbeski Church. W. Beer.

Alten Clemens Hospital. Manfred Hülsbusch.

Helpers in the Aegidistreet. W. Beer.

Russian prisoners are brought into town in the morning to work and then returned to their prison in the evening. W. Beer.

The neighbors are looking to the departure of the helpers from Bortan and asking, "Will you come back tomorrow?" "No, tomorrow other helpers will come." W. Beer.

Carrying water back to the ruins after it has been delivered by the water wagon. W. Beer.

A water-pipe break has blocked the street and all cars must go back.

Ludgen Street after the air raids. W. Beer.

After the raid, the citizens can get some food at a "soup kitchen."

W. Beer.

The water wagon brings water to the inhabitants. W. Beer.

Otto Schuett's parents outside their destroyed home on 11 October 1943.

The sun is shining while residents try to rescue what they can from the ruins of their homes. W. Beer.

The Nazi funeral service for victims of the raid. W. Beer.

Burial of some of the victims of the raid. W. Beer.

The Prinzipalmarkt.

Manfred Holsbusch.

Two light flak batteries (20mm calibre) near Münster. Hans Hohler.

A group of young Luftwaffe helpers at a Münster flak battery in Münster. H. Hessling.

88mm flak guns at Münster. Date of this action is unknown. W. Beer.

The 100th Bomb Group B17, Royal Flush, *with one engine feathered, lags behind the 390th Bomb Group formation after bombing Münster. Shortly after this photo was taken over the Holland/German border* Royal Flush *lost another engine and came back to England alone. The 390th plane at the right is* Rose Marie, *piloted by Lt. Dougherty. Rear elements of the 96th Bomb Group are at the top right.*

Part of the 390th formation after dropping their bombs on Münster. Official U.S.A.F. Photo.

The 95th Bomb Group under attack from German fighters shortly after dropping their bombs at 1503. Münster is burning at the left and the Dortmund-Ems Canal in the foreground. **Official U.S.A.F. Photo.**

A 95th Bomb Group plane under attack. **Official U.S.A.F. Photo.**

The encircled airplane is Herky Jerky II, *piloted by Rodney Snow as it crossed the Dutch coast on its return from Münster. The plane at the top is* Rhapsody in Flak.

Flak damage to B17F 498 (piloted by Lt. Reiley) which crash landed at Framlingham on two engines.

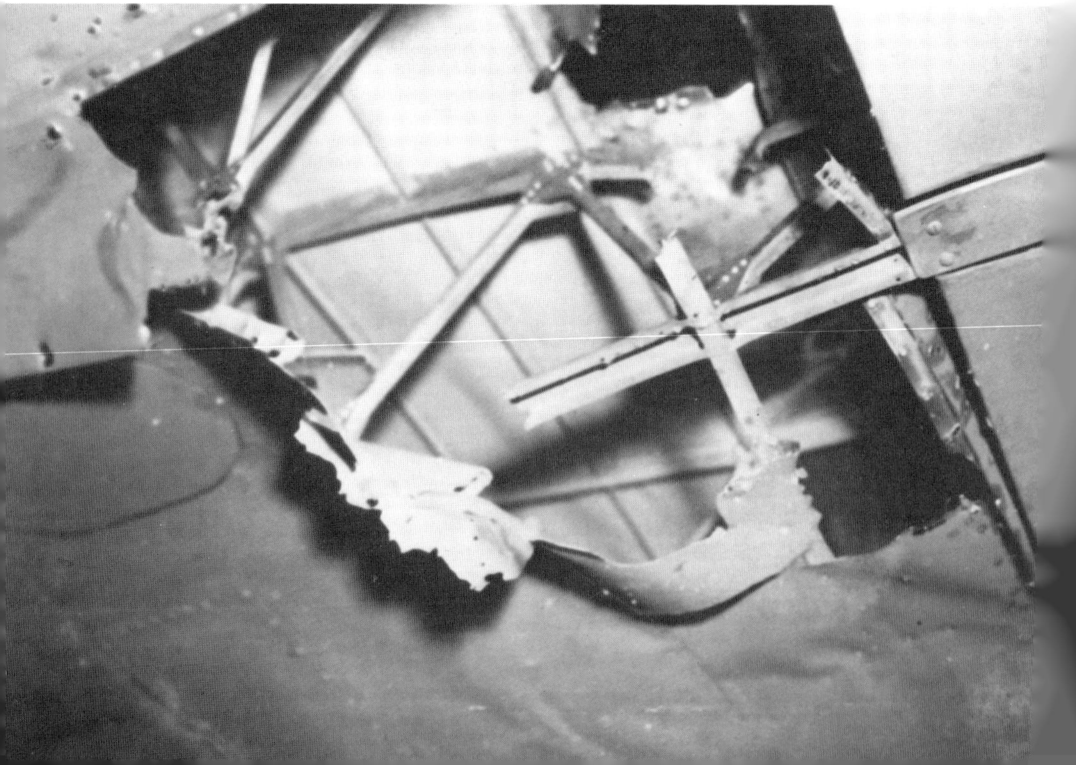

Flak bursts near the 95th Bomb Group formation. Official U.S.A.F. Photo.

Heavy flak during the Münster mission of 10 October 1943 as seen from a 95th Bomb Group B17. Ellis Scripture.

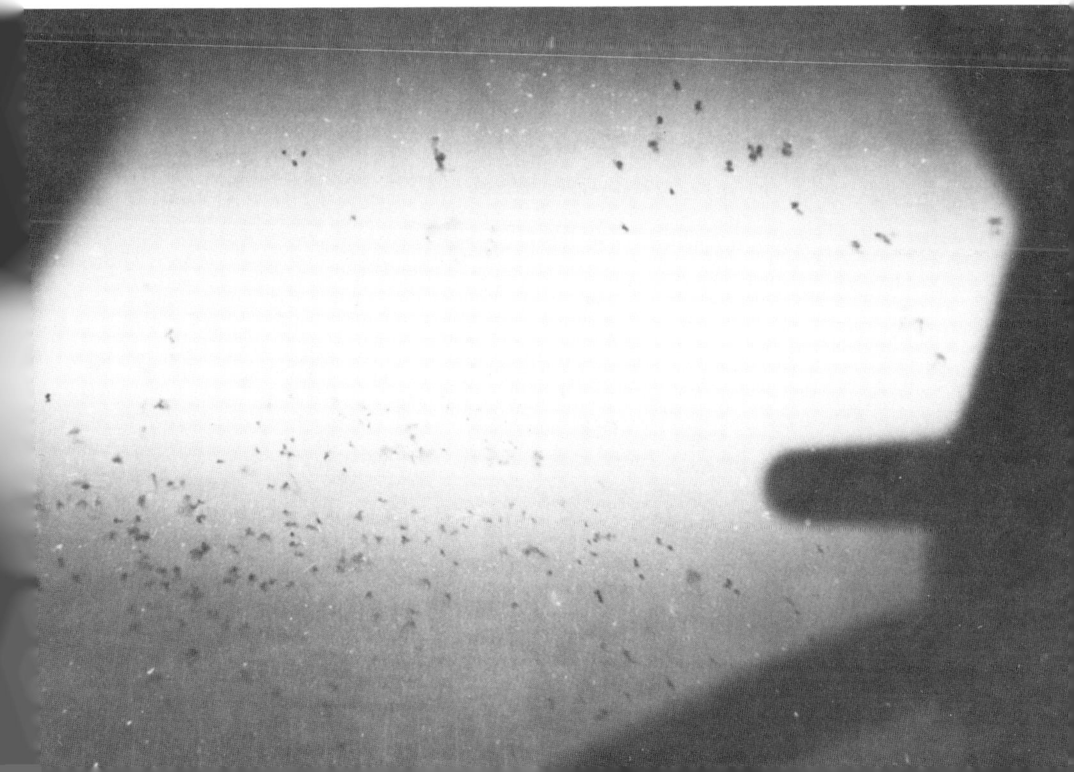

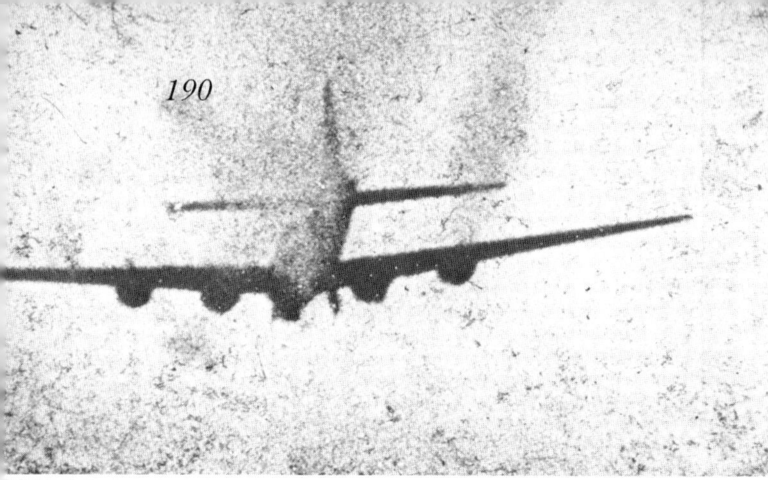

B17 (Group Unknown under fighter attack from an Me 410 of ZG on 10 October 1943.
Hallerback.

A work party refilling a bomb crater after th raid.
H. Hessling.

The 94th Bomb Grou formation on the wa home after bombing Münster on 11 November 1943.
Official U.S.A.F. Photo.

The crew of Rosie's Riveters *that flew* Royal Flush *on 10 October 1943. Lt. Robert Rosenthal is second from left in the front row. Crew Chief J. Woodall is second from left in the back row and the Assistant Crew Chief, J. Dell is third from the right in the back row.*

The original crew of Fritz Blitz. *Pilot Eldon Broman is standing second from the left.*

The Lead Crew of the 388th Bomb Group on the Münster raid, flying 230215, Slightly Dangerous, *Lt. James A. Wisehart, Pilot, is standing, second from the left.* William Goldenberg.

The crew of Stupefier *of the 379th Bomb Group, Kimbelton, Hunts. They crashed on take-off on 9 October 1943 but flew another B17 on 10 October October 1943. The pilot, Lt. Robert Haughy, is second from the left in the back row.*

Flak damage to Rusty Lode *of the 390th Bomb Group which landed at Thorpe Abbotts. Pilot is Lt. Robert Sabel.*

Official U.S.A.F. Photo.

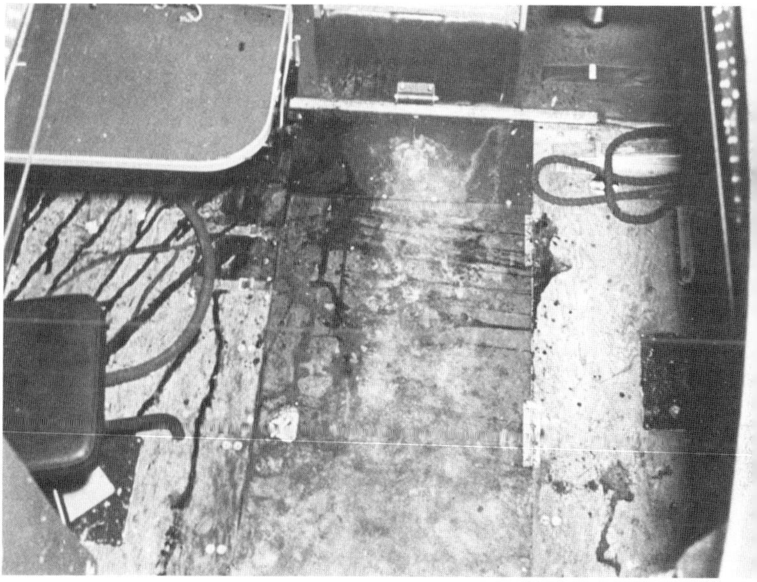

he radio room of Rusty ode.

Top of the wing of Rusty Lode.

Top of the wing of th *390th B17* Eightball *showing rocket damag*

From this view of Eig ball's *wing you can se that it was virtually sheered off.*

The 91st Bomb Grou B17G Air Baboon McGoon *after it cras landed out of fuel at Tarrington, Suffolk, returning from Müns*

crew members.

A dramatic collision between two 100th Bomb Group Fortresses and a German fighter is recalled by Lt. Robert Schneider, Pilot of the 100th Bomb Group's plane, *Little Mike:*

What little was left of the 100th Bomb Group's formation was flying low and to our left. Shortly after bombing the primary target, two of their ships collided with an Me 109. This I only partly saw when one of my Waist Gunners called me on the interphone. I glanced to my left just in time to see the aftermath of the explosion. I only remember seeing one chute and was told later that it was the German fighter pilot. We were also in trouble — a fighter shot out our right wing flap almost to the number three engine fuel tank.

Sgt. Dan James, Top Turret Gunner in one of the doomed Fortresses *Sexy Suzy, Mother of Ten,* recalls the collision:

Germans were coming in from all directions in flights of four at about nine or ten o'clock high. I began shooting and one went down smoking. 20 mm fire from all sides hit my oxygen tank. My right shoulder was bleeding from flak splinters, and the seat of my flying suit had been blown away. There were now only three ships in our formation.

About five minutes after the target, something hit our left wing and made a hell of an explosion. Flames were all over the ship. Then our Pilot, Lt. William Beddow, yelled over the interphone, "This is it, boys. Everybody bail out!"

It was my duty at this time to open the bomb-bay doors, but when I opened the door behind the cockpit the whole bay area was aflame. Nobody could possibly escape by that exit. And as I turned back towards the cockpit, the airplane went out of control and started downwards. This threw me into the lower level of the nose area where there was another escape hatch. Lt. Beddow was still struggling to regain control of the airplane as I climbed quickly through the hatch, leaving the plane which was then in a vertical dive. I opened my chute after free-falling about 2,000 feet. When I looked up there wasn't a B17 left in the sky. At about 10,000 feet a German fighter nosed in on me, and I thought he was going to open fire but he turned away and left me.

While coming down I saw another parachute far below me. Later I learned that it was Lt. Brooks, our Co-Pilot. Only two others from my crew survived — our Bombardier and the Tail Gunner. A German soldier and several policemen were waiting for me when I landed.

I was well treated in a Luftwaffe hospital where my wounds quickly healed.

The other Fortress involved in the collision was *Sweater Girl.* Its Pilot, Lt. Richard Atchison, was among the six surviving crewmen to parachute safely from the disintegrating bomber. All three aircraft crashed near Ostberven, eight miles north of Münster.

Local farmer Heinrich Stadtbaumer remembers:

I was in my farmhouse about 5 kilometres north of Münster when I saw a large formation of four-engined bombers over Münster on a heading towards Handorf, east of my farm. Between the Dortmund-Ems Canal and my farm, 500 metres south of my position, were two 8.8 cm flak batteries, twelve guns in all, which were firing salvoes of shells into the formation. In the distance I saw dense clouds of smoke rising from Münster.

Very shortly afterwards I saw one of the big bombers spiralling down in a vertical spin directly over my farmhouse. It crashed in a meadow without exploding about 200 metres west of my farmhouse, killing one cow. I also saw several parachutes drifting down.

Ten minutes after the raid I went to the crashed plane and saw the bodies of six crewmembers in and near the aircraft.

(Author's note: This was the 100th Bomb Group's *Sexy Suzy.)*

There were now only four 100th Bomb Group Fortresses left in the air, apart from Captain Harris's aircraft which had caught up with the 390th formation just beyond Münster. Captain Charles Cruikshank, piloting *Aw-R-Go,* Lt. Robert Rosenthal in *Royal Flush,* Lt. John Justice, Pilot, flying *Pasadena Nena,* and Lt. John Stephens at the controls of *Stymie.*

Recalled Captain Cruikshank:

We dropped our bombs on target and very shortly afterwards my aircraft received severe battle damage. I gave the order to bail out. Almost immediately after I had bailed out the ship exploded. I learned later that two of my crew were killed and six wounded. I was very fortunate to come through unscathed.

I was captured a few minutes after reaching German soil, and had a very close call with some irate civilians before a German soldier appeared on the scene. It was the end of our 21st mission.

The remains of Captain Cruikshank's Fortress crashed to earth at Lienen, 15 miles northeast of Münster. Tail Gunner Sgt. Charles Clark was trapped in the exploding B17, and although Radio Operator Sergeant Orlando Vincenti managed to clear the tumbling wreckage, his parachute was ablaze following a fire in the radio room.

Captain Frank Murphy, Navigator of *Aw-R-Go,* gives a detailed account of the final desperate minutes of his Fortress.

Very shortly after our Bombardier, Lieutenant "Gus" Gaspar, had released our bombs over the target, fighter attacks became increasingly severe. I was operating the 50 calibre machine gun above the navigator's table in the nose when there was a violent explosion behind me and I was knocked to the floor. It felt as if someone had struck me with a baseball bat. I felt a stinging sensation, like a bucket of very hot water being thrown over my left arm, shoulder and back. My left side immediately began to feel numb and stiff. I knew I had been hit by something and wondered if I was going to die.

However, I started pulling myself up by my right arm, slipping and sliding on expended shell casings which were by then covering the whole floor of the nose section of our airplane. Lieutenant Gaspar saw me struggling and pushed me down on the floor, motioning me not to move. He then turned back to his gun and continued firing. I had lost my intercom connections and as it transpired later I had been hit by fragments from an exploding 20 mm cannon shell.

At this point, Lieutenant Glenn Graham, our Co-Pilot, came down from the cockpit, pulled the handle to release the forward hatch, motioned for us to follow him and then bailed out. I checked my parachute and crawled to the hatch. I dangled my feet in the opening and recall a very sickening feeling as I looked at the ground several miles below. Despite near hysteria, I knew that I had to leave the airplane and that I must clear the B17 before opening my chute. I eased through the hatch, holding my arms to my sides so as not to be tempted into pulling the ripcord too soon.

It was suddenly very quiet. I was tumbling. The ground appeared miles away as I glimpsed it intermittently. I shut my eyes and pulled the ripcord. There was a loud "thwack" and my parachute canopy opened above me. It was the happiest sight I have ever seen in my life . . . before or since.

I heard loud anti aircraft explosions. I looked up and saw what must have been the 390th Bomb Group passing overhead. A lone Me 109 fighter nearby turned and flew directly at me. I almost stopped breathing thinking he was going to fire at me. However, he simply passed close by, almost collapsing my parachute and flew away.

I had removed my gloves to fire my machine gun. My hands were freezing. The first finger of my left hand was badly lacerated by a splinter from the cannon shell that hit me. I thought of my mother and how she would be affected by this as I suddenly realised I was falling into Germany.

I had opened my parachute at high altitude and it took me approximately twenty minutes to reach the ground. I looked at my watch. It was 1517. As I got lower and lower I realised how rapidly I was falling. I could hear voices and as I looked around I saw several people running towards my anticipated landing place near a group of trees in a large field.

My one and only parachute descent ended as the ground appeared to rush up unexpectedly. I landed awkwardly and sprained my left ankle. I was very thankful that it was all over. As I staggered to my feet I had some difficulty, due to my injuries, in extricating myself from my parachute harness.

Two German men warily approached me. It was obvious that they were as nervous and apprehensive of me as I was of them. One of them then asked, "Deutsch?" I replied, "Nein — American." They then motioned me to pick up my chute and they led me to a group of people at the edge of the field

A German lady, about 35 years old, then said to me in perfect English, "For you the war is over." Then she noticed the blood on my arm and hand and asked me if I had been injured. I said, "Yes, but not badly." She then asked me to come to her house nearby and she would do what she could for my wounds.

An argument then ensued between the two men who had first approached me and the lady — but she prevailed. The small group of curious bystanders, the lady, the two men and myself then proceeded to her small house. One of the German men accompanied me as I hobbled inside, while the lady got a basin of warm water. I took off my jacket and shirt and she bathed my wounds and bandaged them expertly. She then asked me if I was hungry. I declined any food, thanking her for her kindness.

About ten minutes later an armed policeman arrived and took me outside. We walked along a narrow road with me still carrying my parachute. We hadn't gone far when a very large touring car came along. It had wooden spoke wheels and in the front seat were two elderly men wearing German Home Guard uniforms, complete with old style German Army helmets with the vertical spike on top.

Sitting in the back seat, to my great relief, was "Chuck" Cruikshank, our Pilot.

« « « » » »

Feldwebel Gerd Wiegand and Unteroffizier Rossner of Jagdgeschwader 26 continued their climb to altitude:

We levelled off and flew parallel with the first box of Fortresses. I wanted to do the same manoeuvre, outrun the box and attack them head-on, but then the box made an unexpected turn to the left. Now we could only attack them from behind, which meant a sharp turn to catch up to them. We came out of the turn directly behind and above a B17 formation. (This was the hitherto unscathed 95th Bomb Group).

What an awe-inspiring sight . . . their whole armada was laid out in front of me. About 20 olive-green camouflaged Fortresses flying in precise formation with their big white stars and glittering machine-guns as they fired long streams of violet coloured tracer bullets at us from long range.

I decided to attack the B17 at the rear and on the left-hand side of the box while Rossner covered me. Diving at full throttle I levelled off at the plane altitude because fewer of his guns could be brought to bear without hitting his own tailplane. By weaving from side to side I rapidly closed the distance between us. Long streams of tracers were curving past me from my target and the other B17's in the box. For every tracer I saw, I knew there were at least three other non-tracer and equally lethal bullets heading towards me.

Finally, I had him in my gunsight and I aimed at his left wing. I wanted to hit his engines. My guns thundered and immediately big chunks of metal came away from his left outboard engine. I then had to throttle back sharply to stay behind the B17. Suddenly, from somewhere near the tail of the Fortress, a brown object came hurtling straight at me, barely missing my whirling propeller and passing within inches of my cockpit. A human body . . .

I felt cold shivers running down my spine . . .

The B17 slowly pulled away from the box, smoking and severely damaged. What now? for a moment I was undecided what to do next. A quick glance behind me showed Rossner was still covering me. As yet no fighter escorts could be seen, so I made another attack on the Fortress, this time from the right-hand side, concentrating again on the engines. Again big chunks of metal, forcing me to dive to avoid the hail of debris, cruised past me in the slipstream. My B17 now had a broad white trail streaming from the right wing. I had hit the fuel tanks.

Bodies were now tumbling from the doomed Fortress and their parachutes were opening below my airplane. At least some of the crew were bailing out. There was enough time for them all to escape, unless they had been hit.

Finally, the B17, slowly turning to the right, banked steeply and went into a short vertical dive before levelling off and climbing again. I considered leaving it to its fate and going after the box now disappearing in the distance, but I had only 20 minutes fuel left and was nearly out of ammunition. The last time that I had downed a Fortress it had exploded in the air with its bomb load, and parts of it had struck my plane damaging it so severely that I was forced to bail out. I hadn't even received official confirmation of my victory on that occasion!

My B17 was now hanging on its two propellers in a 45 degree climb — The other two engines were gone. Suddenly it stalled and plunged towards the ground. The unforgiving force of gravity claims all things eventually. I followed it down to 5,000 metres as Rossner came alongside. The bomber then levelled off and climbed again. The machine guns hung uselessly from their mounts. Black smoke poured from its left wing, contrasting sharply with the white vaporizing petrol streaming from the right. It was like a huge menacing dragon in its death throes. Such sights are indelibly imprinted on my mind for all time.

Three more times it repeated this same manoeuvre before crashing in a forest clearing from a height of 300 metres, near Saarbeck, 20 kilometers north of Münster. Parts of the bomber and trees whirled high into the air amidst a huge fiery mushrooming ball of black smoke. It was the end.

My engine began to bang, it was rapidly overheating, so I throttled right

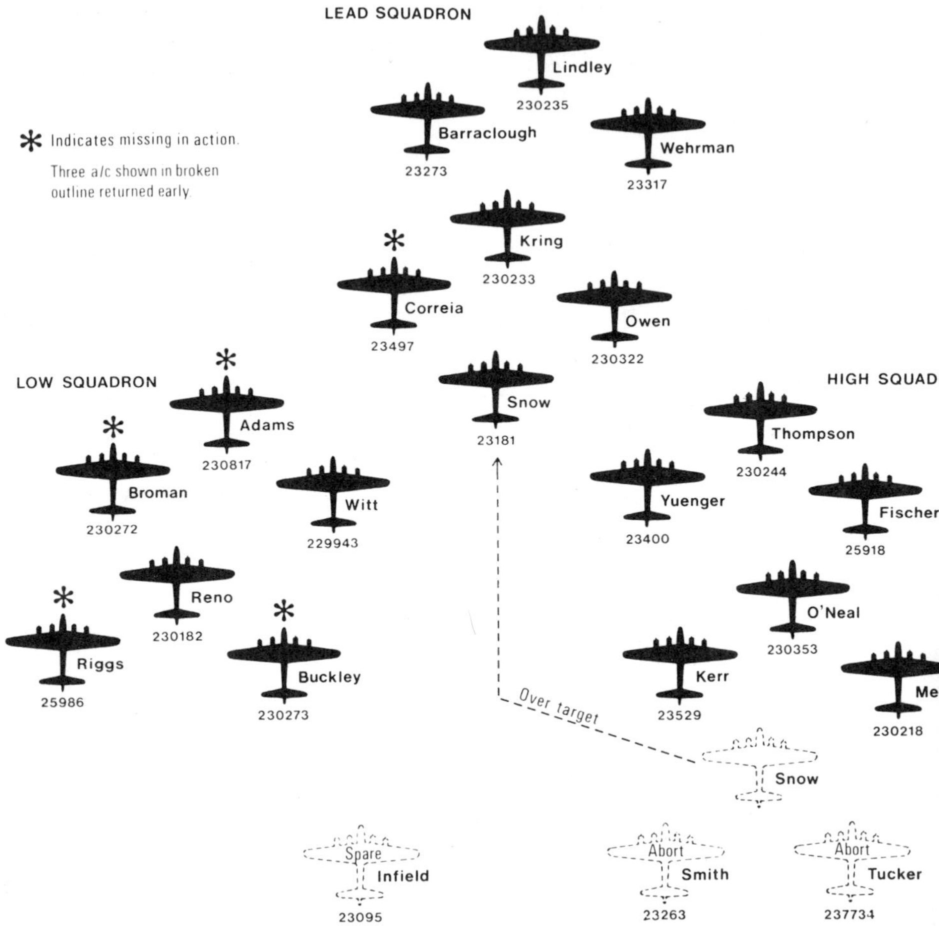

95th Bombardment Group Formation Chart for the Münster raid of 10 October 1943.

back and set course for the nearest airfield, the night-fighter base a Münster-Handorf. As we passed over Münster five minutes later at 1,00(metres, a huge cloud of smoke hung over the city. The middle of the olc town had been devastated. There had been no military target . . .

The Fortress which Sgt. Wiegand had shot down was B17I 986 *Browns' Mule* of the 95th Bomb Group, piloted by Lt John Riggs. The crew were on their 6th mission. Eight para chutes emerged from their aircraft.

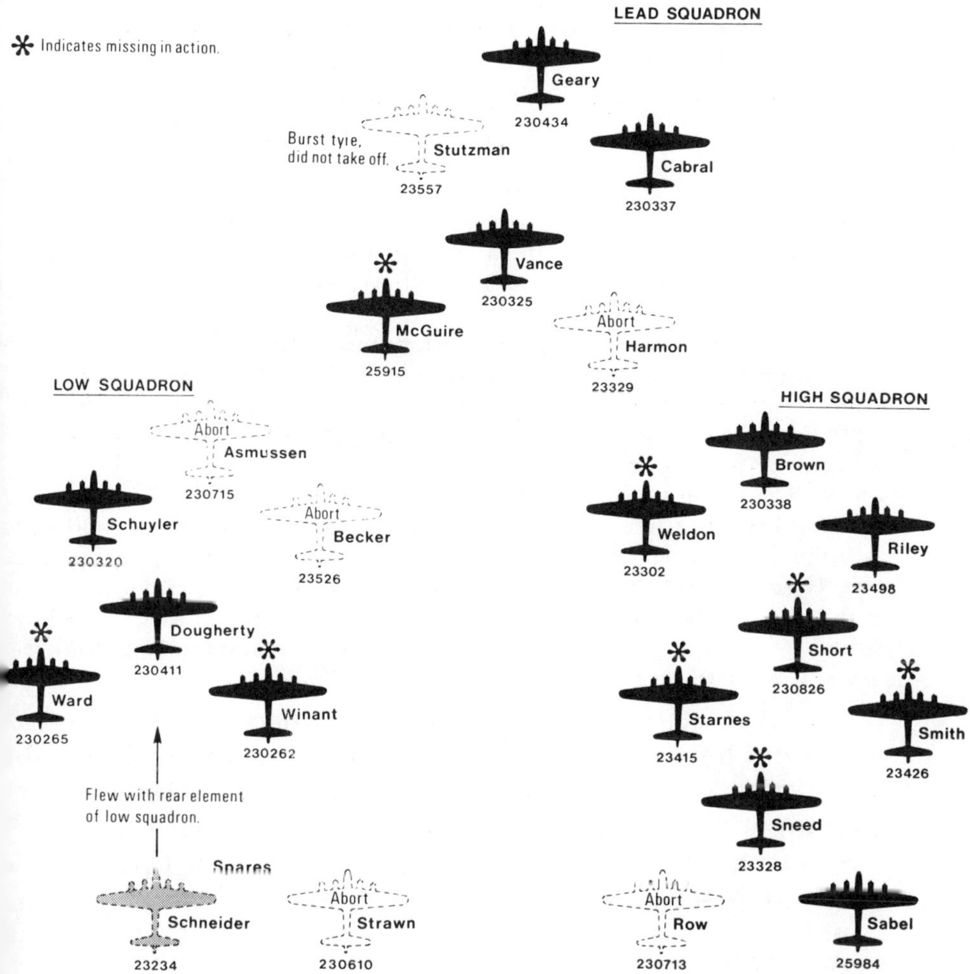

390th Bombardment Group Formation Chart for the Münster raid of 10 October 1943.

Co-Pilot Lt. Ashford Morrison recollects:

I saw Waist Gunner Sgt. Joseph Kelly wave to me and bail out of the waist door. The rest of the crew were positive his chute opened. It is my firm belief that the Germans on the ground shot and killed Kelly as he was coming down, since our other Waist Gunner, Sgt. Charles Davies, went out right after he did and was shot at by rifles.

A German interrogation officer told me that Kelly had been killed, but didn't say how, although the crews of other shot-down Fortresses from our Group shortly afterwards saw eight chutes leave our ship.

The 100th Group's *Royal Flush* was also in trouble. Said Co-Pilot "Pappy" Lewis:

By this time we had already lost our number one engine to fighters, and we had no hope of increasing our speed in level flight to catch up to the 390th Bomb Group.

After we made our turn westwards from the target, the sky suddenly seemed vacant. Our two Waist Gunners had been seriously injured and were receiving first aid from the other crew members in the rear of the ship. They were also busy looking out for fighters, but I couldn't see any serious action.

Our next problem came from our number three engine which was running rough, and evidently damaged by a hit that had opened up a large hole in our right wing. The number three oil gauge indicated a fast drop in pressure, so we reluctantly feathered the propeller while we still had enough pressure to do so.

We were losing altitude very rapidly, but it was good that we were leaving high altitude since our oxygen system had been punctured and most of it was gone. I remember seeing our Top Turret Gunner/Engineer, Sgt. Clarence Hall, spinning round in his turret. I nudged him to ask for a report on our gas supply, and he answered with a glazed look caused by anoxia from lack of oxygen. His oxygen supply hose and intercom connections were swinging completely free.

Had Sgt. Hall been able to look in a mirror at that moment he would have seen that his complexion had a slightly bluish tinge, characteristic of anoxia. The external symptoms are accompanied by an inner feeling of drowsy well-being and optimism, akin to being pleasantly intoxicated. Unless precious oxygen can be restored within minutes, then death is an absolute certainty.

Sgt. Hall said later:

We were hit by fighters, mostly 109's, coming out of the sun in flights of five or six at a time from topsides. They cut right through our formations, seemingly taking out a B17 on every pass. The 110's would line up, just out of range of our point-fives, and lob missiles at us.

Soon after we had lost two of our engines to either flak or fighters, my oxygen system was shot out. Everything was very hazy for a while and it wasn't until we were forced down to a lower altitude that I came round.

I was asked for a gas supply report, and climbed down and tried to transfer fuel from the tanks of the damaged engines to the good ones. But the fuel transfer pumps were frozen solid. I finally worked them loose, however, and completed the transfer.

By this time, our two Waist Gunners were shot up quite badly. Our Tail Gunner was hit in the butt, and I collected a nick between the eyes.

At one stage, the fighters seemed to be going down like flies all around us. We claimed fifteen. It was more a nightmare than reality.

Finding his aircraft *Pasadena Nena* completely alone after bombing the target, Pilot Lt. John Justice sought out another Group of B17's on their way home from the target, and joined up with them.

But the crew of another 100th B.G. plane, *Stymie,* was less fortunate, as Radio Operator Sgt. Carl Battin recalled:

During the short time we were over Münster we were hit by flak. Lt. John Stephens, our Pilot, immediately took us down to a lower altitude in an attempt to hedge-hop back to the Channel. We were under very severe fighter attack. We flew low over a fighter base, and the enemy swarmed in on us, forcing a belly landing. Ball Turret Gunner Sgt. Max Drudge had a 20 mm hit in his right wrist, and I had a broken arm. The rest of the crew were uninjured, but we were all taken prisoner soon afterwards.

Stymie crash-landed at Aalten, Holland six miles from the Dutch/German border.

Meanwhile, more than 200 German fighters were concentrating their efforts on the remainder of the 13th Combat Bomb Wing. The 95th Bomb Group in the Lead position, with the 390th flying 1,000 feet higher and behind them, faced the very real possibility of complete annihilation. The P47 Thunderbolts of the 56th Fighter Group were now mere minutes away from their rendezvous with the beleaguered bombers.

A small force of German fighters met the other four Bomb Groups of the 3rd Air Division just as they made their turn over Haltern towards Münster. From their altitude of almost five miles, the Fortress crews could plainly see the funeral pyres of towering black smoke which marked the crash sites of numerous B17's from the Lead Wing.

The 96th Bomb Group, leading the 45th Combat Bomb Wing, suffered the first casualty. B17G 516, with Lt. Daniel Williams at the controls, was last seen curving downwards and on fire following concentrated fighter attacks. Other 96th crews reported seeing all ten parachutes emerge in quick succession from the stricken Fortress as it spiralled earthwards.

After the 96th had successfully bombed the target, the 388th Bomb Group approached Münster, with Lt. Wisehart piloting the Lead B17 *Slightly Dangerous II.* Shortly before reaching the target, Lt. Wisehart's Fortress was rocked by a near miss from an exploding flak shell. His Bombardier, Lt. Alford, was struck in the left eye by fragments of glass shattering from his instrument panel when his bombsight was hit by ricocheting shrapnel. The delicate gyros in the bombsight were tumbled out of position, and Lt. Alford was unable to refine his sighting further. He then released the bombs by sighting with his unaffected right eye. Consequently, about 50 tons of high-explosive bombs from the formation's 18 B17's, fell harmlessly in open fields three miles short of the target.

At 1508 hours, *Little Lass,* a Fortress leading the Low Squadron of the 388th Bomb Group, was attacked by fighters immediately after dropping her bombs.

Top Turret Gunner Sgt. Raymond Harwood, describes what followed:

As we left the target area our main problem was our number three engine. It had been hit by 20 mm fire and was feathered. We had lost our intercom system earlier, and although our Pilot, Lt. Williams, had contact with other ships using the command frequency the rest of the crew had no voice communication at all.

Suddenly, a twin-engined fighter seemed to appear from nowhere off our right wing-tip. I gave him a long burst and saw his canopy fly off. But too many things were happening to follow him. Shortly thereafter, the point-five ammunition belts suddenly appeared at the top of my turret canopy. For a second this bewildered me, and I then realised that we had gone completely on our back and were in a spinning, vertical dive out of formation. Again, without interphone communication we could not receive instructions from Lt. Williams. At this point, Lt. Garver, our Navigator, tapped me on the leg and indicated to bail out. A quick glance into the cockpit revealed our Co-Pilot Lt. Rogg getting out of his seat. Our airspeed was up to around 350 mph and the altimeter was unwinding too fast to read.

I immediately put my chest chute on and dropped into the nose section crawlway. Here I found Lt. Macy, our Bombardier, who had tried to bail out without first jettisoning the nose hatch door. Consequently, he was hanging by the back straps of his chute on the curved inside hatch door. I lifted him by the chute harness at his shoulders and released him. I then closed the door, pulled the release handle which freed the hinge pins and kicked the door away. Lt. Garver then left.

Just as I bailed out we took another hit in the nose section, and I received several small fragments in the top of my head. I fell free until I stabilized on my back, pulled the ripcord and got a perfect opening. Suddenly it was so quiet that the war seemed a million miles away.

As I floated down I heard a strange sound behind me. Turning, I saw a German fighter coming straight at me, and I thought he was firing his machine-guns. Actually, he had throttled back and it was only the popping engine sounds I had heard. He banked steeply around me, and I could clearly see the pilot. He then wobbled his wings and flew away.

I landed in a high pine tree and had quite a difficult time getting down. Once on the ground, I started removing my heavy flying clothes while on the move, but before I could do so I encountered a German soldier who took me into custody to a town called Greven. It's a lucky thing he did, because soon after my landing some armed civilians appeared and I feel sure they would have shot first.

So passed Sunday, 10 October 1943, my 23rd birthday and the end of my 18th mission.

Elsewhere, the Lead 13th Combat Bomb Wing was suffering further casualties.

Miss Flower III, leading the 95th Bomb Group Low Squadron, staggered as it received a direct flak hit, and slowly glided down with an engine on fire, its propeller feathered. Captain John Adams held the plane steady enabling all his crew to bail out safely before he too, abandoned the aircraft over the Rally Point. The time was 1509 hours.

Flying left wingman and Deputy Lead to Captain Adams, was Lt. Eldon Broman, piloting B17F 272 *Fritz Blitz.* Said Navigator Lt. William Fowler:

After we had turned away from the target the FW 190's began coming in again, and at this point the Low Squadron Leader started to turn out of formation. We followed for about 30 seconds, but after it became clear that he was going down, we went full throttle back towards the formation which was now about 500 feet ahead and above us. The 190's were really boring in and two of them passed so close that I could see the pilots as they passed under us.

We then took hits in the hyraulic system under the top turret guns and fire started. The signal was given to bail out and the aircraft was put on auto-pilot. Lt. Broman and I had difficulty getting the top turret gunner's body out of the nose hatch. He had been killed by 20 mm hits. The pilot and I then bailed out, and we were picked up immediately on landing by Luftwaffe personnel.

In the radio room of *Fritz Blitz* Sgt. Warren Thomas describes the last desperate moments of his aircraft:

The fighters were now hitting us with everything they had. Suddenly a bomber that had been hit loomed over and in front of us. Our Pilot, Lt. Broman, swung clear. We were then hit by flak or a rocket, setting our hydraulic and oxygen systems ablaze. The entire bomb-bay area was on fire as was the right wing.

I fought to open the door leading to the ball turret area since it had been jammed by spent cartridge cases. Frantically I forced it open, kicking and hammering until the gunner exited and bailed out. The tail and waist gunners had already left.

I reached the waist door and jumped. Almost immediately afterwards the bomber exploded. I yanked the ripcord and was overjoyed to have the chute deploy in a normal manner. I then noticed I had several nicks and burns during my descent.

I landed in a nice, soft ploughed field, and a young lad armed with a rifle approached. He motioned me to a nearby farmhouse where his mother looked at my burns. She brought a handful of damp tea-leaves and applied them to my face which soothed the pain.

A policeman eventually arrived and escorted me and two other airmen who had also been picked up, to the local gaol. We were then taken to a Luftwaffe base. The two captured airmen carried me around wherever we went as my wounds had stiffened up and I was unable to walk. A Luftwaffe Doctor dressed my burns and lacerations, and he informed me I would be taken to a prison at Lingen, Germany, to recover from my wounds.

I thought myself lucky to be alive at all after 25 missions.

A traumatic scene was witnessed by a 95th Bomb Group Co-Pilot, Lieutenant Paul Perceful in B17F 218:

I vividly recall seeing a B17 which had been simply cut in two halves by the concentrated cannon fire from a German fighter. I think that the mental process does strange things to you at times like that because the whole incident, from start to finish, appeared to me to happen in slow motion. The Fortress was struck and slowly came apart at the radio room. The front half of the fuselage, wings, still functioning engines, and the cockpit, seemed to slowly rise upwards, completely separate from the rear fuselage and tail unit. Then both halves twisted and tumbled down and away. The battle continued without respite.

Lt. Lesley Kring piloting *Rhapsody in Flak* of the leading 95th Bomb Group recalls:

Following the bomb run Sergeant Cunningham, our Tail Gunner, called me on the interphone and yelled, "Move this damn airplane around a little . . . Jerry is behind us and shooting rockets . . . I can't reach him . . ." I took instant evasive action even though I was leading the second flight of three ships in our Lead Squadron.

Almost immediately after that, while glancing over the left wing at numbers one and two engines, I saw an air-to-air rocket streak past about a foot above the wing. My heart skipped a beat . . .

The tail gunners in the 95th Bomb Group's High Squadron had an exceptional view of aircraft in distress belonging to their own Group, the 390th flying 1,000 feet above and behind, and the 100th Bomb Group flying 1,000 feet below and to their right.

Lt. Theodore Bozarth, Navigator, *Heavenly Daze,* 95th Bomb Group recalls:

During and after the bomb run our tail gunner kept up a running commentary on the battle; ". . . two Forts from the Low Group going down . . . both on fire . . . six chutes from one . . . B17 from the High Group leaving formation . . . one engine feathered . . . .under control . . . no chutes yet . . . there goes another one from our Low Squadron . . . two . . . three . . . four chutes . . ."

It only seemed a matter of time before it became our turn to come under the hammer.

« « « » » »

The 2nd Air Task Force's nine Bombardment Groups were now approaching the I.P. of Haltern. Rapidly overhauling the rear formations were P47's of the 4th Fighter Group on schedule to escort the bombers through to Münster and thence cover their withdrawal.

The 1st Air Division, too, had several abortive B17's mainly due to the excessive drag associated with externally slung 1,000 pound bombs, one under each wing, which six of the nine Groups carried. The remainder of the bomb load — 4,000 pounds — was carried in the bomb bays of each Fortress. Advanced power settings — in order to maintain formation — resulted in overheated engines and flaking of the piston rings. Consequently, a number of externally carried bombs had been jettisoned in the North Sea.

Leading the 1st Air Division was Major Howard Turner in B17F 461 flown by Captain Sterling Basler of the 92nd Bomb Group, located at Podington. Just six miles short of Haltern, a burst of flak struck the ball turret in Captain Basler's Fortress, mortally wounding the gunner. His interphone transmitter button was jammed in the "on" position, and the dying gunner's screams prevented all crew inter-communication. In the resultant confusion, as the two Waist Gunners tried frantically to remove their comrade from his turret in the now smoke-filled B17, Captain Basler veered his bomber to the left while his Navigator, Lt. Kissinger, desperately sought in vain to pinpoint and locate Haltern. The remaining 14 Fortresses of the 92nd Bomb Group, and the two following Groups of the 40th Combat Bomb Wing, followed Captain Basler's turn, still short of the I.P. The Wing was now on a direct course to Coesfeld, 20 miles West of Münster, and another important rail link with the industrial Ruhr.

The escorting P47 Thunderbolts encountered very little opposition as the bulk of the Luftwaffe fighter force were still heavily engaged in battle against the B17's of the 3rd Air Division in the Münster area.

Rocket-equipped Me 110's of the Zerstoerergeschwader (Destroyer) Group ZG/26, "Horst Wessel", were guided unerringly by Ground Control into the fray to intercept the 13th Combat Bomb Wing, now withdrawing towards Holland. The 35 Me 110's approached the bombers from behind and, from a range of 800 yards, loosed a whole salvo of 21cm. rockets into the bomber formation.

About 70 air-to-air rockets, each weighting 240 pounds, sped from the launching tubes under the wings of the Me 110's. The 80 pound warhead missiles were detonated by a time fuse set to explode after four seconds of flight, as the Luftwaffe had at this time no effective proximity fuses. A telescopic sight with graduation marks on it to indicate the span of a B17 at different ranges, was used as a range-finder by the German pilots. They had to be accurate within 60 yards if the attack was to stand any chance of inflicting any significant damage. Their judgement was to prove terribly effective.

Tech Supply, a 390th Bomb Group Fortress commanded by Lt. John Winant, Jr., the son of the then United States Ambassador to Great Britain, took a direct hit and immediately exploded. As the flaming wreckage plummetted to earth five miles below, six parachutes emerged at rapid intervals before the remains of the bomber crashed at Ladbergen 10 miles northwest of Münster.

B17F *Miss Fortune*, flying in the 390th's High Squadron and piloted by Lt. Wade Sneed, shuddered as it received a direct rocket hit. At once the doomed Fortress broke cleanly in half at the waist gun windows. The front half nosed up and collided with another B17, *Miss Behavin* flown by Lt. George Starnes. Eight whirling propellers were instantly transformed into horrific quarter-ton buzz-saws, speeding at 2,300 revolutions per minute. Hundreds of gallons of high octane petrol gushed and streamed from wing tanks sliced open by blurring blades. Following B17's in the High Squadron frantically manoeuvred to avoid the now exploding Fortresses in an effort to dodge wreckage and bodies being hurled in all directions.

The stricken aircraft's Radio Operator, Sgt. Clarence Payne, recalls:

> It was our 13th mission over Germany. We had been engaged with many fighters when, shortly after dropping our bombs, I heard and felt a very loud explosion. It threw me upwards and I was stuck between the ring carriage and the gun-mount. I found myself fighting to get in or out, when another explosion blew me out of the position in which I had been trapped. I instinctively pulled my ripcord and all that was left of our ship was many different sized pieces of metal fluttering to the ground. I saw three parachutes way below me.
>
> I was knocked unconscious upon hitting the ground. When I came to, three German soldiers were pointing to my watch. It said 5 o'clock, and they were trying to tell me that I had been unconscious for about two hours. They took me to the gaol in Münster where I saw three of my crew members, Waist Gunners John Danielson and William Wenckins, and Tail Gunner Carl Spirito. They too, had been thrown clear following the collision.

Only Tail Gunner Robert Coles survived from the 10-man crew of Lt. Starnes' bomber. The widely-scattered wreckage of both aircraft crashed at Burgsteinfurt, near Saarbeck. The 15 crewmen who were killed were buried in local Protestant and Catholic cemeteries with full military honours. Major Karl Boehm-Tettelbach, the Commander of ZG/26, was later credited with the destruction of both B17's.

Lead Navigator, Lt. 'Gus' Mencow, flying in *Pistol Packin' Mama* saw all three B17's from his Group go down as a result of this latest rocket attack. He said:

> It was absolutely incredible to me that anyone could have possibly survived those explosions. Huge sheets of crimson flame, pieces of wreckage and debris flying in every direction . . . then eventually and miraculously, these pitifully few white parachutes opening and drifting far below, which our gunners reported by interphone.

Another witness, Sergeant Bob Banta, Radio Operator, *Rose Marie,* 390th B.G., recalls:

Following the collision one of our gunners reported a crewman being hurled clear without a parachute. Another airman fell clear with his chute but pulled the cord too soon. As it billowed out and arrested his fall a large flame from an explosion licked the canopy and ignited it. He descended faster and faster, trailing a thin column of smoke as his parachute was consumed.

To my right a Fortress exploded with a blinding flash into countless small pieces — the four flaming engines streaking earthwards. For endless minutes the scene was a fantastic panorama of the ultimate in air warfare and one to stun the imagination of even the most hardened and experienced combat flyers.

An ironic thought came to mind. Hollywood could never reproduce scenes such as these . . . Never!! . . . Never!!

« « « » » »

Heinz Hessling, a teenage student at Beckum School, south of Münster, was a Luftwaffe Helper manning the 2 cm flak battery protecting the Dortmund-Ems Canal bridges at Joanning, 7 kilometres to the north of Münster. He remembers:

In addition to the 88 cm and 2 cm flak batteries defending Münster our Battery Commander informed us that mobile 105 cm batteries, mounted on railway flat waggons, happened to be located at Gievenbeck 4 kilometres south of Münster, near the Aa Lake, on that Sunday.

At approximately 1500 hours I saw through my binoculars the largest formation of B17's, about 30, I had ever seen approaching our position from the south. They were flying at an altitude that was well beyond the range of our light 2 cm flak battery.

As they flew over, about 3 kilometeres to the west of our position, a Fortress suddenly exploded. Through my binoculars I could clearly see the wings, engines and fuselage slowly disentegrating in mid-air. Seconds later another Fortress, in the immediate vicinity of the first B17, also exploded and seemed to fly apart. Then slowly the wreckage of both aircraft, trailing long plumes of black smoke, curved downwards and crashed to earth north of our position. *(Author's note:* These two B17's were almost certainly *Miss Fortune* and *Miss Behavin* from the 390th Bomb Group's High Squadron.)

I ran towards higher ground and looked towards Münster. Huge clouds of black smoke were billowing up from the city.The explosions from bombs, and our 88 cm and 105 cm flak batteries sounded like thunder in the distance. I also saw several parachutes slowly drifting down.

Spider, another 390th Fortress in the High Squadron, was

hit by flak while over Münster. The burst killed Tail Gunner George Emerich and severely damaged the rudder. The Pilot, Lt. William Smith, and Co-Pilot, Lt. Joseph Miller, fought a losing battle to regain the comparative safety of the formation. Seven parachutes billowed away from the bomber before it broke in two at the radio room and exploded, crashing at Isendorf, 12 miles northwest of Münster. The crew had completed 18 previous missions.

Recalled Navigator Lt. Donald Callahan:

> Lt. Smith often mentioned to me that he as First Pilot, should be the last to leave the plane in an emergency. Both pilots prevented the aircraft going into a spin, although it was flying very erratically after we had been hit.

Top Turret Gunner, Sgt. William Nicholas, added:

> I went to the nose escape hatch and bailed out after Lt. Smith, who was holding the ship steady, shouted at me, "Go ahead, Nick . . . you're holding up the show . . . jump!"

The two pilots had sacrificed their lives for their crew.

From a full frontal attack by an Me 110 a rocket tore through the right wing, fortunately without exploding, of another 390th Fortress, *Eightball,* flown by Lt. William Cabral. The B17 Navigator, Lt. Gordon Wharton, relates:

> The missile struck our right wing, about 12 feet from the tip, almost severing it from the aircraft. We began to fall in an erratic fashion and the crew was notified to prepare for bail-out. Miraculously, our two Pilots, Bill Cabral and Dick Perry, with the assistance of Bombardier Dean Ferris, who stood behind them and helped pull back the control wheels, succeeded in forcing the nose up and setting the airplane up on the auto-pilot at an altitude of 18,000 feet.
>
> The rocket had badly affected the airflow vital to the "lift" of the right wing. As we could not rejoin the formation, we came under heavy and persistent attack from enemy fighters. I then gave our pilots a heading back to England.

Bringing up the rear of the 3rd Air Division, the 385th Bomb Group (aptly named "Van's Valiants" after their popular Group Commander, Colonel Elliot Vandevanter) were the next to suffer two further losses directly after bombing, virtually within a minute of each other at 1512 hours. Recalls Top Turret Gunner, Sgt. Jack Leahy of B17G 155:

> We were on our 19th mission, well past the average, and we all knew that we were on "borrowed time." Our regular ship, *Vibrant Virgin,* had been

lost over Bremen two days before with another crew. It proved to be an ill omen. Consequently, we were flying a replacement B17G.

As we approached the target area, we came under flak and fighter attack. I got a 190 right over our aircraft while shooting nearly vertically. It was the first time I had been quick enough to catch anything smaller than a two-seater, and I was quite pleased. After the bomb load dropped we continued on course for 30 seconds or so. As the right wing rode up for our left turn, after the bomb run, we were hit consecutively by the shrapnel from two near misses which set our left wing on fire and damaged the controls to some degree. Sgt. Sanborn, our Tail Gunner, was hit twice in the leg by one of those flak bursts, but he still had mobility.

Our Pilots had partial control as we pulled away from the formation, firing off our ammunition. We watched the fire grow in intensity until the whole wing was a sheet of flame. Lt. John Pettenger, our Pilot, had no alternative but to bail us out.

Our pay, and our ammo, had run out at about the same time. So we did the drill.

Lt. Pettenger added:

The fighters were firing on us, and more were getting into line to fire, so we bailed out. The ship blew up soon after we left it.

I landed in a field on a small farm. A farmer with a double-barrelled shotgun captured me. The military then arrived and took me to an airfield near Münster. The remainder of my crew were already there. In fact, Lt. Dorney, my Bombardier, had landed right in the middle of the airfield. On landing, he pulled off the long white scarf he always wore, and headed for the nearest boundary fence. But a few uncomfortably-close rifle shots changed his mind.

Recalled Lt. William Whitlow, Pilot of B17G 539:

Shortly before turning on our bomb run we ran into heavy fighter resistance. As we turned towards Münster we received a direct hit in our number two engine by an FW 190 from 12 o'clock low. We feathered the propeller. At that altitude it was impossible to remain in formation with only three engines. However, we remained close enough to drop our bombs with the Group. Flak was heavy, and we incurred substantial damage to the tail section and lost about four feet from our left wing-tip.

Immediately after releasing the bombs, being a "straggler" we headed for the deck. No luck!! The fighter pursuit was tremendous. We then lost number four engine to fire. Sgt. Richards, Tail Gunner, reported additional damage to the tail section, and also his personal injuries, but he stayed with it. Our ball turret became silent, and we feared the worst for Sgt. Ennis, its occupant. However, he managed to climb out of the turret with substantial injuries. This left our underside free to the fighters. Sgt. Schaumburg, our Left Waist Gunner reported serious injuries to Sgt. Walker, our other Waist Gunner. About this time, Sgt. Ashcraft, Radio

Operator, advised dense smoke in the radio compartment, with the comment, "Let's get the hell out of here . . ."

I was still hoping to reach the "deck" for protection, but then we lost number three engine. With our loss of firepower and the heavy concentration of fighters, it became obvious that we could not make it. So I gave the order to bail out at about 15,000 feet. A later report stated that our ship had disintegrated shortly after I left. It crashed near Nijverdal, in Eastern Holland.

During the battle, my crew claimed five downed fighters and two probables. They did a magnificent job.

Lt. Whitlow continues:

Following the long, tiring mission the previous day to Marienburg, I had a very sore back and my buttocks was bruised from sitting on my parachute buckles. This set the stage for a near miracle. Having released my leg straps for comfort, I unaccountably forgot to fasten them again before I bailed out of the bomb bay. Fortunately, I am a relatively small man, about that time weighing around 150 pounds. When the chute snapped open I slipped halfway through the harness, hanging on by my hands and by extreme outward pressure with my shoulders, the chest strap having slipped up under my armpits. The front portion of the chest strap was now across my eyes and I couldn't look down or sideways, only upwards.

As I was totally unable to anticipate my landing clearly, I sprained both ankles when I finally hit the ground. As luck would have it, I had landed on a grassy meadow which, of course, was as soft as any terrain I could have chosen. I am certain that a harder surface would have broken both my legs.

A parachutist descends at a rate of 1,000 feet a minute. Lt. Whitlow's ordeal had lasted for a nerve-jangling fifteen minutes and unbeknown to the breathless and pain-wracked airman, every foot of that descent had been observed with more than the usual amount of interest from the ground.

Although Lt. Forrest Poore and Lt. Irving Frank, two other 385th Pilots, reported ten parachutes coming from Lt. Whitlow's Fortress, Sgt's. Thomas Ennis and Howard Walker died from their wounds.

The 92nd and 306th Bomb Groups of the 40th Combat Bomb Wing, leading the 1st Air Division, bombed Coesfeld at 1511 hours. The third Group in the Wing, the 305th, had realised the error during the bomb-run, bypassed Coesfeld, and swung around in a gradual right-hand turn to attack the primary target of Münster from the northwest.

The next Wing (91st, 351st and 381st Bomb Groups) of the 1st Air Division had formed a Composite Group of three Squadrons en route totalling 16 aircraft due to several aborting B17's. The Wing had set out from England with 27 Fortresses. As the 1st Combat Bomb Wing approached the primary target from the I.P. (Haltern), it was on a direct collision course over Münster with the 305th Bomb Group, now coming in from the northwest.

A potential disaster was averted as the 13 B17's of the 305th veered desperately away at the last possible moment. Cursing and sweating, the pilots of the 305th swung northwards to seek another target. "SNAFU! . . . SNAFU! . . . (Situation normal, all fouled up!)" sounded vehemently and simultaneously through a hundred headphones.

At 1517 hours, the 1st Combat Bomb Wing unloaded its 1,000 lbs. high-explosive and 100 lbs. incendiary bombs through the dense smoke and dust clouds now boiling upwards from the primary target. The bombers were escorted to Münster by Thunderbolts of the 4th Fighter Group which thereby established a new penetration depth record. A number of these P47 pilots had served in the famous RAF 'Eagle' Squadrons. (Americans who had volunteered their services to Britain before their country had entered the war).

Enemy fighter activity during the bomb run had been sparse, and the P47 pilots were only briefly engaged. Lt. Duane Beeson damaged an FW 190 and Lt. Archie Chatterley damaged an Me 410.

Feldwebel Alois Slaby, a Radio Operator/Gunner with the Me 410-equipped II Staffel of Zerstoerergeschwader 26 (Destroyer), remembers:

> We were based at Hesepe, 30 kilometres north of Osnabruck. The 4th and 5th Squadrons were also based at Hesepe and the 6th Staffel at nearby Vorden. My pilot was Leutnant Friedrich Stehle.
>
> Although the alarm had been sounded sometime earlier, we didn't take off until 1420 hours. With Leutnant Stehle leading our Staffel we headed westwards. We didn't know at that time which city was being attacked but later on radio instructions from our ground-control centre directed us to the enemy bombers. We then saw the city of Münster burning.
>
> We were too late to prevent the initial bombardment, but we had to try to

stop any further attacks. We then sighted a formation of B17's while we were southeast of the burning city. Leutnant Stehle then manoeuvred into position behind the bombers and opened fire. Dense smoke immediately poured from a B17 and as we emerged from the clouds of smoke there were bombers over, under and in front of us. Suddenly it was raining bombs all around us and the air was full of metal.

Our Squadron then tried to launch another attack on the B17's but it wasn't easy. Firstly, the enemy bombers were not flying in such close formation as before the bombing and were taking evasive action. Secondly, enemy fighters suddenly appeared and our close attacking formation was split up into individual planes and dispersed. Our wingman, however, managed to rejoin us and we eventually reached airspace over Holland.

Then we saw an Me 410 from our Squadron heading eastwards with one engine feathered. The pilot told us over the radio that he'd been in a dogfight with P-47's and was having difficulty in getting back to base due to compass and direction-finder failure. We turned back to escort him and hopefully protect him from enemy fighters. During this turning manoeuvre we inadvertantly put ourselves in great danger.

Then it happened . . .

Leutnant Friedrich Stehle describes ensuing events:

Dogfighting in the Me 410 was to be avoided at all costs. It was too heavy and could not turn sharply enough or maneouvre very well at the high altitudes at which the B17's and B24's flew. Our top speed was only 15 m.p.h. faster than that of the B17, and against the Thunderbolts it was like entering the Kentucky Derby on a carthorse. The added drag of four rockets and their launching tubes did not help matters.

As we turned, we saw four or five Thunderbolts coming in to attack us out of the sun. During the short exchange of fire, I heard a "Wrrrrrush" and I thought, "Now we've really had it . . .". We had taken about 25 hits through the right side of the fuselage between myself and Alois Slaby. The whole cockpit canopy literally disappeared and the left engine was hit in its cooling system. The engine rapidly over-heated and was successfully shut down. We were now at the Thunderbolt's mercy, but for some reason they left us alone.

Radio-Operator/Gunner Alois Slaby recalls:

During the exchange of fire with a P-47 something struck my head hard and I suddenly noticed our cockpit canopy had gone. I wanted to bail out but the pilot shook his head. I then radioed an S.O.S. and almost immediately afterwards I blacked out.

Leutnant Stehle continues:

It was extremely difficult to keep our aircraft flying on only one engine with the additional drag with the canopy sections gone. But by using almost full power on the good engine we were just able to maintain an altitude of 3,000 feet. We were ready to bail out at any time but we managed to hold on and land safely at Hesepe. It was the end of our 62nd combat flight and we felt very fortunate to have survived it.

Feldwebel Slaby concludes:

I regained consciousness as I was being lifted from the aircraft and taken to the base hospital. I was suffering from exposure and an acute lack of oxygen. However, I quickly recovered and I flew again in the next big American raid against Schweinfurt shortly afterwards.

« « « » » »

Almost at the same time as the 1st Wing was bombing Münster, two of the three Groups of the 41st Wing (384th and 303rd) bringing up the rear of the 1st Air Division, released their bombs on a now blazing Coesfeld.

Recalled Captain 'Ev' Frink, Lead Pilot in the 384th Fortress *Patches:*

Although I had two Navigators on my crew that day because we were the Lead ship, one of them, Lt. "Red" Hegstad, had his interphone cut out while we were crossing the North Sea with near disastrous consequences. As a result, we took a course into the target area which was too far south and we hit the northern tip of the Ruhr Valley, notorious for having the most powerful flak defences in the world. The 88 mm gunners had our range and altitude, and at that time I very much doubted whether we would ever make it back to England. But after what seemed an eternity we got through the barrage and headed north for our target.

Several towns in the vicinity were on fire and smoking from hits by earlier Groups. Numerous smoke screens added to the confusion. What we thought was Münster had already been hit very hard, but this later turned out to be Coesfeld.

During the bomb run I had much difficulty in setting up the auto-pilot. After I had turned over the controls to Lt. Clyde Carlson, our Bombardier, the first turn that he tried to make almost threw us out of formation. I immediately un-clutched the auto-pilot and told Clyde that we would fly the run manually. This was done, and a very good pattern on the town was observed.

P-47 Thunderbolts gave us excellent close support throughout.

The 41st Wing's third Bomb Group, the 379th, had seen Captain Frink's Lead Fortress fire flares as it passed over Haltern on a northerly heading.

Recalls Captain Joseph Wall, Lead Navigator in B17F 237:

We then saw Münster burning off to our right, but the other two Groups seemed to be "essing" and we thought they were trying to get into a better position to attack the Primary target. We then followed them further towards the east. However, we saw them drop their bombs on a town we thought to be Coesfeld, which was already burning from the hits of the earlier Groups. Our Pilot then asked me for another target of opportunity while we were still heading north.

A 95th Bomb Group Fortress commanded by Lt. Lionel Correia, then came under concentrated attack by fighters over Greven, northwest of Münster. Nine parachutes spilled fom the blazing bomber before it eventually exploded in the air and crashed near the Dutch/German border.

Over Emsdetten, northwest of Münster, Captain Robert Brown, piloting *Cabin in the Sky,* the Lead B17 of the 390th's badly-mauled High Squadron, spoke tersely to warn his crew of the streams of white vapour trails now closing menacingly in on the formation: "Ahead . . . Eleven o'clock high . . . Thirty-six more . . . fighters . . ."

Tail Gunner Sgt. 'Ike' Adamson, flying in the 390th's Fortress *Miss Carry* recollects:

We had been under the most concentrated attack of all my missions. It had continued without a pause for a full 25 minutes and by then I was sure that it was only a matter of time before the whole Wing was completely wiped out. Remember that we were still over Germany at this time. Suddenly, the interphone came alive with everybody seeming to shout and yell at once. "They're P47's . . . Little Friends!! Little Friends . . .!!"

At first I was bewildered, because I still could not see any signs of our escort, only more German fighters lining up for yet another attack from the rear. I strained forward and looked up from my cramped position in the tail turret. I'll never forget that sight . . . big, ugly, red-nosed Thunderbolts hurtling down in almost 90 degree dives. One after another, in quick succession, they swept down firing in short bursts trying to break up the enemy formations which, I am sure, never knew what hit them.

The P47's were the most beautiful sight in the world. It was a very emotional moment for us all.

Lt. Douglas Gordon-Forbes, Bombardier, *Cabin in the Sky,* 390th B.G., recalls:

It is difficult to adequately express the feelings which swept over me at that moment. I felt like yelling and praying at the same time. Our Group was being decimated. Our ammunition was almost exhausted, empty cartridge cases were piled almost a foot deep on the floor. Down below, our ball-turret gunner tracked each enemy fighter, protecting the ships belly whenever a Jerry came near. Only his guns were empty.

Suddenly I felt completely drained and spent as though I'd lived a hundred years in those last twenty five minutes.

The 56th fighter Group ("Zemke's Wolfpack") had taken off from their base at Halesworth, Suffolk, through worsening weather conditions at 1400 hours. Poor visibility and low cloud had made take-off and assembly extremely hazardous. They flew a direct course to the rendezvous point at an altitude of 30,000 feet.

Upon sighting the bombers, now withdrawing 6,000 feet lower, the Thunderbolt pilots led by Major David Schilling, could see the carnage below as the German fighters bored in mercilessly on the dwindling and beleagured Fortress formations.

P47 Pilot Lt. Robert Johnson remembers his surprise attack:

We sighted the "Big Friends" west of the burning city and suffering grievously from a savage mauling by swarms of single and twin-engine fighters. We immediately dropped our belly tanks.

Conditions were ideal for a "bounce" — the sun was directly behind us as we plunged down from high altitude at full power. All the German pilots could see was the glaring sun instead of our planes.

The sky seemed filled with German fighters, black crosses everywhere! I lined up on an Me 110, one of three as they dived shallowly to get into range to fire rockets into the bombers. The pilot, warned by his gunner, twisted and turned to evade me. My P47 responded to every move of the rudder and stick like the thoroughbred it was. One short burst, eight streams of bullets from my guns converged on the Me 110 which instantly blew up. I was so close to him that my Thunderbolt shook from the explosion and I heard and felt chunks of metal thudding against my plane as it hurtled through the smoke and debris of the shattered aircraft.

I hauled back on the stick and at full throttle zoomed back up to the safety of altitude. Everywhere I looked I saw FW 190's, Me 109's, Me 110's, and the new Me 410's. I levelled off and saw three FW 190's below closing in on the B17's. I was now the only P47 between them and the bombers. I immediately dived to intercept them.

At our tremendous closing speed it was a 90 degree deflection shot. Aiming ahead of the leader I opened fire. White flashes appeared all over the German fighter, the cockpit shattered and the plane exploded. Very shortly after that, my aircraft was hit by cannon fire which severed the rudder cable and I nearly bailed out there and then, but by using the rudder trim tabs I had sufficient manoeuvrebility to ease round in a gradual turn and head west for home.

That FW 190 had brought my total up to five aerial victories. I was now an "Ace!" Strangely, I felt more elated about getting number five than my precarious position warranted. I started calling for help, and suddenly found myself in the battle area again. Bombers and fighters all over the place. Right in front of me another FW 190 . . . I prepared to fire.

A Thunderbolt dropped like a stone, guns blazing, and before I could fire the German aircraft disintegrated into flying wreckage. The P47 kept diving, the pilot had spotted another target below. While I was climbing, I saw two more of our P47's and headed towards them.

Major David Schilling also became an "Ace" during the mission by destroying an FW 190. Summing up Major Schilling's ability as a Pilot, Colonel 'Hub' Zemke said of him:

Since April 1943, when the 56th became operational in England, he'd emerged from a jovial, carefree and likeable junior pilot to a hard-driving, cool-headed and aggressive combat leader.

Although heavily outnumbered, the 56th Fighter Group battled courageously and skillfully to prevent the Luftwaffe's thrusts at the strung-out bomber formations. Their valiant efforts could not, however, prevent the further loss of four 13th Wing Fortresses.

A 390th Bomb Group crew on their 18th mission under the command of Lt. Edward Weldon, went down at Diesettrup, 20 miles north of Münster. Flying as an Observer in that aircraft was Lt. Keith Neubaur, the Station Gunnery Officer at Framlingham. It was his first mission.

Narrates Top Turret Gunner, Sgt. Marion Laird:

The name of our regular ship was *The Bad Penny*,but due to it being battle-damaged during the Marienburg raid the day before, we flew a spare B17. After bombing the assigned target, an 88 mm shell went completely through our number four engine and exploded about 25 yards above us. It set the engine on fire, and we were forced to leave the formation.

We dropped to about 7,000 feet heading for the Dutch coast and were attacked almost immediately by a flight of FW 190's. During the short running battle we received major damage. A fighter straffed the full length of our right wing to just short of the cockpit, which increased the flames. Lt. Weldon hit the bail-out bell, and I went out through the nose escape hatch with the Navigator, Co-Pilot, Bombardier, Observer and finally the Pilot. The rest of our crew bailed out via the rear door and the bomb-bay. Our ship exploded on its way down very soon after Lt. Weldon had jumped clear.

All 11 crew-members were unhurt, except Tail Gunner Sgt. Harames, who received some 20 mm fragments in his left leg. Radio Operator Sgt. Roth, was on the loose for three days before being captured. The remainder were picked up almost immediately on landing.

Patsy Ann III a 95th Bomb Group Fortress, piloted by Lt. William Buckley, curved slowly away from the formation with both its wing fuel tanks blazing and a fire in the radio room. Navigator Lt. Robert Barto recalls:

Our interphone was not working during this emergency. A few seconds later we received a direct hit, either by flak or rocket, which broke off the entire tail assembly, and the plane went into a spinning dive. Our Bombardier, Lt. Ed Jannly, and I, bailed out through the nose exit hatch. I then saw our aircraft crash and explode in a corner of the same field where I landed.

Co-Pilot Lt. Frederick Kennie, Tail Gunner Edward Burlingham and Waist Gunner Donald Reinhart also managed to parachute to safety before their B17 crashed near Lingen, 25 miles northwest of Münster.

The eighth 390th Bomb Group Fortress to go down was *Pinky*. Its Pilot, Lt. Frank Ward, managed to reach Eastern Holland before ordering his crew to abandon the aircraft. Navigator Lt. Harold Wolosin, revealed:

After we had bombed Münster our plane was severely damaged by both flak and fighter fire. We had to leave the formation near Enschede, and after it became obvious that we were not going to make it, Lt. Ward ordered us to bail out. All ten crewmen got clear of the ship, but I learned later that our Bombardier, Sgt. Lester Look, had tragically broken his neck on landing. Earlier, while over the target area, Sgt. Look had displayed exceptional coolness and courage in shooting down two German fighters. I was unfortunately unsuccessful in my efforts and recommendations for an award for him.

Eight crew members of this Fortress were taken prisoner. The remaining survivor, Tail Gunner Sgt. Theodore Converse, was lucky enough to find friendly help.

There were now only two 100th Bomb Group Fortresses still in the air.

Lt. John Justice, at the controls of *Pasadena Nena,* describes the last desperate minutes of his aircraft:

I saw a group of B17's to our left returning from the target area. They were some five or six miles away and lower, so we dived to meet them and joined their formation, taking a position between all three squadrons. It seemed a safe place, and we headed homewards. But the formation soon came under attack, and we took a hit in our number four engine which sent us into a fast spin.

From about 20,000 feet, my Co-Pilot John Shields and I, tried to pull the aircraft out of the spin. At about 5,000 feet we succeeded, but the plane was still in a dive. John and I continued to try and right the aircraft and we levelled off below 1,000 feet, at which time we knew the rest of the crew had bailed out.

Without discussing it, John and I decided to head for home, crewless and crippled. The number four engine was still on the aircraft, but there was no cowling on it all the way back into the wing. We were able to control the Fortress and John decided to take up a position in the top turret to protect us from further attack. We had no communication, so it is my supposition that John saw a German fighter following us down and rotated the turret to take aim. The German, seeing the turret move, realised that there was still life aboard and sprayed us from one wing tip to the other with 20 mm cannon shells. Both wings were completely on fire, and the whole side of the cockpit, my side, was blown away.

John, realising our situation, came forward from the top turret. There was blood across his forehead. He reached under my seat and handed me my parachute, then he put his own on and bailed out through the nose escape hatch. I then clipped on my chute and headed for the bomb bay. The top turret had been turned, so I was unable to get out that way. For some reason, I stepped up into the cockpit to retrieve something and then went down and out the nose exit hatch. To this day I do not know what it was I took from the cockpit.

My chute snapped open at 500 feet from the ground. All I could see were trees and a sandy patch ahead. I decided to try and land in the sand. Not knowing how to guide a chute, I grabbed an armfull of shroud lines hoping to make the sandy area, but found that I was going away from it. I released the shroud lines and decided to drift into the trees. Fortunately, the trees had been planted at the same time and were all about the same size. When my chute collapsed, after being caught in the upper branches, I was left suspended about two feet from the ground. Apart from the wound on the back of my neck received when part of the cockpit had been blown away, I was unhurt. I unbuckled my chute harness and dropped to the ground. At about that time, to the south, the aircraft crashed about a mile away.

What Lt. Justice did not know was that his plane crashed two miles east of Harskamp near Barneveld in Central Holland, and that the bodies of Lt. John Shields and Tail Gunner Sgt. Gaetano Sportelli were soon to be found near the scene of the crash by German search parties.

The 13th Combat Bomb Wing had penetrated the target area with 49 Fortresses. Only 24 now remained, some having sustained severe battle damage, to continue their withdrawal towards the Dutch coast.

Captain Ellis Scripture, 95th Bomb Group Lead Navigator, remembers the bravery of his colleagues:

One memory stands out on this and other difficult missions which I flew. That was the calm way young men reacted to extreme danger, and especially during the vicious air battles with German fighters. This stands out as a lasting tribute to the men of the 8th Air Force.

On this mission, calm prevailed in all situations. When planes were going down, we heard their Pilots say over the command radio such things as: 'We're hit badly' . . . 'We're going down' . . . 'Carry on' . . . 'We'll be O.K.' . . . 'We'll see you later' . . . No panic, no rapid talk, just men doing a difficult and hazardous job well.

On the way home, the remnants of the 390th and the single survivor from the 100th gathered around us. We heard one statement from the Group Leader of the 390th. Speaking to Colonel Gerhart he said, "Thanks, it was a good show with a great lead."

But the battle was not yet over for the 1st Air Division.

While in the Münster area, a 91st Bomb Group Fortress had sustained fatal damage. Said Co-Pilot of B17G 737, Lt. Joseph Rose:

We were hit by flak or fighters in our number two engine from which streamed dense smoke. We tried to feather the propeller, but without luck. Smoke continued to pour from the engine nacelle for the next ten minutes. We were now well behind the formation with no hope of catching up. Our Pilot, Lt. Earl Verrill, then gave the order to bail out over Holland as we were losing both power and altitude. After checking that everyone was out, I jumped via the nose exit hatch while Lt. Verrill held the ship steady.

It wasn't until some time later that I learned that Lt. Verrill had crash-landed the plane following a complete loss of power, near Apeldoorn, Holland, and that our Bombardier, John Lilley, had pulled his ripcord too soon as he went out of the nose hatch. His opening chute caught on the horizontal stabiliser of the tailplane and he was tragically dragged to his death.

« « « » » »

Münster's railway station complex received five direct hits from 500 pound bombs. One of these completely demolished the roof of the main entrance hall. The Reichsbahndirection (railway administration offices) on Adolf Hitler Strasse, which ran parallel to the North/South railway tracks, was also heavily damaged and set on fire. The marshalling yards and a goods depot were also hit by both high-explosive and incendiary bombs, causing single-track traffic for days afterwards. Teams of mobile specialist railway repair gangs worked in shifts round the clock to restore normal rail traffic so vital to the German war effort.

An army barracks complex on Rothenburg Strasse, an army supply depot and the Law Courts on Bisping Strasse, were also partly gutted by fire.

In the Raphaelsklinik on Klosterstrasse, near the railway station, a conference of the Clemens Sisters (Catholic nuns) from the surrounding Westphalian and Rheine districts was in progress. The building was heavily hit and there were many casualties. Fifty-two Sisters tragically lost their lives.

The Apollo Theatre, on Konigstrasse, also received direct hits. Theo Ladner, an eye-witness recalls:

I was 16-years-old in 1943, and I was in the Apollo Theatre on this particular Sunday. The film being shown was "Der Nachtfalter" (The Moth) when the air-raid sirens sounded and everyone left the cinema. All the civilian audience and several passers-by went into the cinema air-raid shelter, but many soldiers of the Wehrmacht remained outside in the open air in front of the shelter. I walked to the Marienplatz where there was another air-raid bunker.

The first waves of bombers came from the direction of Hindenburgplatz and flew over the Apollo Theatre in the direction of the Altstadt. Then all that could be heard was a fearful rushing sound and a terrible inferno erupted. I was lying in the gutter about five metres in front of the shelter at the Mariensaule. This bunker got a direct hit and there were 79 killed. The square in front of the Apollo Theatre also received a direct hit where the many Wehrmacht soldiers were standing. More than 80 soldiers were killed, some of their bodies being ripped to pieces.

Later, I was ordered by the authorities to help clear away these bodies. I felt so ill that I simply ran away. In addition to the great damage to the city centre, among other targets bombed was the Military Police Station near the entrance to the main railway station. It got a direct hit and apart from a huge crater nothing else was ever found.

Air Defence Helper Karl-Friedrich Bell, from his flak battery on the northern perimeter of Münster, recalls:

The indescribable volume of noise from the exploding bombs and our flak batteries ceased, as suddenly as it had begun, to be replaced with a deathly silence. From the shattered city centre immense columns of smoke drifted silently skywards.

It was all over . . . the raid had lasted for twenty minutes.

At the Show Ground on the Southern edge of Münster an unreal silence descended following the raid. Otto Schuett resumes his recollections of that Sunday afternoon:

There was nobody in sight. While I stayed outside flat on the ground everybody else seemed to have taken shelter in the basements of nearby houses. Dust from the explosions and dense smoke from the many raging fires stung my eyes and clogged my throat. But there was no water — the water mains had been destroyed.

Suddenly the concern for my family became paramount in my mind. My fears intensified when word was received that the area of town where we lived had been hit the hardest. In my anxiety to get home as quickly as possible I used my Youth Movement Identification Card as a receipt for a bicycle which a trusting lady gave me. I started for home but had to carry the bike when I found that most of the streets had become practically impassable because of huge piles of smoking rubble over which I frantically clambered. Finally I arrived at the end of what, half an hour earlier, had been our street. (Aegidii Strasse, 200 yards south of Münster Cathedral)

I immediately feared the worst. The bombs had literally ripped our street and buildings apart and practically no stone remained unturned. Only the front wall of our house remained standing, the second and third floors and the roof had been totally demolished. By now the stunned survivors were beginning to crawl out of their basements. They were the lucky ones. Neighbours of ours had died in their basement shelters when their house was hit and it had caved in on top of them.

Finally, to my great relief, I saw my mother, two sisters and brother. They too, had been buried but were able to escape through a small opening in their shelter, close to where they had been sitting, during the raid. Other occupants of that shelter had not been so lucky and would never see daylight again.

My father was missing. Very fortunately he turned up later but with his left arm and hand heavily bandaged. He was the assigned Air Raid Warden for our local community. As the sirens had signalled an impending air raid, a local cinema (The Apollo Theatre) around the corner from our house had stopped the performance. The people had gathered outside, waiting for the "All Clear" siren to sound. When the attack had started, my father tried to get the crowd into the shelter. Bombs started falling and a piece of shrapnel struck my father's left hand, embedding itself and lacerating the muscles and tissue. The bomb fragment was later removed but his hand, with its now stiffened fingers, was almost completely useless. But he had survived.

Fires were raging all around us. What little we could salvage of our worldly belongings we took into the garden of our house. There wasn't much to be done, little was left. I wish I had had my plum cake . . . The cake, miraculously still on the oven plate, was resting against the garden wall full of dust and debris, a mess and no longer fit for human consumption. The four rabbits had not survived either, They had died of concussion and shock in their small hutches.

Our neighbourhood was a complete shambles and in complete ruin. What had initially survived the explosions of the bombs was now rapidly becoming food and fuel for the raging fires, now totally out of control due to the lack of adequate water supplies. Some of the larger conflagrations would continue to smoulder for days afterwards.

For the second time in two years my family's existence had been shattered.

Although the official police report of casualties of the Münster raid state that there was a total 361 killed, of which 60 were soldiers, Theo Ladner asserts:

My father was called up as a policeman during the war and was serving with the B.D.O. (Befehlshaber der Ordnungspolizei — Commander of the Security Police) on the Kaiser-Wilhelm-Ring. Risking his life, my father brought home copies of the documents which listed the casualties. There were exactly 765 deaths on that day, civilians and soldiers. After memorising the contents of these documents, they were destroyed for safety reasons.

In 1954, the Münster City Council issued a summary of the total of 102 air raids on the city. For 10 October 1943, this report states that total casualties (i.e. killed) were "473 civilians and almost 200 soldiers." It is highly probable that the exact figures will never be known.

It is a fact, however, that if the additional six Bomb Groups of the 1st Air Division, and 388th Bomb Group, had bombed the primary target as scheduled instead of being diverted by the defences, and by pure chance, the casualties would have been considerably higher, not to mention the additional devastation to Münster's factories and rail facilities

Nevertheless, the raid on that "Black Sunday with sunshine" proved to be, by far, the heaviest of the war for Münster. The city's main electricity transformer station was heavily damaged and put out of action, as was the main water pumping station (Kanalwasser Pumpwerk) located beside the Gartenstrasse on the northern outskirts of the city. Also heavily damaged, were three banks, two insurance offices, ten factories partly destroyed, and six warehouses containing timber and food partly gutted by fire. Two schools, fortunately unoccupied, were also heavily hit.

The police report reveals:

The electricity supply and water mains leading to the city centre were totally destroyed. The only way out was through the rubble-filled and burning Prinzipalmarkt (market place), Lambertikirchplatz and then through the Kircherngasse. All other exits and streets were completely blocked by demolished houses, raging fires, wreckage of all descriptions and the hidden danger of unexploded or delayed-action bombs was ever-present.

It was this central area of the city which bore the brunt of the attack. Whole rows of tall, elegantly imposing and historical "Burgerhauser" (citizens town houses) dating back to the Middle Ages were totally destroyed. Thirty-five major fires and a far greater number of smaller conflagrations were fought by 28 separate fire brigades, hurriedly brought in from throughout Westphalia, and rushed to the city from the nearby Ruhr Valley. Four heavy-duty excavators especially adapted for rubble clearance, were brought into action to clear the main streets first.

Rescue teams of specialist Technische Nothilfe (TENO's) and miners tunnelled and clawed their way through tons of masonry, brick rubble and assorted debris by the eerie light of candles and torches in order to reach the trapped and injured. For some 500 of Münster's citizens, however, there was to be no rescue.

Colonel Alkire's grim words of warning to the combat crews of the 100th Bomb Group, spoken almost a year previously in far-off Washington, echoed starkly and terribly clear on this day: "Don't get the idea that your job is going to be glorious or glamorous. You've got dirty work to do, and you might as well face the facts . . ."

« « « » » »

The Thunderbolts of the 353rd and 78th Fighter Groups met the surviving bombers during their withdrawal near the Dutch/German border, thus reinforcing the hard-pressed P-47's of "Zemke's Wolfpack."

Major Eugene Roberts, leading the 78th Fighter Group, in P47 *Spokane Chief,* describes his part in the battle:

> I saw dense smoke coming up from Enschede and a group of B17's flying through fairly accurte and heavy flak. From our position at 28,000 feet, I saw some straggling Fortresses being attacked far below the main boxes, so I commenced a long, steep dive. Earlier, I had seen a Fortress on fire, breaking up and spilling parachutes heading down towards Haaksbergen.
>
> I lined up on an Me 110 which was itself firing on a B17. The damaged

Fortress went into a steep diving turn to the left, pouring white smoke. I rapidly closed on the Me 110, swinging in behind him, and opened fire at about 350 yards. I was now closing at a terrific rate, and at about 100 yards range I completely smothered the enemy aircraft in strikes. I was practically jamming my guns into him. The left engine belched smoke, and at about 30 yards I broke sharply to avoid a collision. The last I saw of him he was in a vertical dive with both engines on fire from 15,000 feet.

I pulled up to about 18,000 feet and then spotted an Me 410 positioning himself on a B17 below and to my left. I dived down and closed from the rear, again opening fire at about 350 yards. I closed to point-blank range and saw dozens of strikes all over the aircraft. Pieces of fuselage flew off and whipped past me, and again I almost rammed my target. Pulling up sharply to avoid him, and to cover my rear, I climbed back to 24,000 feet to rejoin the bombers on their route out. From their observations, other pilots in my Group later confirmed these two aircraft as destroyed.

Fighters of both sides were now involved in numerous and vicious dogfights which ranged over a broad belt of northwestern Germany and eastern Holland, as the P-47's strove to prevent further Fortress losses.

German Me 109 Pilot, Oberleutnant Heinz Knoke, 5 Staffel JG/11, takes up the story:

Suddenly, we sighted a formation of Thunderbolts which apparently spotted us at the same time. It seemed as if they did not expect us to attack them. I got into position behind one of them and opened fire. It suddenly blew up and fluttered down.*

At that moment the formation broke up, and in the melee which followed my aircraft was badly damaged in the left wing and tailplane. It instantly flipped over on its back and went down vertically out of control. I couldn't do anything, but the engine seemed to be undamaged and running normally. I went down to 3,000 feet, frantically pushing and pulling the stick. I broke into a cold sweat and my hands began to shake. "Knoke," I thought to myself, "this time you've had it!"

In utter desperation I tried pushing the stick over to one side. It had jammed. I took my feet off the rudder pedals and as a last desperate resort kicked hard against the stick. Suddenly there was a violent jolt, the aircraft whipped and rolled upright and my head struck the side of the cockpit canopy. But everything functioned properly again.

---

*Although this P47 is not on the official loss list for 10/10/43 at the National Archives in Washington, bomber crews of the 306th B.G. later confirmed seeing a Thunderbolt (Group unknown) spinning down out of control and its Pilot successfully bailing out between Münster and Coesfeld. Similar discrepancies between the War Diaries of the German Fighter Groups and the Official Luftwaffe Loss List for 10/10/43 appeared during research for this book.

I wanted to land at Rheine but could not find it, so I decided to return to Twente. I couldn't get the under carriage down, so I had to make a belly landing beside the runway. I climbed out and inspected the damage to the tail and rudder. Just then an FW 190 landed on the runway. Perhaps one of its undercarriage legs had been damaged because it suddenly flipped over on its back and instantly exploded in flames. There was nobody to be seen on the airfield. The sirens had sounded to signal an air raid, and everyone was in the shelters. A few moments later I heard the thunder of bombers and then the airfield was hit by bombs.

The FW 190 that Oblt. Knoke had seen crash-land and explode was piloted by Leutnant Hans Meyer of IIJG/26. His aircraft's undercarriage and engine had been damaged during the air battle. Just before touching down, Lt. Meyer, although wounded in the arm, had unbuckled his straps and when his aircraft cartwheeled he was catapulted clear of the flaming wreckage, breaking and grazing his left forearm and suffering burns. He eventually recovered in the hospital, only to be killed in action on 15 March 1944.

At 1530 hours the 305th Bomb Group, still seeking a target of opportunity, had mistaken the burning Enschede for a German town and released its bombs, some of which fell on the nearby Luftwaffe airfield of Twente. Although the military target of Enschede's railway system warehouses and factories in the southern section of the city were heavily damaged, 151 Dutch civilians lost their lives as a result of the unintentional aerial attack.

On his arrival at his bomb-shattered home in Enschede, 18 year-old Joop Ziglstra was shocked and stunned to discover that his 20 year old sister had been killed by an incendiary bomb. He reported:

It must be remembered that this tragic accident would never have happened if the Nazi's hadn't started the war in the first place, then invading and occupying Holland. For this reason there is absolutely no way that I could attach any blame to the Americans for the death of my sister.

Thunderbolts of the 353rd Fighter Group had rendezvoused with the bombers at 1529 hours, and were almost immediately in action, diving down almost vertically to protect the battle-damaged stragglers, limping their perilous way westwards.

Captain Walter Beckham, in his aptly named P47 *Little*

Demon, destroyed three German fighters in rapid succession. Recalls Captain Beckham:

Tracer bullets appeared while I was shooting down the third German fighter, indicating that I was running out of ammunition. I closed to very short range and emptied my guns from dead astern. A fourth Me 110 banked round to attack me, so I instinctively turned sharply towards him. He then broke off the engagement, diving violently downwards, evading a P47 with empty guns.

I turned towards home and looked around to clear my tail. Eight or ten single-engine enemy aircraft were behind, but a bit too far away to fire at me. I used full throttle and nosed down at about 1,000 feet a minute dive, and turned slightly off my homeward course to the left so as to be flying directly into the sun. I must have begun to widen the gap, because after about five minutes I was about one third of the way across the Zuider Zee heading directly towards Amsterdam when the enemy fighters gave up the chase and turned away.

Captain Beckham's three victories had raised his score to five enemy aircraft destroyed, and had made him the first 'Ace' of the 353rd Fighter Group. His remarkable achievement was witnessed by the crew of a straggling B17.

Sergeant Leo Hotis,Ball-Turret Gunner, B17F *Queen Jeanie*, 384th B.G. reporting on the mission said:

Very shortly after bombing Coesfeld our ship lost power and we began to lag behind the formation. Several twin-engine fighters lined up on our tail when our Bombardier reported an FW 190 about to hit us from 1 o'clock high. Fortunately, an instant later Lt. Bedsole, our Pilot, yelled "P47!!. . . Hold your fire!!"

The Thunderbolt dived right under us and took on all of the German fighters, single-handed. I saw him destroy two of them and the last I saw he was giving all hell to a third..

« « « » » »

Little Lass of the 388th Bomb Group was still in the air, its Pilots, Lt. Paul Williams and Lt. Israel Rogg, having managed to pull the aircraft out of its terminal dive after it was struck by flak while in the target area. Sgt. Raymond Harwood, who had bailed out with the Navigator and Bombardier at that time, was reunited with his crew several days later and discovered what had happened. He said later:

According to the rest of the crew, the ship had continued earthwards but no-one else had managed to bail out because of centrifugal force. The pilots were fortunately able to pull the ship out of the dive very close to the ground. At that time they thought everyone else had bailed out, having no interphone. The fighters who had initially hit us, were still with them, and the sound of gun-fire from out ship told the pilots that they were not alone.

There were still three engines running on good old *Little Lass* and the boys kept pecking away at the fighters. By that time, they were approaching the Dutch coast, badly shot-up and unable to gain any altitude. They were flying so low that the aircraft hit its ball turret and tail on the top of a dyke bank and then number two engine struck a steel pole while flying across the marshes. It was feathered successfully.

With the two remaining engines overheating they lost power and the crew started dumping equipment over board when they reached the North Sea. The fighters had been driven off or left due to shortage of fuel. But they gradually lost flying speed and ditched about three miles off the Dutch coast. Their hopes were still high as they clambered into the two life-rafts, thinking that the British Air-Sea Rescue had a good chance of picking them up, but it was a German minesweeper that rescued them at about 3 am the following morning. By this time, they were very relieved to see anyone.

Chapter 13

AS the 95th Bomb Group led the survivors of the 13th Wing across the North Sea, Captain Rodney Snow in the Group's Lead Squadron had his own problems with *Herky Jerky II.* He remembers:

During the flight home we were attacked only occasionally. However, I lost pressure on my number two engine and was unable to feather the propeller, so that it was aimlessly and harmlessly windmilling. There was nothing I could do about it except add extra power in an effort to stay up with the formation.

On crossing the Dutch coast, I advised our Group Leader that I was going to have to leave the formation because of the considerable drag the windmilling propeller was causing. Also, my gas supply was getting uncomfortably low. To lighten the plane we dumped all excess equipment into the sea. An Englishwoman, either a WAF or a WREN, picked up our "Mayday" signals and gave us directions.

The injured Pilot of *Miss Carry,* Lt. Paul Vance of the 390th Bomb Group, had been moved into the nose compartment of his Fortress when the battle had subsided over Central Holland. He had been given morphine injections to counteract the onset of shock and pain from his still bleeding lacerated thigh, and wrapped in blankets. His place in the cockpit was taken by Sgt. Henry Glende, the Engineer/Top Turret Gunner.

A number of 13th Wing B17's were in similar trouble.

Commented Lt. Marshall Thixton, Bombardier aboard the 95th Bomb Group's Fortress *Liberty Belle:*

We'd had to shut down our number three engine after sustaining battle damage while in the target area and were forced to leave the formation near the Dutch coast. Our ship was badly shot-up, and we'd lost most of the plexiglass nose to cannon fire. We crossed the North Sea fully expecting to ditch at any time.

And Lt. William Isaacs, Bombardier in the 95th Group's

plane *Holly Terror* recalls:

From our position in the High Squadron, the last I saw the only remaining 100th Bomb Group plane over Holland was trailing smoke and lagging further behind our formation. I didn't think that he could possibly make it back to base.

Royal Flush, one of the two 100th Bomb Group survivors, had only two engines still functioning and running at full power. Said the plane's Co-Pilot, Lt. Winfrey Lewis:

We continued to lose altitude, so Lt. Rosenthal gave the order to jettison everything possible — guns, ammunition, bomb-sight, etc. As we got lower, and had almost crossed the Zuider Zee, I could see the Bombardier and Navigator still busily throwing things out of the nose hatch.

Our two wounded Waist Gunners had been made as comfortable as possible in the radio room. We sweated out our aircraft on the return flight over the North Sea at very low altitude, just hoping that we could make the English coast. Through sheer luck, Lt. Rosenthal's perseverance, good navigation by Ronald Bailey, and various and assorted prayers in all faiths, the English coast finally came into view through the gathering mist and undercast at about 1630 hours.*

The low cloud and patchy ground fog covering most of East Anglia presented a very real hazard to the returning battle-damaged bombers and their exhausted crews.

The bulk of the escorting P47's were safely down, despite the poor visibility, but two tragedies marred their return.

Lt. Fred Olson of the 352nd Fighter Group, having sustained damage in what was probably the very first action of the battle on the outward flight, had ditched his P47 15 miles off Lowestoft, Suffolk, at 1544 hours. But despite an extensive air and sea search of the area, no trace was ever found of either plane or pilot.

Another Thunderbolt, flown by Lt. James Jones of the 56th Fighter Group, who had shot down an FW 190 during the battle, was forced to land at Boreham, Essex, an airfield still under construction. On landing at 1639 hours in limited visibility, his aircraft struck a tractor, setting both it and the careering Thunderbolt on fire, and instantly killing the tractor driver. Lt. Jones was pulled from the blazing fighter by members of the U.S. Corps of Engineers. He suffered second-

*The name Royal Flush is derived from the perfect hand in the card game called Poker. A Royal Flush is 'Unbeatable.'

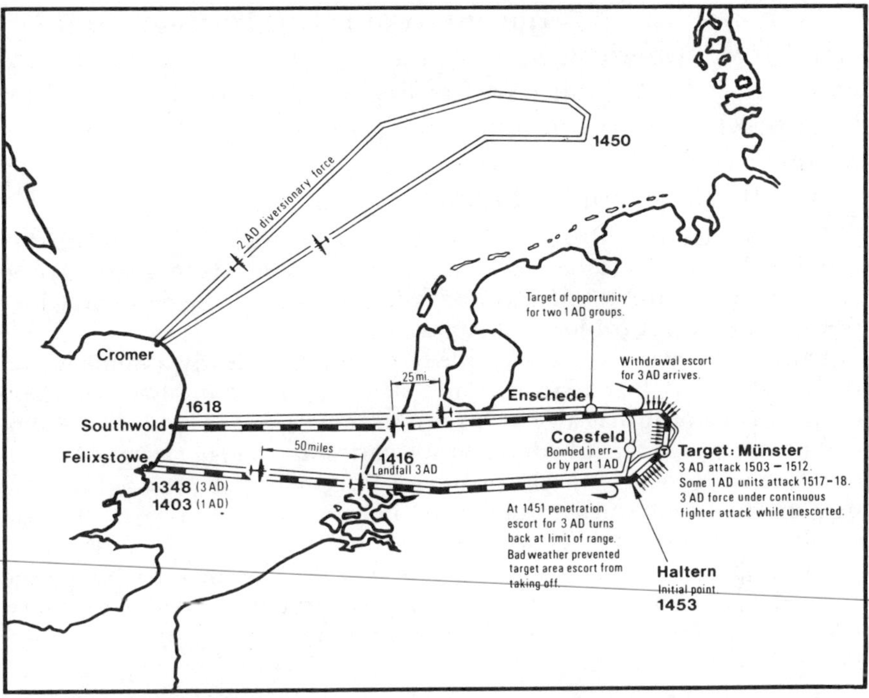

Mission Plan Summary of the Munster Raid of 10 October 1943.

degree burns.

B17's with wounded crewmen aboard were given priority as soon as they appeared in the landing patterns circling the airfields, firing red flares.

Lt. Paul Vance, now weak from loss of blood, was positioned behind Sgt. Glende and Lt. Murdoch in the cockpit of *Miss Carry* to add his considerable experience and expertise as they prepared to land at a fog-shrouded Framlingham. The time was 1650 hours. He said later:

> Conditions could not have been much worse on our arrival over the base. Sgt. Glende and Lt. Murdoch were having a tough time finding the runway. I helped talk them in. Two attempts to land were thwarted by the fog and jangled nerves, which was very understandable under the circumstances. On their third pass they made as smooth a landing as one could ever wish for. It was a team effort all the way.
>
> The ambulance was waiting just off the runway, and as I received a blood transfusion I could feel the pain in my leg gradually easing.

Lt. Vance was subsequently awarded the Distinguished Service Cross, America's second-highest award for gallantry, as was P-47 Pilot Captain Walter Beckham of the 353rd Fighter Group, who was promoted to the rank of Major following the Münster raid.

Recalled Captain Beckham:

I was desperately short of fuel and set down happily on the first airfield I could find, so I missed the debriefing at my base. When I eventually arrived at Metfield, I found that I was in the dog-house. Having destroyed three German fighters, I couldn't understand it.

Our orders were to stay with the bombers. It is clearly a fundamental principal that fighter planes should stick together but I had lost radio contact. It seemed that all our Group Commander and Squadron Commander knew was that I had left the formation and had not rejoined it. But if my job was to stay with a formation of 48 fighters with plenty of fuel and no guns fired, and watch a straggling B17 being shot to pieces, then I want another assignment . . . or become a plumber!

Lt. Colonel Loren McCollom, our Group Commander, was kind enough, and honest enough, to first ask me to tell my side of the story, which I did. He said, "Walter, you did the right thing," and he recommended me for a D.S.C.

Another 390th Fortress came in to land at Framlingham on only two engines. Said Sgt. James Shields, Bombardier in the 390th's Fortress 498:

Captain Bruce Reilly told everyone to go to the radio room, considered to be the safest place in a crash-landing, and brace ourselves as he was about to try a landing. Our ground crew told us later that we narrowly missed hitting several buildings.

Lt. Colonel Thomas Jeffrey, Deputy Group Commander at Framlingham, remembers the return of this Fortress to its home base:

Colonel Ed Wittan, the Commanding Officer of the 390th, and I were in the Control Tower at Framlingham awaiting the return of the aircraft from the Münster mission.

It became obvious that some very bad weather was rolling in from the North Sea over East Anglia and there was a question in our minds as to whether or not the returning aircraft would be able to land at the base. Evidence of this bad weather, which in a very short time restricted visibility at ground level to less than 50 yards, was confirmed by the fact that a large number of P47 aircraft had already come in and landed at our base due to the fact that they had been unable to get into their own respective airfields.

Since we didn't want to park these fighters on our B17's hardstands, they had been lined up on one side of one of the three runways that wasn't expected to be used by our returning bombers on this day.

As I recall, one or two or our returning B17's did manage to get in, with very restricted visibility shortly afterwards, using the main runway. We knew, from the numerous distress flares, that there had been severe battle damage, that there were wounded people aboard those aircraft and we hated, very much, to have to turn our Group away from Framlingham and divert them to other bases.

However, the weather conditions which had deteriorated so rapidly necessitated that we do this. As a matter of fact we didn't even have time to ascertain what alternative airfields were available and we had to advise our pilots to simply look for somewhere else to land.

As Ed and I were descending the steps on one side of the Control Tower we heard the roar of an approaching B17 and looked up just in time to see one of the " Square J" airplanes attempting a landing at Framlingham. The B17 was not lined up on any runway and he was at extremely low altitude, not more than 40 yards away. The propeller on Number 4 engine was gone, Number 3 was feathered, the other two engines appeared to be functioning normally as it hit the grassed area. Apparantly the pilot applied the brakes immediately after touch-down at a speed of about 90 miles an hour. Directly after he'd applied his brakes the nose of the airplane dipped dangerously close to the ground and the tail rose up accordingly. The careering B17 disappeared rapidly into the fog that had, by that time encompassed the entire field.

Ed and I ran to his staff car and drove across the airfield in the general direction of the airplane. We found the B17 on the perimeter track at the far side of the base parked in a normal attitude. In addition to the missing propeller from the right outboard engine the cowl ring was gone, a large piece was gone from one of the three blades of the feathered number 3 propeller and there were countless holes of varying sizes in the airplane as we walked around it.

Captain Reilly, the B17's Pilot, lowered himself down from the nose hatch. In a very slow and deliberate manner he raised his right arm and saluted us. He then said to Ed what must have been the understatement of the year; "Colonel, when I found out that after having lost numbers 3 and 4 that we were also losing number 2 I thought, for a couple of minutes back there, that we weren't goin' to make it . . . . ."

Recalled Sergeant Bob Banta, Radio Operator *Rose Marie* 390th B.G.:

Our Pilot, Lt. Dougherty, elected to attempt a landing at fog-shrouded Framlingham. As we began our our final approach we could see the parapets of Framlingham Castle faintly through the mist. The sound of the engines changed and the lowering flaps slowed the plane noticeably as we glided over the dim and hazy countryside and bounced in for a safe landing. That day, with its many narrow escapes, brought only numbness once our hearts had stopped pounding. We had narrowly missed colliding with another B17 on landing.

There was a mountain of material for conversation but we were unusually quiet as we inspected the countless holes in our plane. It would take weeks to repair.

We were only halfway through our tour of missions. Almost all the 390th's original crews were gone, to say nothing of their replacements. Where do you find optimism for the future in statistics like these??

The six other surviving 390th Group Fortresses, their fuel dangerously low, had sought out other East Anglian airfields on which to set down.

Thirteen surviving B17's of the 95th Bomb Group eventually arrived back safely at their base at Horham between 1632 and 1652 hours, including the battered *Liberty Belle,* where visibility was only marginally better.

One of the Group's bombers to return was *Herky Jerky II.* It's Pilot Captain Rodney Snow, recalls:

As we approached the vicinity of our own base the weather was rapidly deteriorating. The scud from the North Sea had moved in quite quickly so that visibility was extremely restricted. Our main concern was the cloud ceiling which appeared to be 1,000 feet or less. We were in bad shape because of our shot-up condition, our near-empty fuel tanks, and the inevitable fatigue which had begun to set in.

After we had cranked the right-hand landing gear down manually because of lack of hydraulic pressure, we prepared to land. We saw a runway, and I tried a big right-hand turn to line the plane up with it. Suddenly the Waist Gunner yelled, "Pull up, Cap!! Pull her up!! You're heading straight for a church steeple!!" With a violent maneouvre to the right we only just missed hitting a church spire which had been obscured by the mist and fog. We then completed the turn, and saying a little prayer let down at an unidentified base.

While we were taxiing back to a hardstand, the Tower told us we were at Thorpe Abbotts. The Commanding Officer of the 100th then inquired as to the whereabouts of his Group as they should have at least been in radio contact with the Tower by that time. The Colonel refused to believe me when I told him, "I'm sorry to say this, Sir, but I don't think that you will have anyone from your Group home this day." But I could not convince him of what we had seen less than two hours earlier, so I advised him to contact Colonel Gerhart at Horham by phone.

Five 390th Fortresses, including Major Hansel and Captain Geary in the Lead plane *Pistol Packin' Mama,* also landed at

Thorpe Abbotts. The crippled *Eightball,* without brakes, and its Pilots, Lt. William Cabral and Lt. Richard Perry, wrestling with the controls, careered off the end of the runway, slewing round crazily and ending up straddling a roadside ditch. Then came the barely-flyable *Rusty Lode* on two engines, with only six crew members, and the body of Sgt. McGregor slumped in the shattered radio room.

The Pilot, Lt. Robert Sabel, recalls:

We had flown a rather jagged course back to England, which put us all well behind the main bomber stream. I was very short on fuel, and I considered bailing out the remainder of my crew when I saw a break in the cloud and made a direct let-down. Our landing gear went down, but it would not lock. Flight Engineer George Woodcock hand-cranked the lock into position. Because I had to fly the aircraft by manipulating the A.F.C.E. control knobs, I had to rely on Co-Pilot Leonard Martin and George Woodcock to line me up with the runway and call out our airspeed and altitude. All manual controls had been severed at the radio room and the bomb bay. I then made a totally blind landing, which was probably one of the best landings I have ever made.

Another B17, the *Royal Flush,* also flying on only two engines, slowly approached the main runway at Thorpe Abbotts through the gathering mist. Said Co-Pilot Lt. Winfrey "Pappy" Lewis:

Sgt. Hall fired flares during our approach to the field to alert the ambulances, and their timing was perfect as they met us at the end of our landing roll in our badly-damaged airplane. Lt. Rosenthal accompanied our two wounded Waist Gunners to the base hospital in the ambulance. The two injured men received good care and attention. Sgt. Darling soon recovered from his wounds, and Sgt. Schaffer was returned to the United States to have some small pieces of shrapnel removed from near his heart.

We learned later that an unexploded 20 mm cannon shell from a German fighter was found rolling around in one of our self-sealing wing fuel tanks. If that one shell had exploded as it was designed to do, ... The Germans employed many prisoners as slave labour in their munition plants, and I can picture some very brave soul risking his all to sabotage and secretly turn out defective rounds of ammunition.

I am still grateful for our deliverance, although I will never really understand, as most of us never understand, the strange tricks of Fate that are played out in our lives.

Stork Club, the only other surviving Fortress from the ill-fated 100th Bomb Group formation, landed at Thorpe Abbotts at 1716 hours. Waist Gunner Sgt. Stanley Smith remarked:

It had been a relatively short mission, but the heaps of spent cartridge cases littering the floor beneath the gun positions told their own story. I was practically out of ammunition, as were all of the other gunners on our ship. We had started out with a total of some 9,000 rounds.

When we were debriefed by the 100th's Intelligence Officers asking about "Our Guys" all we were able to tell them was of those we had seen going down. They gradually came to realise the full enormity of what had happened was nothing short of a catastrophe. Our two Groups (390th and 100th) had lost 20 B17's.

Captain Keith Harris, Pilot *Stork Club,* 390th Bomb Group reports:

During the de-briefing at Thorpe Abbotts, an Intelligence Officer approached me and asked me to go to the telephone as General LeMay, Commander of the 3rd Air Division, wanted to speak to the 390th Pilot who had flown with the 100th formation.

It was the first, and only time I had spoken to a General. He wanted to know when and where the 100th airplanes had gone down, how far from the target, how many had reached the target, enemy fighter tactics, etc., etc. I related to him what had happened and that in effect our formation had been literally overwhelmed by German fighters around the Initial Point area. General LeMay then thanked me and congratulated my crew on our safe return.

Thorpe Abbotts was a sad, sad place that day . . .

My crew were credited with four enemy fighters destroyed. I personally can only confirm one as the Pilots view from the cockpit is extremely limited. It was a single-engine fighter which came in at 11 o'clock and it was totally demolished by my Navigator.

The 390th apparently were credited with destroying 62 fighters during that mission, although I'm highly suspicious of these claims.

None of my crew suffered injury, somewhat miraculously, as our airplane was badly shot up. We were subsequently assigned another new ship for our next mission which we flew on the 14th October 1943 to Schweinfurt.

The last Fortress of the Wing, *Little Mike,* arrived over RAF Wattisham, Suffolk, at 1720 hours. It's Pilot, Lt. Robert Schneider, will never forget that crash-landing. He remembers:

The fog was widespread and quite dense. We nearly collided with a barrage balloon which had only its top showing above the mist and scud. By this time I was getting confused, knowing that we were over East Anglia — but where? With near empty fuel tanks I was considering bailing the crew out, and believe me, I'd have to be pretty desperate to use a parachute!

At about this time, a gap suddenly appeared in the fog, and we could see the end of a runway with construction equipment parked along both sides. We immediately made a very steep descent, lowering the landing gear, but I did not risk using the flaps as the right flap was damaged and I was unsure of the landing characteristics with only the left flap usable.

After the airplane touched down we lowered both flaps and they functioned satisfactorily. By this time, however, we had used up far too much runway to stop in time, and with brakes locked on, tyres skidding and smoking, we slid off the end of the concrete runway and ploughed into the soft soil beyond the perimeter track. The two main wheels immediately dug in and the airplane went up on its nose and then fell back. The tail wheel struck the concrete, driving it up through the vertical stabiliser and breaking the fuselage in half at the ball turret. Fortunately, nobody was hurt, and you never saw ten people exit from anything so fast in your life.

We were driven back to the mess hall where we learned that we had crash-landed at RAF Wattisham, Suffolk. The Mess Sergeant opened a big can of sliced peaches, and I have never tasted anything so good in my life. The wreckage of our airplane was salvaged a few days later.

The 13th Combat Bomb Wing, having lost 25 Flying Fortresses in as many minutes during the raid, had been to Hell and back.

Captain Frank Murphy, the injured Navigator on the shot-down 100th Bomb Group B17 *Aw-R-Go,* who was to spend the next twenty months as a prisoner-of-war at Stalag Luft III, Sagan, Silesia, summarises those traumatic twenty five minutes:

Historically, the correct perspective for judging the men of a Military Unit is not the final outcome of the battle but their dedication in carrying out their mission and, in the last instance, how they performed when called upon to fight to the end against impossible odds as was the case at Münster.

In this proper historical sense, the performance by the men of the 95th, the 100th, and the 390th Bombardment Groups over Münster on 10th October 1943, as I saw them, could quite rightly, and with full justification, be considered the United States Air Force equivalent of The Charge Of The Light Brigade in the Crimea or General George Pickett's Charge at Gettysburg during the American Civil War.

« « « » » »

The 3rd Air Division's four remaining Groups all managed to land their aircraft, with a few exceptions, on their home bases at Great Ashfield, Knettishall, Rougham and Snetterton Heath. Many of the returning Fortresses carried varying degrees of battle damage.

The B24 Liberators' of the 2nd Air Division also returned to their bases in Norfolk without mishap, but the return of the

1st Air Division Fortresses was not without incident.

Following battle damage, the 351st B.G. B17 *Argonaut II*, crashed into the North Sea off Covehithe, Suffolk. The Pilot, Lt. Argiropulas, had bailed out with his crew over Norfolk after first putting his plane on auto-pilot and pointing the nose towards the sea.

In similar circumstances, a 384th B.G. Fortress still carrying a 1,000 lb. bomb which unaccountably refused to jettison, was over Suffolk when Lt. William Wilson ordered his crew to bail out after he too, had put his aircraft *(Wahoo II)* on an easterly heading. The crew all landed in the Ipswich area, but unbeknown to them, a potential disaster now threatened the residents of the small North Suffolk town of Eye.

Peter Smith, then a 15-year-old schoolboy, describes what happened next:

> I was standing with my father in his meadow on the outskirts of Eye when we heard the sound of a plane and saw a B17 coming very low towards us. One engine had stopped and the propeller on another was only turning very slowly from the force of the airstream. The bomb-bay doors were open as it roared directly over us. Then it hit a large tree which ripped one of its wings off, about 200 yards from Eye church. Huge branches were hurled in all directions. The aircraft then slid across two smaller meadows, killing two unfortunate cows who happened to be in its path, and finally ending up on the far bank of the River Dove about 400 yards from us.
>
> I was the first person to reach the wreckage, blood from the cows was everywhere, and much of the debris was in the river which was only three or four feet deep at that point. Very soon about 100 American servicemen from the nearby Red Cross Club arrived on the scene to look for survivors, but it turned out that the plane had been empty when it had crashed.
>
> Police arrived shortly after and cleared the area because of a suspected unexploded bomb thought to be still on board.

A search was made, and the bomb was found in the river near the crashed aircraft. It was removed by a Bomb disposal Team from RAF Feltwell.

The 91st Bomb Group B17G *Sir Baboon McGoon* made a wheels-up landing on a partially harvested sugar beet field near the Suffolk village of Tannington, without injury to the crew. Geoffrey Pipe, then a schoolboy, recollects:

> I can remember the B17 flying very low over Saxted. The aircraft then turned to the left, disappeared from view and crash-landed in a field belonging to Mr. Reggie Harvey at Tannington. I hurried to the scene, and

to my surprise, was allowed to look over the B17. Many other local people did the same. The damage was mainly to the underside of the plane. The nose section and propellers had been badly bent. There were hundreds of empty shell cases on the floor of the aircraft, which suggested that there had been a lot of action during the flight.

Another schoolboy, Tom Perkins, noted that the ball turret had been ripped off, and the chin turret underneath the nose had been badly buckled in the landing. During the next few weeks, however, the Americans brought in pierced steel planking and laid a temporary runway, repaired the aircraft, and flew it back to its original base at Bassingtowne, Cambridgeshire.

The 384th Bomb Group Fortress *Yankee Gal* was not so fortunate. It collided with a hangar after landing at RAF Desford, a small grass airfield near Leicester, but luckily without injury to the crew. The badly damaged B17 was written off and salvaged a few days later.

Three Fortresses of the 379th Bomb Group had left their Group's formation just before crossing the English coast and had finally landed, with near-empty fuel tanks, at Biggin Hill, Kent, the famous RAF Battle of Britain fighter base. Said Pilot Lt. Robert Haughy, of the B17G 824 *Fearless Forsdike:*

> Our crew had completed its 21st mission, and we were glad to get down in one piece before the weather closed in completely.
>
> We were invited to the Officer's Mess that night where we found that the British officers were treated like royalty and were waited on hand and foot by young and very attractive WAAF's. After a few drinks, we all let our hair down and "jolly well" raised a little hell much to the "Limey's" amusement, as they also joined in the merriment until the bar ran dry. We had also completely demolished the dignity of their domain by flirting and joking with the WAAF's which was apparently strictly taboo.
>
> The RAF officers were glad to see us arrive, but I think that they were far happier when we departed.

At Thorpe Abbotts the stunned groundcrews, who had waited and hoped in vain throughout the late afternoon for the remainder of their Group's aircraft to return, drifted silently away from the empty hardstands all hope now gone as darkness descended.

The mood was summed up by Line Chief Sgt. Robert Spangler, of the 351st Squadron:

"Coming so soon after the Bremen losses just two days earlier, the Münster mission . . . well . . . I simply couldn't believe it . . . grief and bewilderment was mirrored on every face.

Thorpe Abbotts schoolboy, Sammy Hurry, recalls:

I'd been in and around the Control Tower for most of that day. The only B17 with a square "D" on its tail — the 100th's markings — came in on the main runway on only two engines and, as I remember, a third engine cut out on landing. As it went past us Billy Taylor could only murmur "They're shot to pieces . . . "

Another former local schoolboy, Ken Everett, added:

At first we thought that the 100th's other B17's may have been diverted to other airfields further inland because of the weather. But as the time passed on well past nightfall, we discovered that this was not so. Apart from one, they had all gone down.

Royal Flush Pilot, Lt. Robert Rosenthal, said:

Later that night we went to the Officer's Club to try and wind-down and relax. We found it to be a very lonely and silent place.

And the plane's Ball Turret Gunner, Sgt. Ray Robinson, observed:

The first night after Bremen we were too scared to sleep, the second night after Marienburg we were too tired, and the third night after Münster we were just through . . . finished.

Lt. Paul Perceful, Co-Pilot of B17F 218, 95th Bomb Group, said:

After the debriefing, I met Captain Dewey Johnson, our Lead Bombardier, in the 336th Squadron operations room. I had already heard that Dewey had been knocked away from his bomb sight shortly after we had passed the Initial Point. It was later discovered that a flattened bullet had struck him. He had climbed back to the bomb sight and placed the bombs right on the target.

I said to him, "How goes it, Dewey?" His quiet reply was, "Perceful, I've got the horrors . . . I think I'll go up to the Officer's Club . . ." I did not go with him.

Captain Dewey Johnson was awarded the British Distinguished Flying Cross, and was personally decorated by King George VI at Buckingham Palace, London, a few days after the Münster raid.

The claims by bomber crews of enemy fighters destroyed during the battle were highly exaggerated. The 390th Bomb Group's gunners alone claimed to have downed 62 German fighters. This can be partly explained by the fact that when as many as ten Fortress gunners from different B17's, flying in a tight defensive formation, were all firing at, and seeing strikes on the same attacking fighter, duplication of claims was bound to occur, especially in the heat of battle when the adrenalin is at its peak.

The official German records reveal that 26 of their fighters were shot down, and another seven severely damaged and written off in forced landings through battle damage.

At Framlingham Airfield, the 390th's Deputy Commanding Officer, Lt. Colonel Thomas Jeffery, listened as some of the Group's surviving crews were being debriefed:

This raid had been the worst to date as far as losses for the 390th were concerned. They were felt very heavily by Colonel Wittan and I who had known each missing crewmember since his assignment to the Group.

It turned out, after talking to Captain Reilly a little later, that on two or three occasions in anticipation of such an event as had occurred that afternoon, that he had learned to make, and practised, an instrument approach to the airfield by passing over Framlingham castle at a specific and precise altitude, which was known only to him, and letting down at a rate of exactly 300 feet per minute. This would then put his airplane over the edge of the airfield at just above zero altitude by using instruments only.

On this day Captain Reilly had accomplished that remarkable feat with nowhere else to go. In other words if he had missed the airfield he would have had to put the airplane down wherever he happened to be at that point in time. It was a successful, if somewhat unorthodox, landing and I consider myself privileged to have been able to have witnessed it person ally.

Lt. Richard (Dick) Perry, Co-Pilot on the badly damaged *Eightball,* recalls:

It was wonderful to be able to get our feet on English soil again after working hard to keep the *Eightball* flying and surviving a very rough landing. We were able to get home principally because of the extremely rugged qualities of the Flying Fortress and its ability to absorb tremendous structural damage and still stay in the air.

After being debriefed at Thorpe Abbotts, we were trucked back to Framlingham, our home base. All the way back, our crew discussed plans for getting a few days leave to go to London and forget about our recent narrow escape. On arrival, our Squadron C.O. Major Joe Gemmill, felt quite differently. His view was that the best way to get the "butterflies" out of our stomachs was to participate in another mission immediately.

I found that he was absolutely correct. Later on I used his approach on many other crews who had been through rough missions when I eventually became an Operations Officer.

On his arrival at Framlingham, Captain James Geary, Pilot of the Group's Lead B17 *Pistol Packin' Mama,* which had also landed at Thorpe Abbotts, had an urgent telephone call from London waiting for him.

Colonel Wittan had me brief the American Ambassador concerning his son's flight and what I had seen following the explosion of his aircraft. The Ambassador asked me what I thought John's chances of survival were. I told him anything was possible, but that I thought it not very probable.

It wasn't until I was on my second tour of operations that I too was shot down following my transfer to the 100th Bomb Group at Thorpe Abbotts. When I finally reached the P.O.W. Camp at Sagan, the first person I met as I entered was John Winant. He told me that he had no idea how he had got clear of the plane, and thought he might have been blown out.

It just proves that nothing is impossible.

Sgt. William Kubitzki made the following entry in his diary that night:

Mission Number 12. October 10th 1943. Plane 230325 *Miss Carry*

Takeoff: 1100. Landed: 1650. Target: Industrial Area—Münster, Germany.

Crew: Vance, Murdock, Fallon, Thompson, Glende, Kubitzki, Martin, Farris, Power, Adamson.

Escort: P47's. Excellent while it lasted.

Bomb Results: Excellent—500 lb. demos.

Flak: Heavy over edge of Ruhr and Target.

Fighters: Entire Luftwaffe were waiting for us. 109's, 110's, 410's, JU 88's, 190's.

Remarks: Vance shot through leg. Murdock and Glende flew plane home and landed in terrible ground-fog.

Fighters downed: Glende 4, Farris 2, Kubitzki 2, Adamson 1.

Rockets: Thousands of them.

After writing his narrative of the Münster raid following the debriefing, Major Robert Williams, Operations Officer of the 306th Bomb Group at Thurleigh, Bedfordshire, put forward his suggestions at the end of his report to his Group Commander, Colonel George Robinson:

It is recommended that missions should not be flown on three consecutive days since it leads to undue flying fatigue, especially on the part of the pilots. This is particularly dangerous when the landing at the end of the third mission is made under conditions of extremely poor visibility. Such landings tax the skill of even a fresh pilot, and are extremely dangerous to one who is extremely fatiqued after flying 22 hours in combat formation in a time-span of 54 hours.

« « « » » »

Meanwhile, in a still burning Münster, by far the most heavily damaged of the three targets, the grim and dangerous task of rescuing the wounded and recovering the dead continued. Among those killed were 14 foreign workers.

As well as the many industrial and commercial buildings destroyed or heavily damaged, 526 houses — mostly in the city centre — had been completely demolished or severly damaged. A further 2,600 homes had been damaged to a lesser degree, ranging from medium to slight. More than 25,000 citizens were made homeless and were subsequently evacuated. Major disruption had undoubtedly been achieved.

Fraulein Hildegard Kosters describes the scene earlier on emerging from the shelter beneath the railway station:

The sound of the sirens signalled the end of the raid. We stumbled out of the blazing station, past several mangled bodies in the main hall where death had reaped a horrible harvest. All around us were burning houses, buildings, heaps of rubble and the hellish crackling of the fires. Our house had been demolished and was now blazing fiercely. We hurried past the burning and smoking buildings through Piusallee, Mecklenburger Strasse, Mondstrasse and in the rough direction of Wolbeck.

We eventually arrived in the late evening, totally shocked and exhausted, with singed clothes and ruined shoes. It took us nearly five hours to cover 12 kilometres. The loss of our home was a great blow, but we were very thankful that we had escaped with our lives.

Gerhard Ringbeck recalls:

After I had done what I could to help rescue the wounded in the immediate vicinity, and by then enough experienced rescue parties had arrived, I continued on my scheduled journey later that evening.

For me, as an experienced soldier at the Front, it was dreadful to realise that our people in the cities and towns of our homeland were so open and defenceless against air raids, and that they would continue to be so for the foreseeable future. It was then that it became perfectly clear to me, more than ever before, that the war under these circumstances could have only one possible ending.

The injured Captain Frank Murphy together with Captain Charles Cruikshank of the 100th Bomb Group were driven to a village north of Münster where they found eight more American airmen at the home of the Burgermeister which was being used as a collection point for prisoners. Captain Murphy remembers:

There was a large picture of Adolf Hitler in the hallway and as the Germans passed this picture they would say, "Heil Hitler", something which I'd only seen previously in films.

At about dusk that afternoon we were all taken in a convoy of cars to an airfield which was about ten miles away. There we were put into what was apparently the base prison where approximately 25 American airmen had preceded us, including Lieutenant John Winant, the son of the American Ambassador to Great Britain.

My wounds were noticed by the Luftwaffe guards and I was taken to the Base Hosptial. Two German doctors washed and dressed my injuries and bandaged my sprained ankle. They decided to leave the small fragments of shrapnel alone to eventually work themselves out. I was returned with an armed guard to the security building with the other prisoners.

Shortly after that three German Air Force pilots came in to talk with us. They had apparently fought against us that afternoon over Münster. My recollections of these conversations was that they were largely exchanges of mutual respect. The Luftwaffe pilots were fairly complimentary of us and we were, rightly, fairly complimentary of them. They were certainly skillful and determined flyers.

The following day we were taken to the local railroad station and from there we went to Frankfurt for interrogation.

The badly-wounded Lt. Howard Hamilton of the 100th Bomb Group, together with several more injured crewmen who were collected on the way, finally arrived at a bomb-shattered Münster in an ambulance driven by an elderly civilian and guarded by his armed grandson. Said Lt. Hamilton:

When we got to Münster there were 13 of us injured Americans. We were placed on stretchers outside the main civilian hospital. There was a great deal of smoke and flame all around the area. There were many German civilian casualties that day, and consequently we were not taken into the operating theatre, which was in the basement of the hospital, until about four o'clock the next morning. Five American crewmen died during the night while they waited for medical help.

Because of the large number of civilian casualties, medical supplies at the hospital were quickly exhausted, and there was no anaesthesia for us by the time they got around to our operations. Fortunately, we were in such a state of shock that it was not that much of an ordeal.

There was only one German surgeon on duty. He was assisted by six or seven nuns who appeared to be extremely efficient and competent in performing minor surgical operations and applying dressings, etc. I recall that one of the nuns did all of the operating on me until she got down to the punctured lung, then the German doctor completed my operation. They did not bother to do anything about the wounds to my hands, but both healed satisfactorily with the passage of time.

We spent from 10 October until 25 November, 1943, in the basement of Münster hospital. When we were thought fit to travel we were taken by rail to Barth P.O.W. camp on the Baltic coast, after an interrogation at Frankfurt. During the long journey, the train had several very lengthy delays while repair work was done on the railway tracks, following the Allied bombing campaign. Almost every town we passed through bore signs, in varying degrees, of bomb damage.

The surviving civilians of Münster and Coesfeld had seen and experienced at first hand what the inhabitants of towns and cities like Warsaw, Rotterdam, Coventry, Smolensk, London, Liverpool, Manchester and scores of other heavily-bombed places throughout Europe had suffered and endured at the hands of the Luftwaffe during the previous four years of the war.

They reacted in exactly the same way as the populations of those cities and towns had done. Despite their grief over the loss of loved ones, they resolutely and courageously stuck to their immediate task of clearing up their shattered communities and got on with living and working. But they now undoubtedly realised, if they had not done so before, that the sands of time were now beginning to run out for Adolf Hitler and the Nazi regime.

Fifteen year old Otto Schuett concludes his narrative:

By about 2100 hours on that Sunday evening, hungry and thirsty, we were sitting amongst the smouldering ruins in our torn and stinking clothes. We were evacuated to a small village not far from Münster later that same night.

The next day we hitch-hiked back to the City to see if anything more could be saved. But the few odd pieces of our furniture and personal belongings which we had been able to throw and carry out into the garden the previous day was all that was left. I climbed into the basement through the cellar window and found a bottle of my mother's home-made fruit juice. The following day I came back in the hope of finding more and to surprise my family. But there was to be no more . . . because in the meantime the whole ceiling had caved in and buried forever what might have remained. I suppose I had been lucky again . . .

The events of October 10th 1943 often pass through my mind and with those thoughts pictures appear of the friends and neighbours who died on that day. A great sadness comes over me and I also often wonder what kind of men the crews of those B17's were that never returned home. A few days after the raid I saw the remains of a crashed B17 at Ostbevern (which is fairly close to Münster). Amidst the twisted and torn metal I noticed a brown shoe which, no doubt, had belonged to one of the crew members. Now and then that one shoe also remains in my memories. I wish and hope that the man who used to wear that shoe managed to parachute safely to earth. Perhaps it's only a small matter, but it remains outstanding in my mind.

October 10th 1943 was the beginning of the end of Germany and the Second World War. Many more air raids were to follow and many thousand were yet to perish in the cities. Both sides would suffer immensely.

Chapter 14

THE following are original Press Releases by both sides which illustrate the vital role Allied Air power was playing over Germany in 1943. The Air Defences of the Third Reich, which had they been able to be deployed to the Eastern and Southern Fronts, could quite conceivably have turned the tide in Hitler's favor.

From the "DEUTSCHE ZEITUNG in the Netherlands," Amsterdam, Monday 11 October 1943. "Latest Communique from the Wehrmacht:"

51 American terror Bombers and 285 Soviet tanks destroyed in two days — 48 Soviet planes shot down on Sunday — Eight ships with 40,200 tons of war supplies sunk by U-Boats.

From the Fuhrer's H.Q., 11 October. The High Command of the Wehrmacht announces:

Between the Sea of Azov and Saporoshje the Soviets increased their attacks with strong support from artillery, tanks and fighter aircraft, but the attacks failed because of vigorous German defence.

In the Middle Dnieper also, in the region south of Somel and in the battle area west of Smolensk, all Soviet attacks were repulsed.

The heavy fighting in the break-through bridgehead area south-west of Welikiji-Luki continues unabated.

In the last two days 285 Soviet tanks have been destroyed, the majority of them in the battle areas of Melitpol and Saporoshje.

In the central and southern sectors the Luftwaffe gave strong support to the defensive action of the Army, attacked enemy reinforcements and yesterday destroyed 48 Soviet planes for the loss of only three of their own.

In the heavy defensive fighting to the west of Smolensk, the "Hesse-Saarpfulz" Infantry Division under the command of Lieutenant-General Boge, particularly distinguished itself.

In Southern Italy the enemy attacked a rail base in the Plain of Campania. It was repulsed in a bloody battle. From the rest of the front there are only reports of local fighting between our advance guards and weaker enemy forces.

German fighters and anti-aircraft artillery of the Luftwaffe and of the Coastal and Marine Artillery shot down, over the Mediterranean, nine bombers, mostly four-engined.

During hard battles in the Kara Sea, East of Novaya Zemla, in the North Atlantic, and in the Mediterranean, German U-Boats sank eight ships with 40,200 tons of war supplies and severely damaged two others with torpedoes.

Yesterday afternoon American bombers attacked West Germany. The explosive and incendiary bombs did much damage to residential areas, especially in Münster. The Cathedral and three other churches were severely damaged. The German defence, especially fighter aircraft units, destroyed a large number of the attacking planes. The destruction of 51, mostly four-engined bombers, has already been reported. As a result, the enemy has lost, in the course of his terror attacks on the territory of the German Reich, a total of 208 bombers in the last three days, most of which were four-engined planes.

Records at the National Archives, Washington, D.C., indicate the following Army Air Force losses for Sunday, 10 October 1943. Eighth Air Force Germany and Holland, 30 B17's and 1 P47. Twelfth Air Force, 1 B17 Greece, 2 P40 Warhawk fighters Italy, and 1 B25 Mitchell bomber North Africa. One B24 of the 13th Air Force was lost over the Solomon Islands in the vast Pacific Theatre.

RAF Bomber Command War Diaries (Martin Middlebrook) state that during night operations for 8/9 October 1943, 641 aircraft were despatched on bombing raids to Occupied Europe. The Main Force was sent to Hanover. Smaller groups attacked Bremen, Berlin, Castrop-Rauxel and Duren. Twenty-seven bombers failed to return.

Also, a further 62 aircraft were sent on sea mining operations over the North Sea and the Baltic, and four aircraft despatched to France to drop propaganda leaflets. Of these 66 aircraft, four were lost.

On 9/10 October 1943, a small force of Mosquitos attacked Berlin. All aircraft returned safely. There were no night operations anywhere by the RAF on 10/11 October.

An Associated Press report issued in London on 11 October 1943, stated:

American planes shoot down 102 enemy aircraft in Münster attack. Raiders also bomb Coesfeld: Invasion this year discussed.

London, Oct. 11 (AP)—Boosting Nazi plane losses to more than 300 in three days, American Flying Fortresses and escorting Thunderbolts shot down 102 enemy planes yesterday as the big bombers tore through stubborn defenses to blast the important German transportation centres of Münster and Coesfeld.

Thirty bombers and two fighters, a communique said, were lost by American formations, which also hit an airfield near Enschede, Holland, in the blazing climax to a weekend of violent Allied aerial activity that riddled the Germans' fighter strength.

While the size of the attacking American formations was not officially disclosed, there was reason to believe that they may have approximated the record concentrations of 400 bombers which hammered German targets on each of the two preceding days.

The American raids reached a new high in strength in numbers on Friday, when Fortresses and Liberators bombed the Stuka factory in Bremen and submarine shipbuilding yards at nearby Vegesack, and on Saturday, when they flew a round trip of 1,800 miles — their deepest penetration of Nazi territory — to hit the former free city of Danzig, the former Polish city of Gydnia and other targets in Eastern Germany.

Lieutenant-General Ira C. Eaker, Commander of the United States Eighth Air Force, disclosed that the attacking force on both Friday and Saturday totalled 400 bombers, and said these and other raids to follow were in preparation for an Allied invasion of Germany "across the English Channel and the North Sea."

"The big push into Germany, when it comes, will cost lives just as the landings at Salerno did," General Eaker added. "It is the task of the Eighth Air Force and the RAF to destroy factories and weapons and transport of the Germans so our invasion casualties will be cut down.

"This is our stern assignment this Winter. We shall not shirk it."

With ten men to a bomber, more than 4,000 American airmen took part in both the Friday and Saturday raids.

"The fight is now at white heat," Eaker declared.

The Americans went out by daylight yesterday only a few hours after Berlin was raided by nightflying RAF Mosquito bombers for the 14th time in less than a month.

In a quick follow-up to Friday's American daylight blow, the British returned to Bremen that night and also hit the rubber and railroad center of Hanover for the fourth time in less than three weeks. Simultaneously Mosquitos struck Berlin.

Berlin reports said the American planes yesterday dropped bombs in the heart of Müster, and added: Casualties among the population were considerable as well as damage to residential quarters, churches and public buildings.

Münster, which has plants turning out chemicals, war machinery and surgical instruments, has been hit many times at night by the RAF, the last big raid occurring on 11 June. At one time reconnaissance showed 260 acres of the city devastated.

London tabulations showed the weekend attacks boosted to 539 the number of German aircraft shot down in the last eight days, against a loss of 241 Allied bombers and fighters.

General Eaker's disclosures started a new wave of "invasion before Christmas" talk.

It has long been acknowledged here that the invasion date would depend largely upon the speed with which United States air power was built up in this theatre. The weekend performance of the Americans clearly demonstrated that the Yankee airmen are through sparring and are ready for the championship bout.

The sizzling three-day pace by the Americans brought showers of praise — and the most space yet — from the British press, which naturally is partial to its own mighty RAF.

At the same time from Stockholm came dispatches saying that Swedish aviation commentators were hailing the American raids on eastern Germany as most sensational, testimony to the growing power of the United States Air Forces.

On the same day that the above press report was written (11 October 1943) Britain's Prime Minister, Winston Churchill, sent the following letter to General Devers:

I shall be obliged if you will convey to General Eaker and his Command the thanks of the British War Cabinet for the magnificent achievements of the 8th Air Force in the Battle of Germany in recent days, culminating in their remarkable successes of last week.

In broad daylight the crews of your bombers have fought their way through the strongest defence which the enemy could bring against them and have ranged over the length and breadth of Germany, striking with deadly accuracy many of the most important hostile industrial installations and ports.

Your bombers and fighters which support them in these fierce engagements have inflicted serious losses on the German Air Force, and by forcing the enemy to weaken other fronts have contributed notably to the successes of the Allied arms everywhere.

The War Cabinet extend their congratulations also to the ground crews of the 8th Air Force without whose technical skill and faithful labor these feats of arms would not be possible.

I am confident that with the ever-growing power of the 8th Air Force, striking alternate blows with the Royal Air Force Bomber Command, we shall together inexorably beat the life out of the industrial Germany and thus hasten the day of final victory.

better fighter escort was provided, bombers and their crews were being needlessly sacrificed.

« « « » » »

On Thursday, 14th October 1943, the 8th Air Force attacked the ball-bearing factories at Schweinfurt deep inside Nazi Germany with a force of nearly 300 bombers, escorted, to the limit of their range, by 200 fighters.

Lt. Colonel Thomas Jeffrey, of the 390th Bomb Group, leading the 13th Wing recalls:

We all knew that Schweinfurt was going to be a tough mission and we expected trouble. Past experience had shown that during the oblique turns to change our course at specific points during the missions as briefed, some Squadrons, or occasionally entire Groups, would become temporarily detached from the tight defensive formation of each Wing during these manoeuvres at high altitude. This inevitably attracted enemy fighters, often to our cost.

During the evening before the raid I contacted each of the other Group Leaders in the 3rd Division and discussed with them a method of avoiding this. The plan was that ten minutes or so before each scheduled turn the rear Groups in each Wing would increase their airspeed and make the turns, at different altitudes, simultaneously with each Wing's Lead Group. It proved to be most effective and our losses were kept to a minimum, despite fighter attacks for long periods. During the mission we could clearly see the B17's from the 1st Division ahead of us going down occasionally as a result of concentrated fighter attacks.

As was the case in preceding missions, the brunt of the fighter attacks fell upon the Leading Wing of the first Air Task Force. The 40th Combat Bomb Wing, comprising the 92nd, 305th, and the 306th Bomb Groups, had 27 of their B17's shot down during the Schweinfurt raid. In total the 1st Division lost 45 aircraft and the 3rd Division 15 B17's on "Black Thursday." Despite these losses, 500 tons of high explosive and incendiary bombs were dropped on the ball-bearing factories which resulted in a 60% fall in production. 38 German fighters were shot down.

Lieutenant Leonard Herman, Navigator B17F *Brass Rail,* 95th Bomb Group, vividly remembers:

As soon as we learned that fresh eggs were on the menu for our pre-dawn breakfast that morning, we knew we were in for a real tough mission. Fresh eggs were always the indicator. The better the chow, the rougher the mission.

Schweinfurt would be our 24th mission. When you've flown that many missions you learn to accept the combat routine and the basics. We were a "no chatter" crew. We didn't get this far without being sharp. Our original pilot had been killed a month previously, several of us had been wounded, but the majority of our original crew were still together and we made it because we were good.

Flak, we can't do anything about. We fly our course, stay in formation and pray we don't get hit. At least with the fighters we can shoot back. We are busy . . . busy watching them as they line up to attack our tight formation . . . busy following them as they swoop in . . . crazy busy . . . short bursts . . . short bursting them to death . . .

We are on pure oxygen and can feel the adrenalin flowing. There is no fear at this time because we are too busy to think about anything but doing our job. We see planes hit, we count the chutes as our buddies bail out and we wonder when the hell the fighters are going to stop coming.

We're on the bomb run, flying straight and level. Then it's "BOMBS AWAY!" . . . "Bomb-bay doors coming up!" . . . "Let's get the Hell out of here!" . . .

We peer down seeing the bombs hit, watching the explosions and the flames and the smoke. Now the purpose of our mission is complete. Good, bad, or indifferent. We know one thing, we are going home. We had dropped our bomb-load. Our planes will be faster on the way back. Sure, there's still going to be plenty of fighters and flak to fly through and there will be further losses, but somehow we got through and got back.

That was Schweinfurt . . .

Although the cost had been high, the 8th Air Force had again demonstrated that a determined attack with a sufficiently large force of bombers could not be turned back. For the accuracy of its bombing on this mission the 390th Bomb Group was awarded a Distinguished Unit Citation.

In addition to the 5 B17's lost by the 94th Bomb Group, Bury St. Edmunds, was *Brennan's Circus,* flown by 21 year old Lieutenant Joe Brennan. After having lost two engines while in the target area Lt. Brennan elected to attempt the long flight home at low level across Germany, Belgium and Holland. Despite attracting constant fighter attacks and fire from ground batteries, *Brennan's Circus* eventually reached the North Sea having lost one of the two remaining engines to ground fire over Holland.

Just five miles short of the English coast Lieutenant Brennan expertly ditched his aircraft on the cold and unforgiving North Sea. His crew, having completed their 25th and final mission, clambered into the two life rafts and were picked up an hour later by a British Air-Sea Rescue launch. As *Brennan's Circus* slid quietly beneath the waves her crew said a prayer of thanks.

Flying from Thorpe Abbotts that day, as composite with the 95th and 390th Bomb Groups, were eight B17's led by 20 year-old Lieutenant Owen "Cowboy" Roan of the 100th Bomb Group. During the Schweinfurt mission only one 8th Air Force Bomb Group suffered no crew casualties or battle damage . . . the eight Fortresses of "The Bloody Hundredth."

Asserts 100th Bomb Group Operations Officer, Major John Kidd:

> The Fall of 1943 was an extremely difficult period in air warfare. The United States Air Forces were pioneering a concept of daylight strategic bombing, and there was a lot on record as to whether or not it would succeed. The losses were high, but we had photographic evidence that positive results were being achieved. However, the predominant question remained. Was it worth the cost? This was being discussed and assessed at the appropriate levels both in London and Washington all the time we were flying these missions.

Bloodied but unbowed, the 8th Air Force attacked Duren in the Ruhr Valley on 20 October, 1943. Fourteen more raids on German strategic targets were flown by December 31, including two on Münster's marshalling yards and six to the shipyards of Bremen, Kiel and Emden. During this same period, five targets in Occupied France and Norway were also attacked, including a raid on a VI Flying Bomb site.

The fact remained, however, that the American daylight bombers, while flying without long-range fighter escort, were enduring unacceptable losses. Although the Luftwaffe itself was suffering a high rate of attrition, it had repeatedly demonstrated that by concentrating its firepower, air-to-air rockets especially, on one bomber formation at a time in massed attacks, they could, and did, succeed in bringing down many bombers.

General Curtis LeMay said at that time:

> The more Fortresses we have here the shorter the war is going to be, and the more fighters we have to protect the Forts, the smaller the losses will be.

On 1 December 1943, the superb long-range P51 Mustang,

generally regarded by experts as the finest all-round fighter of the war, made its debut in support of the 8th Air Force. Its fuel consumption was about half that of the P47's thirsty 130 gallons per hour, but before it was accepted for service in December, the substitution of a lighter Merlin engine, and relevant design flaws, caused several of the early P51's to lose their tail sections in high speed tests. These problems were successfully overcome, and with larger capacity auxiliary fuel tanks now available to the P38 Lightning and P47 Thunderbolt fighters, the 8th Air Force resumed long-range deep penetration raids in early 1944 with telling effect.

The Americans had been flying daylight raids from England since mid-1942, supporting the night attacks on Occupied Europe by RAF Bomber Command. By mid-October 1943, the 8th Air Force in England had grown to 21 Bombardment Groups and 9 Fighter Groups. Barely eight months later, in early June 1944, the 8th had more than doubled its air strength to 46 Bomb Groups and 18 Fighter Groups. This mighty force was quite capable of putting nearly 3,000 combat aircraft into action at any one time, and very often did so.

Among the hundreds of Polish fighter pilots who had fought a very valiant rearguard action while flying, since the outbreak of war in 1939, with the Polish Air Force, the French Air Force,and then the Royal Air Force from bases in England, was the vastly experienced Witold "Lanny" Lanowski. He recalls:

> In May 1944, I transferred from the RAF and joined the 56th Fighter Group, "Zemke's Wolfpack" with their red-nosed Thunderbolts.
>
> After covering the bombers we were easily able to go looking and seeking at random for the Luftwaffe. We would pounce on them as they were taking off, we attacked them when they were landing. There was no place in the whole of Germany which we could not reach.
>
> Gone were the days when I almost wept with despair and frustration at the dreadful sight of our bombers returning over Holland and Belgium from a raid inside Germany being literally chopped to pieces by the German Air Force in the distance, simply because our Spitfires and Thunderbolts had insufficient range at that time.
>
> I was very proud to have fought by the side of those young British and American fighter pilots, some of whom were no more than boys, who fought extremely bravely above foreign soil.

Chapter 16

LIEUTENANT Jack Nosser, Bombardier of the 390th Bomb Group Fortress *Cash and Carrie,* resumes his narrative following his B17's crash-landing.

While I was trying to put on my shoes we held a hurried conference. It was obvious that Lt. Drouhard our injured Navigator, could not travel. So we made him as comfortable as possible with chute packs before we had to leave him. We then agreed to split up. Pilot Lt. McGuire and Top Turret Gunner Sgt. Auger would go in one direction, while Co-Pilot Lt. Oster and myself would head-off in another.

We had no idea where we were, but guessed we must be somewhere between Münster and Holland, and absolutely no idea how far we were from the Dutch border. We headed off immediately through a group of trees, trying to put as much distance as possible between ourselves and the crashed plane, as we had been instructed to do during our briefings. We constantly changed direction, crawling on all-fours over exposed areas until we reached the next clump of trees, and so on.

Finally we stopped to rest since my heavy flying suit was about to overcome me. I then made a serious error. I removed the suit and buried it. I was left with only thin cover-alls over light underwear. I also talked Glen Oster into getting rid of his pistol, as I was afraid it would get us into even deeper trouble than I thought we could handle. We kept moving until we found a place to hide, a ditch overgrown with bushes and brush, to await nightfall. Throughout the afternoon we heard German search parties yelling to each other, and the sound of motor vehicles which told us the hunt was on in earnest. We also heard the spine-tingling howls and barking of tracker dogs, and then knew just how a hunted animal feels and fears. Sheer terror is not a pleasant experience.

While we waited we examined our escape kits, ate some chocolate, and studied our silk escape maps. But they told us very little, as we had no idea of our location when we crashed. We both felt, however, that we were still inside Germany.

We left our temporary refuge at dusk and continued heading westwards, using our button compasses. (These were small enough to hide on one's person in the most obvious place imaginable!) We walked all night across flat fields, avoiding roads and bridges. Our shoes, socks and pants were soaked by the heavy dew from the thick, grassy meadows. When dawn finally came we found a large haystack, well away from any houses or farm buildings. We burrowed our way into the centre of the stack, after first removing our socks and shoes. We hung them on a fence outside our hole, hoping that the sun would dry them during the coming day. We realised that it was a calculated risk which we had to take. The myth that haystacks are warm is completely false — I shivered so much from the cold that I was able to get little rest, which of course, was so vital to our predicament.

At about noon on 11 October, Glen looked out to check things, and found a teenage boy close by watching him. The lad then took off at high speed. We hurriedly put on our shoes and socks, and when we got out into the open saw the boy with a group of adults watching us. They made no effort to help us or make themselves known. Soon after they had gone away we approached an old lady who spoke a little English. She kindly gave us some carrots to eat, and told us we were in Eastern Holland, near Arnhem. She was to prove the only Dutch person to help us.

We wandered around aimlessly for the rest of the day, hiding in remote and secluded places, and going into open spaces where we could be seen in the hope of some friendly contact. We also approached people, but they repeatedly waved us away. We made sure they were alone and nobody else was in sight. We then walked through a village and saw people hiding behind their window curtains as they watched us.

The failure of the American Intelligence Section to give us any information on the Dutch Underground was critical. We had considerable briefing regarding the French Resistance, but I can recall nothing at all on the Low Countries. It would seem to me that belonging to the Underground was in itself a risk, and taking a risk was part of their contribution to freeing their country from the Nazis. But didn't they realise that those American and British aircraft that flew over their country almost every day and night were crewed by people who were also taking risks to help them?

Just after nightfall we ended up on a fairly busy bicycle path, where we again tried to get people to stop. Finally, we physically had to halt a lone cyclist. After rather a pantomime, we eventually made him understand our plight. He motioned for us to follow him and led us to a farmhouse where he invited us inside.

The farmer and his wife got us something to eat and made extreme efforts to converse. Then I noticed that the man who had led us to the farm had suddenly disappeared, and that the hitherto convivial atmosphere in the room was becoming markedly strained. The desire for somewhere warm and comfortable to sleep that night made me ignore the warning of something being unsettling. When my growing apprehensions became strong enough for me to act, both doors into the room suddenly burst open and in rushed about eight burly Dutch policemen. They certainly did not take any chances.

They took us outside and we started walking down a dirt path. I said to the nearest policeman, "What are you going to do now — shoot us?" He laughed, and raised the flap on his holster. He had no gun. "Oster," I said, "we've got it made. The Underground have got us now!" "I don't think so," he replied.

We spent that night in a police cell.

The next morning the Dutch Sergeant and another policeman took us into Arnhem and handed us over to the German S.S.

What happened next more than confirmed and heavily underlined my deeply held conviction that what we were fighting were the worst possible examples of mankind.

At the German Headquarters Building we were taken to a large office and pushed behind a counter that stretched the whole length of the room. The Dutch Police were ordered out and a short time later a German Corporal motioned us to take seats. He and a German Military Policeman and an enlisted man who was busily typing were the only other occupants in the room.

We waited patiently to see what was going to happen next. Suddenly from outside the door came the sounds of a loud furor. There was the clicking of heels and loud yelling of "Heil's" that seemed to go on for several minutes. I began to anticipate that no less a person than Hitler himself was about to make his entrance. As I watched the door, half in amazement and half in apprehension, in strode an SS Colonel who was at least six feet six inches in height . . . a giant. The three Germans came to "Attention" with their eyes staring directly in front. Glen Oster and I sat in our chairs and watched the proceedings with astonishment as the Colonel walked, looking to neither right or left, directly to a desk on the far side of the room. He seemed to fold in unusual places in order to seat himself behind the desk.

The Colonel called the Corporal to the desk and, as the Corporal stood at quivering attention, the Colonel angrily, and at great length, bellowed at him. When he was dismissed the Corporal turned and came straight to Oster.

"Do you men not know enough to stand when an Officer enters the room?", he demanded in English.

Oster stared hard at the Corporal for a few seconds. He pulled himself straight in the chair. "We are officers and we certainly do not stand when other officers enter the room.", he replied haughtily.

A precarious silence fell over the room. I felt a glow of pride at Oster's words. "That's telling them", I thought. My eyes were suddenly pulled toward the Colonel by the noise of the man unfolding from behind the desk. The Colonel almost ran to Oster's chair. His face was bloodless and viciously angry. The Colonel's eyes became wild and his mouth began slavering as he began ranting and raving like a madman. As I watched and listened to the outburst of hysterically malicious petulance, my insides coiled violently. This sudden close perspective of the enemy I had been fighting from the distances of altitude gave me confirmation of some of the reasons for the war. This Nazi was a man completely devoid of tolerance or reason; a bubbling mass of hatred and terror. From the geyser that was his mouth poured molten cruelty and the live steam of fanatacism. He seemed completely oblivious of his audience and became lost, like a pagan priest in a secret ritual, in the black void of uncontrolled passion.

"This is the end", I thought apprehensively and comprehensively, "another hour will not see us alive." I began thinking and wishing Oster had kept his mouth shut just once.

Finally, like a spring driven toy that had been wound too tightly and then snapped, the Colonel subsided into silence and stood, panting and glaring around the room, with the expression on his face of a man finding himself lost in the wilderness. Oster sat stiff and upright carefully studying the floor. The German soldiers were standing transfixed and almost paralyzed, their eyes shifting rapidly to avoid the direct stare of the Colonel.

The silence of the room became deep and profound, which made the sudden opening of the office door sound like an event of catastrophic consequence. Everyone watched with undivided fascination as two SS soldiers marched into the room and snapped rigidly to attention, their right arms thrust straight out in the Nazi salute. "Heil Hitler!", they yelled in unison to the Colonel.

"Heil Hitler", responded the Colonel with equal fanatacism and then he spoke rapidly in German pointing to us.

The SS soldiers motioned us out of our chairs and through the opening of the counter. I hardly remember the walk to the street until the bright morning sunlight hurt our eyes. One of the Germans said something to me and I shook my head indicating I didn't understand. The SS man pulled up the flap on his holster and wrapped his hand around the grip of his luger. He glanced at me meaningfully. It was a thousand words.

"Watch out, Oster", I warned. "this bastard wants an excuse to shoot us here and now."

"They're depraved and that Colonel wanted . . .", Oster began and stopped as the luger cleared its holster and was pointed an inch from his face.

The SS men said something venemously in German. We were to remain silent.!

It was a three block walk to Arnhem prison. The first solitary cell brought the soul searing realization of captivity and the painful gnawing began its burning within me.

This then was my first meeting with the Germans but it was to prove by no means the last. The next day we were transferred to Rotterdam prison.

We were being taken across the prison yard to the latrines when the first B17's of the Schweinfurt raid passed overhead on 14 October, on their way to the target.

I have no idea why they sent us to Rotterdam, near the Dutch coast.

From there we were put in a barred railway coach and escorted to the Interrogation Centre at Frankfurt-on-Main in Central Germany. At Frankfurt railway station several old men tried to attack us with sticks. Frankfurt itself had hardly been touched by bomb damage at that time. If only those people had known what was in store for them . . .

Lt. McGuire and Sgt. Auger had evidently been picked up as they tried to cross a bridge during the late afternoon of 10 October. We arrived at Frankfurt just as the American prisoners were filtering in following the Schweinfurt raid. We talked with some of them through the partition in the next very cramped room, and discovered a navigator and bombardier from the 390th whom we knew well, as we came from the same Squadron, the 570th. Apparently, when they were descending after bail-out they saw their plane explode, and assumed their pilot and co-pilot had been killed. But about three months later, at Sagan Prisoner of War camp, the co-pilot arrived there with his face and hands terribly scarred from burns. The Pilot, Lt. Cole, was killed holding the ship steady while his crew bailed out . . .

Lt. Joseph Rose, Co-Pilot of the 91st Bomb Group B17G 737, continues his recollections of the Münster Raid:

I took a free-fall of about 15,000 feet and landed very quickly after pulling my ripcord. It was sometime in the middle of the afternoon of Sunday 10 October 1943. I was in a rather large, uncultivated field with a hedgerow not too far away from me. My first action was to bury my parachute in a shallow grave along by the hedgerow. The warm flight clothing and boots, together with the escape kit, would hold me in good stead for the October journey to freedom, at least until I could get some warm clothing which would not be so conspicuous.

At that time I was still professing a belief in the Jewish religion, and as I walked along the small backroads and across fields, I could not help but reflect on the words I had heard the day before from our Squadron Commander. "You fellows of the Jewish faith all know that tomorrow is Yom Kippur. Those of you who do not wish to participate in tomorrow's mission will be excused." I made no effort to reveal my heritage. "Coincidence or punishment?" I thought as I trudged along towards darkness. The reader must judge for himself. I know that four years later I married a Christian girl and am still living a healthy, satisfying and rewarding life at the age of 61.

Early next morning I continued in a southwesterly direction, but had still not come across anything to pinpoint my location. It was not until some time around noon that the sight of a lone farmer near a cottage, and my desire for a hot meal, combined to form the rationale for my first contact.

I was lucky. He pointed to his barn and bade me wait there. Presently he appeared with a large bowl of beef stew and cold milk. It was like ambrosia. However, the farmer was literally scared to death. He explained that if he were caught giving aid to the "enemy" both he and his wife would be shot. I understood his plight, although very little of his language, and after he showed me my position on the escape kit map I thanked him and continued on course.

It was towards dusk that I came upon a single brick kiln with several large haystacks somewhat distant from the kiln. I do not remember seeing any other buildings. I decided to spend the night in one of the haystacks, and the next day if things looked all right, I would try and establish contact. Having made myself comfortable by burrowing in at the top of the stack, I was able to observe the coming and going of three men working at the kiln.

I stayed in the hay until mid-afternoon the next day, only to get down at night for pump water and to relieve myself. Since being shot down two days earlier I had not seen any type of military presence, so I reached the conclusion that these men were a calculated risk, and that I was never going to make it without somehow being put in touch with the Dutch Underground.

I came down the back side of the stack and walked slowly down and into the kiln. I don't remember the physical layout, only the heat of the kiln, the three men and some chairs around a small desk.

They were cordial and offered to help me as much as possible. I was elated. Maps were put in front of me, and one of the men left to bring me civilian clothes and official papers. As I enjoyed the proffered apples, the remaining two men explained how I was to proceed and the next person that I would contact a bit further down the Escape Line.

It seemed to be only a matter of a very few minutes before the door was flung open and two Dutch policemen rushed in with pistols drawn and the third man right behind them. After seeing that I offered no resistance (I was unarmed) the charged atmosphere disappeared and the same reason for their actions was voiced by them all, "The Germans are here in large numbers, and we are afraid for our lives." Of course, the Dutch Underground was there too, but I had simply made the wrong choice of people.

There were three bicycles outside, and the two policemen and myself made off for what, if I remember correctly, turned out to be the little town of Markelo, Holland, some five or six kilometres away. There, after some more hot beef stew served to me by the Mayor's wife, and observed by a dozen or so curious, but "understanding" townspeople, I was put in an automobile and driven to Amsterdam.

The German soldiers in charge of the jail there were anything but hostile. However, the accommodation left a great deal to be desired — straw on a cold concrete floor in a cell of what must have been a medieval fortress. Fortunately, I left Amsterdam the next day on a train which followed the route of the Rhine River, in the company of two civil, but military-bearing, German soldiers who made the long trip as pleasant as possible under the circumstances.

I spent the next 10 or 12 days at the Interrogation Centre at Frankfurt where I first became acquainted with the deafening sound of German flak guns and the terrifying roulette of a British night bombing attack. I seriously question if a seven point Richter scale earthquake could cause such panic and horror.

My time at Dulag Luft was spent in solitary confinement in a four by eight foot cell with a translucent window and a burlap mattress half full of straw on the floor. The ersatz coffee and watery barley soup was calculated to only sustain life.

My one trip to the interrogator produced the only bit of humour (although I didn't know it at the time) during my stay there.

After offering me an apple and cigarettes, he asked several questions about my attachment to what Squadron and which Group, its location and airplane insignia. After informing him that I was obliged only to give my name, rank and serial number (a phrase I am sure he had heard enough times to cause him apoplexy) he said, "Well, Lt. Rose, perhaps you will be good enough to tell us your religion?"

Although my dog-tag had a "P" for Protestant on it since my first combat mission, I could still feel my head and torso dropping through my anus. I managed to give the same trite phrase . . . name, rank and number.

"Oh, you don't have to tell me, Lt. Rose. I can look at you and see what you are." My Semitic features had spoken for themselves. In my entire months as a Prisoner of War at Sagan my religion was never alluded to again. This is not to say, however, that those of us who espoused Judaism at the time did not suffer just a little higher level of emotional trauma than our Christian counterparts.

Here follow some excerpts from the personal diary of Lt. John Pettenger, Pilot, B17F 155, 385th Bomb Group, written in December 1943:

A day to remember is definitely October 10, 1943, on which day I had some difficulties over Münster on a routine bombing mission.

My first recollection is of gazing down the barrel, or perhaps I should say up the barrel of a 12 gauge (hammer type) shotgun held by some German Home Guardsman I assume, after having jumped from my aircraft. Apparently I had been knocked out by the fall. I enjoyed the fall through space very much — all except the sudden stop at the end.

After bailing out I made about three tumbles, head over heels, then settled down on my back, my feet sticking straight up in the air. Turning my head over to see the ground so as to tell when to open the chute, I went into a tight, flat spin so I pulled the ripcord. By this time I was at 10,000 feet. Different from other cases, there was no jar when the chute opened. I remember the sudden reaction I had to the quietness and stillness about me. I looked up and could see other chutes up above me, and others below, hitting the ground. To the west could be seen large pillars of smoke rising over Münster. Then I seem to have felt quite happy, and repeating to myself, "Well, here I am, right in the Fuhrer's back yard."

My legs kept getting tired on the way down so I would double up and hold them to rest them. I might have thought of my wife at home, and many other things, but they were only fleeting remembrances for I was fast approaching the ground. Getting closer I could hear the flak guns and the wind whistling in my ears. There was a small field under me but I was heading for a barbed-wire fence bordering it. As a last desperate chance I spilled the chute, causing me to fall faster and backwards, but carrying me way from the fence. I landed on my back with my legs folded under by back. (Today, December 13, 1943, I still have a sore knee from the fall.) I still had my steel flak helmet on, which accounts for my being alive, for I had hit the back of my head, also. Then, complete oblivion. Falling through space is such a pleasant sensation, I should like to repeat the same experience if I could eliminate the sudden stop at the end.

The guard kept asking if I had a pistol and started to search me, not too thoroughly. By this time I had regained my senses and could see that we were not alone. Beside the guard, there was a most beautiful horse in the field. I can't give an opinion whether German or possibly a Polish horse, but just the same, a wonderful bit of horseflesh.

Suddenly I knew how an animal in a cage must feel. Leaning on the fence were about ten civilians, mostly women. Just staring at me, not unfriendly, but just a stare of curiosity. I must have been a sight to make anyone curious, standing there in heavy flying clothes with a steel helmet still on.

The guard had me pick up my parachute and walk over to the road. The women kept feeling the silk of the chute and seemed to be amazed at its smoothness. I would look at them and they would stare back at me with no emotion, except perhaps curiosity. I felt like a monkey in a cage.

It was now about 1530 in the afternoon, flak guns were still going off, the sun was getting through a thick haze of smoke from Münster to the west. Presently, a stormtrooper came putt-putting down the road on a small motorcycle, shouting with one lung the size of a Canadian Spam can. He instantly searched me and inquired the time I had come down. Looking mostly for a gun, he took my escape kit. He looked pretty sharp with his light-green dress uniform. He tied my chute on the back of the machine, tied my hands behind me, and ordered me to get on the back of the machine. There was no place for my feet — strictly a one-man affair.

It must have been a rare sight, we two going down the road. I still had my steel helmet on, hands tied behind me, and holding on with my knees for dear life. Quite a few people on the road, walking or riding bicycles, all stopped and stared at such a strange sight.

After a ride of about a mile-and-a-half, we came to a parked station-wagon (I think built by Ford). We stopped here and I was put in the car in which there was another shot-down flyer. The trooper left us with the

Home Guards. After a ten-minute wait, they all piled into the station-wagon, about ten of them, and we drove a short distance to a farmhouse. Here I kept motioning to my hands until they untied them. My, what beautiful houses here. It was a very rustic and artistic farmhouse, if you like that sort of thing.

A little girl kept asking us what we were (British or American), how many men were on the ship, our Squadron, if we were married, and other questions. She spoke fairly good English, and laughed at us when we played dumb, calling us "dumb kaputs." Not getting any information, the guards chased her away. All of this time we were locked in the car. After thirty minutes the guards piled back in and we drove to a small town, about ten miles northeast of Münster. We made quite a commotion as we came to the centre of town. We left the station-wagon and went into the Town Hall or Court House. We entered a small office overlooking the square from which I could see and hear the people outside talking and chattering a mile a minute. Presently, a civilian lawyer arrived who spoke English. He asked me different questions, among them if I was married. They could see the ring on my finger so I admitted same.

After thirty minutes or so, another civilian arrived who also spoke English, and took us outside to a small car. We got in the car with a civilian guard and proceeded to an airfield just outside town. On the way there, the driver said that he had lived in the States before the war, and he tried to get information. He made comments like, "You are fighting for the men with the money. There isn't any sense in all these wars. I would like to be back in the States." He said he had to return to Germany.

We came to the entrance of the field and entered the gatehouse. I remember taking particular notice of the blackout curtains, saying to myself, "Hell, the Germans have their air raid troubles, too."

This field was permanent and well-built, having large, two-story tile and brick buildings, and every type of plane in the Luftwaffe. While waiting here about an hour-and-a-half, I received another search. Women passing through the gatehouse stopped to stare at me and feel the silk in my parachute, always remarking how smooth it was.

One by one the rest of my crew filtered in. Lt. Dorney, my Bombardier, had actually parachuted right into the middle of the airfield from our ship, miles from where I landed, and was the first to arrive. He'd been kept in a separate part of the building since capture. When he landed, he headed for the nearest fence, but a few rifle shots changed his mind.

Funny incident happened here. A real sharp-looking Captain had been waiting for his driver for about thirty minutes, pacing back and forth with his dog. Finally the driver arrived and immediately tried to give some excuse, but the Captain didn't give him a chance. He ordered him to a stiff "Attention" and started shouting at him. The Captain would keep pacing back and forth, and each time he passed the luckless one he would howl at him so hard the room shook, while the driver was shaking in his boots.

Finally, the Captain got tired of shouting and they left. As soon as they had gone the remaining enlisted men all gave sighs of relief and shook their heads.

A small guard then took us to the main administration building. The moon was coming up and it held promises of a truly beautiful night, for more reasons than one. I thought about overpowering the guard (an easy matter) but couldn't see the percentage, being on an airfield with a steel fence and guards all around the planes.

In the morning, after getting more meat and bread to eat, we were lined up in front of the building. Here the Germans commenced to confiscate any excess clothing (in their opinion) that we were wearing. They took leather flying helmets, leather jackets, and all sheepskin clothing. "It is warm in Germany," one guard remarked as he relieved me of my flying boots, but oh, how they lied.

Next thing we knew, we were on our way to the railroad station at Münster in a bus with the curtains drawn. They drive fast here, about 45-50 m.p.h.

What a contrast, the people here and in the small village. Here they stare at you also, but with a look of hate, or in some cases just a blank expression as if they were lost on a sea of darkness. Just a blank stare looking through you. I feel sure they would have made quick work of us if the German guards had not been with us. I heard they have every respect for the Army.

Nearby buildings were still burning or smoking. As we walked by the people, they never missed a chance to trip us if a guard wasn't looking.

We waited for a train for about an hour, during which time the civilians kept staring with hatred at us. The train was a welcome sight.

I would imagine a person would be extremely upset if his home had been destroyed or family killed in the bombing. I can appreciate their feelings towards us somewhat. You might say, "Well, they bombed the Poles, Russians and others." But can these folk, who bear the brunt of the bombings, be held responsible? Then perhaps the pilots or bombardiers? Then again, a pilot or a bombardier is a soldier who is only doing his job taking orders and executing the same, regardless of his desire to do them. Is he to blame? Which all leads back to those responsible members of the political party. Most Germans fear the Party and its members. The majority of the soldiers all want to quit and go home, they don't want to fight, at least the ones I have spoken to. All are not fooled, some know that Germany is losing the war. The Party being so strong they can do nothing.

On our way to Frankfurt we passed through the Ruhr ("Happy Valley"). Every town we passed had been hit by bombs. City block after city block had been totally destroyed, yet the factories and the railroads were still going strong.

We ate lunch at some large town in the lower Ruhr during a stopover. They had Russian prisoners repairing the buildings. Some officer had just made Captain after serving in the army for 14 years. He was so happy about it that he came over to tell us about it too. When we said some of us were Captains in the army after less than three years he exclaimed, "Only in America could such a thing happen!"

It's hard to describe a trip alongside the Rhine by train. Ancient castles on hilltops, rugged mountains and hills, river-boats ploughing along, and small picturesque towns. It is impossible to describe such beauty.

Following the raid several other crewmen who had managed to temporarily evade the German search parties, most of which had tracker dogs to assist them, filtered through the Interrogation Centre at Frankfurt and thence to Prisoner of War camp during the following weeks. One of the very last to be caught in the net following the Münster raid, was Major John Egan of the 100th Bomb Group, who had bailed out of the crippled *Mlle. Zig Zag* in the Haltern area, and had spent the next two weeks living off the land and sleeping rough in Western Germany during which he had managed to "acquire" civilian clothes. When he eventually arrived at Sagan, Stalag Luft III, his hands and face were marked with festering sores from minor flak wounds, but he soon recovered with adequate medical attention.

Majors Egan and Cleven had served together at ten air bases in the United States and at Thorpe Abbotts, England. On his arrival at Sagan, Major Egan was greeted by his fellow Squadron Commander, who said, "You're late. What kept you?"

Chapter 17

LIEUTENANT Arthut Horning, the Navigator of the crash-landed 91st Bomb Group Fortress, had parachuted to the ground in the same area of Holland as Lt. Rose during the Münster raid. He was fortunate in making almost immediate contact with friendly Dutch farmers who supplied him with civilian clothes, and spent the next three days trudging southwards towards the Belgian border, sleeping in haystacks during the nights. He relates:

My feet were still aching and I did not know which way to turn. I wanted to go south, but the roads ran east or west. After flipping a coin I headed east. Soon the road curved too far north, and I had to retrace my steps. The road going west was all right. Having to go back over the same ground was very tiring, and I found that my maps were very inadequate.

When I reached a town, I got off the main road and looked for a place in which to spend the night. I intended stopping at the first house I saw, but some sixth sense told me not to do so. A boy then approached on a bicycle. He was wearing wooden shoes (clogs) and had his hair plastered down straight like a good Dutchman. As I was dead on my feet, I told him who I was. He told me to keep walking and then rode slowly some way ahead in case anyone was watching. We eventually reached his farmhouse.

There I met his parents. Hot water was brought to soak my feet, and I sat there feeling wonderful while they discussed how to get me out of Holland. We all agreed that the most important thing, for the time being, was for me to have some welcome rest. My friend thought he had heard that I could be flown back to England, but I was highly sceptical. He then said, however, that he had a friend who could arrange it, and would see him that night.

I slept in the best bed in the house that night and all through the next day, 14 October. That evening, the friend was brought to the farmhouse. He spoke good English. He asked my name and checked my identity. He assured me that I would be flown out, and said that he would return in a day or two, to let me know the final arrangements. He vanished after that, and my friends could never contact him again.

After waiting for two days my friends became nervous, and I knew for their sakes that I must move on. They volunteered to buy my railroad ticket for me. It was such a small place, however, that I was afraid the ticket might be traced if I was captured, and I certainly did not want to put them in jeopardy after all their kindness.

I went to the railroad station on the morning of 17 October, and bought a ticket without any trouble. Now I was faced with the problem of which train was going where. People had also told me that the Wehrmacht and civilians travelled in separate rail cars, and I did not know how to tell the cars apart. I decided to wait until someone was running for a train then running beside them, say "Naar" and then my destination. Doing this would, I hoped, eliminate giving them the chance to notice my accent and get suspicious. When the third train came in I heard someone name the town I wanted, and I got aboard.

There was an elderly lady in the carriage and I sat next to her without anyone paying any attention to me. At the very next stop a whole crowd of German soldiers joined us. The lady, who had been sitting so nicely and quietly beside me, promptly started a conversation with me. Of course, I couldn't understand a word of it. When she would not stop, I said "Ikben doof." (I am deaf). She made several sympathetic clicking noises with her tongue and the crisis passed. All was quiet again and I silently prayed that the soldiers wouldn't notice the perspiration on my forehead.

When I reached the town of Hilvarenbeck, still in Holland, I got off the train and followed the highway towards Belgium. I reached the proximity of the border and had no idea how to cross the frontier checkpoints without the necessary papers.

Then a man came along the road on foot and I stopped him. I explained the position and asked for his help. He guided me for a short distance and then, pointing to something conspicuous, indicated that the border was there. He wished me luck, we shook hands, and then he left.

I hid in some bushes and observed the location for half-an-hour. There were no control points or German patrols in sight. I gathered up my courage and walked straight on over the border. I walked for about six kilometres into Belgium before I met a farmer who I asked for food. So far I had been incredibly lucky.

« « « » » »

Following Lieutenant William Whitlow's hazardous parachute descent from his blazing 385th Bomb Group Fortress his next stroke of extreme good fortune arrived almost immediately, a young English-speaking Dutchman who reports:

I had watched the airman coming down after his bomber had been set on fire by several FW 190's. He landed only a hundred yards from where I watched from the edge of a large wood. I ran across to him and clearly remember asking him, "Are you American?", and his answer, "Yes. Am I in Germany?"

For his own safety 19-year-old Joop Noest, who was himself a fugitive from the Gestapo as a result of his Underground activities in the Hague of Holland previously, had dug a hole within walking distance of the farm, near the village of Holten, where he stayed when there was no danger. He continues:

After I had asked the local farmers, who had gathered round to see Mr. Whitlow, to leave (one of them took his parachute for making new clothes), I took him to my hiding place. I told him that he would be safe but if he was discovered by the Germans he was to tell them that he had discovered the hole by himself.

I then returned to the woods a few hundred yards away and watched the Germans concentrate their search in the numerous farmhouses and buildings. They were asking everyone whether anyone had seen the airmen coming down. One farmer, I heard later, told them that he had seen "the paratroopers" land, form up and then march off in the general direction of Holten!

It was several hours before the Germans departed, however, and I clearly remember my cold perspiration.

Recalls Lieutenant Whitlow:

The hideaway which Joop Noest had used previously was a long, narrow hole dug in tunnel fashion, parallel to the surface, in a ridge between double hedgerows. It had a corrugated iron roof and the opening was hidden by shrubs and undergrowth. It proved to be a most effective hiding place because on several occasions during the next 48 hours German search parties walked through the hedgerow literally within inches of our hideout.

Continues Joop Noest:

I also remember how very cold and damp the dugout was during those long October nights. While I was being given food and drink for us both by different farmers, they warned me that the German search parties were using tracker dogs in the surrounding area. During the next few days and nights that we stayed in the hideout, I only dared to venture out in the dead of night, or in the very early hours, to collect food from friendly farmers.

Lieutenant Whitlow had another surprise coming. He relates:

Eight days later, Joop told me there was another American in the area and he asked if I would go with him and help accomplish his identification. After discarding my flying clothes and changing into civilian clothing obtained by Joop, we rode bicycles for about two miles to where the airman was hiding.

The American was John Ashcraft, my Radio Operator.

Joop Noest concludes:

When I was forced to leave the Hague of Holland to evade the Germans, the Underground organization there gave me the specific task of making contact with shot down Allied airmen who were hiding from the Germans in Eastern Holland. I was also supplied with a list of safe hiding places and addresses in Holten, Wierden, Nijverdal, Rijssen and Almelo. From these locations the escapers were guided through Holland, Belgium, France and eventually Spain and freedom.

Although nearly forty years have gone by since that beautiful sunny Sunday of the 10th October 1943, I vividly remember that day because Mr. Whitlow and Mr. Ashcraft were the very first airmen that I helped to keep from the Germans. I took them to an address in Nijverdal for the next stage of their journey. Quite a large number of escapees were to follow those two during the remainder of 1943 and 1944.

« « « » » »

Lieutenant John Justice, Pilot of the 100th Bomb Group's Fortress *Pasadena Nena,* landed in a thick forest between Barneveld and Ede in Central Holland. His parachute had caught in the branches of a tree but he managed to reach ground without difficulty. Using his button compass he took a southwesterly direction, not knowing if he was in Germany or Holland, and soon came to a very large clearing. It quickly became apparent that he had stumbled on a German Army Camp.

He watched several truckloads of German soldiers, rifles slung, drive out of the camp, presumably he thought, to search for him and his crewmembers. He returned to the depths of the forest and continued walking, eventually coming to a narrow dirt road.

A little later he fortunately made contact with two young boys on bicycles who confirmed that he had parachuted into Occupied Holland. Recalling the incident later, Lt. Justice said:

They thought I was asking them if they were "Deutsch" (German) because they do not use the word "Dutch" — they use "Netherlanders." We finally got the communications worked out. They then had a discussion between themselves which I did not understand, and after a few minutes they motioned for me to follow them, and we went about half-a-mile up the road. They hid me in a roadside ditch and one lad went away on his bike. I think he went to his home to see if his parents would help me. He came back soon after, and evidently his parents had said "No!"

But more positive help and medical treatment was forthcoming during the next few days for the wounded airman at the home of Jacob Boueman at the small village of Kootwijkerbroek in a lonely farmhouse just south of Barneveld where his host introduced him to an Englishman:

The other man was a British spy who had been parachuted into Holland. His job, in my case, was to verify that I was an American and not someone planted by the Germans to infiltrate the Underground. He questioned me very, very thoroughly, but being sent by the British his prime objective was quizzing British escapees, and he did not have too much knowledge of Americans. However, he was satisfied with my answers, and asked me to provide him with questions and situations which he could use in the future when interrogating Americans.

The next evening, after dark, I was introduced to yet another man. I was instructed to follow him on a bicycle to another hiding place and stay about 50 yards behind him. We rode for many miles alongside railroad tracks, dirt roads, paved roads, until we finally came to a small town and went into the home of the Chief of Police of the City of Barneveld, Sergeant Jan Beute.

It was here that I discarded my flying clothes and uniform and was given a set of civilian clothes. Because they spoke no English, communication was difficult. There were three in the family; husband, wife and daughter, who was about 22 years old. I was given a bedroom in the attic which was to be my "home" for the next 30 days.

To relieve the monotony of hiding out in the Beute family's attic, I noticed that they had clocks in various rooms which chimed on the half-hour and the hour. So during my stay, I started a project to adjust all the clocks so that they chimed in unison, a task which I successfully completed.

After 30 days, I was told that I would be leaving the next morning, and that I had been held there for so long because the Germans had maintained checkpoints in an effort to capture me. Now that the checkpoints had been raised, the Underground were taking me on my way.

It must be remembered that the risks people took on my behalf were enormous. If I was caught, then all I had to lose was my freedom, but anyone caught helping me faced torture and death at the hands of the Gestapo.

Very early the next morning a man came and collected me, and after hurried farewells to the Beute family, we cycled to the City of Arnhem. Leaving the bicycles at the railroad depot, my escort bought tickets to Tilburg, Southern Holland.

On his arrival at Tilburg Lieutenant Justice was taken to a small Art Shop owned by Kees van Hombergh, who remembers:

Joep Terhaar brought John Justice to my shop on 11 November 1943. In those days we had only one thought and one purpose; to make our country free again as soon as possible.

Over a period of time I had made a detailed map of the nearby Luftwaffe airfield at Gilze-Rijen using detailed drawings which had been smuggled out by a relative, Frans Mutseers, who worked as a carpenter at the airfield. Nico Hoogers and I explained to Mr. Justice the importance to the Germans of this airfield. We asked him to memorize the positions of local landmarks relating to the airfield's workshops, the under-ground fuel tanks, bomb dumps, and those sort of things.

Although the Allies had attacked this airfield in the past they had not achieved very much, mainly because the Germans had built a dummy airfield about eight miles from Gilze-Rijen near the villages of Riel and Brakel. In late October the Royal Air Force had attacked this decoy. It had rained bombs, and inevitably there were a few casualties. If it could be attacked effectively it would indeed be a great blow and a great triumph for us.

Mr. Justice was also given the description of a British Intelligence agent who would contact him on his arrival in England regarding the details of the plan.

Needless to say, if anyone had been caught by the Germans with the plan in their possession it would have meant instant arrest, and almost certain death. This meant suspense and tension for us all with the constant threat of discovery. The very real possibility of treason was never far away.

Lieutenant Justice also recollects:

During my stay in this area, I became familiar with Radio Free Orange, which was the British broadcast to the Netherlands. The Dutch underground workers wanted a code word or a song that could be played to them so they would know of my safe arrival in England. They explained just how this would work, and that whatever song I came up with had to be something of my very own. After thinking it over for a while, I asked them if they had ever heard the song, "Yes, We Have No Bananas." They were not familiar with it, so they translated the words of the tune into their own language.

On the night of 15 November 1943 Lieutenant Justice was guided across the border into Belgium by 24-year-old Wim Martens, who recalls:

Nico Hoogers brought John Justice to my home from Tilburg. At that time we lived near Alphen, two miles from the Belgian border. As my father was a miller and corn-dealer we often crossed the border into Belgium.

Before leaving I explained to John that he was to follow me at a distance of 100 metres and that when I eventually turned into a building he was to follow. I took him across the border to the village of Poppel where there was a pub for working-class people. The owners, Madame Yvonne de

Jongh van Abeele and her husband had connections with the Belgian Resistance Movement. From Poppel the escapees were guided via Weelde and Turnhout to Brussels.

Lieutenant Justice continues:

There were about five people in the bar on our arrival. The owner was a quiet little man, his wife very outspoken and she carried on most of the conversation. Everyone was drinking beer and I was invited to join them.

The next morning, after having my photograph taken, a new guide and I cycled to a small town which had a railroad station. My guide bought tickets to Antwerp where we changed trains and went on to Brussels.

I was taken to a very impressive apartment in Brussels and greeted by Madame Olders and her sister, who were expecting me. But it transpired that it was too dangerous to stay there and Madame Olders made arrangements for me to be guided across the city by tramcar to another location.

After about four days in this home, I was joined by another American, Carl Spicer, who was also from the 100th Bomb Group. He had been shot down during the Bremen raid on 8 October. On our last day there, the lady of the house was called across the street to answer the telephone. This was at about noon. She returned very nervous, and said she was going to be investigated by the Gestapo for some activity prior to our arrival.

Carl and I had all our clothes on, including overcoats, and were ready to leave immediately. We waited all afternoon and evening, and at about eight o'clock a group of men came to the house. There was a lot of talking which we could not understand, so we cornered a middle-aged gentleman and asked what was happening. He said that a woman down the street had reported our host to the Gestapo for aiding Frenchmen on the run from Germany's forced labour camps. We asked why we were not being taken away immediately, and he replied, "You are not to worry. The Gestapo would take some time to get the investigation started." When we asked what would happen to the informer, he replied, "Oh, don't worry about her, either. I've just shot her . . ."

« « « » » »

After short stays at Nijverdal and Wierden, Lieutenant Whitlow and Sergeant Ashcraft of the 385th Bomb Group were taken by Dutch guides to Hengelo where they stayed with another Dutch family for three days. They were only too well aware of the risks taken by their guides and helpers. It was an acknowledged fact that the percentage of helpers was low, which is wholly understandable considering the consequences which followed discovery or betrayal.

Following their stay at Hengelo, the two escapees left by train for the Roermond area in southeastern Holland via

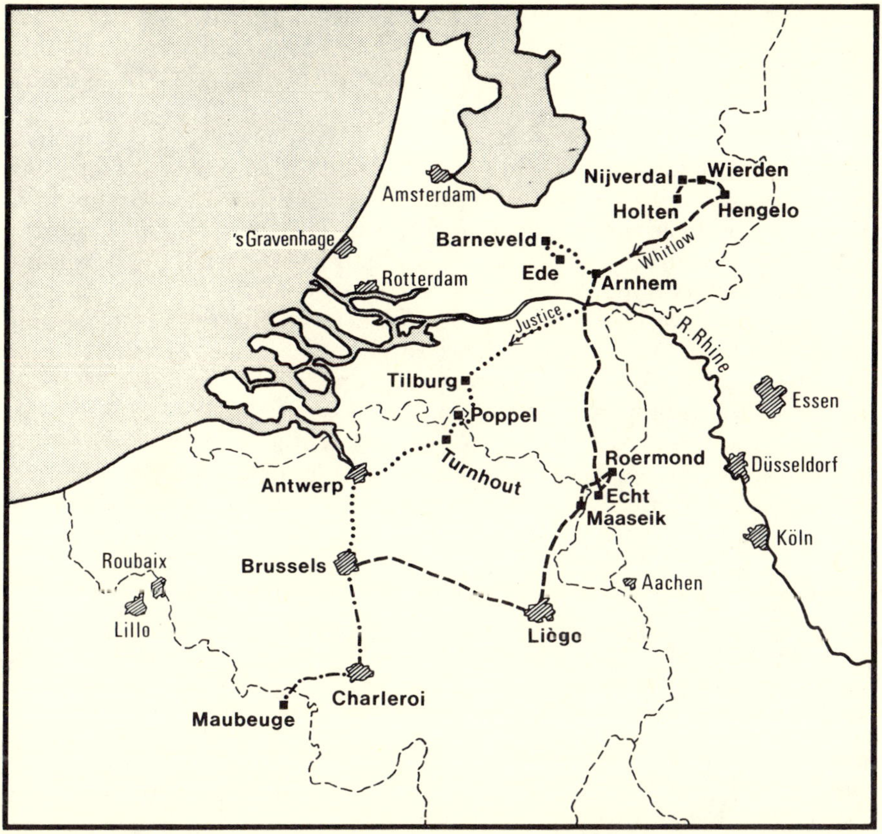

Escape routes taken by Lt. John Justice, 100th Bomb Group, and Lt. William Whitlow, 385th Bomb Group through Holland and Belgium following the Münster raid on 10 October 1943.

Arnhem, accompanied by a Dutch guide.

It was at the Arnhem railroad station that Lieutenant Whitlow had an alarming experience. He recalls:

We never actually came into contact with the Gestapo except in passing through boarding gates at railway stations, and in displaying our tickets and forged passports while travelling by train. Nevertheless, their presence was very often obvious and the fear of our discovery was always triggered off by our own mistakes or by unfortunate circumstances.

I recall one of my first "heartstoppers" to have been at the railroad station at Arnhem while we were waiting for the train to arrive. A very dignified German officer approached me directly and, in either Dutch or German, spoke to me emphatically. Of course, I had no idea what he said, although the inflection in his voice seemed to indicate that he was asking me a question. Fortunately, I noticed that he had an unlit cigarette in his mouth. I was smoking, so I promptly took out a match and lit his cigarette. He then thanked me and walked away.

The next close call was at Roermond. We had been staying at a farmhouse with the Loven family near a wide canal for several days. One night we left the farmhouse, boarded a small boat, crossed the canal and went to the home of a Chinese medical doctor, Mr. A. Wong. The next evening after dark, we got into the back of his big black Oldsmobile sedan and crouched down on the floor. The bridge back across the canal was heavily guarded, but when the guards ordered Doctor Wong to stop, he slowed down, shouted "Doctor" and drove rapidly across the bridge. We were absolutely appalled at the risk he took. If we were discovered, our only punishment was imprisonment — his was death. Soon after we had crossed the bridge we heard the roar of motorcycles behind us. But Doctor Wong merely pulled over to the side of the road to let them pass.

It was that evening, 5th November 1943, guided by resistance members, that we walked across the border from the Dutch village of Neeritter into Belgium.

« « « » » »

During their three week stay in Brussels Lieutenant's Justice and Spicer were moved to two more seperate addresses, the homes of the Cyprien and Depaye families. They were given a complete change of civilian clothes, forged documents, passports and false backgrounds for the next stage of their journey through France by the highly efficient "Comete" escape organization.

The founder of the "Comete" escape line, Madame Andree de Jonghe, had been inspired by stories she had heard about Nurse Edith Cavell, of World War I fame, which her schoolmaster father had read to her as a young girl in Brussels. She subsequently guided many Allied airmen personally to distant Spain. Eventually however, she was betrayed and arrested by the Gestapo and sent to Ravensbruck Concentration Camp.

On the 4th December 1943 the two escaping American airmen arrived in Paris by train. During their seven day stay in the French capital they were helped by a small Frenchwoman whose code name was "The Little Lady in Black", and who was apparantly an original member of the French Resistance Movement.

Lieutenant Justice remembers:

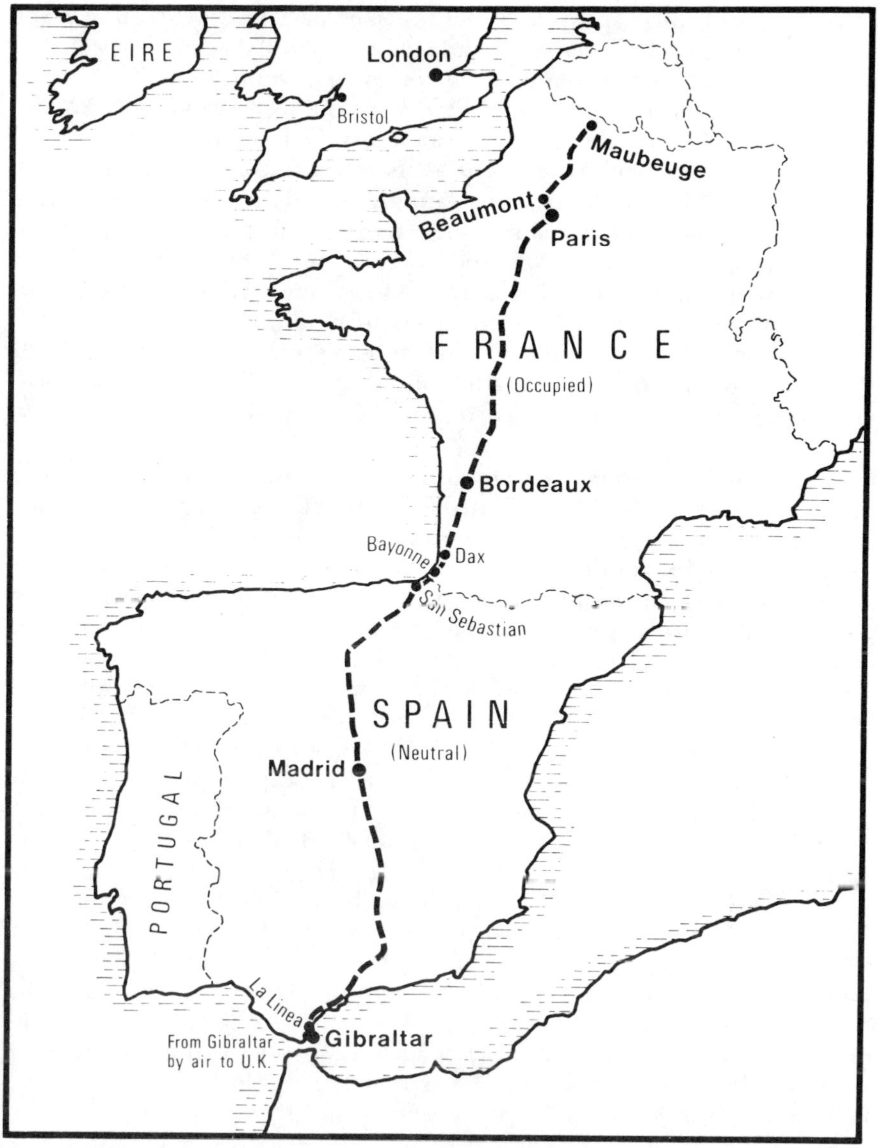

The escape route through France and Spain takes by Lts. Justice and Whitlow.

The "Little Lady in Black" gave us full instructions. She was turning Carl and I over to another lady who would accompany us to Southern France. We met our new lady guide who told us we were going to have dinner in a cafe before going to the railroad station. She also advised us that whenever we were around anyone we were not to speak unless she spoke to us, and our only answer was to be "Oui." She asked if we liked rabbit, if so, when we arrived at the restaurant and read the menu, she would say did we like "lapin", which is rabbit, and we of course, would say "Oui"

Everything went well. The waiter took our order and went to the kitchen, only to reappear and yell clear across the restaurant — there were several uniformed Germans present — that the cooks had no more rabbit. This caused all kinds of confusion. Our guide and the waiter were yelling and hollering at each other across the packed restaurant, and all the time this exchange was going on Carl and I were saying, "Oui . . . Oui . . . Oui!!"

I don't remember what we finally had for dinner. All we wanted was to get out of that very tense and dangerous situation.

We boarded the train, and our guide sat between Carl and I. We travelled all night to Bordeaux, and all night long she talked to us, asking questions, and when we would start to give an answer she said, "Don't say yes, say oui."

On reaching Bordeaux we were turned over to four Frenchmen, as were the other American and British airmen who had been on the same train. They told the four of us what to expect next. Then they bought tickets to a small town to the South of Bordeaux, and we all boarded separately. On arrival, we left the station and were provided with bicycles which we pedalled out of town and into a small forest where we stopped for lunch, and were told we would have to ride for another 15 miles.

We resumed our ride, and after about 35 or 40 miles, we stopped in another wooded area to await darkness before going through the next village which apparently was occupied by many German troops.

While waiting, I complained to the other escapees, saying, "Fifteen miles . . . My God!" One of the Frenchmen heard me. He came over to me and asked, "What is twenty, twenty and ten?" He then explained that his English was not good enough, and he had said fifteen when he meant fifty.

After dark, we proceeded silently through the village without incident and stopped at a French mountain inn among the foothills of the Lower Pyrenees Mountains, the natural barrier between France and Spain. They looked extremely forbidding and virtually impassble from a distance. We were housed for the night, fed a lovely meal and all the wine we could drink. I slept well that night, 11 December, despite knowing that crossing the Pyrenees in December would be extremely hazardous. We were almost free men again, instead of being very wary and frightened fugitives.

Following the dangerous journey across the Pyrenees on foot and travelling through Spain by train to the British base of Gibraltar, the four airmen were flown to England during the night of December 24th 1943. Lieutenant Justice relates:

We arrived at Bristol, England, early on Christmas morning, and were given train tickets to London. We were told to go to a British Security Agency which was occupying a certain hotel. Late in the afternoon we arrived at the Agency in London, and were immediately put under house arrest until we could be positively identified. It was long after the dinner hour, but the British cook did everything he could to ensure that we had a Christmas dinner.

Two days later, Lt. Daniel Smucker from the 100th Bomb Group, arrived, identified us and we were released.

Soon after our release by the British, the American Intelligence people opened an office, complete with living quarters, and we moved in. We had a lot of free time, but we were interrogated daily by a W.A.C. Captain. During one of these sessions the Captain was called away, and returned with a British gentleman. I immediately recognized him as being the man who was described to me when I was shown the map of the Gilze Ryjen airfield. I had lost the small map, made by the two saboteurs, while I was moving from one address to another in Brussels, but I had memorized the important installations on the airbase, the trees where something was camouflaged, the gasoline tanks and so on. When the Captain was again called out of the room, he flew into a rapid fire interrogation of his own and I drew a map of the airfield for him. By the time the Captain returned, he had received from me all the information he wanted, and a short time later departed.

« « « » » »

On the evening of Wednesday, 29 December 1943, the announcer of Radio Free Orange in London, broadcast the following message to the Netherlands:

"En nu, voor onze nieuwe verzoek, hebben we het liedge 'Ja, we hebben geen bananen.' " (And now, for our next request we have the song 'Yes, We Have No Bananas.')

Later, in February 1944, the Luftwaffe airfield at Gilze-Rijen was heavily damaged by a highly-accurate bombing raid carried out by B24 Liberators and B26 Marauders.

« « « » » »

After crossing into Belgium from Neeritter, Lieutenant Whitlow and Sergeant Ashcraft stayed for a week in Maaseik, then travelled on to Liege for a further twelve days. Their Belgian guides changed constantly, sometimes from journey to journey, sometimes from hour to hour. They eventually arrived in Brussels on 24 November 1943 where they came under the care of the highly-organized "Comete" escape line. They left Brussels, after an eventful stay of three weeks, on Wednesday 15th December, and after changing trains and guides three times en route, arrived in Paris the following day.

Both escapees stayed in Paris only two days before leaving by rail for the French Atlantic port of Bordeaux on Saturday, 18 December 1943. They arrived there early the following morning. Unbeknown to them, travelling on the same train but with a different French guide, were Sergeant Walter House, a 384th Bomb Group Radio Operator, and 100th Bomb Group Top Turret Gunner and Flight Engineer Sergeant Thomas Combs.

Both these evaders had vivid memories of hair raising incidents they had experienced during the previous four months "on the run" since being shot down on separate missions over France during the first week in September. They met for the first time as they boarded the train for Southern France, and had originally been scheduled to leave Paris in mid-November, but the arrest and imprisonment of a number of French resistance workers by the Gestapo at that time had meant for them a further month's stay in the French capital. Sergeant Thomas Combs recalls:

> At that time, the Allied Air Forces were dropping supplies to the French Maquis at pre-arranged dropping zones near Paris. Prior to one particular drop, someone apparently tipped off the Germans and they ambushed the dropping zone. During the ensuing battle a red-headed Maquis Captain (I never did discover his name) killed two Germans during his escape. He came to the apartment where I was being hidden in Paris and wanted me to team up with him. As I did not know who he was at that time, and I felt that I was in enough trouble already, I declined his offer. Later on I met him again, and by this time he had a price on his head. To this day, I do not know if he survived the war.

Sgt. Combs describes the tensions of the train journey to Bordeaux — the rear of the train he was on had three carriages filled with German troops:

> They were coming and going through our carriage all night long. You can imagine how we felt. A small female French guide sitting between two escaping American airmen, with inquisitive glances every so often from the passing German troops . . . needless to say, we were both scared, mainly for her sake.
>
> At Bordeaux we changed trains for Dax. We also changed guides, and the last I saw of this very brave young French girl was looking back and seeing her wave goodbye to us over the milling German troops at Bordeaux railroad station.

Lt. Whitlow describes the meeting of the four escapees on Sunday, 19 December:

We first met Sergeants House and Combs when we arrived from Bordeaux at Dax railroad station. Apparently they had been on the same train but with a different guide. From there we were to continue the journey to Bayonne on bicycles. It was only then that we discovered that Sgt. Combs could not ride a bicycle, and we had an experience which was both comical and nearly disastrous.

After several attempts we got him started. He could keep his balance while underway, but he had to walk up the hills. After travelling several miles on Sunday afternoon, we were moving at a good pace downhill when we noticed a group of three German soldiers approaching on foot from the opposite direction, and on the other side of the road. This unnerved Sgt. Combs so badly that he lost control and actually ran into them, knocking one of them down and falling off his bike.

We kept right on moving assuming that we would never see Sergeant Combs again, and that we would soon be overtaken by the German Authorities. After about an hour of hard cycling we stopped for a rest at the side of the road. Sure enough, here came Sergeant Combs, travelling at tremendous speed, down the road on his bike to rejoin us . . .

He breathlessly reported that the soldiers, all of whom were very young Privates, had graciously accepted his hurried apology, which he said he had blurted out in English, and helped him back on to his bike. From what had seemed almost certain discovery and subsequent imprisonment had turned into a very humorous, although dangerous, exchange.

We then continued on our journey at a more sedate pace and in silence.

Finally, came the crossing of the Pyrenees. This was an extremely difficult journey, made worse by the very cold December weather and the lack of adequate footwear. Although we started with shoes, they were so cheaply made that the nails came through to our feet and the moisture of the mud and snow destroyed the soles quickly.

The Germans patrolled the mountains with tracker dogs and there were many occasions when we heard the animals barking at very close range, so it was absolutely essential to cross and re-cross freezing cold mountain streams to avoid capture. One close contact with Germans occurred, when we seemed to be at the ridge of the mountains and on the very border between France and Spain. We were resting at a mountain farm which was the home of a shepherd. We were in the barn, all the sheep being out to pasture, when suddenly the shepherd rushed in to tell us that the Germans were on their way up the hill and that we should hide under the straw and sheep dung, using only straws to breathe through. How we managed to do this without coughing and sneezing I will never know. However, our real good fortune, and that of the shepherd, was that the Germans were without tracker dogs on this occasion.

Sgt. Thomas Combs takes up the narrative:

When we finally came to the border between France and Spain we found that it was guarded. It was night time, and we had to judge when the patrolling border guards were the furthest distance away from where we wanted to cross. When we could no longer hear their footsteps crunching in the icy snow we rushed over into Spain.

We made it — or so we thought — because the very next morning we ran into another guard who fired on us from the top of a small hill. We ran around the hill and came up almost behind him and hid beneath a large rock. We waited for what seemed like forever, hardly daring to breathe, listening to him searching for us. When, at long last he had gone, we moved on very cautiously.

The soles of our shoes had practically disintegrated by this time. Our feet were bleeding and almost frozen with the snow, ice and slush, but the knowledge that we were almost there kept us going.

Lt. William Whitlow describes their final bid for freedom:

On Christmas Eve, again in a shepherd's hut, we were briefed by our guide that we would be taken to a lonely country road, and we were to hide out of sight until we saw a car approach with only one headlight working. I am not really sure what happened at the roadside, either we showed ourselves too soon, or the car was incorrectly identified. In any event, we all made a frantic dash back to our hiding place in the hills. Our guide then left, apparently to make radio or telephone contact, and returned later with a new time schedule. This time we met the "one-eyed" car without any hitch at one o'clock on Christmas morning. What a Christmas present!!

An agent of the British Consulate drove us to San Sebastian, and the following afternoon we all managed to undo the pleasure of our new-found freedom — we gorged ourselves on a fantastic seven-course meal (not to mention wine and cognac) provided by our hosts. Having been on a diet barely above starvation level for months, without any rich foods of any kind, we all became violently ill. Recovery was rapid, however, and on the next day, 26 December 1943, we were chauffered to Madrid in the Consul's limousine for processing and the necessary formalities for our return to England. We were billeted in a luxury hotel for three days and travelled by train to Gibraltar, where we celebrated New Year's Eve with friendly Scottish soldiers.

We returned to England on 4 January 1944.

« « « » » »

During their interrogation by Allied intelligence officers in London, Lt. Whitlow and Sgt. Ashcraft learned of the deaths of fellow crew members Sgt. Thomas Ennis, the Ball Turret Gunner, and Left Waist Gunner Sgt. Howard Walker, on the day of the Münster raid. They were also told that they were not the only members of their crew to make the hazardous and courageous journey down through Occupied Europe to the sanctuary of Spain.

Co-Pilot Lt. Jim Burch, although injuring his leg while bailing out of the stricken plane, and Lloyd Stanford, the Bombardier, together succeeded in making the perilous journey, by a different escape route from Holland, through Belgium and France, across the daunting Pyrenees Mountains to Spain. Virtually at the final barrier between himself and certain freedom, Lt. Burch was so weakened by the strength-sapping ascent and descent of the mountains that he tragically drowned in the icy waters of a swiftly flowing river near Irun, just north of San Sebastian, on the afternoon of 22 December 1943. His body was never found.

« « « » » »

On 30 January 1944, a tired, haggard and underweight but triumphant Lt. "Art" Horning, Navigator of the 91st Bomb Group B17G 737, arrived back in England. His dangerous and arduous journey through Occupied Europe since being shot down over Holland on 10 October 1943, had taken him 112 nerve-wracking days to complete.

One other successful evadee, however, did not reach Spain. Sgt. Theodore Converse of the 390th Bomb Group, after bailing out from his crippled Fortress over Holland on 10 October 1943, made contact with some students who were members of the Dutch Underground at s'Hertorganbosch. From there he crossed into Belgium, where he met and worked with Gaston Mathys, one of the Underground's commanders. "Ted" Converse was eventually liberated by Allied Forces when they reached Brussels in August 1944.

Chapter 18

An American Airman's Prayer

Dear God, please listen as I begin my prayer to You. As I start, I do not find it difficult to express my thoughts. Phrases of truth, constructed in my mind, easily find their way through my heart and on to You.

Bless us, Lord and Savior, not only we men in this bomber; but every man up here in Your cold blue backyard of clouds. We're climbing now; higher and higher to the sun, feeling more and more Your Holy presence.

Slowly, but steadily, we continue to approach enemy territory. Here we ask for guidance . . . as well as forgiveness. Please, dear God, help steer us through the flak-filled course in and out. Protect us in this vast sky en route and from the enemy fighters who lie in wait, like unto the tiger stalking his prey in the jungle.

Forgive us also, for what we are about to do; the spreading of death, horror and destruction among a people . . . forced by crazed leaders to continue a war of bloodshed, hunger, disease and continual strife.

God grant Thy loving kindness and grace that someday soon we may all return to our homes and loved ones. Those who are single to their girls and sweethearts; those of us who are married to our wives, waiting in anxiety and patience; those who have neither, but yearn for the guardian love of a mother or father; those who have no parents or friends, but yearn, fight, and die for a Nation that will live forever for freedom, justice and equality.

Some of us, it is true, may not be so fortunate to come back. But we who are still left to carry on the struggle know that they have not died in vain . . . that their souls and spirits will shine brightly in the heavens at night . . . watching over us who remain to lead the struggle onward to final victory.

Humble and insignificant as we may appear now, high in this unfriendly sky above the crazy patchwork quilt of enemy soil below us; we do solemnly ask that Thou grant us . . . this prayer of an American airman.

Amen.

(From the original pencilled copy written by Lt. Paul Chryst, Bombardier, 91st Bomb Group's Fortress *Time's A'Wastin'*, on the back of his Flight Log Book while en route to the primary target of Merseburg, Germany, 2 November 1944).

Chapter 19

THE following extracts were taken from the diaries and memoirs of American Airmen who were shot down during the Münster mission. The first is from the diary of Lieutenant John Pettenger, Pilot 385th Bomb Group.

Kriegie.

Down in the Ruhr Valley, flying so low,
Some chairborne bastard said we must go.
Flak loves big bombers, fighters do too;
P47 boys, what's happened to you?
Write me a letter, send it to me;
Send it, "In care of Stalag Luft III."

—*An Airman's Lament.*

Kriegie's Song

A little bit of something fell out of the sky one day
It landed near Berlin, just ninety miles away
And when the Luftwaffe saw it, it looked so cold and bare
They said, "That's what we're looking for,
We'll put our Kriegies there."
So they got a few old Goon-guards and combat crews enough
And put them in that bloody hole and called it "Stalag Luft"
Oh Mother dear, it's worse out here than all the lands remote
Until I die you'll hear me cry, "Send me that bloody coat."

—*Anon.*

Reflections

When this bloody war is over, Oh, how happy I will be
Just to put my civvy clothes on, no more soldiering for me

No more flying raids on Sunday, when we should be out "On Pass"
We will tell the Group Commander to shove those bloody passes right inside his "tum de tum . . ."

—*John Pettenger.*

Kriegie Slang and Expressions

Kriegie .... A prisoner of war.
Purge .... A new group of arrivals.
Appel .... Roll call, twice daily.
Gash .... Something extra.
Kein Trinkwasser..................... Water container.
Goon or Kraut .... A German.
Tally Ho .... Cry used when a Goon enters the block.
Block .... Barracks.
Combine ....Section of a block composed of 14 men.
Compound .... Camp area
Around the bend .... Mentally unstable.
Taking the pipe .... Same as above.
You've had it .... Finished, that's all.
Brew .... Hot tea or coffee.
Fuhrer .... Leader, "Combine Fuhrer."
Pea Shooter .... Fighter pilot.
Paliasse .... The sack, bunk or bed.
Lager .... The camp.
Abort .... A toilet,
or on a mission when a ship leaves the formation.
Goonbox .... Guard box.
Luftgangster .... Term Krauts used for Allied airmen.
Flieger Alarm .... Air raid warning.
Uncle Joe ....Stalin.
Verboten .... Forbidden.
Bleed .... To gripe.
Kapute .... Finished, broken.
O.K.W. .... Official German News.
Cooler .... Solitary confinement.

Memories of Stalag Luft III, Sagan

Here follow extracts from John Pettenger's diary:

First Day. The new arrivals, after the lecture by Colonel Spivey and issue of utensils, were given a bowl of barley and a cup of cocoa. By this time it was about 1300. We spent the afternoon finding a place to live and getting straw to make our sacks. Willie Bemis and I managed to get in a combine with two older Kriegies who showed us the way around.

Leventhal showed up in about ten days. Rather pale and downcast looking. The civilian police and the Gestapo had caught him. He had had quite a rough time of it. He was also minus a tooth.

The camp had eleven barracks holding 1,100 men, a theatre, two cook-houses and five latrines.

Searches. Once every month or so, our block is searched for tunnels and contraband. Any canned goods which are not holed, the Krauts put holes in them so that we can't save anything to help in an escape attempt. We have to stay outside the block from three to eight hours while the search is on. Meanwhile, the Goons go poking around outside with long, thin rods searching for tunnels. After the search we can put in for any personal equipment that might be missing.

A Prisoner's Prayer.

by William Counihan.
December 1, 1943.

Dear Lord I pray Thee,
To guide my friends and watch o'er me.
To keep me strong in body and mind
For the coming future and the passing of time.
To keep my mind from going astray
In the passing thoughts of yesterdays
To keep looking forward to a shining tomorrow.
Forgetting war, evil, and its passing sorrow
Help me to work and pray as a man
Living this life as best I can
We pray Thee to help draw this war to a close
Helping us as You have those
Who have lost their sons, brothers and fathers
By helping us look for better tomorrows
If it be Thy will, Thy will be done
And our long lost Peace will finally be won.

—Amen.

Lieutenant David Paris and his doomed crew plunge earthwards over Merseburg, 2nd November 1944. This fortress, **Blue Streak** *was based at Sudbury, Suffolk, with the 486th Bomb Group.*

The crew of Miss Behavin' *with the exception of Robert Coles (third from left in back) were all killed in the mid-air collision with* Miss Fortune *over Münster.*

The crew of Patches II of the 384th Bomb Group flew the lead position of their Group. They bombed Coesfeld. Pilot "Ev" Frink is at the left in the back row.

The crew of Tech Supply, *piloted by Lt. John Winant of the 390th Bomb Group. Winant was the son of the then American Ambassador to England.* Tech Supply *was shot down on the Münster mission.*

The wreckage of Tech Supply *at Lodbergen, near Münster.*

The crew of the 91st Bomb Group B17G 737, piloted by Lt. Earl Verrill, third from left in the front row. Lt. Arthur Horning, at the right of the first row, evaded capture and returned to England 30 January 1944.

The B17G 737 after crash landing in Holland. Bart Rijnhout.

The crew of Little Lass *of the 388th Bomb Group which ditched in the North Sea off the Dutch coast while returning from Münster. Paul Williams, Pilot, is at the left of the back row.*

Captain Nathaniel "Gus" Mencow, Lead Navigator of the 390th Bomb Group is pictured in front of the strike photos of the Schweinfurt raid of 14 October 1943. The 390th Bomb Group was awarded a Distinguished Unit Citation for the accuracy of their bombing on that mission.

John Pettenger's crew (he is second from left in the first row) of the 385th Bomb Group.

Crash site of Aw-R-Go *of the 100th Bomb Group. The Pilot was Captain Charles Cruikshank and the Navigator, Captain Frank Murphy.*

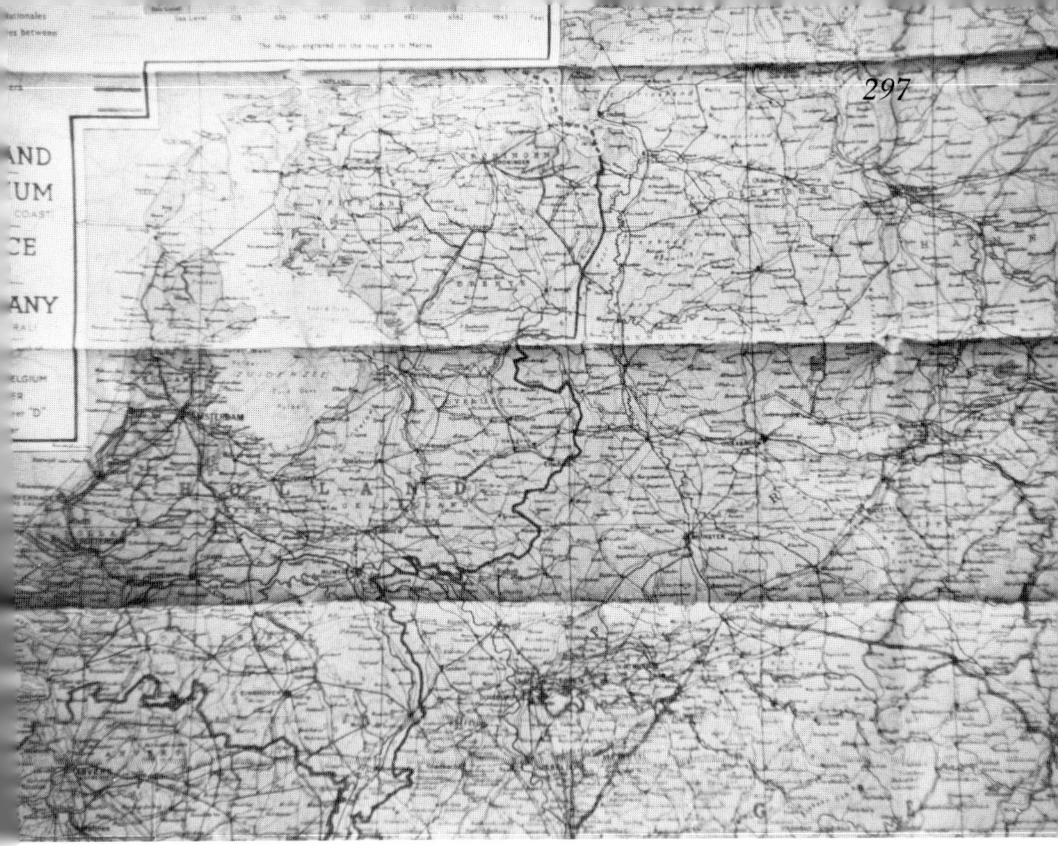

Silk escape map as carried by all combat crewmen of the Eighth Air Force.

The identity papers of Kees von Hombergh.

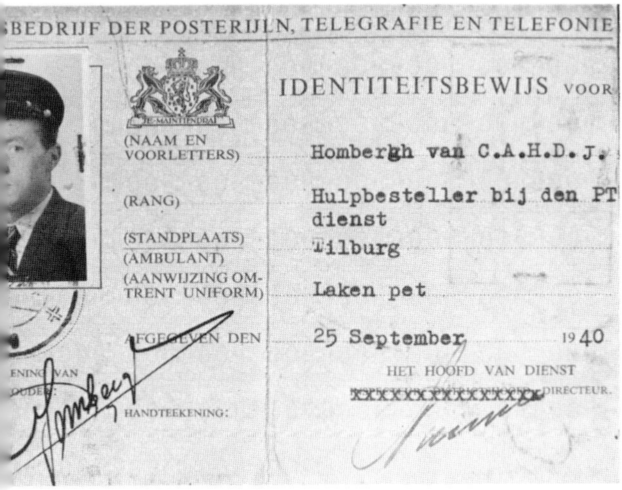

BEDRIJF DER POSTERIJEN, TELEGRAFIE EN TELEFONIE

JE MAINTIENDRAI

IDENTITEITSBEWIJS VOOR

(NAAM EN VOORLETTERS) Hombergh van C.A.H.D.J.

(RANG) Hulpbesteller bij den PT dienst

(STANDPLAATS) (AMBULANT) Tilburg

(AANWIJZING OMTRENT UNIFORM) Laken pet

AFGEGEVEN DEN 25 September 1940

HET HOOFD VAN DIENST

XXXXXXXXXXXXXX DIRECTEUR.

HANDTEEKENING:

Kees von Hombergh in a concentration camp near Berlin in 1944.

John Justice, taken by a member of the Dutch underground in November 1943 while Justice was on his evasion route.

Madame Yvonne de Jonghe with John Justice in Poppel, Belgium, November 1943.

Thomas Combs in Paris en route to his escape.

Thomas Combs picture taken for his French Identification papers used during his escape.

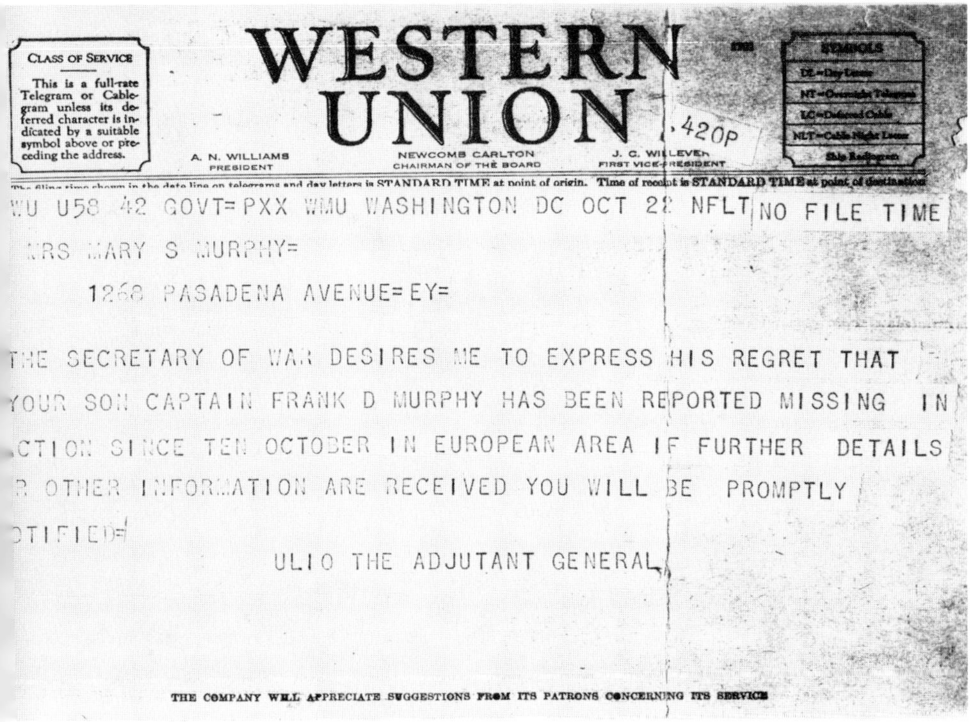

CLASS OF SERVICE

This is a full-rate Telegram or Cablegram unless its deferred character is indicated by a suitable symbol above or preceding the address.

WESTERN UNION

A. N. WILLIAMS, PRESIDENT — NEWCOMB CARLTON, CHAIRMAN OF THE BOARD — J. C. WILLEVER, FIRST VICE-PRESIDENT

SYMBOLS
DL=Day Letter
NT=Overnight Telegram
LC=Deferred Cable
NLT=Cable Night Letter
Ship Radiogram

420P

The filing time shown in the date line on telegrams and day letters is STANDARD TIME at point of origin. Time of receipt is STANDARD TIME at point of destination

WU U58 42 GOVT=PXX WMU WASHINGTON DC OCT 22 NFLT NO FILE TIME

MRS MARY S MURPHY=

1268 PASADENA AVENUE=EY=

THE SECRETARY OF WAR DESIRES ME TO EXPRESS HIS REGRET THAT YOUR SON CAPTAIN FRANK D MURPHY HAS BEEN REPORTED MISSING IN CTION SINCE TEN OCTOBER IN EUROPEAN AREA IF FURTHER DETAILS R OTHER INFORMATION ARE RECEIVED YOU WILL BE PROMPTLY OTIFIED=

ULIO THE ADJUTANT GENERAL

THE COMPANY WILL APPRECIATE SUGGESTIONS FROM ITS PATRONS CONCERNING ITS SERVICE

Telegram received by Frank Murphy's mother informing her that her son was Missing In Action.

Barth P.O.W. Camp (Stalag Luft I). William Nicholls.

Another view of the Barth P.O.W. Camp (Stalag Luft I).

William Nicholls.

Looking down the fence line of the Barth P.O.W. Camp (Stalag Luft I).

William Nicholls.

Prisoners of War at the Barth Camp (Stalag Luft I) in May, 1945.

William Nicholls.

The dance band at Stalag Luft III. John Pettenger is third from the left, and John Brady is seventh from the left. John Brady.

Stalag Luft III, Prisoner of War camp, in which John Pettenger, Robert McGuire, Jack Nosser and Glenn Oster were imprisoned.

American and British Prisoners of War at Barth (Stalag Luft I) in May 1945. Howard Hamilton of the 100th Bomb Group and William Nicholls of the 385th Bomb Group were imprisoned here. Colonel Hubert Zemke was the Allied Commanding Officer here. William Nicholls.

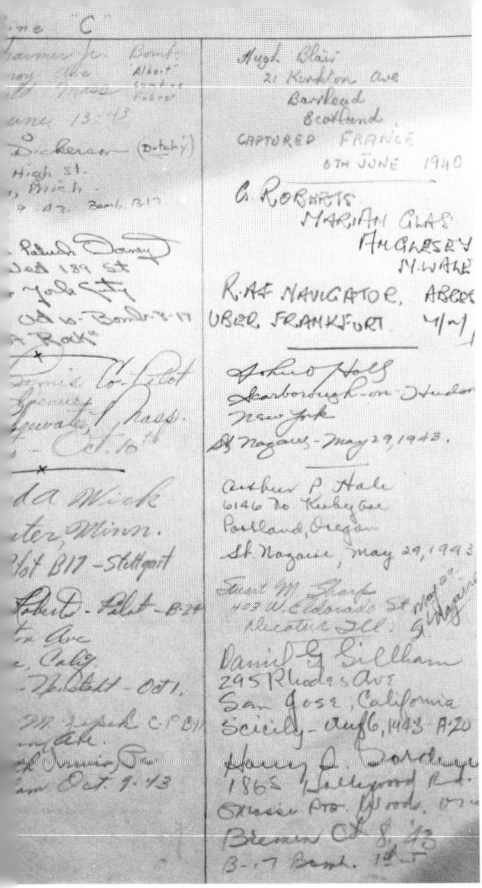
Hugh Blair
21 Kirkton Ave
Barrhead
Scotland
CAPTURED FRANCE
6TH JUNE 1940

C. ROBERTS
MARIAN GLAS
ANGLESEY
N. WALES
R.A.F. NAVIGATOR, ABERD
UBER FRANKFURT

John Holt
Scarborough-on-Hudson
New York
St Nazaire - May 29, 1943.

Arthur P. Hale
6146 No Kirby Ave
Portland, Oregon
St. Nazaire, May 29, 1943

Daniel G. Gillham
295 Rhodes Ave
San Jose, California
Sicily - Aug 6, 1943 - A-20

B-17 Bomb.

Some of the signatures of Prisoners of War collected by John Pettenger in his diary.

Some of the relics and souvenirs of P.O.W. life collected by Jack Rogers at Stalag Luft III and other P.O.W. camps. Sergeant Rogers was on the crew of El P'sstoffo of the 100th Bomb Group.

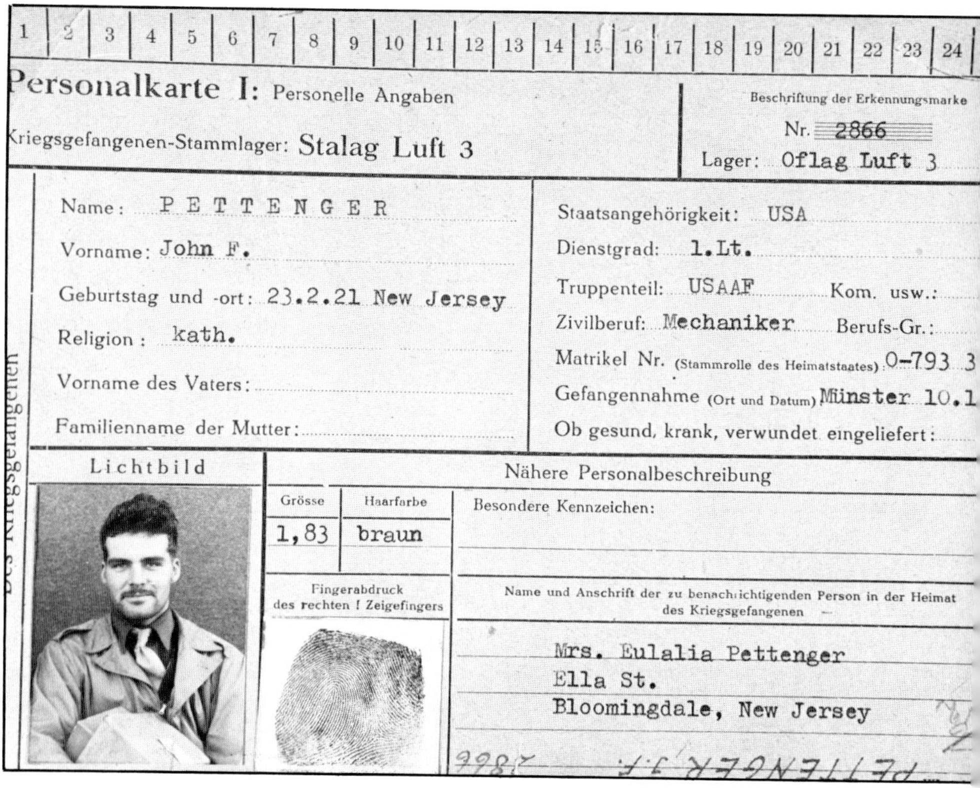

1	2	3	4	5	6	7	8	9	10	11	12	13	14	15	16	17	18	19	20	21	22	23	24

Personalkarte I: Personelle Angaben

Kriegsgefangenen-Stammlager: Stalag Luft 3

Beschriftung der Erkennungsmarke
Nr. 2866
Lager: Oflag Luft 3

Name: PETTENGER
Vorname: John F.
Geburtstag und -ort: 23.2.21 New Jersey
Religion: kath.
Vorname des Vaters:
Familienname der Mutter:

Staatsangehörigkeit: USA
Dienstgrad: 1.Lt.
Truppenteil: USAAF Kom. usw.:
Zivilberuf: Mechaniker Berufs-Gr.:
Matrikel Nr. (Stammrolle des Heimatstaates): 0-793 3
Gefangennahme (Ort und Datum): Münster 10.1
Ob gesund, krank, verwundet eingeliefert:

Des Kriegsgefangenen

Lichtbild

Nähere Personalbeschreibung

Grösse	Haarfarbe
1,83	braun

Besondere Kennzeichen:

Fingerabdruck des rechten ! Zeigefingers

Name und Anschrift der zu benachrichtigenden Person in der Heimat des Kriegsgefangenen

Mrs. Eulalia Pettenger
Ella St.
Bloomingdale, New Jersey

John Pettenger's record card as a Prisoner of War.

A record card with pictures of Dan James of the 100th Bomb Group. He had bailed out after his B17 had collided with a German fighter plane after bombing a target.

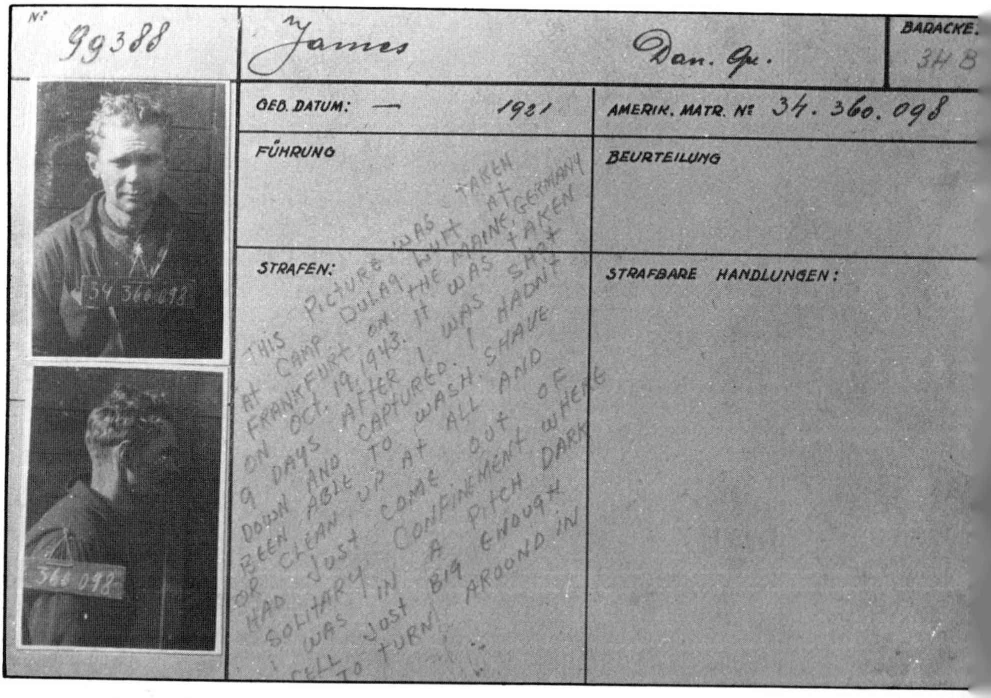

Nr. 99388 James Dan. Gr.

BARACKE: 3HB

GEB. DATUM: — 1921

AMERIK. MATR. Nr. 34.360.098

FÜHRUNG

BEURTEILUNG

STRAFEN:

STRAFBARE HANDLUNGEN:

THIS PICTURE WAS TAKEN AT CAMP DULAG LUFT AT FRANKFURT ON THE MAINE, GERMANY ON OCT. 19, 1943. IT WAS TAKEN 9 DAYS AFTER I WAS SHOT DOWN AND CAPTURED. I HADN'T BEEN ABLE TO WASH, SHAVE OR CLEAN UP AT ALL AND HAD JUST COME OUT OF SOLITARY CONFINEMENT WHERE I WAS IN A PITCH DARK CELL JUST BIG ENOUGH TO TURN AROUND IN

One group brought the sounds of home to the airmen on special occasions. Glenn Miller and his orchestra at Thorpe Abbotts (100th Bomb Group) on 1 September 1944.

The B17 Silver Dollar *of the 100th Bomb Group which Colonel Thomas Jeffrey flew over the bombed out areas of Germany after VE Day to survey the damage to industrial targets. This B17 had flown 106 combat missions.*

There are approximately 75 combat crewmen of the U.S. Eighth Air Force in this photograph. Just over four times that many were lost during the Münster raid in a period of twenty-five minutes. (The author believes that this picture was taken at the 381st Bomb Group in Ridgewell, Essex, in 1943.)

Christmas 1943. For some of us Christmas started on the afternoon of 24 December. After drinking raisin wine quite a few were pleasantly intoxicated. Raisin wine always leaves a hangover, headache and sickness. Despite this, it is always a major product of Stalag Luft III.

With special Christmas parcels from England there was plenty of excellent food, including plum pudding and fruit cake. The Krauts issued beer which is the best I have tasted since leaving the States.

The Camp Choir gave a programme at 1430 which was very good.

The Goons who were not working came around and wished us all a "Merry Christmas."

Quite mild outside with a little snow, but not enough for a White Christmas though.

Funerals. Latest news on the Bulletin Board on Saturday, 22 January, said: "Men on aircrews will not be given military funerals in the future because they were terrorists and Luftgangsters and couldn't be classified with a regular soldier." The German Kommandant expressed his sympathies, but said it came from higher sources and that he could do nothing about it.

Hypnotism. About two weeks before Christmas, hypnotism swept the place. The British were the chief exponents of it. We were given demonstrations in the barracks which were quite amazing. They have the victims thinking they are flying, driving a car, or drinking. Some we could stick a pin in their finger and it couldn't be felt. We would suggest things to them while they were asleep, and they would do them after they woke up, not being able to say why they did them. Another fellow was told to wake up in ten minutes time. He missed it by just a few seconds. They could even make a person have a headache or be sick to his stomach when they woke up if the hypnotist suggested it to them.

Interest died out in about two weeks. The next craze to hit us was Bridge, which is still going strong. Quite a game. Chess came also but has since died out.

Bombings. Quite often we hear the bombing of Berlin which is 70 miles away. We hear it early at night, during the air raids. The guards are placed every 10 yards along the fence during the raids, which last from 30 to 60 minutes. Sometimes the windows, doors and the whole building shakes during a raid. Some fellows that were 60 miles from Hamburg when it was bombed said they could read a newspaper at that distance.

We don't make lamps out of oleo any more because one of the men was shot in the legs at the South Camp. The guards are instructed to shoot at any lights during an air raid. The oleo lamps are comprised of a tin can, a wick, and some oleo margarine.

Goons. They are the guards, or I should say workmen, who go snooping around. They wear overalls and carry a screwdriver and a flashlight. They fill up the tunnels that we dig. They all speak English, although they act dumb. They wander around under the barracks, or up in the roofs trying to overhear conversations and get information. They look like the result of the last draft. Quite a rough lot, all look about 50 years old. Every time we see one go in the block we holler "Tally Ho", so everyone can be on their guard. Sometimes they holler "Tally Ho" themselves if they come into the building and no one sees them. They are a friendly lot, and we have quite a time with them.

Appel. Is nothing more than roll call. We fall out at 1000 and 1600 each day, 1100 on Sundays. Some of the Goons go through the block while others count us. They go through this routine two or three times if a mistake is made in the count. There always seemed to be a mistake on a cold day.

West Cook House. This building is used to store potatoes and to heat water. German food such as barley is cooked there. The front section, which has a full length porch, has a bulletin board. Theatre notices, Gefangen Gazette, and news from the German papers are put up there. Above it there is a loudspeaker which has music on it all day. It comes from a nearby German radio station with no advertisements.The music is excellent. Two or three times a week a special programme comes over for the benefit of the prisoners. Comments in English and all American tunes are played.

East Cook House Has a small bulletin board which usually has a list of prisoners recently taken. The building contains a classroom, infirmary, library, reference library, camp office, the food exchange, and a boiler room. We use this room to get all our hot water.

The library has many fine books of all kinds. The reference library contains more technical books and magazines, also quite a few German books and magazines.

Popeye. He is the Number One Sergeant when it comes to taking roll call each day. He got his name because he's lost one eye, and is all Army from the Old School. Very efficient, to say the least!

Sad Sack. Is where I spend my time from midnight to ten in the morning. It has a straw mattress and pillow. The Germans do our sheets and pillow cases about every two or three weeks. The first weeks I slept in it, it fairly crippled me. But after a time I have gotten hardened or used to it. It is a two-deck affair with boards instead of springs.

Packages After we are notified, a guard takes us to the Vorlager to get the parcels. There, an American and a Kraut open the parcel in front of us. Great care is taken to see that nothing is lost. Some things from some parcels are confiscated. Anything that could be used for escape is taken.

Tunnels. The Krauts have discovered about five or six tunnels since November. They seem to find them just as they reach the fence. There are wires leading into the ground all along the fence so we think that the ground is wired for sound by the fences.

Air Raids. We are beginning to become air raid conscious here of late. Starting tomorrow, 15 March, we are going to have air raid drills. The guards holler "Flieger Alarm" and a siren is blown. At these signals we have to return to our blocks. As soon as it gets warmer we are going to be allowed to dig slit trenches.

Day Air Raids. Since the middle of January we have been getting air raids. Although we can't see the Allied bombers we can feel the earth tremble when the bombs hit. We also see the 190s and twin-engine fighters take off and come limping back home. The raids last between 30 and 60 minutes.

More on Tunnels. The Krauts found a tunnel last week at the North Camp which was about 400 feet long and had electric lights inside for illumination. Eighty-six men escaped, and so far only 23 have been caught. This tunnel was started last Summer and just used to escape this Spring. Two men are in the cooler now who tried to escape last week during a snow storm. They put white sheets over their heads, and were caught just outside the fence. It seems the "Hund-Fuhrer" caught them. As a result of these endeavours we now have three Appels a day, and the Krauts insist on cooking the food that the Red Cross sends because the boys save it for escape purposes. We have decided we will not take them up on that, so at present we are at a standstill.

Betting. The men here will bet on almost anything or anybody. One bar of chocolate is worth five packs of cigarettes. For the last week or two the bets have been on "When will the Compound cat, Timoshenko, have kittens?" These cats here only come to you when you call 'Katz", not "Kitty."

The Escape. Latest news as of 6 April 1944, via Colonel Spivey: There are six men in the cooler, and eight more on the way there. Forty-one men of the 82 who escaped have been shot, either by S.S. troops or the Gestapo. The men of the Luftwaffe are quite harmless. They said some were shot while resisting arrest, and others trying to escape again after being captured. This seems a very high proportion. No other news.

Morale. Today, 11 April, was a wonderful day for the camp's morale. My own went up 200%. At about 1230 we saw either five or six Groups of B17s flying about 12,000 feet two miles west of the camp. We think they bombed Foest, about 15 miles away. It is now 1800 and the smoke is still overhead from the fires started. We saw one B17 shot down, and one Jerry fighter which made a straight dive into the ground. These were the first friendly ships I have seen since 14 October at Frankfurt. They certainly looked swell.

Kommandant. Due to the escape at the North Camp, the old Kommandant was removed from his office. We have a new one now, and as yet there have been no changes made. The other Kommandant was a real old officer and a gentleman. Only 10 haven't been caught that escaped from the North Camp.

Jitters There are all kinds of speculations as to when the invasion will come. The German papers have the opinion that it will come sometime between 19 May and 25 May. They keep repeating how surprised the Allies will be when they try to invade.

Weather. We have so much rainy and cloudy weather here that it is quite easy to see why the Krauts are always fighting. They are trying to win a place to migrate to.

Memorial Day. On 28 May, Colonel Spivey gave a speech which was very moving. He stressed why Memorial Day is held. In memory of those who have died that we might live as we wish. It should mean more to us, now that we have known so many men, personal acquaintances, who have given their lives.

INVASION. 6 June 1944. A dull, rainy day. All the men here at Stalag Luft III were in the barracks. About noon it was announced over the German news that the invasion had started. Immediately, there was a very different atmosphere. Men running all around outside and hanging round the radio for more news. The British nearly went mad in the next camp, jumping out of the windows, among other things. Quite a few of the British have been prisoners for four years now. We tell the Goons that "Alle ist Kaput." Everyone's morale is up 100%. Oh happy day! I'm beginning to think that I will not know how to act, or what to do, when I get back to civilization.

Russians. We always wondered what the Goons did with our flying equipment that was taken from us. We now know where some of it went. We see quite a few Russians wearing flying suits with a large "SU" painted on the back. It is probably a good idea. The Russians have no Red Cross service and have no way of getting clothes to wear. On Invasion Day, the Russians went wild. Running around and making "V" signs to everyone with their fingers.

New Plane. The Krauts have a new jet-propelled ship that flies near here. It is fast and makes a whistling noise. It has a high tail, like a Mosquito's. The wings are set way back on the fuselage. It has two jets on each wing, and the ship is very streamlined and graceful.

Bulletin Board. On 23 September, the Goons put up a notice stating: "Anyone escaping will be shot." Because there are many areas in Germany where people are shot on sight, and due to the unfair methods of war, we are considered gangsters.

Unluckiest Kriegie. He is probably the guy who ditched while on a training flight over the Gulf of Mexico. He was picked up by a Kraut submarine. There are several Kriegies here from the Mediterranean Theatre with similar tales of woe.

Christmas, 25 December 1944. The band played in Block 52 on Christmas Eve. They changed the Block to look like a nightclub. Everything was there except the bar. With Xmas parcels we certainly had some swell food during this festive season. As we said last year, "We'll be home by Christmas next year. Jawohl . . ."

Morale. The Camp morale has gone up since the Russian offensive began. I expected the Russians to start during the first two weeks of January, and to finish the war by the middle of February. They have been bringing men and material up since November 7. Also the Krauts have been taking men to the Western Front. The Goons say that this is the drive that means everything.

« « « » » »

Many of the other American officers who had been shot down during the Münster raid were also imprisoned at Stalag Luft III, Sagan in Silesia. These are some of the recollections of Lieutenant Jack Nosser, 390th Bomb Group:

I wasn't involved in the Escape Organisation at Sagan. No one in our room did more than the occasional duty of dispersing from the few unsuccessful tunnels which went from the various barrack blocks and headed towards the fence. Incidentally, the camp radio was in a room next to ours, but to this day I still do not know where it was hidden. When it was time for the BBC news broadcasts, the room was cleared. The Germans also knew that it was there and they looked for it several times, but even they failed to find it during their thorough searches.

It was sometime during March, 1944, that Glen Oster thought out a plan which the Escape Organisation accepted. He wanted me to go with him, of course, but to me it was too risky and stood little chance of success. He finally found someone else for the attempt. His plan was to dress in white sheets to blend with the snow, crawl to the fences, cut their way through with wire-cutters and into the forest. From there they would try and make it to the nearest airfield, steal an airplane and fly to Russian Occupied territory.

There was a roadway between our camp and the camp North of us. At the end of the roadway was a single wire fence and then the surrounding coniferous forest. They had first to get through the double wire fence of our camp compound, then past the guards at the gate, before crawling to the single wire fence, and of course under all the searchlights and machine guns from the guard watch-towers.

To digress for a moment. The previous Christmas, the Germans had permitted us to move about the camp later than usual. The Colonel in charge of the Escape Committee had taken this opportunity to go through the fence to the British Compound who provided him with the detailed information on how to start various types of German aircraft. I would guess that the British had detailed procedures and information on almost everything the Germans possessed.

Glen Oster and his companion started through the fence a short time before the barracks were locked for the night. They made it through the double fence into the roadway, and they made it past the gate guards. Unfortunately, it was at the time that the Germans were bringing their guard dogs back into the compound for the night. It must have been a young or inexperienced dog that picked up their scent first of all. He ran over to them lying in the snow and sniffed without making a sound. He returned when his handler called to him. The second dog sniffed and barked immediately, and that was the end of the attempt. Both Oster and his companion were sent to the Cooler.

In the late Spring of 1944 about 80 Allied Kriegies tunnelled their way out of Sagan in what later became known as "The Great Escape." The tunnel, which took many months to complete, even had electric lights for its whole length and a crude, but very effective air-conditioning system. We later learned that about 50 of the escapees had been caught and executed by the Gestapo while "resisting arrest." The true facts were very different . . .

Lieutenant John Pettenger, of the 385th Bomb Group, resumes his diary entries during the forced march from Sagan to Spremburg as Russian forces approached from the East:

Adieu to Sagan. On Saturday evening, 27 January at 2130, the guards told us we were leaving in two hours. After several delays we left at 0530. We were issued a Red Cross parcel which we carried on a home-built sled. We marched 18 kilometres before noon, arriving at a village called Halbau. On the way, hot water was given to us by civilians or we traded cigarettes for it. It was the only thing that kept us warm. Cigarettes will buy almost anything. We stayed overnight in a church. Seventeen hundred of us in a church built for 400 people. We had to sit up all night. We slept on pews, altars and anything that was level. I was sick that night.

Monday, 29 January. We left Halbau at 0900 and marched 19 kilometres to Siligersruhe. The guards are having as bad a time of it as we are. They throw those that fall by the wayside up into a truck that is travelling with us. It's so cold marching that the water freezes my moustache solid. We cannot even keep warm when we are marching. Had a headache all day. Had two hats on and kept my ears warm. We are stretched out over a mile when on the march. That night, we were quartered in a huge barn — 800 of us. We sleep with our hats on. The straw is warm and comfortable. We stayed all the next day in the barn, which was owned by Polish people. There were many foreign workers in this area and the people were very friendly and helpful to us.

On Wednesday we left Siligersruhe at 0730 and covered 20 kilometres to Maskau via Prebus. We arrived at 2230. We march an hour and rest for five minutes. Today was the coldest days march — the temperature averaging below zero. We stayed in a large pottery factory at Maskau. What a Godsend! I didn't think I would ever be warm again. We are crowded but there is plenty of heat from the kilns. We found a tunnel under the street by which to escape, but were too tired to even try.

We stayed at Maskau during February 1st and 2nd. Our morale is getting pretty high. The guards issued the first food to us while we were here. We had lived on Red Cross parcels up to this point.

We left Maskau on Saturday at 0700 en route to Spremburg. We are supposed to march 15 kilometres to Graustein today, and seven kilometres the next day to Spremburg. We had a thaw today and all the snow is gone.

My right leg gave me trouble today — all kinds of pain. I won't be able to march seven kilometres tomorrow. About 80% of us are sick with the "G.I.'s" or throwing up. We could hear the bombers today. The ground really vibrated. We slept here — 130 men to a barn. The people at this farm were very kind to us. They gave us plenty of hot water, and we even had a light in the barn.

On 4 February we left Graustein and arrived at Spremburg at 0930. Just made it with my bad leg. I now have blisters all over my feet. We were housed during the day in a huge garage at a large German motor-pool or training base. Here we were issued some soup which really tasted good. Rumoured the Russians are just behind us. The Germans are digging trenches all over this area.

At about 1630 we were marched through Spremburg to the railroad station where we were loaded aboard French boxcars — 52 men to a car. It is so crowded that we can't stretch out but must sit with our feet doubled up all night. The guards tried to get us to sing to keep up morale. They want us to harmonize. We all sang *Lilli Marlene* together.

Had an air raid during the first night on the train. During February 5th and 6th we were side-tracked most of the time and covered very few miles. The train certainly moved during the air raid. Every time the train stopped everyone went out to defecate, regardless of the people about.

During the 6th we passed an airfield near the Slovakian border. It was very hilly here and very pretty country. All kinds of rumours as to where we are going. Nurenburg is the favourite. The majority of us are still sick.

We arrived at Moosburg on 7 February 1945.

« « « » » »

Rumours were rife as the crumbling defences of Hitler's "Thousand Year Reich" reeled under the sledge-hammer blows of the Russian forces on the Eastern Front and the Allies from the West. One of the more persistent rumours being that the S.S. were about to take hostages to Switzerland and use them to secure favourable surrender terms. The prisoners at Moosburg were only too well aware that the S.S. were not particular who they took.

Lieutenant Jack Nosser concludes:

Glen Oster, who had tried unsuccessfully to escape from Sagan and had consequently spent many days in the Cooler there, "Rod" Rodriquez, an absolutely fearless Mexican-American, and myself decided to make a break for it while we were on a working party in Augsburg. One of our closest calls, and there were several, came when we walked straight past an S.S.

roadblock on a bridge when their attention was diverted while they questioned the occupants of a German staff car. We finally met up with an American armoured column north of the River Danube a few days later.

It had been a very eventful two years with long periods of boring monotony in between. We had made it and had luckily survived. A large number of very fine men had not been so fortunate . . .

« « « » » »

Far to the north, at Barth on the Baltic coast, was Stalag Luft I Prisoner of War Camp. Among the many injured crewmen who recovered from their wounds there were Lieutenant Howard Hamilton and Lt. Harold Weachter, both of the 100th Bomb Group.

Lt. Hamilton recollects:

We had a long roundabout train ride from Frankfurt, through the outskirts of Berlin, up to a town called Barth, located on the Baltic in Pomerania. This was our permanent camp. The closest town of any size was Stralsund. At the time I arrived the only occupants were about 40 or 50 British officers.

Camp life was not too bad except it was boring, and we were situated near a Hitler Youth Flak Training School. We were also due north of Berlin and directly on the route that the British bombers took on their way out after bombing Berlin. At night, after the RAF had bombed Berlin, they would come down to the deck and fly directly over our camp, and of course, the Flak School. The Hitler Youth would go out and open up with their flak guns on the British bombers for target practise, also of course, trying to shoot them down. This seemed to irritate the British bomber pilots and they would circle around and then spray the area with machine gun fire. Fortunately, we did not lose anyone to the machine gun fire, but it made for very exciting nights!!

Being officers, we did not work. But we did the usual things which prisoners did to pass the time. We dug many tunnels trying to escape. Tunnelling was tough because, being beside the Baltic, we always encountered water about six feet down. I don't think anyone made it via the tunnels, but one or two men succeeded in escaping by going over the fence during construction periods when there were blind spots to the tower guards. We also played a little baseball.

Occasionally we received food parcels from the Red Cross, but probably for three quarters of the time we did not have food parcels, and we had to eat the food the Germans provided which was about a 900 calorie daily diet. I personally lost about 30 pounds.

We received a change of bedding every six weeks at the same time as we had our eagerly awaited shower bath. We had one typhus epidemic and the Germans got quite concerned about it. They vaccinated everyone and also issued razor blades with instructions that one razor was to serve about four or five men. The razor blade was for shaving off all of the hair, and I mean all!! We drew lots to see what order we would use the razor. A very stinging situation. After we had shaved ourselves they marched us over to the showers, then they turned the water on for a minute or so. They gave us kerosene to smear on the head and pubic areas (where we had shaved) and then withheld the water from us for about five minutes. They finally turned on the water again and let us soap down and then rinse. The purpose of all this was to kill the lice eggs which were the carriers of the typhus.

Life was very monotonous until early April, 1945, when the Russian Cossacks arrived and liberated us. The Germans had planned to march us to the west, but the Russians crossed the River Oder at Stettin, turned north, and cut us off before we could march. This was about three weeks or so before the formal ending of the war.

The first night we were free things got pretty wild. Many of our Russian liberators were Mongolian troops with no concept whatever of our Western way of life. We lost 23 men from our camp that night through small-arms fire or from stepping on land mines. Things finally quietened down and a couple of days later the Russian Commander told us there were 4,000 S.S. troops on the island of Rugen, a few miles offshore, near our camp.

The Russians, with no assault craft of their own, gathered up fishing boats along the coast, and planned to assault the island. Unfortunately, the Germans had sabotaged the boats before leaving, and the Russian Commander appealed to us, as Americans with a lot of supposed know-how, to repair the boats. Several of us volunteered for this and we got the boats in running order. The Russian Commander then told us that he was going to give us the honour of steering the boats for the Russian troops in the assault on the island.

This was not very appealing to me since I knew that the German S.S. troops had 88 mm guns and could blow us out of the water long before we could reach the island. So a friend and I walked off. We finally joined up with a Russian infantry platoon, and marched with them. The platoon comprised foot-soldiers and a horse-drawn wagon loaded with bread and vodka.

Typically, we would be moving down a road and would attract small-arms fire from pockets of cut off Germans. The platoon would pull over, stop, break out the vodka and pour a ration all round. Suitably fortified with a glass or two of courage, the unit would then assault the pockets of resistance in the woods.

Considerable rapes and lootings went on when the troops entered a town or farmhouse. And there seemed to be no restrictions on drunkenness as far as the Russians were concerned.

The only problem I had with the Russian Commanding Officer was that he kept wanting to give me the honour of leading the charge at the head of the assault troops, simply because he thought I had it coming to me, based on my time in prison camp. I managed to convince him that, since he had come all the way from Stalingrad, the honour was really his. Somehow I survived the ordeal and returned to Stalag I.

Luckily, the war had ended, and the S.S. troops on Rugen had decided to surrender prior to the actual assault against the island. It would undoubtedly have been a very bloody assault had it taken place.

I began to worry about how to get out because the nearest Western Allied Unit was a Canadian Division at Rostock, some 60 miles away. The Russian Commander at Barth really wanted all of the Americans out as soon as possible, but he had nowhere he could march us to. We started work repairing the runway at Barth, and finally got it in shape for the B17s to come in and pick us up. We were then flown to Rheims, France, and boarded trucks for the drive to camp "Lucky Strike" on the northern coast of France, near St. Valery. Then home.

« « « » » »

The legendary fighter "Ace", Colonel Hubert "Hub" Zemke, former C.O. of the 56th Fighter Group, and also C.O. of the 479th Fighter Group (Wattisham, Suffolk), was the senior Allied officer at Barth. He had the unnerving experience of bailing out from a P51 Mustang fighter when it broke up ("Became unglued," to use his own laconic expression) during a violent storm near Celle, Germany, on 30 October 1944. By that time he had shot down 19 German aircraft and had won the Distinguished Service Cross for valour over Berlin, 6 March 1944, a day on which the 8th Air Force had suffered its heaviest loss of the war — 69 heavy bombers.

By a strange quirk of fate, Colonel Zemke's German father, a railway engineer, had been born in nearby Stralsund, 30 miles to the northwest of Barth. His mother was also German born, and they had met and married after emigrating to the United States before the First World War. Recalled Colonel Zemke:

Major General Borisoff, the Russian Divisional Commander, asked me if the Allied Prisoners of War wanted to assist, as infantry, in the assault against the island of Rugen. To this I replied that we were anything but infantry assault troops, although we had some small arms. The Russians would have had to equip us and train us in ground tactics. Many of our men had never even fired a rifle.

The camp POW's under Colonel Gus Lundquist, had captured a handful of FW 190's at Barth Luftwaffe Airfield prior to the Russian takeover. We volunteered these aircraft and our crews against the island for close ground support, but because of language difficulties, communications and logistical support problems, this gesture was turned down.

My Chief of Staff, Group Captain "Pinkie" Weir, RAF Bomber Command, had several lengthy discussions with Major General Borisoff on these particular aspects. There were 1,500 RAF airmen who were also POW's at Barth, and were in one of four compounds under the command of Group Captain Greene, RAF Fighter Command.

Before the Russians over-ran the Barth area, and during which time we took over the camp, a cadre of some 200 American and British airmen was organised and equipped to guard the camp and run foraging parties for food. (9,200 people eat a stack of food.) These foraging parties were under the joint command of Colonel Mackenzie, USAAF, and Major "Tag" Pritchard, a Royal Marine Commando who had been captured in Italy.

« « « » » »

At Stalag 17B near the Northern Austrian town of Krems, Allied prisoners (enlisted men) lived under the most primitive conditions. These are some of the recollections of Sergeant Raymond Harwood, 388th Bomb Group:

At Stalag 17B there were 4,300 Americans after the camp was filled in April 1944, plus Russians, Siberians, French, English and Italian prisoners, bringing the total to about 15,000 men. Each of the different nationalities were kept apart, and we Americans lived far better than the others, but only because we got some Red Cross parcels. Our barracks were overcrowded so that we lived like sardines in a can. Each barracks was split into two parts with a washroom in between. Each half was about 100 feet long and 40 feet wide, housing 150 men. The camp was divided into compounds of four barracks each. We stood roll call about three times a day and shakedowns for prohibited articles two or three times a week. They were apt to be pulled at any time of the day or night. The food that the Germans gave us was very poor, consisting mostly of dehydrated soup which had more maggot-like worms in it than anything else.

A number of times men were killed trying to escape. And escape from this camp was nearly impossible. The Russians died like flies, and I saw as many as thirty taken out for burial in one day. Their casket was a piece of canvas wrapped around them. But the American dead were given a regular military funeral.

In Stalag 17B we were allowed to mingle with the English prisoners, even though they were housed in another compound. There were only a few of them, and we enjoyed talking to them. One night I remember a group of British bombers coming in. The pathfinder marked out our camp, we thought, to ensure the bomb-laden craft would know where we were. then they dropped the so-called "Christmas Tree" flares directly over us and we knew we were the target instead of an airfield a short distance from the camp. I heard men actually pray in fright as we huddled in slit trenches waiting for the bombs. I guess someone found their mistake at the very last minute, and the bombers turned away and the bombs missed us with no damage.

Another time, two P-38 Lightnings flew over camp to start a straffing run on a bridge and river traffic on the Danube River near us. They made two passes in which they wobbled their wings at us obviously knowing we were there. On another occasion a group of 15th A.F. bombers came in from a direction we had never seen before with their bomb bays open. They bombed Krems, the town outside the camp. These events were very good for our morale.

Most times we could tell if things were going badly for the German forces. The worse they were doing, the less water we had. They would only turn it on maybe twice a day for thirty minutes. If they seemed to be doing well, as in early 1944, the water was on all day.

On April 7, 1945, we were marched out of Stalag 17B in the face of oncoming Russian forces. We were put in groups of about 500 men and marched directly across Austria towards the American lines. The following is a word-by-word untouched copy of the diary I kept in pencil on the forced march:

7 April 1945. For the past few days rumour has it that we evacuate the camp in face of the advancing Russians. We are supposed to go tomorrow and all that we can't carry is being destroyed. Our march is supposed to take seven days and we leave here in groups of five hundred. The way I feel I don't think I can make ten miles. Food is really scarce. I really hate to leave under German guard but I have maps and other essentials for escape except food. I'll see what the future brings.

8 April 1945. We left camp this morning at about 1030 and marched 26 Kms. to Maigen where we slept in a barn, all tired men. The Germans haven't fed us all day and all we have eaten is what we were carrying with us. The country is rough mountain country and we are using rural roads. We are doing much better than I thought men in our physical condition could.

9 April 1945. Travelled 18 Kms. to Zening, Austria, today and again no food. A barn for shelter as last night. Legs sore but I'm taking it much better than I thought I would. Maybe the Germans think we don't need to eat. Once in a while when the guards will allow it we are able to buy bread with soap or cigarettes.

10 April 1945. Eighteen months as a P.O.W. today. We remain in Zening all day and tonight. Two meals of barley (dish water) soup, our first since we left camp. Aside from this, five of us (Conners, Gardin, Cornwell, Moore and myself) had a hen we stole. Reported that our old camp, 17B, was bombed by Russians. Also four men from my old barracks, 34-A, were killed or wounded trying to escape. There are storm troopers and volkstrom men everywhere.

11 April 1945. We made 16 Kms. to Bergen, Austria. The last two uphill, to stay in another barn. No food today. All is going as well as can be expected, but I'm pretty hungry. What little food we had with us when we left camp is about all gone and our rations are below that of starvation.

12 April 1945. Made 14 Kms. to St. Oswald, Austria, and another barn for shelter tonight. Rained nearly all day and all got plenty wet. Hard marching in the mud. Received small bread ration (18 men to a loaf). Good weather for ducks but pretty cold even for them.

13 April 1945. A hard day today. Twenty-five Kms. in the rain and mud and over the worse mountains we have hit yet. Staying in Grein, Austria, tonight in a barn and, of course, no food. It's Friday the 13th for sure today. Looks like we are the flying infantry going on a foot.

14 April 1945. We didn't move today and the weather is fair. Getting our clothes dried out. Two hot meals today. They must have broken their hearts to give us those. Saw our first game yesterday — three deer, and they sure looked swell, so free and beautiful. It must be wonderful to be free. It's been so long since I have been that way that I'm not sure what it is like. I'm sure a lot of the people back home don't appreciate the fact that they are free and have enough to eat and a place to stay, to say nothing of not being pushed around with a gun.

15 April 1945. Made twenty Kms. to Naarn, Austria, and sleep. To date we have been moving southwest from Krems towards Linz, Austria. Today has been nice and we have broken out of the hills into the Danube Valley which makes marching easier. To date we have received six hot meals from the Germans such as they were. Also two bread and biscuit rations. Four potatoes was our food for today.

16 April 1945. Made twenty Kms. today and reached Styregg, Austria. Bread and biscuits before we started and after three Kms. we got hot soup.

17 April 1945. Rest today and one meal from Jerrys with a small ration of bread. Hot all day. We go through Linz tomorrow. Plenty of bombs, craters and dead bombs around here, and also quite a bit of air activity. We stole a chicken today.

18 April 1945. We made thirty-one Kms. today and our only meal a small dish of soup and a piece of bread. Went through Linz and crossed the Danube to the Southern side. Staying in Weifing, Austria, in a barn tonight. Linz was pretty well bombed out, and the Americans hit it again today about two hours after we passed through.

19 April 1945. We made seventeen Kms. today with a small food ration (two spoonsfuls of pork, 1/5 loaf of bread, three potatoes and margarine). We sleep in a barn tonight in the town of Kaltenton. It's surprising what a man can do on so little to eat. Passed by an airdrome with mostly Messerschmidt 109's all old and Hungarian pilots. We were buzzed by two P-38's and some of the boys hit the ditch in fear of being strafed. All the German guards did too. The Germans fired anti-aircraft guns at them directly overhead.

20 April 1945. Made twenty-five Kms. today to Kallham, Austria. Not too bad a day and we lay over tomorrow. Soup for supper, and we sleep under the stars tonight. Rumour has it only three more days on the road.

21 April 1945. A big surprise today. Red Cross parcels came in by truck from Switzerland and we sure needed them. All the trucks were American Chevrolets and GMC's driven by English POW's. Sleeping in a wagon bed under a shed tonight. It looks like rain. Just soup from the Jerrys for supper.

22 April 1945. It rained all night last night. Made twenty-three Kms. today to Aurolmunster, Austria, in a bitter, cold rain, wind and hail storm that lasted all day. Had a small ration of bread and soup for the day's ration.

23 April 1945. We made twenty-two Kms. to Althein, Austria. No food today. Rain, hail, wind all day. The roads muddy and hard hiking. A lot of the boys have G.I.'s. We expect to lay over tomorrow. Only one day left to reach our destination.

24 April 1945. We layed over today. Cloudy but no rain. Soup from Jerrys and a small ration of bread.

25 April 1945. We made thirty Kms. today to end our trip. A hard day. The new camp is a spruce forest and we built a lean-to for tonight and probably will fix it up more tomorrow. We have to walk a mile for drinking water. We passed through Braunau, Hitler's birthplace. Quite a few American P-51's strafing while we were on the march.

26 April 1945. Improved on our shelter, and received parcels today, three to four men. Jerry ration was eighteen men to a loaf of bread, one spoonful of salt, one spoonful of barley and a little horsemeat. Gardin has been sick for the last few days. Medical Officer Major Beaumont (American) has charge of us, ordered us not to escape.

27 April 1945. We're still trying to fix up our shelter. It's rough with only two pen knives. Jerry ration of three potatoes today.

28 April 1945. It rained all day and last night. All of us wet to the skin and a wet bed for tonight. This is really roughing it. The Jerrys can't feed us. We had 1/2 cup of barley for four men, and 1/2 cracker per man today. Conners and I have G.I.'s coming on. Gardin is still sick.

29 April 1945. The weather is fair today and maybe we can get some clothes dry. We took Gardin to the hospital which is in an old barn. It's wonder more aren't there. The rumour last night was that the war is over, but guess it's not true. Sure wish the end would hurry up and come. I don't feel so good today. We received Red Cross parcels — one to two men. The five of us got one English, one American, and half a French parcel. I saw my first jet-propelled plane today. It's starting to rain a little. Probably means another wetting but I sure hope not.

30 April 1945. Not a bad day today. It's tried to rain all day but nothing to amount to anything. Gunfire not too far away, and I sure hope it's the Yanks, they can't come too fast. The Russian prisoners are starving to death, those that the Jerrys don't shoot. Sometimes it sounds like the first day of the deer season here.

1 May 1945. It was damp and cold all day which made it miserable. A few potatoes and some horsemeat from the Germans. The Yanks are not far away. We can see the tanks and hear the guns just across the Inns River. Got the G.I.'s worse, not feeling good.

2 May 1945. It snowed last night. Up most of the night with G.I.'s. What a life! Americans within a few miles of us. They can't come too soon. 6:30 pm. We're free men! Captain Summers from California, of the 13th Armoured Division with the 3rd Army, came into camp to tell us we were no longer Prisoners of War. If I wasn't sick, I'd be the happiest man in the world. Still under German guard tonight.

3 May 1945. A rainy day. Today I saw something I have been waiting a long time to see. U.S. Infantrymen came in and disarmed the few German guards left with us. They were plenty rough and we, the ex-POW's, took everything they had except the clothes they had on, and personal property. We captured a lot more Germans in this area with guns we took from our former guards plus a few we got from the Yank infantry boys that freed us. Five of our boys ran into twelve Hitler youth kids and had to shoot five before they would surrender. We eat tomorrow from food we have taken from the Germans. It's take what you want off the Jerry, they did it to us and now it's our turn. And they don't like it! Gardin has already been moved, probably back to a base hospital. He is pretty sick. We should move out of here in a day or so. Most of our former guards have seen their last sunshine.

4 May 1945. Fair weather until evening and then the usual rain. Conners is sick. Moore has been gone all day and it now looks like he will stay out tonight. Since recapture we haven't had anything except one-tenth loaf of bread. A lot of the boys have gone out to towns and farms to get food against direct orders from the Lt. Col. in charge of the recapturing forces. It's either go out and find some food or forget you have a stomach. I never was so hungry! But I'm getting too sick or weak to even go after water. A lot of the boys are getting sick from lack of food or from sleeping on the wet ground. About seventy-five percent of the camp have dysentery or diarrhea or both. Quite a lot of confiscated German food came into camp but only the so-called big wheels got any of it. They are wonderful camp leaders.

5 May 1945. A little rain this morning. Conners has gone to the hospital. We haven't seen Moore since yesterday morning. Just two of the original five still together (Cornwell and myself). No-one seems to know about food or when we move out. Hope one or the other takes place soon. I'm surprised not to be at least fed after being in United States hands again.

Later: Received K rations and marched eleven Kms. in the rain to a factory and shelter. We left the forest camp around 7 pm and carried but very little of our clothes or bedding. We left those to the Russians who needed them worse than we did, because they will have to make their own way home.

6 May 1945. We are in a very modern aluminium factory, untouched by bombs. Millions of dollars worth of equipment in it, and well supplied stock rooms. We start processing tomorrow and move out. All of us are supposed to be out in the next five days. We're still sleeping on the floor but it's dry. Still eating K rations, but it's a million times better than what we've had during the last eighteen months. It's been a month since I've had a bath or been undressed. I sure would like a hot bath, clean clothes, and a good bed. Nothing could be better at present.

7 May 1945. THE WAR IS OVER!!

« « « » » »

What Sgt. Harwood did not record in his diary, fearing that it would be confiscated on reaching Allied Forces, was the following horrifying account — since also confirmed by Sgt. Warren Thomas of the 95th Bomb Group — by Sgt. Dan James of the 100th Bomb Group:

I weighed 98 pounds at the end of the forced march. I was so weak and sick that I had to be lifted into a jeep and driven about 10 kilometres to an abandoned factory where we were given good American food. From a nearby airport, American planes landing and taking off every 10 minutes, took us to Le Havre, France. From there we went home to New York by sea.

During that march I witnessed the most pitiful and dreadful sight.

When we were trudging past Mauthausen Concentration Camp, after about a week on the march, we passed a few thousand Jewish people marching along the road. Each one had a yellow star on his clothes. Some did not have shoes, and their clothing was so ragged that it was falling off them. They stank very badly, and were so thin that their bones almost protruded. They were going to their deaths in the gas chambers of Mauthausen.

The Jewish people were guarded by S.S. troops, and many were falling by the roadside because of their exhausted condition. Their S.S. guards would club their heads with rifle butts. At one small hill on the road, about 200 yards in length, I counted eight bodies.

This was the most tragic and barbaric sight that I have ever seen in my life.

Chapter 20

AS the Allied Armies approached, then encircled Münster, Otto Schuett remembers:

> As a Hitler Youth Leader I was standing at a major highway just outside Münster during the closing days of the war and warning the Allied convoys to slow down because Germany's secret weapons would soon be in action against them. That's how convinced I was at the young age of 17 that Germany was still going to triumph, even at that late stage.
>
> When I had been on the receiving end of Allied air-raids, rest assured that I was angry and bitter . . . homes lost . . . close friends killed. At the time I had thought of nothing but revenge but to be honest I simply did not know the other side of the story and of all that had gone on before.

On April 2nd 1945 British troops of the Sixth Guards Tank Brigade, consisting of the Grenadier and Scots Guards together with units of the American 17th Airborne Division, stormed their way into Münster, which they captured the following day.

The Cathedral city, dating from the time of Charlemagne, was invited to surrender, but the Germans decided on a suicide stand whereupon heavy British artillery guns pounded it, and was followed up by the forced entry of the British tanks with the American airborne troops in close support. The city was little more than a heap of rubble, even worse than Cologne.

Its destruction was significant in that Hitler had announced that he would hold his peace conference there, hoping that it would erase the memory of the disastrous Thirty Years War which had ended at Münster three hundred years previously.

The war in Europe was over. The victors and the vanquished made their way slowly homeward during the Summer of 1945 to try and pick up the threads of shattered lives and to rebuild for an uncertain future.

Heinz Knoke, a German Fighter Pilot, who had miraculously survived over 400 operational missions, often against overwhelming odds, and was credited with destroying 52 Allied aircraft, wrote in 1945:

During the last two years I have become very lonely. Not many of my comrades have returned from what we ourselves call "The Great Fighter Graveyard." Even in defeat, however, we can still remain victors in one sense . . . victors over ourselves, victors over the baser instincts which threatened to rob us of courage and faith. Those of us who survive have been wounded more than once. I myself, wounded five times, am now a cripple.

Our world is reduced to rubble.

We are dazed by all the sensational disclosures and events which occur in rapid succession. For us, the road to the future must lead through poverty and want. Despotism without conscience has been revealed among the Nazis in the background behind Hitler. Disgusted and indignant, the German fighting soldiers and officers turn away from these whose brutal war crimes and atrocities are now exposed. These criminals, whose activities were as a rule restricted to the Concentration Camps and Labour Camps in rear defence areas, have dishonoured the name of Germany. The atrocities committed under the sign of the Swastika deserve the most severe punishment. The Allies ought to leave the criminals to the German fighting soldiers to bring to justice.

Communism has now reached the heart of Europe. Over Berlin the Red Flag now flies. There we have the real victor in this war. When will Stalin's tanks roll across Europe?

« « « » » »

Conservative estimates put Russian casualties of the Second World War and Stalin's purges at 21 millions.

Contrary to popular belief, the majority of Nazi war criminals did not flee to South America after the war. Many are now living and prospering in Germany and other wartime Occupied European countries after having assumed false identities and backgrounds. They have successfully, it seems, concealed from increasingly reluctant investigative authorities their appalling wartime activities.

Humanity can take hope however from a survivor of one of the most notorious death camps, Auschwitz, who said, "I can forgive but I can never forget. Peoples are not evil, only individuals."

Just how secret was that terrible secret? When a desperate, stateless 17 year old Polish Jew shot the nephew of the German

Ambassador in Paris, Lord Rothschild wrote a letter*, which was published, to *The Times,* one of Britain's most respected and internationally read newspapers:

> In the name of a reprisal began an organised campaign of plunder, destruction and violence. It has been announced in the newspapers that any criticisms made in foreign countries of the treatment of the Jews will only increase their torments in Germany.
>
> I have no fear of doing this, because their torments cannot be increased. Almost the only thing left for them is death; for many that would be a welcome and blessed relief.
>
> Some people may think from reading the newspapers that pogroms (organised plunder and massacres) are something new in the treatment of Jews in Germany. That is untrue. The difference between the treatment of the Jews in the last three or four days and their treatment during the last three or four years is quantative. Qualitatively these things have been going on continuously.

Not that the wartime Allies could claim a clear conscience. Following Hitler's invasion of Poland in September 1939 (thus leaving western Germany, including the industrial Ruhr Valley almost entirely undefended, a golden opportunity which the dithering and undecided Allies failed utterly to exploit) Stalin grasped his chance to invade Poland from the east.

During the bitterly cold winter of 1940/41, on the direct orders from Stalin, more than 15,000 Polish Officers, the intellectually elite of their country and who had been taken prisoner during the attack, were murdered in cold blood by shooting in the back of the neck, using German made ammunition. The frozen bodies were buried in shallow graves in the Katyn Forest, north-west Russia.

This mass murder of defenseless prisoners of war was discovered in April 1943 by the German Army.

At the end of the war, which by conservative estimates cost the lives of at least 52 million people world-wide, some 50,000 Russian Cossacks, men, women and children, found themselves in Germany, Austria and Britain. Many were prisoners of war, many were political refugees from the tyranny of Stalin's Communism. Many of them had ended up fighting

---

*Lord Rothschild's letter appeared in *The Times* on December 12, 1938.

for Hitler, believing that when the war was over they could surrender to the Allies and be granted political asylum.

Such was not the case. Their death warrants had already been signed at Yalta between the wartime Allied leaders, President Roosevelt, Prime Minister Churchill and Marshal Stalin. This agreement said that at the end of the war all Russian nationals were to be returned to Soviet Russia.

At Lienz, in southern Austria, 6,500 Russian Cossacks and their families were forcibly herded into trains for transportation and 'repatriation' to Russia. Many of them committed suicide rather than face Stalin's execution squads. The orders came direct from the British Foreign and War Offices in London.

The Reverend Kenneth Tyson, Padre of the 8th Battalion, Argyle and Sutherland Highlanders, a very famous Scottish Regiment, and who had been given these appalling orders, described the operation as "an evil event."

Battle hardened Scottish soldiers, who had fought their way through many savage battles during the heat of the North African Campaign and then through the freezing mud the length of Italy,** found themselves facing Cossacks and their families, begging to be shot as an alternative to facing Stalin's revenge.

Reverend Tyson remembers that a few broke down completely:

> One or two of our men just couldn't take it. There were soldiers pushing people along with their rifle butts . . . not hitting them but just pushing them . . . with tears streaming down their faces. It was the first and only time I ever saw an Argyle and Sutherland Highlander in tears.

In similar circumstances, British soldiers found themselves in the unenviable position of having to forcibly repatriate 26,000 Jugoslavs, many of whom had served in the German Army and many of whom were subsequently tortured, then executed, by President Tito's partisans. The orders had come

---

**Prime Minister Churchill, in 1942, described Italy as "The soft underbelly of Europe." United States Army General Mark Clark, who personally experienced the bitterly fought Italian campaign, Sicily, Salerno, Anzio, Monte Cassino and the rest, preferred the much more realistic and accurate description; "Tough old gut."

from Harold Macmillan (who later became one of Britain's post-war Prime Ministers) and the late Field Marshal Lord Alexander who overrode instructions from London and Washington that the Yugoslavs should be screened and only genuine Nazi collaborators handed over to Tito. British Foreign Office documents dated September 1945 describe the forcible repatriation as "a ghastly mistake."

In January 1984, the British Broadcasting Corporation produced a documentary, "The Klagenfurt Affair", for nationwide television, which described the repatriation. Mr. Macmillan declined to be interviewed by the B.B.C.

« « « » » »

As former airfields throughout Eastern England, which had reverberated with noise and bustling activity by both day and night, were abandoned and left derelict to the elements, stripped of all the modern paraphernalia of war, an unreal silence gradually descended.

Gone forever were the huge, sky-swamping formations of the Allied Air Fleets and only one final question remained. What did they achieve? Had it all been worth the tremendous cost in lives and aircraft that had been lost? During the daylight raid to Berlin on 6th March, 1944 for example, the U.S. 8th Air Force lost 69 bombers, 27 of which were from the 13th Combat Bomb Wing, its, and the 8th's, heaviest loss of the war. During the night of 30th-31st March 1944, the Royal Air Force Bomber Command lost 97 aircraft while attacking Nuremberg.

In 1944 the German Army Commander, Field Marshall Erwin Rommel said, "Stop the bombers or we will lose another city every night."; German Economics Minister Albert Speer stated, "The Allied bombing offensive was Germany's greatest defeat. The real importance of the air war was the fact that it created a Second Front long before the invasion of Europe in June, 1944. That front was the skies over Germany."

According to the German High Command the Allied Air Forces had kept nearly one million German servicemen and over 20,000 heavy guns fully occupied on the Western Front as

"TAXI!" Courtesy of The Sunday Express

a part of the German air defences. "Without this great drain on our logistics, weapons and manpower," Speer concludes, "we might well have knocked Russia out of the war before the

"Have you boys seen the bad news?"

To Winfrey & Lenase, Best wishes from "Giles"

Yes I remember well this is where we first discussed the age of consent you also discussed it with Florrie Finch, Queenie Quinn, and most of the other WAAFs in my outfit

Daily Express, September 16th, 1979

Allied invasion of Europe."

General Dwight Eisenhower, Supreme Allied Commander, asserts: "The Allied Air Forces had achieved the impossible."; General Bernard Montgomery, Commander of the British Army in Europe, added, "The bombers did more than anyone towards winning the war." And Luftwaffe Field Marshall

"Mac . . . Sergeant says how do you spell this 'Hogmanay'?"

Sunday Express, Jan. 1st, 1956

With best wishes from "Giles" to William Whitlow.

Hugo Sperrle confirmed emphatically, "Allied Air Power was the chief factor in Germany's defeat."

In early 1942 Air Marshal Arthur "Bomber" Harris, Commander of Royal Air Force Bomber Command had said; "There are a lot of people who say that bombing can never win a war. Well, my answer to that is that it has never been tried yet . . . and we shall see."

Sir Arthur Harris died in early April 1984. A former Flight Engineer of R.A.F. Bomber Command, Sergeant Ray Piper, said of his Commander:

He was affectionately known to us as "Butch", and he fought for a campaign medal for us afterwards, but it did not happen.

All the aircrew looked on him as a benign father-figure . . . I never heard anyone criticise him for where he sent us.We did not resent it. It was part of the job.

« « « » » »

In May 1944 Lt. Colonel Thomas Jeffrey, the Deputy Group Commander of the 390th Bomb Group at Framlingham, was given the choice of becoming Group Commander of either the 95th or the 100th Bomb Group by General Curtis LeMay. He chose 'The Bloody Hundredth' at Thorpe Abbotts.

In March 1945, with the war in Europe almost concluded, he was again promoted, becoming the Deputy Director of Operations of the United States Air Force in France and Germany.

Shortly after V E Day in May 1945 Colonel Jeffrey flew over many of the bombed out cities and devastated industrial targets of Germany, surveying at low altitude the results of the Allied bombing campaign in which he, as a senior officer of the 13th Combat Bomb Wing, had played a significant part. He remembers:

It was a most interesting and educational flight.

I had the last B17 (as far as I know) from the 100th Bomb Group, the *Silver Dollar,* transferred to the flight section of U.S.A.F.E. Headquarters at Wiesbaden, Germany. This airplane had flown 106 bombing missions to these same targets, and the bomb symbols, representing each of these missions, were painted along the fuselage.

The reader can imagine the large numbers of curious onlookers who gathered around this airplane the day I took it to Templehof Airport in Berlin.

I returned to England in 1951 with the 509th Bomb Wing (B29 Superfortresses). This was the Wing which had dropped the atomic bombs on Japan in 1945. While in England, as Director of Operations during the establishment of the U.S.A.F. 3rd Air Force at South Ruislip, I re-visited Framlingham and Thorpe Abbotts . . . things were rather quiet. . . .

'The wheel had turned full circle.''

« « « » » »

In Britain in 1939 there were only about 150 airfields, mostly grass, but by 1945 a total of 720 airfields bore testimony to the largest single construction project every conceived and completed in this country.

Nowhere were these airfields more crowded than in the gentle undulations of the East Anglian countryside. In Suffolk, Norfolk and Essex alone, there were 103 bases, each of which averaged 500 acres. Indeed, no other country before or since, has been so densely crammed with airfields, and it was said that in these three counties of rural England, the granary of Britain, there was an airfield at about every fifth village.

Roger Freeman, who as an Essex schoolboy had witnessed much of the activities of the Allied Air Forces during those eventful years, as indeed had a whole generation of East Anglians, cycled his way up to a small Norfolk village shortly after the war. He remembers:

I first visited Thorpe Abbotts on a beautiful summer's day. The airfield there was still complete but deserted. Nature had begun to regain her hold, brambles were entwining some of the buildings and well-trodden footpaths had become overgrown. Much of the camp was in woodland, which gave an added emphasis to the deserted scene. Rabbits scampered about between the Nissen huts and trees. There was no absence of bird life, but the feeling of a special and extraordinary stillness was there. I recall the unsecured door of a hut creaking gently, presumably in a breeze.

It is very easy to let one's imagination establish a charged atmosphere in such circumstances, but I truly recall some intangible feeling of ghostliness about that airfield; perhaps it had something to do with having witnessed the intense activity and volume of noise at a wartime Fortress airfield and finding it difficult to contrast it with the wide, deserted landscape of gaunt black hangars, empty hardstands and runways stretching away to the wooded horizon.

The sun was warm and that part of Norfolk was a beautiful and peaceful place. It was not a day for ghosts . . . but they were there. . . .

Chapter 21

LONDON, 11 November 1979. Remembrance Sunday. Throughout the length and breadth of the British Isles, from the wartime training ground of the Royal Marine Commandos in the rugged Highlands and sheltered glens of Scotland, to the long steep-sided valleys of Wales, the emerald-green sunlit meadows of Ireland, and the rolling Shires of England, a Nation mourned its dead of the horrific holocausts of two World Wars. British casualties in the Great War amounted to a million and a quarter, those of the Second War 400,000.

Young Men, the elite of their generation, cruelly cut down in the very prime of their lives. Three of the Allied casualties of the First War were later discovered to be just 14-year-olds. They had come from Canada, Ireland and South Africa, and had falsified their ages on enlistment.

To some, the apathetic and fortunately ignorant, the names of Ypres, Arras, Paschendael, Cambria, Dunkirk, Dieppe, Caen and Arnhem, are just names on a glossy tourist map where they might have stopped enroute for hurried refreshment before hastening on to their holiday destinations. To others, of an older generation, they bring back memories of a very different kind.

In a poignant and very moving ceremony at the Cenotaph in London's heart, Whitehall, veterans of both wars gathered with their relatives and friends to pay tribute to long-lost comrades who had given their all for that most cherished and valued of all man's possessions, freedom.

The resonant chimes of Big Ben, towering about the Houses of Parliament on the Thames Embankment, clanging across the City of London, signalled the beginning of the two minutes of total silence at the eleventh hour, the eleventh day, and the eleventh month. The wreath-laying ceremony at the foot of the Cenotaph then followed, led by the Nation's Monarch.

A little later, in a time-honored tradition, leading the march-past of the Cenotaph were veterans belonging to the Association of the Royal Navy, Britain's Senior Service. These veteran's ships had seen action in the seven great oceans of the world. From the long, hazardous Atlantic, Arctic and Mediterranean convoys, shepherding laden tankers and freighters crewed by the gallant men of the Merchant Navy, to the great surface battles, fought over thousands of square miles of lonely sea.

Following them, in the bright November sun which reflected glittering campaign medals, marched the proud Associations of the British Army, the Desert Rats of El Alemein, the Dunkirk Veterans Association, the Far East Prisoners of War Association, the Burma Star Association marching at a hundred paces to the minute with the valiant and fearless Ghurkas, and the white sticks of the blind mingling with the Red Berets of the Parachute Regiment.

Finally, came the youngest Arm of Britain's three Services, the veterans of the Royal Air Force Association. Saviours of their country during the savagely fought Battle of Britain in the late Summer of 1940, Fighter Command had won the respect, admiration and eternal gratitude of the whole Free World. They had bought priceless time in which to rearm while Bomber Command carried the offensive to the enemy in a blood-ridden campaign that lasted the whole length of the war, and which added a decisive contribution to the ultimate victory.

These elderly veterans had faced nightmares of fear and danger, from the freezing waters of the Actic Ocean off lonely Bear Island, the burning heat by day and the bitterly cold nights of the Western Desert, the stifling jungles of Burma and the fiery skies over the Rhur Valley, which were so unnaturally extreme that they continue to haunt them to this day.

Coinciding with the Cenotaph Service, at innumerable cathedrals and churches in cities, towns and villages throughout the Nation, congregations reverently observed Remembrance Sunday.

In the very heart of rural Suffolk at the 13th Century All Saints Church, Great Ashfield, Lay Elder John Ellis conducted the service. As the congregation sang that most beautiful and stirring hymn *"For All The Saints Who From Their Labour Rest,"* he walked across to the Memorial Altar before reading the Names of the Missing in Action.

From this small Suffolk village nine local men had made the supreme sacrifice during the two wars. The hymn ended, and John Ellis intoned their names to the hushed congregation.

"John Brown, Nelson Brown, George Carter, Arthur Hawes, George Hawes, Arthur Scase, Cyril Scase, Leslie Walpole and Arthur Wyatt."

From the Roll of Honour commemorating the 415 American airmen who died in missions over Occupied Europe while flying from the nearby airfield with the 385th Bombardment Group, he read 12 names.

"Mercer Abernethy, Robert Bayne, Clifford Canterberry, Harold Fredericksen, James McKee, Ned Mirabel, Paul Sommers, Arthur Spikos, Harry Swift, Anthony Vespasiano, Charles Wardle and Leonard Wasilewski . . . their bodies rest in Peace, but their names live for Evermore."

"They grow not old as we that are left grow old
Age shall not weary them nor the years condemn.
At the going down of the sun and in the morning we will remember them."

Epilogue 1

ALMOST 40 years after he had served at various 8th Air Force bases in England as a Sgt. Radio Technician with the 95th Bomb Group, Ted Lucey now living in Lakeville, Connecticut, recalls:

I know that in the ebb and flow of the fortunes of war I was lucky. I wasn't in combat. Not as the flyers were. They were the ones who took all the risks and who did the dying. The flyers of the 8th Air Force were the bravest men I have ever known, together with the men of the RAF and those of the Luftwaffe.

If I had been assigned to a B17 or a B24 I would have flown. If the selection process had put crossed rifles on my lapel, instead of a propeller and wings, I'd have slogged along with the infantry. If my uniform had been blue I would have taken my chances with a U-Boat or a kamikaze.

Time has gone by and places far away exist only in my memory. Neither I nor anyone else will ever again see a thousand planes in the sky. I will never again know the same excitement and boredom . . . the comical and the sad . . . the brilliance and the stupidity . . . the selfishness and selflessness . . .

I will never again see Framlingham, Horham, Elveden and Knettishall as they once were. For time has worked its changes, and nothing is quite the same.

Another veteran, a Fighter Pilot who saw a great deal of combat while flying with the 78th Fighter Group from Duxford, Eugene Roberts, still residing at Spokane, Washington, remembers:

My memories of my tour of England are still rather vivid. As a young man I saw the mightiest air armadas that probably will ever be seen, and I was part of them. The worries, fears and anxieties are gone now and only the pleasant memories remain. I visited Buckingham Palace and met the King and Queen, and the then Princesses. I met many famous people such as Lord Trenchard, Lord Halifax and Anthony Eden. How many young men in their early twenties had such opportunity? Truly, it was a most exciting time and after nearly forty years is still well remembered.

Another 8th Air Force veteran, Frank Murphy who flew 21 missions with "The Bloody Hundredth" from Thorpe Abbotts and who is still living in Atlanta, Georgia, has his own memories of those dramatic days over war-torn Europe:

> You never forget . . . even after four decades. For many years my business has required that I pass through England several times each year on my way to European cities and to the Middle East. On those clear days when we lift off from London Airport and turn towards Europe, I always remember. As we approach the Continent I feel the airplane shudder as the guns are test-fired. I hear the co-pilot admonishing the crew to watch for German fighters and I hear the responses . . . I still look for enemy aircraft. . .
>
> It is all in an old man's memory of course. But they are there . . . the men and the Forts of the United States Eighth Air Force flying into the great daylight air battles over Europe during those grim wartime days.
>
> If you were there, you never forget.

What happened to some of the other veterans and civilians who were involved in various ways in the Münster raid? Where are they now?

Madame Yvonne de Yonghe van Abeele of the Belgian Resistance passed away in 1980. Her namesake, Madame Andree de Yonghe, founder of the famous "Comete" Escape Line, was awarded the George Medal, Britain's highest gallantry medal for civilians. She survived the horrors of Ravensbruck and devoted the remainder of her working life to helping and caring for the sick and needy of Africa with Belgian medical teams. In June 1981 Madame de Jonghe, G.M., retired and returned home to Belgium after a lifetime of helping others in need.

Clemens Von Galen, the Bishop of Münster, died in 1946 and was laid to rest in his now rebuilt and beautifully restored Cathedral. John Egan, who had led the 100th Bomb Group to Münster, died several years ago, virtually on the eve of being promoted to the rank of Brigadier General. Keith Harris, 390th Pilot of one of only two B17's in the 100th's formation to return from the raid, Glenn Infield, Major General John Gerhart both of the 95th Group, Thomas Combs of the 100th and Joe Scarlett of 103 Squadron, R.A.F. Bomber Command, have all passed on in very recent years.

David Schilling, who led the 56th Fighter Group to Münster, eventually became that famous Group's Commanding

Officer and accumulated twenty three air victories. While serving as a Staff Officer with the post-war U.S.A.F. in England he was tragically killed when his sports car struck a concrete bridgepost at Eriswell, Suffolk in 1956. To this day that bridge is reverently known as "Schilling's Bridge."

Walter Beckham now lives in Alburquerque, New Mexico. When he was eventually shot down over Germany on 22nd February 1944 he was the leading 8th Air Force Fighter Command "Ace" with 19 confirmed air victories to his credit. In July 1982 he went to the world famous Oshkosh, Wisconsin, Air Show, where he saw Ray Stutsman receive the highly coveted "Grand Champion Warbird" Trophy for his magnificently restored P47 Thunderbolt fighter in the colours of Colonel Beckham's *Little Demon*.

William Lindley, the indestructable 95th Group Pilot who had led the 8th Air Force to Munster and Rodney Snow's former pheasant shooting partner at Horham, also served with the post-war U.S.A.F. and rose to the rank of Major General, before retiring to San Antonio, Texas. Similarly, Major General John Kidd, former Operations Officer of the 100th Bomb Group, is now living in California. Major General Kidd played a key role in the organisation of the massive Berlin Airlift in 1948. Also now living in California are the two escapees, John Justice and William Whitlow who is now an Attorney at Law.Colonel "Hub" Zemke also lives in California, He is now a busy and successful ranch owner. Arthur Horning now lives in Florida.

Raymond Harwood, 388th Bomb Group, is a National Parks Superintendent at Clarendon, Vermont. Bill Kubitzki completed his 25 missions as Radio Operator/Gunner with the 390th Group then transferred to the 15th Air Force in Italy and flew a further 51 missions to targets in Occupied Europe. He now lives in Louisburg, Kansas.

All the original crew of *"Rosie's Riveters"*, the 100th Bomb Groups' most famous B17, are still in touch with each other. Winfrey "Pappy" Lewis is close to retirement from managing the affairs of a construction and property company in Houston, Texas. He occasionally meets Clifford Milburn who also lives in Houston. Ray Robinson now lives in Kansas and

Clarence Hall in Georgia.

Sammy Hurry now teaches Retail Management at a Technical College in Kings Lynn, Norfolk. Billy Taylor works for a Coach Company at Harleston, Norfolk and John Watson is a co-owner of a Construction Plant Hire Company near Ipswich, Suffolk.

Joop Noest was arrested by the Gestapo in July 1944 as a result of his underground activities, and sent to a concentration camp in Poland. He escaped and made his way homewards only to be re-arrested and imprisoned near Munich. During a bombing raid he again escaped and was liberated by the advancing American 3rd Army in the late Spring of 1945. On his return home to Holland in early July 1945, he volunteered for service in the Dutch Army as the Dutch East Indies were still occupied by the Japanese. In 1948, he resigned from his driving instructor post and went into insurance, and in 1960 started his own insurance office in Haarlem. The business prospered so that he was able to sell his company in 1976. Joop Noest now lives in semi-retirement in Northern Holland.

Sergeant Beute, the Barneveld Police Chief, was arrested by the Gestapo, and sent to a concentration camp where he died in late 1944. Doctor Adolph Wong Lun Hing, the Chinese aircrew helper, was also arrested but fortunately survived to continue his medical practice in Southern Holland after the war. Dr. Wong died in 1968.

Kees van Hombergh was also arrested and imprisoned near Berlin. He survived and is still living in Tilburg, Holland, enjoying retirement with his wife Lena, who also played a very active role in the Dutch Underground. Wim Martens is now also retired, and living in the same area of Holland, near the Belgian border. They survived to receive well-earned awards from grateful governments.

More than 20,000 resistance workers were not so fortunate.

On 10 October 1980, Joseph Hallerbach, who is a now retired mining engineer, re-visited the site of his crash-landing on a meadow near Holten, Holland. He found that very little had changed geographically over the intervening years, and he was given a cordial welcome by the same Dutch farmers

The devastation of Münster can be seen in these photographs taken in April 1945. In the top photo the Dortmund-Ems Canal can be seen.

John Archer.

The restored Münster Cathedral and center of the city.

The Münster Cathedral in 19

H. Ko

The Münster Cathedral in 1980. H. Kosters

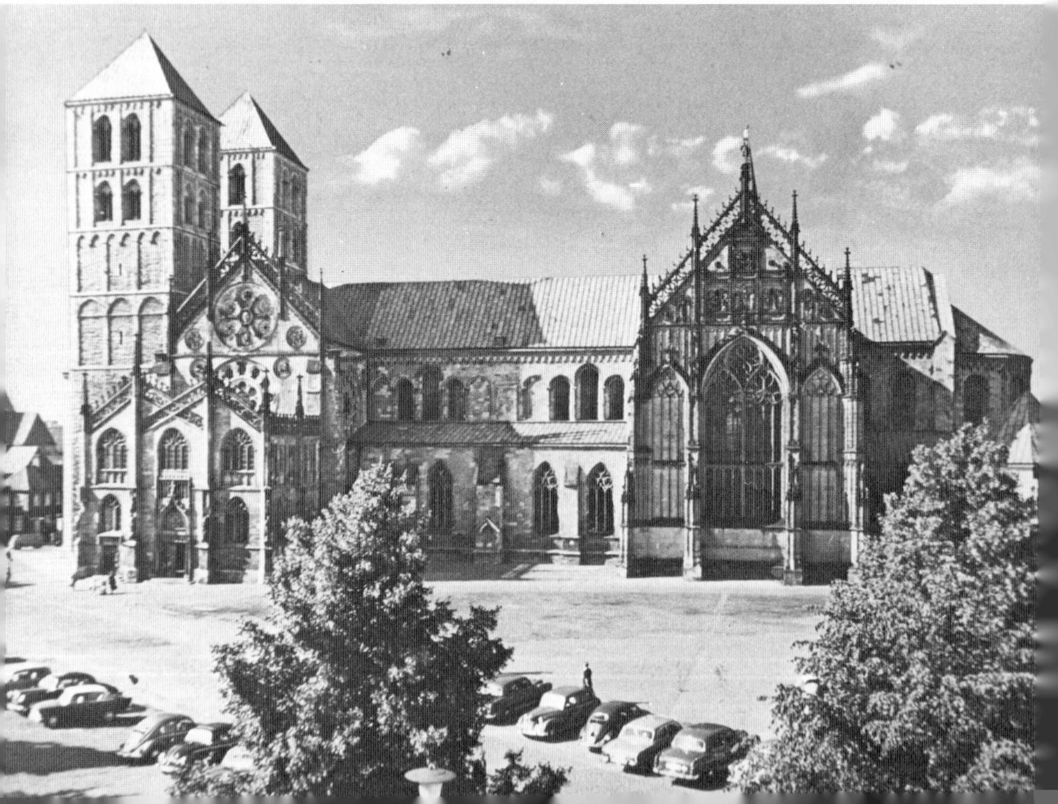

Colonel Walter Beckham, U.S.A.F. (Retired) standing beside the completely restored Little Demon, *the P47 which he flew on 10 October 1943 when he shot down three German fighters.* Walter Beckham.

Witold "Lanny" Lanowski in 1977. He is holding a model of a P47 which he flew in the 56th Fighter Group.

Colonel Hubert Zemke in 1980. Colonel Zemke was the Commanding Officer of the 56th Fighter Group.

"Lanny" Lanowski standing beside the only P47 still in the United Kingdom. Richard Lucraft.

Seymour "Buck" Feldman greets Gerd Wiegand in Munich, June 1981. These two pilots had last met in air combat over Belgium on 5 October 1943.

Joseph Hallerbach with Dutch farmers at the scene of the crash of his Me 410 on 10 October 1943.

Otto Schuett looks through Dick Perry's scrapbook when Dick visits Otto's home in New Jersey.

Dick Perry.

Richard Perry, Teresa Schuett, and Otto Schuett in 1983.

Dick Perry.

d Kosters, Sammy y, and Hubert Kosters 25 May 1981 dedica- of the 100th Bomb p Memorial Air um. **Bill Stonestreet.**

Warren D. Thomas of the 95th Bomb Group, Fritz Blitz, *shot down on his 25th mission on 10 October 1943.*

Gale House, Bob Hook and Major General William Lindley (Retired) in 1983 at the 95th Bomb Group Reunion.

Rodney Snow, Pilot, 95th Bomb Group in 1981.

William "Ed" Charles, Lead Navigator of the 95th Bomb Group in front of his former barracks in September 1981.

William Charles in front of the Combat Crew Messhall. The lettering behind him is the original.

B. Scripture at Horham in ber 1983. The mural behind is at the former "Red her Club," the N.C.O. club e 95th Bomb Group.

William Charles remembers a bicycle ride to Horham.

Major General Thoma
Jeffrey (Retired) at the 390th Control Tower, now the 390th Bomb Group Memorial Air Museum.

General Jeffrey locates his former living quarters at the site of the 390th Bomb Group.

General Jeffrey and hi
wife Helen with Mick Tipple, Curator, and
Buxton, Chairman, of 390th Bomb Group M
orial Air Museum.

ıck Nosser, Bombardier of the
'0th Bomb Group.

"Gus" Mencow, Group Navigator of the 390th Bomb Group standing on the former runway at Horham in August 1982.

obert Schneider, Pilot of Little
'ike on 10 October 1943. He flew
'l four of the missions during
Black Week."

Robert Schneider outside the former Officer's Club at Framlingham with the Combat Mess Hall in the background.

James Geary and his wife Betty in 1983. He was pilot of the Lead Ship of the 390th Bomb Group on the Münster raid.

William "Ike" Adamson, Tail-gunner of Miss Carry *at Framlingham in July 1980.*

Colin Durrant.

Paul Vance, Dick Perry, Stanley Smith and Dick Rowland, all of the 570th Bomb Squadron, are reunited at the 390th Bomb Group Memorial Air Museum Dedication on 13 May 1981.

Major General John B. Kidd, his wife Bete and pets.

Major Horace Varian of the 100th Bomb Group in front of his old barracks.

Frank Murphy on the roof of the Control Tower at Thorpe Abbotts on 19 October 1983.

John Brady, Lead Pilot of the 100th Bomb Group, at Thorpe Abbotts in October 1983.

John Parmentier, Crew Chief, 351st Squadron, 100th Bomb Group in forn of B17 Sally B *at Duxford, England.*

Bob Spangler and Harold Wildric Crew Chiefs, 351st Squadron, 100t Bomb Group, with Sally B *in the background.*

Howard Hamilton, Bombardier, 100th Bomb Group, in nose of B17G Mary Alice *at Duxford , England.*

Jack Rogers of the crew of El P'sstofo, *100th Bomb Group, at Thorpe Abbotts, May 1980.*

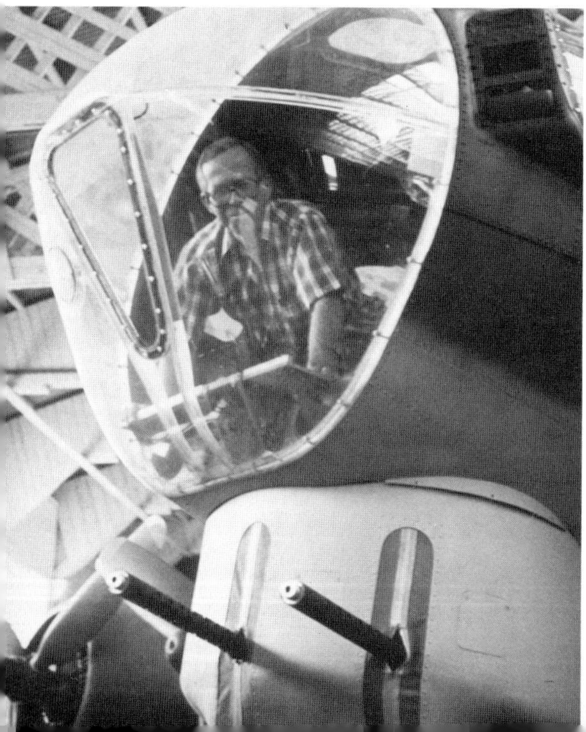

Winfrey "Pappy" Lewis, Co-Pilot of Royal Flush *on 10 October 1943, on* *he Thorpe Abbotts Control Tower* *n April 1980.*

Clifford Milburn, Bombardier of Royal Flush *on 10 October 1943, in 1977.*

Harry Crosby, Group Navigator; Robert Rosenthal, Pilot of Royal Flush, *and Everett Blakely, Pilot of* Just-a-Snappin' *at the Reunion of the 100th Bomb Group in June 1978.*

John Justice and his wi Edna, at the Reunion o the 100th Bomb Group San Antonio, Texas in 1978.

(L. to R.) Jim Brown, Navigator; Harold Weachter, Navigator; Howard Hamilton, Bombardier; and Thomas Casey, Navigator at Thorpe Abbotts in June 1983.

James Stewart, a Squadron Commander of the 445th Bomb Group (B24 Liberators), returns to that airfield in Tibenham, Norfolk.

Ray Harwood and his wife Florence in 1980. Sgt. Harwood was the Top Turret Gunner on Little Lass, *385th Bomb Group, on 10 October 1943.*

John Pettenger and Jack Leahy of the 385th Bomb Group at All Saints Church, Great Ashfield, in August 1976.

John Pettenger at the re-built railroad station in Münster in 1965.

Thorpe Abbotts Airfield, Norfolk, home of the 100th Bomb Group, 13 November 1946. Department of the Environment

Thorpe Abbotts Airfield taken at approximately the same directional reference as the previous photograph, in June 1983.

The entrance to the Group Operations Building of the 100th Bomb Group at Thorpe Abbotts in June 1983.

The wall mural in the "Red Feather Club," the N.C.O. Officer's Club, at Horham, Suffolk, home of the 95th Bomb Group. This picture was taken in 1981.

The Framlingham Airfield Community Site. The Officer's Club, Combat Crew Mess Hall, and other buildings are now used as storage for farm machinery. This was the home of the 390th Bomb Group.

Stewart Evans.

The Hospital Buildings of the 95th Bomb Group at Horham Airfield in 1981.

The Operations Room of the Operations Building at Thorpe Abbotts in June 1983.

Richard H. Perry unveils the Memorial Plaque on the Control Tower Building, now the 390th Bomb Group Memorial Air Museum, at Framlingham, 13 May 1981.

East Anglia Daily Times.

Fly-by of a B17G at the Dedication Ceremony of the 390th Bomb Group Memorial Air Museum, 13 May 1981.

East Anglia Daily Times.

390th Bomb Group veterans return to Framlingham for the Dedication of the Memorial Air Museum. East Anglia Daily Times.

The Sally B *buzzes the Control Tower at the Framlingham Airfield, 13 May 1981.* East Anglia Daily Times.

Major Horace Varian speaking at the Dedication Day, 25 May 1981, at the 100th Bomb Group Memorial Air Museum.

95th Bomb Group veterans at their memorial in front of St. Mary's Church, Horham.

Rev. Werrell, Major Varian and Colonel Mallory (in center of the picture, from left to right) with those responsible for renovating the 100th Bomb Group Memorial Air Museum at the Dedication Day, 25 May 1981. 100th Bomb Group (U.K.)

Veterans of the 100th Bomb Group arrive at their former base at Thorpe Abbotts, Norfolk.

95th Bomb Group veterans (from L. to R.) John Miller, Robert Prest, Dave McKnight, Floyd Kyzer, Earl Underwood, William Charles, "Doc" Steele, Waldo Cleveland, "Lefty" Nairn, Zach Stanborough, Art Frankel, Robert Kopke, and Al Brown, around their Group's Memorial.

The Dedication Services of the 95th Bomb Group Memorial 19 September 1981.

The American flag on the altar of the All Saints Church, Thorpe Abbotts, Norfolk. The flag was presented to the church following the morning service 5 June 1983 by veterans of the 100th Bomb Group.

At the gravesite of Lt. Robert P. Kramer, Pilot of the 100th Bomb Group, K.I.A. 10 October 1943 on the Munster raid. This grave is at the Lambeck Cemetery near Gelsenkirthin. Donal Glaze and George White of the same crew are also buried in this cemetery. the picture was sent to Lt. Kramer's widow after World War II by the German authorities.

The American Military Cemetery at Madingley near Cambridge, England. Many of the dead from the Eighth Air Force are buried here. The American Battle Monuments Commission.

The Wall of the Missing *contains the names, Group, and home state of members of the Eighth Air Force.*

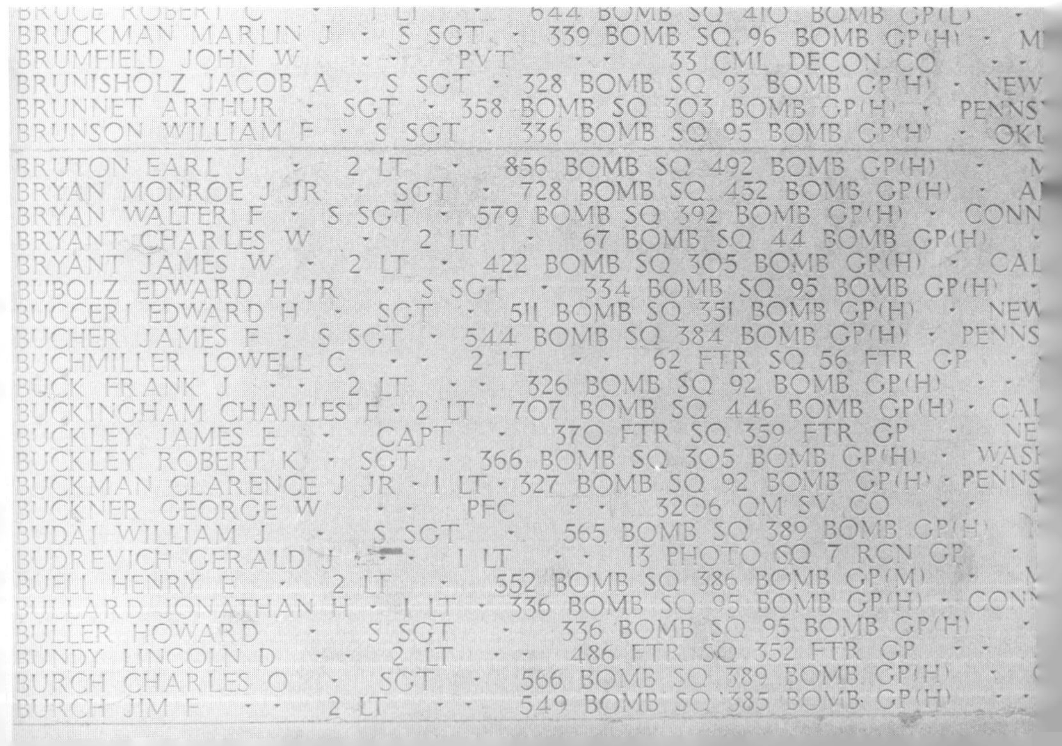

The War Memorial Cemetery near Münster where many victims of the Münster raid are buried.

Hubert Kosters.

Hubert Kosters

Wreaths at the Cross at the War Memorial Cemetery.

This stone from Coventry Cathedral, England, is now installed in the rebuilt Münster Cathedral. Both Cathedrals were destroyed during war-time bombing raids.

All Saints Church, Great Ashfield, Suffolk. Stonestreet

Memorial Plaque to the Officers and Men of the 385th Bomb Group at All Saints Church. Hammond

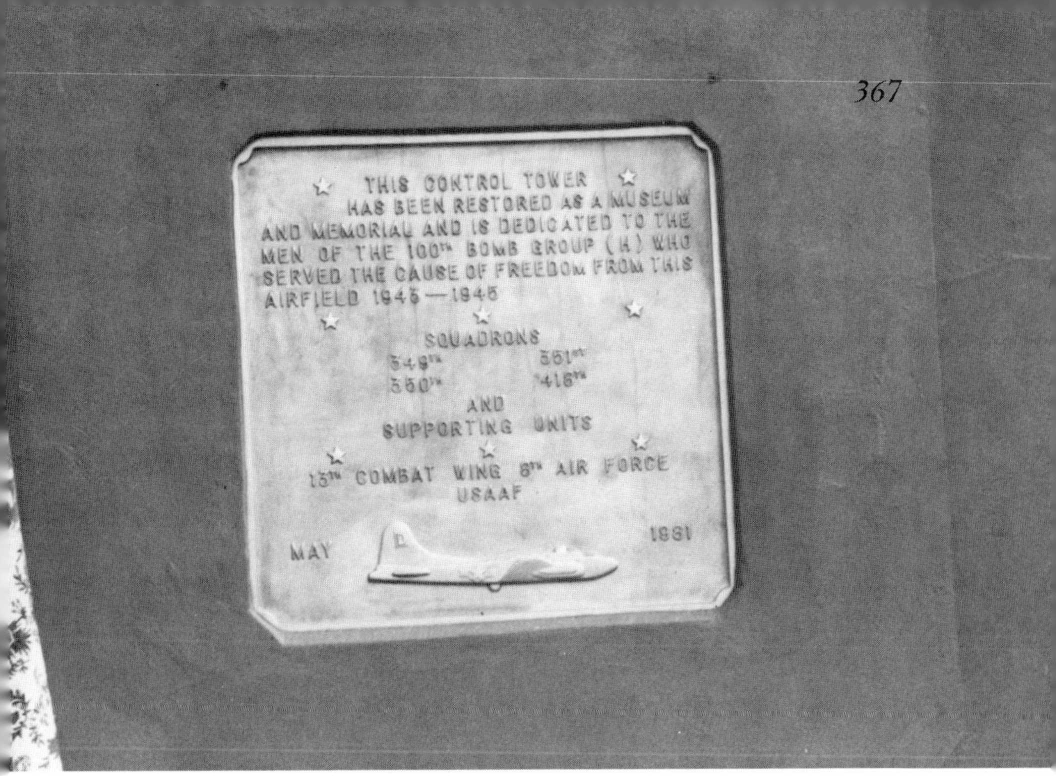

Memorial Plaque to the men of the 100th Bomb Group at Thorpe Abbotts.

Memorial Plaque to the men of the 95th Bomb Group at St. Mary's Church, Horham.

The President

OF THE UNITED STATES OF AMERIC

has directed me to express t

KEES van HOMBERGH

the gratitude and appreciation of th
American people for gallant servic
in assisting the escape of Allied
soldiers from the enemy

Dwight D. Eisenhower

DWIGHT D. EISENHOWER

General of the Army

Commanding General United States Forces European Theater

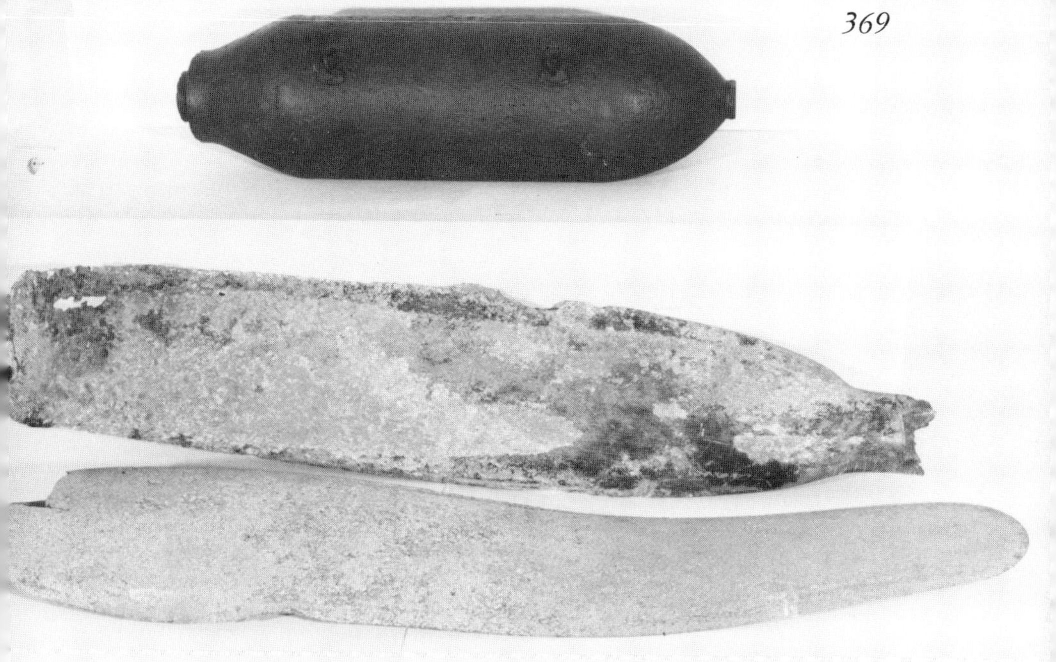

Relics of the Münster raid now in the Münster Museum. At top, a 500 lb. bomb, a propeller blade from Miss Fortune *of the 390th Bomb Group, and a propeller blade from* Sexy Suzy, Mother of Ten *of the 100th Bomb Group.* Heinz Hessling.

Second propeller blades on display at the Münster Museum. The top one is from Sexy Suzy, Mother of Ten *and the lower one from* Miss Fortune.

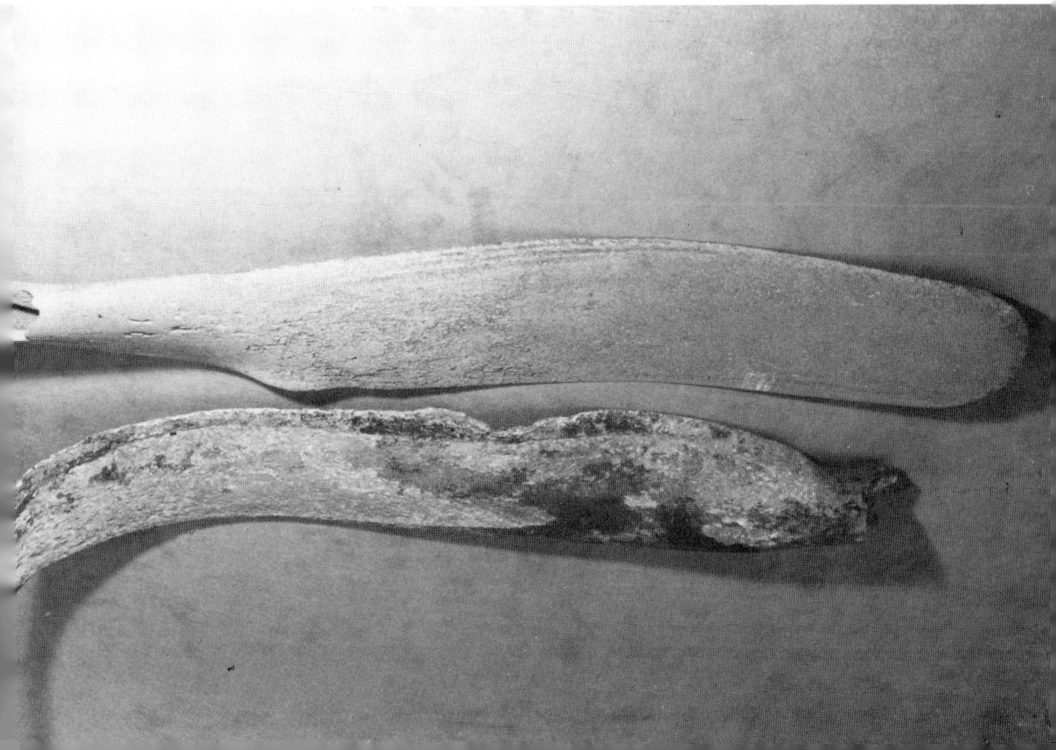

Turbo-supercharger junction box recovered from the crash site of Pasadena Nena *in Holland. This plane was piloted by John Justice.*

Kees van Hombergh.

Unidentified piece of wreckage from Pasadena Nena *crash site in Holland.* Kees van Hombergh

Flare pistol from Pasadena Nena *of the 100th Bomb Group.*

Part of the chin turret from Lt. William Whitlow's B17G of the 385th Bomb Group which crashed in dense woodland at Holten, Holland at 1525 on 10 October 194 after bombing Münster. Recovered by Mr. Martin Hols of Holten, March 1981. Kees van Hombergh

who remembered well that same day in 1943. The passage of time heals old wounds.

The WWII Luftwaffe Fighter Pilot's Association, whose Chairman is the renowned General Adolf Galland, enjoy reunions on a regular basis at various locations in West Germany. These veterans too, have their pride.

Heinz Knoke, although partially crippled, worked in local government after the war and retired in 1982. Alois Slaby is now working in radio at Wien, Austria, after surviving many more anxious and dangerous moments as a radio operator-gunner in the cumbersome and vulnerable ME 410's. In June 1944, Gerd Wiegand's FW 190 was involved in a mid-air collision with a P38 Lightning during an air battle over Compiegne, Northern France. He was severely injured, and as a result of his wounds never flew in combat again. After the war he formed his own architectural firm in Munich. One of his major contracts was the design of the Munich Olympic Village in 1972.

Corporal Rossner, Gerd Wiegand's wingman, was killed in action a few weeks after the Münster raid. Hubert Kosters is now Deputy Director of Münster's Chamber of Commerce. Walter Hoeckner, a Berliner, was killed in August 1944, when his aircraft ground-looped during takeoff from Ziegenhain Airfield, in Central Germany, for yet another combat mission. Altogether, Major Hoeckner had flown over 500 combat missions during which he had been credited with 72 confirmed aerial victories, 56 of which he had shot down while serving on the Russian Front.

Ellis Scripture, now a Vice President of a large national Corporation, returned to Horham Airfield in October 1980 where he had served as Group Navigator with the 95th. To his great surprise and delight he found that his former barracks, where his room-mate was David McKnight, was still standing virtually intact.

Jack Nosser, 390th Bomb Group, retired in March 1983 after working for a California Company since 1948, apart from service in the Korean conflict when he was attached to a B29 Superfortress Reconnaisance Wing. He wrote:

Secretly I dreaded the thought of being taken Prisoner of War again. Propeller-driven bombers, the Norden bombsight and myself faded from the Air Force at about the same time.

He had said, after his successful escape in April 1945:

We had made it and luckily we had survived. A large number of very fine men had not been so fortunate.

Among those thousands who didn't survive was Major Ralph Hansel, the 390th Group Operations Officer who had led his Group to Münster. He was killed while leading the 390th to Emden in December 1943. Lieutenant William Bedsole, a Pilot with the 384th Bomb Group, volunteered for a second tour of operations and was killed during his third raid to Schweinfurt in early 1944. Colonel Edgar Wittan, Group Commander of the 390th, was also killed in early 1944 while flying a P47 Thunderbolt. Lieutenant William Mencow, the younger brother of the 390th Group's Lead Navigator, lost his life while flying with the 401st Bomb Group, Deenethorpe, during one of the missions to the heavily defended oil industries of Merseburg in early November 1944. "Gus" Mencow, who was promoted to 13th Wing Navigator at Horham, now lives in retirement at Worcester, Massachusetts.

Frank Murphy, today a Vice-President of a large Aircraft Manufacturing Company, felt the loss of two of his fellow crewmembers over Münster very deeply:

Orlando Vincenti, our Radio Operator, and Charles Clarke, Tail Gunner, were two of the finest young men that it has ever been my pleasure to know. They were both very quietly spoken, polite, dedicated to doing their job to the utmost of their ability in the most trying and testing circumstances imaginable. They were very respectful of authority despite the relaxed familiarity with which we knew each other. After all that we'd been through together as a closely welded unit their loss, during our twenty first mission, was even more harder to accept and to bear. I know that the other surviving members of our crew felt exactly the same way.

Among those who survived the war and who returned home to a more peaceful world in 1945 were two pilots of the 13th Combat Wing who, between them, had flown more than eighty missions.

A fellow crewman wrote of one:

"There is a saying that if you really want to know a man either gamble with him or travel with him. Well, we didn't gamble, except maybe with our lives, but I did get to travel with him quite extensively and after all these years I still consider him to be the finest all-round man that I have ever met. To my mind he has grown even more impressive over the years and I am not alone in my admiration of him. Like good wine he has improved with age and I am convinced he is still growing in all his good qualities of gentleness, modesty, wit and wisdom. A truly remarkable man and worthy of emulation."

Larry Weltin wrote an obituary in tribute to Rodney Snow, an advertising executive in Atlanta, Georgia, until his untimely death after a short illness in August 1983:

Rodney Snow was a giant of a human being. He was not afraid to work in the trenches, was patient with the youngsters and always had a smile, a kind word and a pat on the back for everyone. He loved all . . . and all loved him.

Those of us who knew him will miss him greatly . . . those who didn't know him missed out. He was truly one of God's most delightful creatures.

Robert Rosenthal returned home in 1945 after flying fifty two missions with the 100th Bomb Group, the last of which was when he bailed out of his exploding B17 over Russian lines near Berlin in February 1945. Many of his friends at Thorpe Abbotts were convinced that it was the end of the legendary "Rosie". But he miraculously survived, and is now a New York lawyer with the distinction of being the most decorated Bomber Pilot in the 8th Air Force.

After almost forty years of active service, Major General Thomas Jeffrey now lives in semi-retirement in Virginia. Among his many decorations are the Silver Star, the Distinguished Flying Cross with four Oak Leaf Clusters, the Polish Cross of Valour, and the French Croix de Guerre with Palm. In the Summary of his outstanding career, the last item, under the heading of 'Unusual Experiences' is the single word: "None".

John Pettenger, a former Pilot with the 385th Bomb Group, has been back to Germany several times since the war. While there, he visited the home of one of the former Prisoner of War camp guards at Sagan, Wilhelm Stranghoner, of whom Mr. Pettenger says:

It was only through Wilhelm's efforts that many of us are alive today.

During our forced march from Sagan to Spremburg, Wilhelm, though only a Sergeant, took over the small towns, and ignoring the petitions and the protests of the town's officials, made sure that we had a place of shelter to spend the night during those freezing temperatures.

I visited Wilhelm and his family five times during the last eighteen years. They are fine people and I consider them some of my best friends. I know of no Prisoner of War that had a bad word to say about Wilhelm. Sadly, he died about five years ago.

« « « » » »

After being put in touch with Gerd Wiegand, Seymour "Buck" Feldman, who is now an Air Traffic Control Specialist with the Federal Aviation Agency in Albuquerque, New Mexico, (and a near neighbor of Colonel Walter Beckham) travelled to Munich in June 1981 to visit relatives. He also contacted Gerd Wiegand who invited him to dinner at his apartment.

After comparing wartime log-books it was confirmed that the two veteran fighter pilots had indeed met in aerial combat over Belgium on that fateful morning of 5 October 1943.

"Buck" Feldman, who later on in the war shot down 11 of the dreaded V 1 flying bombs, describes the reunion:

We talked at length of the causes, problems and the horrors of war. We had both always aimed at destroying the enemy plane, not the pilot, and we decided that he had to do what he did for his country, just as I did.

After dinner we went out onto the balcony. As we looked at maps, log-books, and photographs, wartime memories became strong. We toasted each other and absent friends with champagne. Tears were shed unashamedly, and we let bygones be bygones. We had both lost many good friends during the war.

I gave Gerd an "Ojo de Dios", a good luck charm made by the Huichol Indians of Old Mexico. In return, he gave me a book about the FW 190 in which he wrote; "First time we met as enemies. The second time, 38 years later, we meet as friends. Never again we want to meet as first time. To my new old friend, 'Buck'."

After being put in touch with Otto Schuett, who now lives with his French-born wife, Theresa, in New Jersey, U.S.A., Lt. Colonel Richard Perry (Ret'd.) and his wife Audrey, who also live in New Jersey, visited the Schuett's home in August 1983. Dick Perry summarises the extraordinary reunion:

Theresa treated us to a very fine lunch which included an excellent plum cake, the first one I've ever had.

It was almost impossible to believe that we could be sitting down and sharing food from someone who, forty years previously, had been on the receiving end of our bombing raids. Otto and I had a very interesting and revealing discussion about the political beliefs that prevailed in Nazi Germany at that time and the almost hysterical dedication the German people had to the objectives of the Third Reich. His very graphic account of the Münster raid, as he saw it from the ground, undoubtedly indicates a great deal of compassion for both sides.

Otto's home was destroyed during that raid and I assured him that I was very happy that we had missed him. He showed me a photograph of his mother and father, holding their total worldy possessions, standing in front of the rubble of their house the day after that raid. (See page 182.) It was a very emotional scene, a part of the war that I was very fortunate to have missed.

It was very strange that we should meet each other after all this time, discussing that day which we both remember so vividly; Otto because of the loss of his home and me because of the tremendous struggle we had to keep the *Eightball* in the air after an Me 110 had almost sheared one of our wings off.

It was a thoroughly enjoyable meeting and I am sure that Otto and I will be getting together again to share many more of our experiences.

« « « » » »

Münster today is a city rebuilt in a manner which presents to its visitors the appearance of continuity since the fourteenth century when some portions of its churches were originally constructed. But so much of it had laid in ruins at the end of World War II — much of that destruction coming in the 10 October 1943 raid.

The city fathers of Münster, while other cities were being rebuilt in modern concrete, glass and steel, decided to rebuild Münster as accurately as possible in the original image. Work was done from centuries-old plans and drawings, if they could be found. Photographs were used where plans did not exist. Stone gargoyles were recarved, arches re-constructed, statuary re-cut, and stained glass windows re-shaped to present the same pre-war face.

The citizens of Münster have succeeded in finding a synthesis that makes Münster so snug, so social and at the same time so practical that it can fulfill the needs of a modern community in every respect.

The citizens of Münster thought it their historical task and obligation towards the present and future to enliven the specific atmosphere of the old Münster with a fine feeling for its traditions and modern needs. The old city gained the new face which it presents today.

The rebuilt city stands now as a monument to the devastation of war and the spirit needed to recover from war.

Epilogue 2

BY a remarkable coincidence, all three Bombardment Groups of the 13th Combat Bomb Wing had their memorials in England dedicated within five months of each other during 1981. Their long-abandonded airfields now bear little resemblance to what once had been a segment spear-heading the theory of daylight strategic bombardment. The 13th Wing had dropped bomb loads totalling 58,000 tons on their assigned targets in Occupied Europe, and had sustained losses of 478 Flying Fortresses, each with a ten-man crew, which were missing in action during that bitterly-fought and bloody campaign in the war torn skies over Europe. Between them, the three Groups earned a total of seven Distinguished Unit citations, more than any other Wing in the United States 8th Air Force. If all these missing aircraft could be parked in a straight line, wing-tip to wing-tip, they would extend for almost 10 miles. Altogether, 9,949 American bombers went down over German-held territory.

The unenviable distinction of the highest losses suffered by a single 8th Air Force Bomb Group belongs to the 91st which had been operating from Bassingbourne, Cambridgeshire, since September 1942. During their 340 missions, the Group had 197 Fortresses shot down. Leading the 3rd Air Division loss list was the 96th Bomb Group, Snetterton Heath, Norfolk, which had 189 B17's missing in action. Their former bomber base is now used as a motor racing circuit, echoing to the roaring engines of a very different kind.

Parts of the crumbling and weed-dotted runways and perimeter tracks are almost all that now remain to be seen by the occasional visitor to any of the three former airfields at Framlingham, Thorpe Abbotts and Horham. Several of the original buildings have, however, managed to survive the ravages of time, the silent, stealthy incursions of nature, and the noisy destruction of the demolition men.

At Framlingham, almost the whole Community Site, now used to store agricultural machinery, is still intact including the Officer's Club, Combat Mess Halls, the Base Chapel and cinema. At Thorpe Abbotts, among the several wartime structures to survive, the Group Operations Building still stands amidst tall, whispering trees. At both Framlingham and Thorpe Abbotts, the Control Towers — the very nerve centres of any operational airfield — have been renovated into Memorial Air Museums of both Groups. At Horham, the "Red Feather Club" for Enlisted Men, its colourful wall murals still miraculously in excellent condition, remains virtually intact, together with the Combat Mess Halls which now form part of a turkey breeding farm. Some distance from Horham Airfield the Base Hospital, now a grain drying store, is virtually the same as when the last ambulance drove out of its entrance in 1945. Its interior doors still bear the white stencilled names of various staff departments.

Most of the wide acres that once accommodated these three airfields have long since returned to agriculture. With each passing year a little more is regained for agricultural purposes, and almost complete obliteration is their certain fate. But an extraordinary fascination and an aura of mystique and ineffable sadness still lingers over these now silent bomber bases. A sense of nostalgia still remains among the local inhabitants who witnessed the great aerial armadas forming up over East Anglia through the early morning mists and the pale dawns four decades earlier.

Among the many returning veterans from each Group was Al Brown of the 95th. He had been the Lead Pilot of the aptly named *I'll Be Around* when the 95th, together with the 100th Bomb Group, failed to receive a recall signal in worsening weather conditions, and struck through to Berlin for the first daylight raid on the German capital on 4 March 1944.

John Miller, who as a 17-year-old Waist Gunner had completed his tour of 35 missions, including six traumatic raids to Berlin, with the 100th Bomb Group. In July 1944 he had returned to the United States in time to celebrate his 18th birthday.

It had also been a long time since Paul Vance had seen his former base at Framlingham. The veteran Pilot, now a retired schoolteacher from Chandler, Arizona, and walking with a pronounced limp as a result of his wartime injuries, was happily reunited with some of his former comrades from the 570th Squadron.

At Parham Airfield on Wednesday, 13 May, the dedication proceedings were opened by Lt. Colonel Roger "Hap" Howell, a former Pilot and Assistant Group Operations Officer at Framlingham, who introduced the principal speaker:

It gives me great pleasure to introduce you to a gentleman who started out as a Co-Pilot in the 570th Squadron here at Framlingham in July 1943, stayed for the duration of the war and was ultimately promoted to Squadron Operations Officer. He flew a total of 43 combat missions and earned numerous awards and decorations during that time . . . Lt. Colonel Richard Perry.

"Dick" Perry took the microphone:

Ladies and gentlemen, distinguished guests. I'm very honoured to be able to participate in this historic dedication. First of all, I would like to express our extreme gratitude and pleasure for the arrangements made by our English friends, especially those who are associated with the 390th Bomb Group Memorial Air Museum. I should also mention that all of this could not have been possible without the generosity and help of Mr. Percy Kindred. We sincerely thank you, Mr. Kindred.

We former members of the 390th Bomb Group, our relatives and guests, really do appreciate the warmth of welcome that we have all received since our arrival in England . . . we're very happy to be here. We are also particularly pleased that you people from Parham, Framlingham, Woodbridge, Ipswich and other locations are joining us today. I would be negligent if I didn't mention the fact that we also have representatives here from the existing 390th Strategic Missile Wing located near Tuscon, Arizona. This Group is doing a very commendable job, and we're very proud of them.

I could spend a great deal of time extolling the history of our two countries. I could talk about the English customs and culture which have helped to guide us as a comparatively new nation in our growth. However, I'm going to leave that to the historians. I could also spend a great deal of time talking about our common enemies, our mutual friends, and some of the similarities in our mutual aims and hopes for world peace. Again, I'm going to leave that to the statesmen and the politicians.

Prior to getting around to the job which I have to do in unveiling the plaque to honour those men who gave their lives for freedom, I would like to share a few things with you as we return to this wonderful country. As I look around this beautiful English countryside my mind drifts back about 40 years, and could I just ask you all to take a minute and listen intently . . . What did you hear? You know, it was rather quiet . . .

I can remember, and I think that all of us from the 390th can recall, when there were very few times when we heard this silence. There was always that constant drone of airplane engines . . . they were either taking off, landing, forming up in formation over this airfield, or going to and from targets on the Continent. We can also remember the almost ceaseless night raids of the RAF attacking those same targets. And we can also recall when we had German aircraft over head. We all hope and pray that future generations will not have to endure and witness those same sights and sounds as we did.

I was rather a young man, like many of the people in the 390th, who grew up very rapidly here at Parham, Suffolk, England. We former 390th Bomb Group members feel very fortunate to have served in this most impressive and what we feel was the best bomber unit in the 8th Air Force, during World War Two. After a very intensive training and organisational period in the United States during the first half of 1943, the 390th Bombardment Group, under the very able command of Colonel Edgar Wittan, arrived at this base in July 1943. We were assigned almost immediately to carry our share on such missions as Regensburg, Bremen, Münster, Schweinfurt, Hannover, Kassel and Berlin. Then there were those shuttle missions to North Africa and Russia.

The record of the 390th is very impressive. We flew 301 combat missions, and from aerial photographs our bombs, totalling about 19,000 tons, did tremendous damage to the targets to which we were assigned. The Group was credited with 377 German aircraft destroyed. All this was not achieved without heavy cost to ourselves . . . 144 of our aircraft were missing in action . . . 1,440 of our men were either killed in action or became prisoners of war. We will never forget these sacrifices and we are very happy to have with us here today many of those who were captured.

The 390th was honoured by two Distinguished Unit Citations, and our men were awarded many individual medals and numerous awards from the Allied countries. The aircraft we flew, the B17 Flying Fortress, was the Rolls Royce, or Cadillac, aircraft of its time and those of us who flew it knew of its ruggedness and its capabilities to perform the daylight strategic bombing role. The success of the 390th was due primarily to a great team, moulded together by superb leadership. This team consisted of ground and air personnel, both enlisted and officers, all with one common objective in mind — the success of the Allied Nations.

We cannot think of a more appropriate location for a memorial to the 390th Bomb Group than on English soil, in a country dedicated with America to the ideals of democracy and the freedom of mankind. This memorial illustrates the close relationship of our two countries in the past, present and in the future. It is very difficult to find appropriate words to adequately acknowledge the hard and dedicated work which went into the restoration of this control tower that is now the 390th Bombardment Group Memorial Air Museum.

Colonel Joseph Moller, one of our former Commanding Officers, who is also present today, handed me a tribute which I've framed to place in the museum and I consider it to be most appropriate. It reads: "The reconstruction of our control tower on the field from which we flew so many missions is a beautiful reminder and a lasting memorial to all the men of the 390th. It is without doubt the most sincere, the most gracious, and the most thoughtful living Unit Citation our English friends could possibly bestow on us. The time, the effort and the loving dedication of those who conceived and carried through this project to completion makes us of the 390th sincerely grateful and humbly thankful to each and every one of you, our friends. We are surely proud of this 'living memorial'."

The time has now come for me to unveil the memorial plaque which is in honour of those men who gave their lives during this period of history. May their sacrifices not be in vain . . .

Lt. Colonel Perry then unveiled the plaque on the West wall of the museum. It was then blessed by the Rector of Framlingham, the Rev. David Pitcher. This was followed by short speeches by Mr. Percy Kindred, Mr. John Gray, Major General Robert Bazeley, Commander of the present American Air Force in Britain, members of the museum's committee, and finally a former Commanding Officer of the 390th, Colonel Joseph Moller, who began his speech with a 'one liner': "At this sort of reunion people look at each other and ask, 'I don't look sixty, do I?' and the answer comes back, 'No, but you did when you were . . .!!" He went on to say:

This control tower was the focal point when we were here. It was far easier to fly a mission than it was to come out here and sweat the boys back in. This was the sweat box for every Group Commander, Squadron Commander and even Divisional Commander. Pounds, gallons, tons of sweat are in this building and on its roof . . . Everything has been said about it.

I would like to simply say we owe a great debt of gratitude to our English friends for preserving our heritage of the past. We who flew from this field and served here in days gone by sincerely thank you.

Colonel Moller also gave a solemn reminder that the way to peace was to maintain such powerful military strength that no potential aggressor dare attack us.

As if to emphasise his point, various aircraft of the current Allied Air Force's swept low over the airfield. A memorable closing highlight was provided by the B17 *Sally B*, the only airworthy Flying Fortress remaining in Britain today, which made several low passes over the control tower.

During Percy Kindred's speech of welcome, he said:

It was as Colonel Perry said, extremely noisy, especially during the early mornings prior to a mission, but during the day we got a little respite. But it was always a very welcome sight and sound when the Group returned in the late afternoon or early evening, and we used to wonder as we watched you peeling off the land "How many are missing today?" A little later the empty hardstands told their own sad story.

Parham Parish Council Chairman, John Gray, added:

When you were here I was only a schoolboy, and my memories go back to the more pleasant things . . . the parties we were invited to . . . the film shows in the Officers Club . . . and the memorable concert and dance in that hangar over there when Glenn Miller and his orchestra visited Parham in 1944.

After the speeches, and the viewing of the many exhibits and relics of the air war, recovered from various crash sites throughout East Anglia over the post-war years, the veterans were transported in authentic and patiently restored jeeps, trucks and ambulances of an era long past, to various locations of their former base.

« « « » » »

At Thorpe Abbotts, Saturday, 25 May, the dedication of the 100th Bomb Group Memorial Air Museum took place. Major Horace Varian, the Group's former Ground Executive Officer, addressed the gathering at the renovated control tower, following opening prayers by the Rector of Thorpe Abbotts, the Reverend Werril. He said:

Ladies and gentlemen, I bring you greetings today from the 100th Bomb Group Association in the United States, and particularly to the 100th Bomb Group Association here in the United Kingdom with which many of you are connected.

I, and many others from the United States were here at this base for 2-1/2 years during World War Two, and I submit to you that this is a considerable part of ones adult lifetime. Consequently, the experiences over the past three days have been very meaningful and very moving to those of us who spent such a portion of our lives in this place.

As I think about all of this today, it seems to me that that which endures are human relationships. The instruments of war, the machinery which was necessary to prosecute that war — if any war can be just — a truly just war — these implements and machines of war are tremendously important, but they are passing — they are transitory. The things that endure and that matter, I am convinced, are the human relationships.

To represent the Group here today I am joined by six other people who are also directly connected with the 100th Group in the United States, Bob and Florence Spangler, John and Rose Miller, and Stan and Doreen Gorski. We are all very happy to be here together to represent the Group and what remains of it in the United States.

I think today, as we dedicate this magnificently restored Control Tower and Memorial to the 100th Bombardment Group, we think about three groups of people. Those of us who served here and returned home to the United States, to honour those known to so many of us who gave their lives flying from this base, and finally those who have done such a magnificent job in the restoration of this nerve centre of the 100th Group.

As we dedicate this plaque and this building today we remember, before God, and before one another all of these people who have had a part in what we do here today . . . I unveil this plaque to the Glory of God and the memory of all those who served in the 100th Bomb Group for the cause of freedom from this airfield.

As Major Varian smoothly pulled the curtains aside to reveal a two-foot square bronze plaque set in an exterior wall of the control tower, spontaneous applause came from the many onlookers.

The plaque and the museum were then blessed by Colonel Wingart, the Base Chaplain at U.S.A.F. Lakenheath, Suffolk. Then a Museum Committee member expressed gratitude to the landowners for their help and encouragement throughout the restoration project. He was followed by Colonel Mallory, Commander at the American Air Force transport base at Mildenhall, Suffolk:

I am personally delighted to be here, today. It's almost like a page from the first chapter of "Twelve o'clock High" . . . I think thanks should be expressed to those of you here, and any who are missing, for undertaking this magnificent project. There is nothing that we can say or do to add distinction to what was done here forty years ago . . . certainly the people who worked here and flew from this field gathered distinction, honour and glory to themselves for all time. What you have done here is an example of the partnership, a partnership that goes back many years which held firm in World War Two, is still going strong and holds firm today between the United States and Great Britain.

Thank you again for inviting me, and I thank you for having the foresight and displaying the tremendous energy to undertake this project.

A reception was held later in the afternoon at a packed Thorpe Abbotts village hall. Following a comprehensive slide show of the 100th Bomb Group's wartime activities presented by a Museum Committee member, Major Varian made an announcement:

We have with us today two guests from Germany, Herr Hubert Kosters, a former member of the Luftwaffe, and his charming daughter. Mr. Kosters has provided much valuable research information on one of the 100th's missions to Munster. In commemoration of what we have done today, we have a letter addressed to the 100th B.G. Association U.K. which I would like to read to you.

"Dear Ladies and Gentlemen,

On the occasion of the dedication of the Air Museum and Memorial to all the fallen airmen, both Allied and German, of the Second World War here at the former control tower of the airbase in England, I send you my warmest and sincere greetings.

All Nations are scarred from the terrible aftermath of the Second World War. We cannot overcome the past by forgetting the discord and sorrow which war has brought, but by willingness to reconciliate we can ensure peace for the present.

So it pleases me, on this day of the dedication, to represent the bond of friendship between our peoples.

May the merciful God hold His hand over us so that we are guided in His way and seek for peace which He has prepared for us.

With my sincerest blessing,

Yours,

Dr. Reinhard Lettman, Bishop of Münster"

After the applause had subsided, Major Varian stated that the Bishop's letter would be framed and placed in the museum. Proceedings were gradually brought to a close and preliminary plans were already being formulated to hold the 100th Bomb Group's annual reunion at Thorpe Abbotts to coincide with the official opening of the Memorial Air Museum in 1983.

« « « » »»

Following a memorial service at St. Mary's Church, Horham on Saturday, 19 September 1981, the impressive memorial to the airmen of the 95th Bombardment Group was unveiled by the United States Vice-Consul from the American

Embassy in London, Mr. Frederick Vogel. The unveiling followed a speech delivered by Colonel Sam Morgan, the Base Commander at U.S.A.F. Bentwaters, Suffolk, during which the Colonel said:

Today we, the Americans and the British, share almost everything we have. The very roots of our nation, the United States, came from Britain. Our values are the same, our language is the same, and I think its marvelous that the Friends of the 95th were able to arrange this ceremony and memorial for the men who were over here with you during the war.

It is a chance to think and talk about what used to be, and it's a chance for me to give thanks for what we have today. This outstanding Air Force, of which I am a part, started long before I came along. Veterans of the 95th who are present today, like "Lefty" Nairn, Al Brown, Col. Arthur Frankel and Dave McKnight, helped put it all together. You have given a great deal to me personally, and I don't need to speak from a prepared text at a ceremony like this. There is so much to it that the challenge is to sort out what should and should not be said.

Years ago you heard the song by Simon and Garfunkle "Where have you gone Joe DiMaggio? We turn our shining eyes to you . . ." It was a plea for the existence of heroes such as we used to have, the men and women who rose to the challenge of the Second World War and fought that great battle. I know very well, I believe, the experiences and thoughts which you had then. When we arrived at Horham today my wife, children and I drove out to your former airfield and drove down the runway. We could see then the ghost of a B17 going off into the distance, joining the orbit where you got the great formations together.

I have been in combat, I have turned with the MIG 21's and seen the missiles as they streaked through the air, and the description of flak being thick enough to walk on is not a misnomer . . . it really does look just like that. I've also known the trauma of seeing a comrade engulfed in a ball of fire and go down, to be with us no longer . . . Notwithstanding all of that, war is a great experience . . . for those who don't get shot down . . . and those are who we have with us here today. But we are also taking a moment to reflect on both those who are here and those who are not, and think about the heroism of the people of the 95th and the heroism of the people of Britain who shared that war . . .

The most important thing to a person is their reputation, followed by a sense of values. In other words, when he is presented with a challenge, how does he rise to that challenge? How does he react? Does he have the courage and stamina to look out ahead of him and see the flak and the fighters and still hold the course even though all around him may be coming apart? Even in the face of odds that look like he will never be able to make it through? It goes back to the Ground Crews who shared the trauma when their planes failed to return and their crews were no longer among them.

In the years afterwards you can look back and think upon those experiences and those challenges which confronted you at that time. All of you here, all the men and women of the 95th . . . the people of Horham . . . the Friends of the 95th . . . you can look straight into any man's eye and know that your values were straight and true and when presented with the problems of the past you met them head on and surmounted them admirably.

Today, you have given me a tremendous opportunity of just by being here for the unveiling of this monument I can tell the next generation that I was somewhat a small part of the tremendous organisation of the 95th Bombardment Group.

Thank you very much, and the least that I can say to you of the 95th is that I, and the current Air Force, salute you and all that you stood for.

Several 95th veterans returned Colonel Morgan's salute amidst applause from the circle of many listeners.

Mr. Vogel then made a short speech during which he summarised the achievements of the 95th . . . and the cost:

It is equally an honour for me to have this opportunity to meet with you all and to participate in this ceremony. It is also most appropriate that an Embassy representative be here. I understand that one of the pilots and comrades was the son of the then United States Ambassador to the Court of St. James and while flying with your Wing, was shot down over Germany and captured. We dedicate a memorial here today so that those events of yesterday will not be forgotten and that tomorrow will not demand the same of you and yours again.

The 95th Bombardment Group flew 320 missions and lost 157 aircraft in battle . . . 157 aircraft . . . 1,570 men . . . comrades . . . fathers . . . husbands . . ., brothers and sons of our people. You have returned here today to commemorate heroism, but more so to honour the sacrifices of those times when you gave up your boyhood, your youth, your very lives to achieve a great and lasting victory. The 95th Bombardment Group won three Distinguished Unit Citations for your courage and daring. It is a tribute to you, and to our Allies and friends as well, that such valour remains strong in memory still.

Let those who would challenge us today note well, and take heed, that the sons of Britannia and Columbia still regard such valour as a highest virtue. We dedicate this memorial to you veterans of the 95th Bombardment Group who have returned. Let us also honour those who could not . . . comrades fallen . . . friends lost . . . they bore the banner . . . they paid the price of victory . . .

Mr. Vogel then unveiled the marble memorial, carved in the shape of a B17's tail surmounting a marble plinth on which was laid out the pattern of Horham's wartime runways. On one side of the B17's tail was a bronze plaque of remembrance, and on the other was the distinctive "Square B", the Group marking of the 95th.

Colonel Arthur Frankel, Secretary of the 95th Bomb Group Association in the United States, then responded with a short address:

Without the seeds that were sown several years ago by our English friends, this truly beautiful memorial to our men would not be here today, because it was the Friends of the 95th, the English, who really gave it the impetus for which we all are so deeply grateful.

Both our countries are pacifists, we don't believe in war. In 1938, Prime Minister Chamberlain stepped from an airplane on his return from Germany, waved a piece of paper in the air and declared, "We shall have peace in our time . . ." Well, we all know history . . .

Yes, we are pacifists, but not the type of pacifist that we find in our world today who actively encourage the dissolution of our strength and so invite our destruction. We are standing here today, the lucky ones, because of that strength.

Again, our very grateful thanks to you all.

The memorial was then blessed by Colonel Caspers the Base Chaplain from the nearby American airfield at Bentwaters.

That Saturday evening, the veterans of the 95th and their wives again joined local people in a convivial dinner/dance at nearby Stradbroke High School. Before the 16-piece band began playing the haunting and nostalgic music of the legendary Glenn Miller, the after-dinner speech was made by Roger Freeman. He said:

I have many personal recollections of Horham. In 1942 I was a 13-year-old schoolboy, and I occasionally stayed with my cousin at Dennington, which is a village about five miles south of here. We young boys were both "aeroplane mad." On this occasion my cousin said, "Let's cycle up to a place called Horham. They're building an aerodome there." So we cycled from Dennington, through Worlingworth to Horham. I remember how impressed I was by the wide, open landscape on our arrival. This was long before prairie farmers and the huge gaps in the countryside caused by the construction of this airfield was really something to behold. It seemed to stretch to the far horizon.

Well, that was not the last association with Horham, because as luck would have it for us both, my Uncle, who had been in the First World War and was a Squadron Leader in the Royal Air Force during the Second War, was given command of Horham Airfield before the construction had been completed. He was, in fact, the first Commanding Officer of Horham

Airfield and he moved here in late 1942. His son and his nephew, which was me, made the most of that. In fact, it was at Horham in December 1942, that I had my first look inside an American bomber.

My Uncle eventually turned the airfield over to the American authorities and moved on to other jobs. After the war I asked him what he remembered most of his stay at Horham when the Americans were there. He answered immediately, saying that his most difficult task was trying to get the Americans to pronounce "Horham" correctly, instead of them consistently saying, "Whore-Ham". . .!

Anyway, my cousin and I continued to cycle over to Horham, peering over the hedge and watching the big bombers . . . and they were Flying Fortresses. Now, in those days we didn't know that the unit occupying the airfield was called the 95th Bomb Group, because there was such a thing as security. We therefore labeled the bombers that flew from Horham as the "B in the Square" because the B in the square was what they all carried on their tails. In fact, the Big B turned out to be a very appropriate marking because "Big B" was the nickname for the enemy capital, Berlin, and it was the 95th that on 4 March 1944, became the first of forty-odd American Bombardment Groups to strike the capital city of Germany.

In fact the 95th, probably unbeknown to the English people around the base, had a very tough time of it during the early days. There was a time when it was suffering a 35% survival rate for its crewmen. Though I say "suffering a survival rate" because if you saw your buddies go down you were suffering too. And the fact was that there was only one in three of the original crews who survived. It was very tough indeed and a very bloody war which they fought.

The 95th, as you have already heard today, was awarded three Presidential Unit Citations — they didn't give these away — they were really hard won. As you also heard, the 95th was the only Group in the American Air Forces in Europe to come away from that war with three such Citations. That gives a fair indication of the sort of battles which it fought. Another indication is that the gunner with the most claims of enemy aircraft shot down while flying in bombers was also based here at Horham. Yes, the 95th had a very hard war . . . very hard indeed. . .

It's all a long time ago now, of course, but when the 95th first arrived at Horham in June 1943, there's no doubt that the local people at least, or at best, viewed them with a certain amount of suspicion . . . these strange, brash young men from across the sea from a place called America with which the locals only associated with the film stars of Hollywood.

There is the story, probably not true at all but it was told in those days, about the farmer who lived near Horham. The base was built around his farm. After a few months following the American's arrival, he went to the local cattle market and there he met another farmer. The other farmer greeted him with, "Well, hello Bill. How are you getting along with them there Yankees?"

Thereupon Bill exploded, "Gettin' along with 'em? Gettin' along with the blighters? I'll tell you how I'm gettin' along!! Why, since they've been here my cows have gone off the milk . . . my chickens have gone off the lay . . . my gatepost has been knocked down . . . my dog has been run over . . . my apples have been stolen . . . my daughter's pregnant . . . my wife's run off with one of 'em . . . and I can't drown my sorrows because the blighters have drunk all the pubs dry . . .!"

Well, it wasn't long before the people of Horham, Denham, Stradbroke and the surrounding district began to realise what was going on. They would watch the bombers go out and they saw them come back, sometimes full of holes, and they also saw some of the terrible crashes which occurred. They got to know the G.I.s in their smart uniforms who seemed to be everywhere in the ubiquitous jeeps, and soon they developed quite a liking for these strange young men from across the water. They soon began to refer to them as "Our boys." It was "Our boys" that went out today . . . It was "Our boys" who had got badly shot up.

By the time they went home in 1945, perhaps the Americans did not realise this, but there was a certain fondness towards them. And as for the Americans? Well, they went home, those that were lucky enough to go home, and what did they do? They married, they had children and they got on with life. They didn't want to remember the war in which they had escaped with their lives. But now, if I may say it, they're sliding past middle age, they are retiring and it's time to think. They think about what must have been the most traumatic moments and days of their lives. They think about the Second World War. And what, specifically, do they think about?

You can't go back to a battlefield in the sky. The 95th struck at targets as far afield as Norway, Occupied Poland, down to Africa, and you can't go back to those battlefields way up in the clouds . . .

So you come back to the only place you can return to . . . the old airfield at Horham . . . Horham in Suffolk County, England. That's the focal point of your interest. To all those men, however short a time they spent here, this little spot in England will always mean something to them. And for the locals? They have realised now that when this airfield was built in their village, it was the most momentous thing that ever happened to this ancient village and probably will ever happen to it. They realise that it is a part of their history just as it is part of the history of the men who flew from Horham Airfield years and years ago.

It is a long time since the inhabitants of Horham have been woken up in the early morning by the dull roar of Flying Fortresses grinding off the end of the runway with their loads of bombs to distant targets . . . a long time since their contrails criss-crossed the sky . . . a long time since Adolph Hitler was a household name. But, as you have seen, veterans of the 95th and your ladies who have returned with you, the sort of welcome extended to you, and you suddenly realise, don't you, that those funny old English have a big soft spot for "Our boys". . .

I've said it before, and I'll say it again. We see lots of Americans over here at American N.A.T.O. air bases. Americans? They are quite nice, friendly people. But anyone who served with the 8th Air Force is something really special . . . Welcome back!

Among the returning 95th Bomb Group veterans was William Charles, a 336th Squadron Navigator, who had flown over 50 missions with the Group. The following day he went for an early morning walk in the chill September mists. He recollects:

I walked alone along the same paths, now overgrown, from my former barracks site in the 336th Squadron area to the combat mess hall. The 38 intervening years suddenly evaporated in the mists of time, and it was as if I was doing it all over again as I trudged towards a breakfast which existed only in my memory.

From there I walked to the Group Operations building, dilapidated but still standing, where we had received our specialised briefings before each mission, wondering if I'd return, and how many of the boys I would ever see again.

Eventually, I reached our Squadron's flight line. I am not a sentimental man, but it was so uncanny how the years seemingly rolled back, just as in the opening scenes of "Twelve o'clock High" when the Ground Executive Officer cycled back to his former bomber base after the war and he stood alone at the end of the runway seeing and hearing the roaring engines of a ghostly B17.

I went to the site of the Officer's Club, now demolished, and the first thing that crossed my mind was how we used to stand around a tinkling piano being expertly played by Dr. Jack McKittrick, our Squadron Flight Surgeon. I recalled the beautiful tenor voice of Lt. Stephenson, a Bombardier on Lt. Bullard's crew, from our barracks.

I also recalled, most vividly, the morning Lt. Bullard's Navigator received a 'Dear John' letter from his wife. He also had a young daughter whom he had never seen. Naturally, we'd joined him in trying to drown his sorrows at the club that night, and we had ended up singing a storm. The very next day John Bullard's crew was shot down . . .

Later that morning, I went to the Red Feather Club with my good friends Dave McKnight, Al Brown and John Miller, all of whom I had known well and with whom I'd flown many, many missions. We were joined by English Friends of the 95th. While there, we drank a toast to our fallen comrades and absent friends, probably the first drinks to be consumed there for almost 40 years. The club, with its colourful wall murals, literally breathes a special atmosphere.

Dave McKnight is, of course, a special friend because he set such as inspiring example for we replacement crews to emulate during those dangerous and eventful years. I have always felt that I was living on borrowed time when I look back, and I wonder how I ever survived all that I did. I am convinced that my mother's prayers had a lot to do with God sparing my life, although I sometimes think that I haven't done much with the life which He gave me, I'm still very thankful.

That Sunday afternoon we went out to the American Military Cemetery at Madingley, near Cambridge, surely the most beautiful and impressive of all American Cemeteries, and surely our comrades of days gone by could not have been laid to rest in greener pastures than these.

It was not until I saw all the names of John Bullard's crew among the 4,000 or so names which are carved on "The Wall of the Missing" that I finally learned their fate. I had never heard whether or not they had survived but the hope had always existed. It was a highly emotional moment for me personally, and it was as if I had secretly known all these years but couldn't accept the fact.

A former Commanding Officer of the 390th Bombardment Group, Colonel Joseph Moller recalls:

I can remember attending so many of the shortened funeral services for the boys during the war, including the service for Edgar Wittan, the 390th's first Commander.

Of course, many of the sons were later taken home and buried in their family plots. However, I was continually surprised by the number of letters I subsequently received from the families of the boys buried at Cambridge asking my opinion as to whether the boys should be brought home or remain at Cambridge.

I tried to avoid making any decision for the families, but I always pointed out to them that their boys were buried where many of their comrades and close friends were. In addition to the graves are the names on "The Wall of the Missing", and the 390th had a great number of them.

In late November 1981, Ellis Scripture the 95th Bomb Group Lead Navigator on the Münster raid, wrote:

We are getting ready to celebrate Thanksgiving in the United States. This is our traditional family reunion each year when we pause to thank God for all our many blessings. Too often we forget!!

I shall always be very grateful that I was allowed to continue my life and to enjoy the laughter of children and grand-children. We hope that they will be spared the heartbreak of war and its terrible destruction.

The great tragedy was that the peoples of the whole world were forced to barbaric acts against each other because of the political ambitions of a few hated men. The world's history has always been thus . . . and unfortunately, the trend continues today in so many areas. All of us grieve for those who continue to be exploited in the name of political gain. Our weapons are now so deadly and uncontrollable that the world would indeed be devastated if man allows his senses to get out of control. We must do all possible to prevent another outbreak of man's hatred.

Man was made to create, not destroy.

The Control Tower at Horham airfield was demolished in the early 1950's following the crash nearby of a Royal Air Force jet training aircraft. But several years ago I climbed the iron staircases of those at Thorpe Abbotts and Framlingham, also those of the now silent Control Tower at Elsham Wolds, in Lincolnshire. They are lonely, wind-swept sentinels, box-like relics from a momentous era that is now but a faint murmur on the distant horizon of memory, and, if there are ghosts, they are here.

You were right, Mr. Deighton . . . be careful . . .

Appendix

WAR DEPARTMENT
WASHINGTON 25 D.C.
4 OCTOBER 1944

As authorized by Executive Order No. 9396, superceding Executive No 9075, citation of the following Unit in General Orders, No. 138, Headquarters 3rd Bombardment Division, 23rd May 1944, as approved by the Commanding General, United States Army Forces in the European Theater of Operations, is confirmed under the provisions of Section IV, Circular No. 333, War Department, 1943, in the name of the President of the United States as public evidence of deserved honor and distinction.

The Citation reads as follows:

The 95th bombardment Group (H) is cited for outstanding performance of duty in action against the enemy in connection with the bombing of an important target at Munster, Germany, on 10th October 1943. The 95th Bombardment Group (H) led the 3rd Bombardment Division and the 13th Combat Bomb Wing (H) in the air, on this highly successful five hour operation which involved a flight of 520 miles at an altitude of 24,000 feet. During the period of no friendly fighter support, the Group was subjected to the violent and concentrated attacks of approximately 250 enemy fighters, chiefly FW 190's, JU 88's Me 110's and 410's. Choosing the 13th Combat Bomb Wing (H) as a focal point, the waves of attackers, after shooting down all but one of the aircraft in the Low Group and eight of the aircraft in the High Group, concentrated on the 95th Bombardment Group (H). Twin-engined enemy fighters, firing 20-mm and 37-mm cannon and rocket projectiles, attacked in Staffels of 12 to 15 aircraft each. Losing five aircraft to this concerted opposition, the Unit maintained a cohesive formation throughout the attacks. The 95th Bombardment Group (H) is officially credited with the destruction of 41 enemy fighters, 5 others probably destroyed, and 19 damaged. Beginning at Dorsten and continuing through the target area, the Group also encountered extremely intense and damaging anti-aircraft fire. Ten of the remaining aircraft in the Unit were damaged. Rallying the remaining aircraft of the Lead Combat Wing, the 95th Bombardment Group (H) led a 6-minute bombing run in a highly effective formation, dropping its bombs directly on the main point of impact. Flying directly through the anti-aircraft barrage, which grew increasingly heavy as the bomb release point was reached, the Unit took more than the usual amount of time on the turns, so that the following Groups which were also undergoing vicious fighter attacks, could rejoin the formation and receive the benefit of defensive firepower. The bombing results were superior to those of any other Bombardment Group participating in the operation. Of the 102,000 pounds of bombs released by this Unit, 36 percent fell within 1,000 feet, and 64 percent hit within 2,000 feet of the assigned aiming point. The bombing pattern was excellent. Testimony to the highly successful bombing of the target was the award of the British Distinguished Flying Cross to the Lead Bombardier for his work on the mission. After the bombing, the Group led the Division's forces to the Rally Point where friendly fighter support was met. As a result of the savage enemy opposition, 51 of the Unit's personnel are missing in action, and 4 were wounded.

Distinguishing itself by courageous resolution in overcoming vicious enemy fighter attacks and heavy anti-aircraft artillery fire, the 95th Bombardment Group (H) displayed extraordinary valor, audacity, and courage under fire. By heroic strength of purpose, it led the way over the target to carry out its mission successfully. This Unit's personnel performed its task with coolness, skill, and self-sacrifice in the face of unusually determined and damaging enemy fire. The extraordinary devotion to duty and disregard for personal safety displayed, above and beyond that of all the other Units participating in the same operation, resulted in a vital blow at the German war effort. The outstanding valor and bold, vigorous heroism displayed on this occasion presented an inspiring example for other Units of the Army Air Forces.

BY ORDER OF THE SECRETARY OF STATE FOR WAR:

G. C. MARSHALL,
Chief of Staff

Distinguished Unit Citations were awarded to the 381st Bombardment Group (H), Ridgewell, Essex, following the Bremen mission 8th October 1943, the 351st Bombardment Group (H), Polebrook, Northamptonshire, for the accuracy of their bombing at Anklam (aircraft factories) on 9th October, 1943, and to the 390th Bombardment Group (H), Framlingham, Suffolk, following the Schweinfurt raid 14th October 1943.

From: 3rd Bombardment Division Headquarters.
T0: Commanding General, U.S. 8th A.A.F. Headquarters.
Subject: Remarks to conclude summary of the mission to Münster 10/10/1943.

(1) On this mission the heaviest losses to date were sustained by the 3rd Division, the result almost entirely of enemy fighter opposition. No new weapons were used by the enemy, but an analysis of their tactics indicate that greater effort was concentrated on the lead combat wing, and more especially on the Low Group of that Wing. This completely disrupted one Group of the bomber force. It is not likely, however, that the plan reduced the losses of the enemy to an appreciable extent.

(2) Despite the heavy opposition, the remainder of the Groups of the formation bombed with great effectiveness, completely obliterating the assigned M.P.I. Such results under adverse conditions prove that hard training and good air discipline pay dividends.

(3) Another change in enemy tactics is that their fighters are now waiting to strike until the escort of the bombers has turned back. This will require a more comprehensive system of diversion in the future.

(4) Flak was again the cause of a few losses, the aircraft being hit and forced out of formation where enemy fighters could easily concentrate on them. Crews are reporting certain areas to be defended by especially accurate anti-aircraft gunners. A record of these districts is being kept and an effort will be made to avoid these areas in the future or to warn formation leaders of their location prior to each mission.

—Brigadier General Curtis E LeMay.

UNITED STATES EIGHTH AIR FORCE LOSSES
FRIDAY, 8 OCTOBER 1943
PRIMARY TARGETS: BREMEN & VEGESACK, NORTHWESTERN GERMANY

AIRCRAFT NUMBER	SQDN.	GRP.	NAME	PILOT	FATE OF CREW
			B17 FORTRESS LOSSES		
42-29520	323	91		John J. Karp	3 KIA, 7 POW
42-3258	527	379		William L. Hickey	10 POW
42-3123	535	381		Leslie A. Kemp Jr.	10 KIA
42-29765	533	381		James W. Hartje	3 KIA, 7 POW
42-29854	532	381	*Ole Flack Sack*	Arthur M. Sample	8 KIA, 2 POW
42-29941	535	381		Edwin R. Manchester Jr.	6 KIA, 4 POW
42-30009	532	381		Jack S. Pry	2 KIA, 8 POW
42-30722	534	381		Dexter Lishon	10 POW
42-30864	535	381		William F. Cormany Jr.	1 KIA, 9 POW
42-37751	365	305		Wallace E. Emmert	10 POW
42-5855	423	306		Dean C. Rodman	5 KIA, 5 POW
42-29959	367	306		Lawrence W. Kooima	6 KIA, 4 POW
42-29985	367	306		Thomas D. Ledgerwood	1 KIA, 9 POW
42-30367	337	96	*Flak Happy*	Edmund I. Bolstad	7 KIA, 3 POW
42-30373	338	96	*Lucky Lady III*	Warren A. Jones	4 KIA, 6 POW
42-37752	339	96		Paul A. Flahive	10 POW
42-3233	350	100	*Our Baby*	Gale Cleven	10 POW
42-3386	351	100	*Marie Helena*	Richard Gormley	10 KIA
42-5864	351	100	*Piccadilly Lily*	Thomas Murphy	6 KIA, 5 POW
42-30154	349	100	*War Eagle*	Arthur Becktoft	1 KIA, 9 POW
42-30358	350	100	*Phartzac*	Frank Meadows	8 KIA, 2 POW
42-30818	350	100	*Salvo Sal*	William McDonald	1 KIA, 8 POW, 1
42-30840	350	100		Herbert Nash	5 KIA, 5 POW
42-30275	551	385	*The Vibrant Virgin*	Ralph M. Jensen	10 POW
42-30292	569	390	*Pulsatin' Polly*	Marshall Shepard	6 KIA, 4 POW
42-30318	570	390	*Devil's Daughter*	Arlin Rennels Jr.	1 KIA, 9 POW
42-30330	568	390	*Blood Guts & Rust II*	James C. Pedersen	4 KIA, 6 POW
			B24 LIBERATOR LOSSES		
42-63958	565	389		Michael J. Fuerst	9 KIA, 1 POW
42-7470	579	392		William W. Clifford	10 KIA
42-7488	579	392		John B. Buschman	3 KIA, 7 POW
			P47 THUNDERBOLT LOSSES		
42-6268	62	56		Fleming	POW
42-7911	335	4		Patterson	EV
42-7915	335	4		Smith	POW

UNITED STATES EIGHTH AIR FORCE LOSSES ON SATURDAY,9 OCTOBER 1943

PRIMARY TARGETS: ANKLAM, MARIENBURG, GDYNIA & DANZIG, POLAND & EASTERN GERMANY

AIRCRAFT NUMBER	SQDN.	GRP.	NAME	PILOT	FATE OF CREW
			B17 FORTRESS LOSSES		
42-5178	322	91	*The Old Stand By*	James D. Judy	1 KIA, 9 POW
42-29711	322	91		Charles B. Pinning	10 KIA
42-29740	323	91		Morris M. Guttu	5 KIA, 5 POW
42-29778	322	91		Alexander W. Stewart	6 KIA, 4 POW
42-30772	323	91		Thomas E. Walsh	8 KIA, 2 POW
42-30554	326	92		William F. Whelan	5 KIA, 5 POW
42-5221	427	303		Bernard J. Clifford	10 KIA
42-3152	508	351		William H. Warring	1 KIA, 9 POW
42-29868	508	351		Joseph H. Turley	8 KIA, 2 POW
42-29603	511	351	*Spitball*	Howard G. Maser	1 KIA, 9 POW
42-30790	511	351		Harry B. Morse Jr.	10 POW
42-30867	510	351		Lloyd A. Christman	4 KIA, 6 POW
42-5407	526	379		Vernon Smith	1 KIA, 9 POW
42-37728	525	379		James K. Lash	10 POW
42-3180	533	381		Herbert Carqueville	9 KIA, 1 POW
42-29958	534	381		James L. Loftin	2 KIA, 8 POW
42-30012	533	381		Landon C. Hendricks	10 KIA
42-29712	546	384	*Philly Brooklyn*	Mark B. Calhoun	2 KIA, 8 POW
42-29814	544	384	*Dallas Rebel*	John T. Ingles	10 KIA
42-30377	412	95	*Rodger the Lodger*	Ralph W. Eherts	10 KIA
42-3543	338	96		Rodney S. Greene	Sweden INT
42-30781	413	96		William C. Hunt Jr.	10 KIA
42-30336	548	385	*Miss Nanalee II*	Glyndon D. Bell	10 POW
42-30371	560	388	*Iza Angel II*	Henry J. Nagorka	2 KIA 8 POW
42-30802	560	388	*Gyndia*	Henry C. Kinney Jr.	2 KIA, 8 POW

GERMAN AIR FORCE LOSSES FRIDAY 8 OCTOBER 1943

MANUFACTURERS' SERIAL NUMBER		STAFFEL	GROUP	PILOT	FATE OF CREW
550513	FW 190A-6	5	II/JG 1	Franz Scherler	KIA
26052	Bf 109G-6	8	III/JG 1	Rudolf Einberger	KIA
550490	FW 190A-6	1	I/JG 1	Rudolf Hubl	Wounded
550729	FW 190A-6	1	I/JG 1	Johannes Kreimeyer	KIA
530715	FW 190A-6	2	I/JG 1	Hans Ehlers	Wounded (Col.* 100th B17)
591	FW190A-4	3	I/JG 1	Alfred Hoyer	Wounded
15726	Bf 109G-5	6	II/JG 11	Gunter Stenzel	KIA
5706	FW 190A-5	10	III/JG 11	Wilhelm Munchrath	KIA
1200	FW 190A-5	10	III/JG 11	Ernst Rumpf	KIA
410266	FW 190A-5	2	I/JG 11	Erich Hondt	Wounded
120010	Bf 110G-2	9	III/ZG 26	Hans Tagge	2 KIA
20318	Bf 109G-6	3	I/JG 3	Erich Hoder	Wounded
20710	Bf 109G-6	3	I/JG 3	Alfred Schmitt	Wounded
20252	Bf 109G-6	2	I/JG 3	Otto Wirth	KIA
15768	Bf 109G-6	3	I/JG 3	Erwin Stark	KIA
20273	Bf 109G-6	3	I/JG 3	Franz Effenberger	KIA
020	Me 410A-2	8	III/ZG 1	Gunther Sonntag	1 Wounded
231	Me 410A-2	7	III/ZG 1	Adolf Wentzel	1 KIA, 1 Wounded
6130	Bf 110G-2	3	I/ZG 1	Robert Wefers	1 Wounded
120010	Bf 110G-2	5	II/ZG 1	Karl-Heinrich Matern	2 KIA
6396	Bf 110G-2	Stab	II/ZG 1	Hans-Bodo Busch	2 KIA
150113	Bf 110G-2	4	II/ZG 1	Gerhard Busse	2 KIA
6400	Bf 110G-2	5	II/ZG 1	Fritz Dotter	2 KIA
20604	Bf 109G-6	4	II/JG 3	Horst Feder	KIA
5611	Bf 110G-2	Erpr. Kdo.	25	Hans-Jurgen Scheer	2 KIA
20295	Bf 109G-6	9	III/JG 54	Heinz Schulz	Wounded
	FW 190A-6	1	I/JG 1	Hans Philipp	KIA

*Collision

GERMAN AIR FORCE LOSSES SATURDAY 9 OCTOBER 1943

MANUFACTURERS' SERIAL NUMBER		STAFFEL	GROUP	PILOT	FATE OF CREW
19874	Bf 109G-6	Stab	II/JG 11	Karl-Heinz Kutzera	Wounded
530365	FW 190A-6	3	I/JG 11	Wolfgang Heinert	KIA
120487	FW 190A-3	1	I/JG 11	Harry Pelzer	KIA
530119	FW 190A-6	2	I/JG 11	Michael Widmann	KIA
637-	Bf 110G-2	Stab	ZG 26	Alfred Anton	1 Wounded
6374	Bf 110G-2	7	III/ZG 26	Helmut Zittier	1 Wounded
6371	Bf 110G-2	8	III/ZG 26	Richard Heller	1 Wounded, 1 KIA
6381	Bf 110G-2	8	III/ZG 26	Heinz Bovers	1 Wounded
6736	Bf 110G-2	3	I/ZG 1	Wolfgang Gunnel	2 Wounded
19696	Bf 109G-6	9	III/JG 54	Emil Hecker	Wounded

UNITED STATES EIGHTH AIR FORCE LOSSES ON SUNDAY, 10 OCTOBER 1943

PRIMARY TARGET: MUNSTER, WESTERN GERMANY

AIRCRAFT NUMBER	SQDN.	GRP.	NAME	PILOT	FATE OF CREW
			B17 FORTRESS LOSSES		
42-37737	401	91		Earle R. Verril	1 KIA, 1 EV, 8 POW
42-3497	335	95		Lionel Correala	1 KIA, 9 POW
42-5986	334	95	*Brown's Mule*	John D. Riggs	3 KIA, 7 POW
42-30272	335	95	*Fritz Blitz*	Eldon Broman	1 KIA, 9 POW
42-30273	334	95	*Patsy Ann III*	William E. Buckley	5 KIA, 5 POW
42-30817	334	95	*Miss Flower III*	John M Adams	10 POW
42-3516	338	96		Daniel M. Williams Jr	10 POW
42-3229	349	100	*Pasedena Nena*	John K. Justice	2 KIA, 7 POW, 1 EV
42-3237	418	100	*Stymie*	John F. Stephens	10 POW
42-3433	350	100	*Lena*	Robert P. Kramer	3 KIA,7 POW
42-30023	349	100	*Forever Yours*	Edward B. Stork	2 KIA, 8 POW
42-30047	350	100	*Sweater Girl*	Richard B. Atchison	4 KIA, 6 POW
42-30087	351	100	*Shackrat*	Maurice E. Beatty	8 KIA, 2 POW
42-30090	349	100	*El P'sstoffo*	Winton L. MacCarter	10 POW
42-30723	351	100	*Sexy Suzy-Mother of Ten*	William M. Beddow	6 KIA,4 POW
42-30725	350	100	*Aw-R-Go*	Charles B. Cruikshank	2 KIA, 8 POW
42-30734	351	100		Charles Thompson	3 KIA, 7 POW
42-30823	350	100		Charles D. Walts	5 KIA, 5 POW
42-30830	418	100	*Mlle. Zig-Zag*	John D. Brady	1 KIA, 10 POW
42-3539	550	385		William B. Whitlow	2 KIA, 4 POW, 4 Ev
42-6155	549	385		John F. Pettenger	10 POW
42-5898	562	388	*Little Lass*	Paul E. Williams	10 POW
42-3302	571	390		Edward W. Weldon Jr	11 POW
42-3328	568	390	*Miss Fortune*	Wade H. Sneed Jr	6 KIA, 4 POW
42-3415	571	390	*Miss Behavin'*	George E. Starnes	10 KIA, 1 POW
42-3426	571	390	*Spider*	William W. Smith	3 KIA, 7 POW
42-5915	570	390	*Cash & Carrie*	Robert A. McGuire Jr	10 POW
42-30262	568	390	*Tech Supply*	John G. Winant Jr	4 KIA, 6 POW
42-30265	571	390	*Pinky*	Frank E. Ward	3 KIA, 6 POW, 1 EV
42-30826	571	390		Robert B. Short	3 KIA, 8 POW
			P47 THUNDERBOLT LOSSES		
42-8635	328	352		Fred D. Olsen	KIA
Unknown			Unknown	Unknown	Unknown

GERMAN AIR FORCE LOSSES ON SUNDAY 10 OCTOBER 1943

MANUFACTURERS' SERIAL NUMBER		STAFFEL	GROUP	PILOT	FATE OF CREW
20495	Bf 109G-6	7	III/JG 1	Wilhelm Hermannes	KIA
937	FW 190A-5	3	I/JG 1	Felix Emmerich	KIA
2632	FW 190A-5	2	I/JG 1	Paul Habranke	KIA
530112	FW 190A-6	2	I/JG 1	Hans Vorhauer	KIA
27067	Bf 109G-6	6	II/JG 2	Albert Rolff	Wounded
15920	Bf 109G-6	12	III/ZG 26	Hermann Staiger	Wounded
530770	FW 190A-6	8	II/ZG 26	Hans Meyer	Wounded
6408	Bf 110G-2	9	III/ZG 26	Oswald Knobloch	2 KIA
6399	Bf 110-2	9	III/ZG 26	Heinrich Ulrich	2 KIA
150137	Bf 110G-2	9	III/ZG 26	Erich Armbruster	2 Wounded
120048	Bf 110G-2	8	III/ZG 26	Julius Baumann	1 Wounded
420025	Me 410A-2	9	III/ZG 1	Wilhelm Berlin	1 Wounded
239	Me 410A-2	9	III/ZG 1	Robert Reck	2 KIA
420031	Me 410-2	7	III/ZG 1	Karl Grinninger	1 KIA, 1 Wounded
116	Me 410A-2	9	III/ZG 1	Josef Hallerbach	1 KIA, 1 Wounded
15651	Bf 109G-6	6	II/JG 3	Karl-Ludwig Seewald	KIA
26074	Bf 109G-5	5	II/JG 3	Paul Draeger	Wounded
15954	Bf 109G-5	2	I/JG 3	Adolf Leib	Wounded
932	FW 190A-6	Erpr. Kdo.	25	Werner Ulrich	KIA
1727	FW 190A-6	Erpr. Kdo.	25	Deiter Eisenlohr	Wounded
740001	Bf 110G-4	6	II/NJG 1	Willi Wurochitz	1 Wounded
	FW 190A-6	3	II/JG 1	Walter Hoeckner	Uninjured
	FW 190A		II/JG 1	Unknown	Unknown
	FW 190		II/JG 1	Unknown	Unknown
	FW 190		II/JG 1	Unknown	Unknown
	Bf 109		II/JG 26	Unknown pilot bailed out after colliding with two 100th B.G. B17's	Unknown

SUMARY OF BOMBING, SUNDAY, 10 OCTOBER 1943

GROUP	ALTITUDE	TIME OF RELEASE	TARGET	BOMB LOAD	NUMBER OF A/C OVER TARGET
		3rd AIR DIVISION			
		13th Combat Bombardment Wing (CBW)			
95th	24,600	1503 hours	Munster	228 x 500 lb.	19
390th	25,600	1504 hours	Munster	192 x 500 lb.	16
100th	23,600	1505 hours	Munster	72 x 500 lb.	6
		45th C.B.W.			
96th	24,700	1509 hours	Munster	216 x 500 lb. (12 x 500 lb.)	18
388th	24,700	1510 hours	Munster	714 x 100 lb.	18
		4th C.B.W.			
94th	24,600	1511 hours	Munster	719 x 100 lb.	17
385th	23,600	1512 hours	Munster	643 x 100 lb.	16
		1st AIR DIVISION			
		40th C.B.W.			
92nd	25,000	1511 hours	Coesfeld	180 x 500 lb.	15
305th	26,400	1530 hours	Enschede	168 x 500 lb.	14
306th	24,500	1512 hours	Coesfeld	216 x 500 lb.	18
		1st C.B.W.			
381st	24,400	1517 hours	Munster	6 x 1,000 lb. (210 x 100 lb.)	5
91st	25,600	1518 hours	Munster	6 x 1,000 lb. (247 x 100 lb.)	7
351st	24,600	1518 hours	Munster	1 x 1,000 lb. (336 x 100 lb.)	7
		41st C.B.W.			
384th	25,300	1517 hours	Coesfeld	22 x 1,000 lb. (630 x 100 lb.)	15
379th	26,800	1525 hours	Enschede	30 x 1,000 lb. (620 x 100 lb.)	15
303rd	24,600	1517 hours	Coesfeld	12 x 1,000 lb. (798 x 100 lb.)	21

95th BOMBARDMENT GROUP (HEAVY), HORHAM, SUFFOLK MID-OCTOBER 1943

AIRCRAFT'S SERIAL NO.	SQDN.	AIRCRAFT'S NAME	OCT. 8th	9th	10th	14th	A/C's FATE
42-3037	412th						Unknown
095	412th	Peggy Ann					Unknown
153	336th	The Devil's Daughter					USA 9/4/44
263	335th	Slightly Dangerous					USA 27/6/44
273	412th	Impatient Virgin			A		SAL 22/12/43
283	336th	Yankee Queen					SAL 31/1/44
317	412th	The Spirit of '76				A	MIA 30/11/43
400	336th	The Gremlin's Sweetheart			A		SAL 21/6/45
462	336th	San Antonio Rose	A			A	MIA 21/2/44
465	412th		A				USA 27/6/44
497	335th				MIA		
529	336th			A	A		MIA 6/3/44
545	334th						MIA 29/1/44
42-5791	334th	Ruthless					SAL 20/3/44
918	336th	Heavenly Daze			A		MIA 11/1/44
986	334th	Brown's Mule			MIA		
42-6039	335th						MIA 29/11/43
080	335th	Wewa Special					Unknown
098	335th	Superstitious Aloysius				A	MIA 4/1/44
42-29943	334th	Situation Normal			A		MIA 6/3/44
42-30114	335th						MIA 20/10/43
120	334th	Patches	B				SAL 6/1/45
135	412th					MIA	
167	336th	Destiny's Tot	A				USA 6/4/44
173	412th	Circe					MIA 10/2/44
178	334th	Darlin'Dolly					MIA 1/1/45
181	335th	Herky Jerky II			A		MIA 24/1/44
182	334th	Blondie II					MIA 11/12/43
218	335th		A		A		MIA 11/12/43
226	336th	Spook VI		A			MIA 29/1/44
233	412th	Rhapsody in Flak			A		MIA 13/4/44
235	412th	The Zootsuiters			A		Unknown
244	334th	Holy Terror			A		MIA 5/1/44
255	412th						MIA 16/12/43
272	335th	Fritz Blitz			MIA		
273	334th	Patsy Ann III			MIA		
288	412th	Louise II					SAL 26/10/43
322	412th	Liberty Belle			A		SAL 23/6/44
342	334th	T'aint a Bird		A			MIA 4/8/44
353	334th	Ten Knight in the Bar Room					MIA 5/12/44
377	412th	Roger the Lodger		MIA			
609	335th	Pistol Packing Mama					MIA 10/2/44
634	412th		A				MIA 21/2/44
674	336th	Kathy Jane III	A				MIA 30/12/43
817	334th	Miss Flower III			MIA		
42-37734	336th	Cuddle Cat				A	MIA 5/1/44
756	335th	Roarin' Bull					MIA 24/1/44

KEY TO LETTERS: **A** — Minor damage sustained during mission. **B** — Major damage. **MIA** — Missing in action. **USA** — Returned to United States. **SAL** — Salvaged for spare parts. **RAF** — Transferred to Royal Air Force.

100th BOMBARDMENT GROUP (HEAVY), THORPE ABBOTTS, NORFOLK
MID-OCTOBER 1943

AIRCRAFT'S SERIAL NO.	SQDN.	AIRCRAFT'S NAME	OCT. 8th	9th	10th	14th	A/C's FATE
42-3229	349th	Pasadena Nena			MIA		
233	350th	Our Baby	MIA				
234	351st	Little Mike			A		SAL 13/10/43
237	418th	Stymie			MIA		
271	351st	Nine Little Yanks & A Jerk					SAL 7/3/44
279	350th	Badger Beauty					SAL 29/5/44
307	351st	Skipper					SAL/24/1/44
386	351st	Marie Helena	MIA				
393	418th	Just-A-Snappin'	B				SAL 12/10/43
413	350th	Hard Luck					MIA 14/8/44
433	350th	Lena			MIA		
474	351st	Queen Bee	B				SAL 27/12/43
508	418th	Bastard's Bungalow III					MIA 18/3/44
534	349th	Ol' Dad					SAL 27/4/44
42-5861	349th	Laden Maiden					MIA 30/12/43
863	350th	Paddlefoot's Proxy					Unknown
864	351st	Piccadilly Lily	MIA				
957	349th	Horny	A				SAL 9/5/44
997	351st	Heaven Can Wait	B				MIA 30/12/43
42-6087	418th	Royal Flush			B		MIA 11/8/44
094	418th						SAL 27/12/44
42-29931	350th	Jaybird					MIA 22/2/44
42-30023	349th	Forever Yours			MIA		
047	350th	Sweater Girl			MIA		
061	418th						USA 28/6/44
062	418th	Terrynten					MIA 10/2/44
066	418th	Mugg Wump					MIA 30/10/44
087	351st	Shackrat			MIA		
088	310th	Squawkin' Hawk	A				USA 17/5/44
090	349th	El P'sstofo			MIA		
091	418th	Blivit	A				SAL 21/4/44
152	418th	Messie Bessie	A				SAL 28/4/44
154	349th	War Eagle	MIA				
170	349th	Oh Nausea (& Miss Carriage)	B				MIA 6/3/44
184	349th	Muggs					SAL 5/8/44
278	418th						MIA 6/3/44
232	350th	Flak Happy					Unknown
330	350th						MIA 6/3/44
358	350th	Phartzac	MIA				
487	349th	Torchy III					SAL 28/4/44
723	351st	Sexy Suzy-Mother of Ten			MIA		
725	350th	Aw-R-Go			MIA		
734	351st				MIA		
758	418th	Rosie's Riveters	A				MIA 4/2/44
788	350th	Missmalovin'					MIA 25/2/44
796	351st	Sunny II	B				SAL 2/1/44
799	349th	The Bigassbird II					MIA 6/3/44
818	350th	Salvo Sal	MIA				
823	350th				MIA		
830	418th	Mlle. Zig Zag			MIA		
840	350th		MIA				

390th BOMBARDMENT GROUP (HEAVY), FRAMLINGHAM, SUFFOLK
MID-OCTOBER 1943

AIRCRAFT'S SERIAL NO.	SQDN.	AIRCRAFT NAME	OCT. 8th	9th	10th	14th	A/C's FATE
42-3279	571st		A				MIA 5/12/43
302	571st				MIA		
312	570th	Sequatchiee		A		A	MIA 22/6/44
327	569th	Tet Tmote				A	SAL 21/10/43
328	568th	Miss Fortune			MIA		
329	570th	Skippy					SAL 5/2/44
415	571st	Miss Behavin'			MIA		
426	571st	Spider	A		MIA		
427	568th	Canadian Club	A				SAL 22/6/45
472	568th		A				SAL 29/10/45
498	571st				B		MIA 8/5/44
526	568th			A			SAL 18/10/43
527	569th					A	USA 10/6/44
557	570th						MIA 30/11/43
558	571st						Unknown
42-5863	568th	Paddlefoot's Proxy					Unknown
915	570th	Cash and Carrie			MIA		
984	568th	Rusty Lode			B		Unknown
42-30223	571st	Rick O'Shay	A			A	MIA 11/12/43
42-29991	571st		A			MIA	
42-30246	570th	Spot Remover	A				MIA 20/2/44
262	568th	Tech Supply			MIA		
263	569th						Unknown
265	571st	Pinky			MIA		
266	569th	Lucky Strike	A				SAL 9/7/44
289	568th	The Dull Tool	A			A	MIA 4/1/44
292	569th	Pulsatin' Polly	MIA				
318	568th	Devil's Daughter	MIA				
320	569th					A	MIA 4/1/44
325	570th	Miss Carry			A	A	SAL 2/5/45
330	568th	Blood Guts and Rust II	MIA				
334	570th	Virgin Sturgeon	A				MIA 29/1/44
337	570th	Eightball			A		MIA 10/2/44
338	571st	Cabin in the Sky			A	A	Unknown
348	568th		A			A	MIA 16/12/43
411	568th	Rose Marie	A		A		MIA 11/12/43
426	569th	Rovin' Ramona					Unknown
434	570th	Betty Boop-The Pistol Packin' Mama			A		MIA 25/2/44
455	569th					A	Unknown
476	568th		A				MIA 20/12/43
610	568th					B	SAL 17/10/43
639	569th						RAF 21/1/44
642	569th	Geronimo	A			A	MIA 19/7/44
667	569th		A				MIA 11/12/43
713	568th	Phyllis Marie				A	MIA 8/3/44
715	569th					A	MIA 21/6/44
719	569th					A	MIA 20/10/43
783	570th	Stork Club	A		A		MIA 16/3/44
42-37723	569th	Paydola					Unknown

Bibliography

The Mighty Eighth by Roger Freeman. Published by MacDonald of London, U.K.

Mighty Eighth War Diary, Roger Freeman. Jane's, London, U.K.

The History of the 95th Bomb Group, Captain David Henderson, USAF, Ret'd. Kentucky, USA.

The Bloody Hundredth, Major Horace Varian, USAF, Ret'd. Massachusetts, USA.

Contrails: My War Record, (100th Bombardment Group), Contrails Publications, New York, USA.

The History of the 390th Bomb Group, Colonel Joseph Moller, USAF, Ret'd. Arizona, USA.

Thunderbolt, Major Robert Johnson, USAF, Ret'd. New Jersey, USA.

Flying Fortress, Edward Jablonski. Doubleday & Company Inc., New York, USA.

The History of the 353rd Fighter Group, Kenn Rust & William Hess, Aero Publishers, Fallbrook, California, USA.

LIFE'S History of WWII, Text by Sir Winston Churchill. LIFE Publications, New York, USA.

I Flew For The Fuhrer, Heinz Knoke. Evans Brothers Ltd., London, U.K.

The History of the 94th Bomb Group, Harry Slater, Tennessee, USA.

388th Bomb Group At War, Edward Huntzinger, Florida, USA.

The History of the 385th Bomb Group, Lt. Colonel Marston Leonard, USAF, Ret'd. Maryland, USA.

The Fall Of The Fortresses, Elmer Bendiner, New York, USA. Pan Books, London, U.K.

Bomber, Len Deighton. Jonathan Cape, London, U.K.

The Last Secret, Lord Nicholas Bethell. Andre Deutsche Ltd., London, U.K.

Battle Over The Reich, Alfred Price. Ian Allan Ltd., London, U.K.

The Bombing Of Munster, Stadtmuseum Munster, West Germany.

Munster, Josef Bergenthal. Regensberg Press, Munster, West Germany.

Rhine and Ruhr, Westdeutsche Landesbank, Dusseldorf/Munster, West Germany.

The Odessa File, Frederick Forsyth. Hutchinson & Company Ltd., London, U.K.

The Nuremberg Raid, Martin Middlebrook. Allen Lane, London, U.K.

Acknowledgments

This book would have been impossible without the extremely generous help and constant encouragement that I have received during the past five and a half years from many good friends all over Europe, the United States, France and the United Kingdom. First, I wish to express my deepest gratitude to Len Deighton who first suggested I try writing as a new career in 1978 after I became disabled in 1976, and who very kindly took the time and the trouble to advise me how to approach the task and what pitfalls to avoid.

Accomplished aviation authors Roger Freeman, Martin Middlebrook and Alfred Price have also very kindly provided me with much relevant information and helpful advice for which I am deeply grateful.

Arno Abendroth, in Germany, and Paul Andrews in the United States patiently researched the details of the aircraft involved from both sides which were involved in some of the most awesome air battles of the war which took place over Germany in October 1943. (Paul Andrews is currently writing the History of the 91st Bomb Group.)

In addition to all the veterans of the 8th Air Force, the Luftwaffe and the civilians whose names appear in this book there are many other people and organisations with whom I have exchanged many letters regarding relevant research material who have, together, provided many missing links in the chain of this story and to whom I am very grateful; *East Anglian Daily Times,* Ipswich, Suffolk, U.K.; *The Illustrated London News,* London, U.K.; *The Sunday Telegraph and Daily Telegraph,* London, U.K.; *The Sunday Express,* London, U.K.; *The Times,* London; *Air War Bulletin: 1939-1945,* Leiden, Holland; *8th Air Force News,* Florida, U.S.A.; *Veterans of Foreign Wars Magazine,* Missouri, U.S.A.; *Air Force Magazine,* Washington, D.C., U.S.A.; *Wings Magazine,* Orbis Publishing, London, U.K.; The American Battle Monuments Commission, Washington, D.C., U.S.A.; Jay Spencer, Aeronautics Research Department, Smithsonian Institution, Washington, D.C., U.S.A.; George Chalou and Staff, National Archives and Records Centre, Washington, D.C., U.S.A.; The USAF Records Centre, Maxwell AFB, Alabama, U.S.A.; The Public Records Office, London, U.K.; The Royal Air Force Association, London, U.K.; R.W. Mack, Curator of Photographs, RAF Museum, Hendon U.K.; Lt. Colonel Douglas Underwood and Lt. Colonel John Woolnough, USAF, Ret'd., U.S. 8th Air Force Historical Society, Florida, U.S.A.; Department of the Environment, London, U.K.; Wimpey Group Services Ltd. (Civil Engineers), London, U.K.; John Laing Ltd. (Civil Engineers),

London, U.K.; The Royal Geographical Society, London, U.K.; The Greater London Council (Library), London, U.K.; The Imperial War Museum, London, U.K.

The following Unit Contacts of the 8th Air Force provided invaluable help in locating the veterans who witnessed the events described in this book: Louis Pennow, 3rd Air Division Headquarters; Leroy Nitschke, 4th Fighter Group; 44th Bomb Group, Joseph Warth; 56th Fighter Group, Leo Lester; 78th Fighter Group, Gary Fry; 91st Bomb Group, Paul Chryst and George Parks; 92nd Bomb Group, Sheldon Kirsner; 93rd Bomb Group, Charles Weiss; 94th Bomb Group, Frank Halm; 95th Bomb Group, Arthur Frankel and Glenn Infield; 96th Bomb Group, Robert Owens; 100th Bomb Group, Horace Varian; 303rd Bomb Group, Van White; 305th Bomb Group, Abram Millar; 306th Bomb Group, W. M. Collins and Russel Strong; 352nd Fighter Group, R. J. Robinson; 353rd Fighter Group, J.M. Balason; 355th Fighter Group, Gordon Hunsberger; 379th Bomb Group, Frank Betz; 384th Bomb Group, Fred Nowosad; 385th Bomb Group, John Ford; 388th Bomb Group, Edward Huntzinger; 390th Bomb Group, Walter Weigle and Carl Anderson.

In addition, the following 8th Air Force veterans kindly provided much relevant information; Ralph Bowling, Paul Burnett, Clarence Cragoe, John Coppers, Grady Deatherage, Ray Derycke, Trammell Hollis, Donald Jones, Eddy Leighty, John Miller, Karle McKinney, William Nicholls, Paul Pennock, John Radojits, Robert Wright, and James Weaver.

My very grateful thanks are also extended to the following kind people in Germany, Holland, Belgium, France and England for their assistance in the research for this book; John Archer, Mike Bailey, Wilfried Beer of Munster Museum, West Germany, Colin Bryant, Cliff Bishop, Martin Bowman, Edward Buckeridge, Ron Buxton, Malcom Cheney, Mrs Marita Clarke who spent countless hours in translating correspondence from Germany, Christopher Coulthard, Gerald Cooper, Stewart Evans (presently writing a book about *Project Aphrodite*, The 8th Air Force Flying Bombs), Mrs. Joke Folmer (Secretary, Dutch Aircrew Helpers Association), Mike Gaffer, Richard Gibson, Steve Gotts, Cliff Hall, Mike Harvey, John Hawkins, Hans Hoehler, Martin Hols (presently writing a book about the History of Holten, Holland, during WWII), Colonel A.P. de Jongh, Royal Netherlands Air Force, Norbert Kruger, Henny Kwik, Edo van der Laan, Ian MacLachlan, Ian Mactaggert, Ron Mckay, Ken Rice, Bart Rijnhout, Adrie Roding, Peter Sadler, George Stebbings, Bill Stonestreet, Gerry Scutts, Graham Shipley, Carl Giles, Bob Jesko, John Chambers, Alan Harris, Roger Anthoine (presently writing a book about Allied escapees during World War II), and Wim Willemsen (who established contact with Joop Noest) Bart Zijlstra, Led Zwaafe, and Gino Kunzla. Last, but by no means least, my wife Mary for her constant support throughout, and my thanks and congratulations to Norman Ottoway for his truly outstanding maps and illustrations which appear in this book and which graphically portray "The Way It Was."

Listing of Crews

M.I.A. 10 OCTOBER 1943

Explanation of Codes

Crew Position

P—Pilot
CP—Co-Pilot
N—Navigator
B—Bombardier
E—Engineer
TTG—Top Turret Gunner
RO—Radio Operator
G—Gunner
RWG—Right Waist Gunner
LWG—Left Waist Gunner
BTG—Ball Turret Gunner
TG—Tail Gunner

Fate

POW—Prisoner of War
KIA—Killed in Action
EV—Evaded

100th Bombardment Group (H) Thorpe Abbotts, Norfolk

B17F 41-3229 349th Squadron

John K. Justice, P, EV
John F. Shields, CP, KIA
Peter Battisti, N, POW
William C. Brothers, B, POW
Richard E. Whitlock, RO, POW
John F. McDonough, E/TTG, POW
Stanley S. Stopa, BTG, POW
Harry Hafko, RWG. POW
Robert E. Bergendahl, LWG, POW
Gaetano D. Sponelli, TG, KIA

B17F 42-3433 350th Squadron

Robert P. Kramer, P, KIA
Edward F. Connelly ,Jr., CP, POW
Hugh S. Geiger, Jr., N, POW
Thomas B. Casey, Jr., B, POW
Deane O. Todd, E/TTG, POW
James A. Watkins, RO/G, POW
Donald M. Glaze, BTG, KIA
George A. White, RWG, KIA
Fred B. Moore, LWG, POW
Harvey F. James, TG, POW

B17F 42-30725 350th Squadron

Charles B. Cruikshank, P, POW
Glenn E. Graham, CP, POW
Frank D. Murphy, N, POW
August H. Gaspar, B, POW
Orlando E. Vincenti, RO, KIA
Leonard R. Weeks, TTG, POW
Robert L. Bixler, BTG, POW
James M. Johnson, RWG, POW
Donald B. Garrison, LWG, POW
Charles A. Clark, TG, KIA

B17F 42-30087 351st Squadron

Maurice E. Beatty, P, KIA
James B. Dabney, Jr., CP, POW
Grady Moyle, N, KIA
Reid E. Griffiths, B, KIA
Alfred Loguidice, RO/G, KIA
George C. Burgess, E/TTG,KIA
Mortin Levine, BTG, KIA
Angelo J. Licato, RWG, KIA
Edward C. Karamol, LWG, POW
Smith J. Young, TG, KIA

B17F 42-30047 350th Squadron

Richard B. Atchison, Jr., P, POW
Willard Secor, CP, POW
Kenneth Baron, N., POW
Sol Goldstein, B, POW
Elder E. Lisch, RO/G, KIA
Russel W. Bennett, E/TTG, POW
Clarence A. Coombs, BTG, KIA
Elliot O. Preble, RWG, KIA
Westley M. Field, LWG, KIA
Van T. White, TG, POW

B17F 42-30023 349th Squadron
Edward G. Stork,P, POW
John S. Minerich, CP, POW
John J. Gibbons, N, KIA
Arthur C. Twitchell, B, POW
Stefan C. Palmer, RO/G, KIA
Laurence Willey, E/TTG, POW
Paul M. Caveny, BTG, POW
Gordon W. Shields, RWG, POW
Douglas C. Brown, LWG, POW
Ira G. Turner, TG, POW

B17F 42-30734 351st Squadron
Charles H. Thompson, P, POW
Ross McEuen, CP, POW
Edward R. Jones, N, KIA
William J. Sprow, Jr., B, POW
Jack Stern, RO/G, POW
Richard E. Derby, E/TTG, POW
Jesse W. Cook, Jr., BTG, POW
Charles L. Nessel, RWG, KIA
Floyd M. Cahall, LWG, KIA
Donald E. Leech, TG, POW

B17F 42-30090 349th Squadron
Winton L. MacCarter, P, POW
Daniel Barna, CP, POW
Harold L. Weachter, N, POW
George H. Ziegler, B, POW
Alexander F. Sawicki, RO/G, POW
Jack C. Rogers, E/TTG, POW
Robert W. Sandy, BTG, POW
Roy B. Graff, RWG, POW
Raymond J. Manley, LWG, POW
Cosimo A Demonica, TG, POW

B17F 42-30723 351st Squadron
William M. Beddow, P, KIA
Richard W. Brooks, CP, POW
Israel Levine, N, KIA
Milton E. Harness, B, POW
John L. Sullivan, RO/G, KIA
Dan Q. James, E/TTG, POW
Walter E. Zoldak, BTG, KIA
Samuel M. Hicks, RWG, KIA
Robert J. Lynch, LWG, KIA
Richard R. Munger, TG, POW

B17F 42-30830 418th Squadron
John D. Brady, P, POW
John C. Egan, CP, POW
David Solomon, N, POW
Howard B. Hamilton, B, POW
Joseph E. Hafer, RO/G, POW
Adolf Blum, E/TTG, POW
Roland D. Gangwer, BTG, POW
Harold E. Clanton, RWG, KIA
George J. Petrohelos, LWG, POW
James A. McCusker, TG, POW
John L. Hoerr, O/CP, POW

B17F 42-3237 418th Squadron
John F. Stephens, P, POW
Hoyt L. Smith, CP, POW
Rudolph Grum, N, POW
William J. Moore, B, POW
Carl E. Battin, RO/G, POW
John Shay, E/TTG, POW
Max U. Drudge, BTG, POW
George F. Knolle, RWG, POW
William F. Young, LWG, POW
Casimir A Paczynski, TG, POW

B17F 42-30823 350th Squadron
Charles D. Walts, P, POW
Jerome H. Wallace, CP, KIA
Louis H. Oss, N, POW
Richard C. Dodson, B, KIA
Travis D. Brumbeau, RO/G, POW
Clyde M. Walker, E/TTG, POW
Henry A Gratzfeld, BTG, KIA
Thomas F. Murphy, RWG, POW
Frank E. Fethersten, LWG, KIA
William O. Higginbotham, TG, POW

95th Bombardment Group (H) Horham, Suffolk

B17F 42-3497 335th Squadron
Lionel Correia, P, POW
Donald W. Dunhaver, CP, POW
Richard E. Coffey, N, POW
Frederick J. Davis, B, POW
Jerome B. Schneider, RO/G, KIA
Otis W. Ashworth, E/TTG, POW
James D. Bailey, BTG, POW
Roland Alexenberg, RWG, POW
Roger D. Black, LWG, POW
Richard L. Crawford, TG, POW

B17F 42-30817 334th Squadron
John M. Adams, P, POW
Thomas F. Barber, CP, POW
Kenneth V. Winegar, N, POW
Earl T. Dewolf, B, POW
Jerome I. Pubantz, RO/G, POW
Marshall R. Crow, E/TTG, POW
Mike Szewyck, BTG, POW
Wallace E. Watts, Jr., RWG, POW
Orwin O. Tilseth, LWG, POW
James E. Baker, TG, POW

B17F 42-30272 335th Squadron
Eldon J. Broman, P, POW
J. H. Chaffin, CP, POW
William H. Fowler, N, POW
P.D. Guiteras, B, POW
Warren D. Thomas, RO/G, POW
R. E. Rightmire, E/TTG, KIA
R. P. Dillon, BTG, POW
J. O. Black, RWG, POW
F.O.Dean, LWG, POW
T. Kelly, TG, POW
C. M. Forney, O, POW

B17F 42-30273 334th Squadron
William E. Buckley, Jr., P, KIA
Frederick J. Kennie, CP, POW
Robert Barto, N, POW
Edison P. Janney, B, POW
Ralph E. Piner, RO/G, KIA
Richard W. Sluder, E/TTG, KIA
Harry F. Balmer, BTG, KIA
Donald W. Reinhart , RWG, POW
Leo Baron, LWG, KIA
Edward C. Burlingham,TG, POW

B17F 42-5986 334th Squadron
John D. Riggs, P, POW
Ashford M. Morrison, CP, POW
Steve Paczolt, N KIA
Joseph P. Cornell, B, KIA
Thomas B. Haller, RO/G, POW
Paul L. Gillern, E/TTG, POW
Hunter P. Page, BTG, POW
Charles R. Davies, Jr., RWG, POW
Joseph P. Kelly, LWG, KIA
Gifford E. Grover, TG, POW

390th Bombardment Group (H) Framlingham, Suffolk

B17F 42-3415 571st Squadron
George E. Starnes, P, KIA
Warren P. Mosegard, CP, KIA
Lavere G. Shofstahl, N, KIA
Richard H. Hatten, B, KIA
John S. Massa, RO/G, KIA
Donald Hatfield, E/TTG, KIA
Charles R. Dean, BTG, KIA
Paul W. Sucher, RWG, KIA
Charles D. Stamiris, LWG, KIA
Robert S. Coles, TG, POW

B17F 42-30826 571st Squadron
Robert B. Short, P, POW
Bud H. Hinckley, CP, POW
Hal K. Hughes, N, KIA
Norton Stolair, B, POW
Donald A. Lowrie, RO/G, POW
Frank Becay, E/TTG, POW
Richard A. Grace, BTG, KIA
Donald C. Armstrong, RWG, POW
Eugene A. Runser, LWG, POW
William H. Esselstine, TG, POW
Joseph W. Easley, O, POW

B17F 42-3328 568th Squadron
Wade H. Sneed, Jr., P, KIA
Darwin E. Michaelson, CP, KIA
Melvin H. Breckenridge, N, KIA
Lewis S. Gardner, B., KIA
Clarence E. Payne, RO/G, POW
Bertil R. Olsen, E/TTG, KIA
Walter J. Swiniuchowski, BTG, KIA
William E. Wenckens, RWG, POW
John W. Danielsen, LWG, POW
Carl R. Spirito, TG, POW

B17F 42-5915 570th Squadron
Robert A. McGuire, Jr., P, POW
Glenn N. Oster, CP, POW
Albert E. Drouhard, N, POW
Jack E. Nosser, B, POW
Joseph E. Chassaing, Jr. RO/G, POW
Norman A. Auger, E/TTG, POW
Hershel N. McFeely, BTG, POW
Hershel T. Rascoe, RWG, POW
George T. Hodgins, LWG, POW
Clifford E. Strang, TG, POW

B17F 42-3302 571st Squadron
Edward W. Weldon, Jr., P, POW
Clarendon M. Barbarus, CP, POW
James B. Smith, N, POW
Robert W. Rhoades, B, POW
Charles Roth, Jr., RO/G, POW
Marion E. Laird, E/TTG, POW
Bernard L. Levin, BTG, POW
Howard Kreiner, RWG, POW
Grant C. McCracken, LWG, POW
Spiro J. Harames, TG, POW
Kenneth L. Neubauer, O, POW

B17F 42-3426 571st Squadron
William W. Smith, P, KIA
Joseph P. Miller, CP, KIA
Donald W. Callahan, N, POW
Vincent J. McDonald, B, POW
Frank R. Whitehead, RO/G, POW
William C. Nichols, E/TTG, POW
Warren L. Smeltzer, BTG, POW
Robert L. Smith, Jr. RWG, POW
Herbert A. Lee, LWG, POW
George H. Emerich, TG, KIA

B17F 42-30265 571st Squadron
Frank E. Ward, P, POW
Lloyd B. McGrady, CP, POW
Harold J. Wolosin, N, POW
Lester S. Look, Jr., B, KIA
Willis P. Roy, RO/G, POW
Elmer W. Leonard, E/TTG, POW
Milton C. Schwedmer, BTG, POW
Arthur W. Judd, RWG, POW
John J. Cleary, LWG, POW
Theodore G. Converse, TG, EV

B17F 42-30262 568th Squadron
John G. Winant, Jr., P, POW
Donald C. Arns, CP, POW
Robert W. Tredinnick, N, POW
Richard F. Walker, B, POW
Paul E. Hurles, RO/G, KIA
Walter E. Weidemann, E/TTG, POW
Elmer Fjosne, BTG, KIA
Robert V. Wirt, RWG, KIA
Alonzo J. Swope, LWG, POW
Frank V. Malone, TG, KIA

385th Bombardment Group (H) Great Ashfield, Suffolk

B17 F G 42-3539 549th Squadron
William B. Whitlow, P, EV
Jim F. Burch, CP, Drowned during escape William D. Fazenbaker, N, POW
Lloyd A. Stanford, B, EV
John T. Ashcraft, RO/G, EV
Willis G. Shaneyfelt, E/TTG, POW
Thomas M. Ennis, BTG, KIA
Howard E. Walker, RWG, KIA
Clarence W. Schaumburg, LWG, POW
Robert L. Richards, TG, POW

B17F 42-6155 551st Squadron
John F. Pettenger, P, POW
Ernest M. Bemis, CP, POW
David S. Leventhal, N, POW
William P. Dorney, B, POW
John L. Shealy, RO/G, POW
John C. Leahy, E/TTG, POW
Richard H. Clairmont, BTG, POW
Robert P. Lewis, RWG, POW
Harry C. Rudberg, LWG, POW
Donald E. Sanborn, TG, POW

96th Bombardment Group (H) Snetterton Heath, Norfolk

B17G 42-3516 338th Squadron
Daniel M. Williams, P, POW
Frederick J. Frey, CP, POW
William M. Taylor, N, POW
Paul P. Butler, Jr., B, POW
Edward G. Miller, RO/G, POW
Harry R. Mowen, E/TTG, POW
Auguste J. Seguin, BTG, POW
Paul D. Schwartz, RWG, POW
Albert C. Sielaff, LWG, POW
James E. Dixon, TG, POW

388th Bombardment Group Knettishall, Suffolk

B17F 42-5898 562nd Squadron

Paul E. Williams, P, POW
Israel Rogg, CP, POW
Edward G. Garver, N, POW
Robert W. Macy, B, POW
Alfred A Gardin, RO/G, POW
Raymond J. Harwood, E/TTG, POW
Harold N. Moore, BTG, POW
Ralph B. Cornwall, RWG, POW
Maynard B. Rollins, LWG, POW
Roland W. Conners, TG, POW

91st Bombardment Group (H) Bassingbourne, Cambridgeshire

B17G 42-37737 401st Squadron

Earle R. Verrill, P, POW
Joseph Rose, CP, POW
Arthur J. Horning, N, EV
John A Lilley, B, KIA
Ross L. Repp, RO/G, POW
Roy M. Jackson, E/TTG, POW
Gilbert L. Taft, BTG, POW
Stanley E. Lepkowski, RWG, POW
Paul A. Lorman, LWG, POW
Robert D. DeGhetto, TG, POW

Index of Names